# Praise for *Rapid J2EE Developm...*

"The author provides a good survey of the techn                                    )-
ment in the J2EE arena. He touches on all areas t                          ....., from
design through testing. He illustrates the different        ... ..pia development by going into
several technologies in depth, and he also lists or otherwise mentions other available technologies. I would recommend this book to anyone looking to get started with developing J2EE applications."
—*Beth Stearns*
*Consultant, ComputerEase Publishing*

"This book has a lot of great material in it. The author really shows his experience in the subject matter. The content is excellent. I haven't seen another book that is as comprehensive or contains as many real-world lessons learned."
—*Madhu Siddalingaiah*
*Consultant, SEA Corporation*

"I think the book does a good job of presenting a set of processes and technologies that enable rapid development. I think this is an extremely useful book and I would recommend it to others."
—*Satadip Dutta*
*Software Engineer, HP*

"The author skillfully presents a collection of tools, technologies, and processes that facilitate rapid development of J2EE applications. I see this book as a valuable addition to any company bookshelf, especially given its broad application across the software lifecycle. It's also quite amazing that a Google search does not reveal any existing publications with this title. This book should neatly fill that hole."
—*Martin Westacott*
*Director and Senior Consultant, Solstice Software Limited, U.K.*

"If you ever needed to put some polish to your J2EE development understanding or would like to move into the role of Senior J2EE Developer, then this is the book for you. The author covers everything you need to take you from design to coding to build process. Along the way he introduces some new valuable 'leading-edge' technologies. All this will leave you with good capabilities to tackle most J2EE projects confidently."
—*Shane Griggs*
*J2EE Architect*

# Rapid J2EE Development

# Hewlett-Packard® Professional Books

## HP-UX

| | |
|---|---|
| Cooper/Moore | HP-UX 11i Internals |
| Fernandez | Configuring CDE |
| Keenan | HP-UX CSE: Official Study Guide and Desk Reference |
| Madell | Disk and File Management Tasks on HP-UX |
| Olker | Optimizing NFS Performance |
| Poniatowski | HP-UX 11i Virtual Partitions |
| Poniatowski | HP-UX 11i System Administration Handbook and Toolkit, Second Edition |
| Poniatowski | The HP-UX 11.x System Administration Handbook and Toolkit |
| Poniatowski | HP-UX 11.x System Administration "How To" Book |
| Poniatowski | HP-UX 10.x System Administration "How To" Book |
| Poniatowski | HP-UX System Administration Handbook and Toolkit |
| Poniatowski | Learning the HP-UX Operating System |
| Rehman | HP-UX CSA: Official Study Guide and Desk Reference |
| Sauers/Ruemmler/Weygant | HP-UX 11i Tuning and Performance |
| Weygant | Clusters for High Availability, Second Edition |
| Wong | HP-UX 11i Security |

## UNIX, LINUX

| | |
|---|---|
| Mosberger/Eranian | IA-64 Linux Kernel |
| Poniatowski | Linux on HP Integrity Servers |
| Poniatowski | UNIX User's Handbook, Second Edition |
| Stone/Symons | UNIX Fault Management |

## COMPUTER ARCHITECTURE

| | |
|---|---|
| Evans/Trimper | Itanium Architecture for Programmers |
| Kane | PA-RISC 2.0 Architecture |
| Markstein | IA-64 and Elementary Functions |

## NETWORKING/COMMUNICATIONS

| | |
|---|---|
| Blommers | Architecting Enterprise Solutions with UNIX Networking |
| Blommers | OpenView Network Node Manager |
| Blommers | Practical Planning for Network Growth |
| Brans | Mobilize Your Enterprise |
| Cook | Building Enterprise Information Architecture |
| Lucke | Designing and Implementing Computer Workgroups |
| Lund | Integrating UNIX and PC Network Operating Systems |

## SECURITY

| | |
|---|---|
| Bruce | Security in Distributed Computing |
| Mao | Modern Cryptography: Theory and Practice |
| Pearson et al. | Trusted Computing Platforms |
| Pipkin | Halting the Hacker, Second Edition |
| Pipkin | Information Security |

## WEB/INTERNET CONCEPTS AND PROGRAMMING

| | |
|---|---|
| Amor | E-business (R)evolution, Second Edition |
| Apte/Mehta | UDDI |
| Chatterjee/Webber | Developing Enterprise Web Services: An Architect's Guide |
| Kumar | J2EE Security for Servlets, EJBs, and Web Services |

# Rapid J2EE Development

## An Adaptive Foundation for Enterprise Applications

Alan Monnox

i n v e n t
www.hp.com/hpbooks

PRENTICE
HALL
PTR

Pearson Education

Prentice Hall Professional Technical Reference

Upper Saddle River, NJ • Boston • Indianapolis • San Francisco

New York • Toronto • Montreal • London • Munich • Paris • Madrid

Capetown • Sydney • Tokyo • Singapore • Mexico City

Many of the designations used by manufacturers and sellers to distinguish their products are claimed as trademarks. Where those designations appear in this book, and the publisher was aware of a trademark claim, the designations have been printed with initial capital letters or in all capitals.

The authors and publisher have taken care in the preparation of this book, but make no expressed or implied warranty of any kind and assume no responsibility for errors or omissions. No liability is assumed for incidental or consequential damages in connection with or arising out of the use of the information or programs contained herein.

The publisher offers excellent discounts on this book when ordered in quantity for bulk purchases or special sales, which may include electronic versions and/or custom covers and content particular to your business, training goals, marketing focus, and branding interests. For more information, please contact:

U. S. Corporate and Government Sales
(800) 382-3419
corpsales@pearsontechgroup.com

For sales outside the U. S., please contact:

International Sales
international@pearsoned.com
Visit us on the Web: www.phptr.com

Library of Congress Catalog Number: 2004116714

Copyright © 2005 Hewlett-Packard Development Company L.P.
Published by Pearson Education, Inc.
Publishing as Prentice Hall Professional Technical Reference
Upper Saddle River, New Jersey 07458

ISBN 0-13-147220-8

Text printed in the United States on recycled paper at R.R. Donnelley in Crawfordsville, Indiana.

First printing, March 2005

*For Mary*

# Contents

## Part IV Dynamic Environments

## Chapter 12    Optimal Builds . . . . . . . . . . . . . . . . . . . . . . . . . .259

# Preface

*"Three months, or you're dead!"*

These were the opening words of the keynote speaker at a conference I attended over what now seems a long time ago. Three months, the speaker's argument went, was the time available to turn an idea into a fully realized solution. After that, the idea would be out of date and the competition ahead.

The specifics of the rest of the presentation have since faded from memory. The speaker went on to cover the intricacies of B2B and C2B for e-business, but by that stage, my thoughts were elsewhere. The point had been well made: The business world had embraced the Internet, and with it, a new unit of measure—Internet-time.

On reflection, the speaker's opening remarks were something of a watershed in my approach to software engineering. Quality is fundamental to all projects. Nevertheless, the need to accommodate change quickly puts another watchword at the top of the list, alongside quality: *rapidity*!

Modern-day business continues to move at an ever-faster rate, and the enterprise systems that underpin those businesses are required to keep pace. As software professionals, we find ourselves under increasing pressure not only to deliver on quality but also within ever-decreasing timeframes. Compounding these demands further is a marked rise in system complexity. Gone are the days when a system's boundaries were constrained to a single organization. The allure of the Internet for e-commerce has led to demands for systems that require integration on a truly global scale.

Meeting this demand is not easy. Indeed, it has never been easy. In his landmark article *No Silver Bullet*, Fredrick P. Brooks argued there would be no new breakthrough in software development technology that would result in even a single order of magnitude increase in productivity [Brooks, 1987]. Although published over a decade ago, Brooks's statement still holds true. Despite this perceived inability to address the essential complexity of software development, the business world continues to make ever-increasing demands of software professionals despite the poor track record of the IT industry in delivering quality solutions to even medium-term timeframes. Further compounding the problem is the current climate of fierce competition between software vendors, who vie to outdo one another in a bid to win work in what is presently a high-risk market.

Therefore, the bar continues to rise for us as IT professionals. In order to keep pace with these steadily escalating demands and rising competition, software developers are turning to a variety of new and exciting methods, technologies, and tools. Agile methodologies are touted as a panacea for those projects that continue to fail to come in on time and under budget. The word *agile* is proving very popular, with proponents of agile modeling techniques promising to revolutionize our entire approach to systems development. Likewise, others are looking beyond the object-oriented paradigm and seeking to embrace aspect-oriented programming, with its weaves and crosscuts. Supporting all of these new ideas and advances is a maturing base of cutting-edge development tools that assist the software engineer in bringing these techniques to the Java 2 platform.

The IT world is indeed changing rapidly, and not just in terms of technology advances. Today, the speaker's words are more true than ever: *Three months, or you're dead!*

## What Is This Book About?

This book does not promote a radically new development methodology that guarantees to slash your development timeframes. Nor is it about rapidity at any cost. It is certainly not about rapidity at the expense of quality. Instead, this book defines a series of solid software engineering practices that target improving both productivity and quality on J2EE projects.

Many of the techniques covered fall just outside of the mainstream. As such, this book offers a fresh perspective on the problems of rapidity for enterprise solutions. Moreover, not all of the techniques will be applicable for every given scenario. Instead, the emphasis is on arming the software engineer with an arsenal of new ideas and practical techniques relevant to the day-to-day process of building cost-effective, quality solutions.

## Who Should Read This Book?

This book is useful to anyone engaged in the development of enterprise-level systems on the J2EE platform. Whether you are an architect, designer, developer, or tester, this book can help you work more effectively and productively.

Primarily, this book targets anyone who considers himself or herself a software engineer. It is also of interest to anyone who works with or manages developers.

The title software engineer is worthy of further elaboration. IT professionals have a propensity for putting all manner of titles on business cards, from systems analyst and enterprise architect to quality specialist and IT consultant. The true software professional, however, is an extremely versatile individual who is fully capable of fulfilling many, but not necessarily all, of the predefined roles on a project. It is to this type of individual that I apply the term software engineer. Putting aside for a moment the technical description of the role and the associated computer scientist tag, a software engineer is someone who not only knows his or her profession but knows it *well*. He or she can effectively contribute in all project phases, whether analysis, design, implementation, or testing. Moreover, a software engineer continually looks for new ideas to improve what he or she does and how it is done. In short, a software engineer understands that self-improvement and continuous learning are fundamental activities for an IT professional.

If you think this description applies to you, then you are reading the right book.

# How This Book Is Organized

The contents of this book are broken up into four logical parts:

## Part I: Adaptive Processes

- *Chapter 1: A J2EE Adaptive Foundation.* This chapter introduces the concepts behind the creation of an adaptive foundation for rapid development.

- *Chapter 2: Rapid Application Development.* Techniques commonly associated with the rapid development of software, including rapid development languages, approaches to prototyping, and timeboxed development methods, are described in this chapter.

- *Chapter 3: Embracing Adaptive Methods.* Chapter 3 explores the importance of lightweight development methodologies that incorporate an iterative approach to building software.

## Part II: Agile Architectures

- *Chapter 4: Designing for Rapidity.* This chapter looks at how the choices we make at design time have implications for the project's timeframe.

- *Chapter 5: Modeling Software.* The topic of this chapter is the use of models for building software architectures, and it examines how UML diagrams enable the communication, validation, and exploration of system designs.

- *Chapter 6: Code Generation.* We discuss the merits of passive and active code generation. The use of XDoclet for generating boilerplate code artifacts for Enterprise JavaBeans is illustrated by example, along with the use of Apache's Velocity template engine.

- *Chapter 7: Rapidity and the Database.* The repetitive nature of data access code makes it a prime candidate for code generation. This chapter looks at the time savings to be had from the use of the code generation tool Middlegen, as well as at how object-relational mapping products can ease the process of mixing object-oriented technology with that of relational database technology.

- *Chapter 8: Model-Driven Architecture.* This chapter brings together models with code generation techniques to explore the MDA paradigm. The use of the open source MDA tool AndroMDA is covered by example.

## Part III: Rapid Languages

- *Chapter 9: Scripting.* This chapter looks at the benefits of scripting languages and introduces the Java-compatible scripting language Jython.

- *Chapter 10: Working to Rule.* This chapter examines the benefits of using rule engines to maintain business logic. The open source, expert system shell Jess is introduced as an example of a rule-based language.

- *Chapter 11: Aspect-Oriented Programming.* AOP provides new language constructs for modularizing crosscutting concerns. The result is a powerful mechanism for applying changes dynamically to an application. This chapter introduces the AOP language AspectJ and the AOP framework AspectWerkz.

## Part IV: Dynamic Environments

- *Chapter 12: Optimal Builds.* Chapter 12 addresses the importance of having a highly efficient and optimized build process in place for conducting rapid development.

- *Chapter 13: The Integrated Development Environment.* We examine the need to invest in sophisticated and integrated development tools. The open source developer's workbench Eclipse is introduced as an example of a suitable J2EE development environment.

- *Chapter 14: Test-Driven Development.* The practice of test-driven development is key to defining an approach that is resilient to changing requirements and designs. This chapter looks at the importance of constructing an automated unit test suite and covers the JUnit framework for writing unit tests as well as the use of mock objects in testing.

- *Chapter 15: Efficient Quality Assurance.* The final chapter looks at using automated testing tools for undertaking functional and performance testing. The open source tools HttpUnit and Apache JMeter are covered by example.

# About the Software

The examples included in this book use open source software where possible. This approach provides a low-cost option for trying out the rapid development techniques covered. Where suitable open source software products are not available, I have attempted to select commercial products that offer free trial versions for evaluation purposes. In a few rare exceptions, examples use commercial products that represent a best-of-breed for a particular technology, regardless of cost.

# What This Book Contains

The content of this book is part software management and part software development, as rapid development is not possible without engaging both disciplines.

Although the content of this book spans the entire development process, it is not a definitive text on the lifecycle of a project. Rather, the content encompasses a detailed collection of ideas, processes, and techniques tailored to enterprise-level J2EE developments.

Not all of the techniques are applicable to every situation. Instead, you should familiarize yourself with the ideas presented, then draw upon your own skills and experience to determine which of them adds the most value to your specific project.

The techniques and practices presented all represent best-practice software engineering. The intent is to introduce a wide range of subjects rather than focus on a small number of topics in minute detail. Rapid-fire examples illustrate each of the concepts introduced, which bring you quickly up to speed with a particular topic. Each chapter includes links and references to further resources for more information on all the techniques and practices covered.

# Acknowledgments

Few books are written in isolation, and this book is no exception. I'd like to express my appreciation to everyone who has assisted me in the writing of this book, either by reviewing chapter drafts, offering suggestions, or just by encouraging me to keep going.

Acquisitions editor Jill Harry at Prentice Hall kept a firm grip on the reins from the start of the project and helped guide me through the process of writing a book. Likewise, development editor Jennifer Blackwell taught me some valuable lessons on the finer points of good writing style.

I had a great team of reviewers in Bernard Farrell, Beth Stearns, Madhu Siddalingaiah, Martin Westacott, Satadip Dutta, and Shane Griggs. Thanks to each of you for being so meticulous and for taking the time to answer my questions.

A big thank you to Ian Macfarlane for sharing his ideas on the book's structure and for being generous enough to review some of my chapters several times over.

I'd also like to thank Garry Downes, who pointed me in the direction of various articles, papers, and Web sites. Garry's input helped immensely in pulling together the ideas and concepts that make up this book.

I can't finish this acknowledgment without mentioning my parents, Sheila and Derek, and my sisters Jill and Ann. Although they are on the other side of the world, they still gave me heaps of encouragement by phone and email.

The final thank you is for my partner, Mary, who put up with an awful lot while I wrote this book but supported me all the way. Thanks, Mary, for your patience, support, and your keen grammatical eye.

# About the Author

Alan Monnox's IT career has quite literally taken him from one side of the world to the other. Starting out in Manchester, England, Alan now works out of Christchurch in New Zealand as a Solution Architect for Hewlett-Packard, specializing in the development of J2EE systems for HP's enterprise customers in the South Pacific.

Alan has more than fifteen years of experience in the IT industry and has worked on applications ranging from banking systems to GPS navigation software.

Throughout his career, Alan has long sought ways to produce software to an ever-higher quality and within an ever-reducing timeframe. His extensive experience with object-oriented development projects has provided Alan with the background to address head-on the issues surrounding the delivery of time-critical enterprise applications for the J2EE platform.

# Part I: Adaptive Processes

*Cost, quality, and speed—pick any two.*

In Part I, we look at the importance of preparing for rapid application development by establishing a core set of best practices and techniques that are of value to all project teams within a company. The main elements of rapid application development are introduced, and we cover in detail the use of iterative development processes that enable the delivery of on-time solutions that meet the needs of the customer.

# 1

# A J2EE Adaptive Foundation

The Java 2 Platform, Enterprise Edition (J2EE) is the premier development platform for distributed enterprise-level solutions. By incorporating a wealth of enterprise services under the umbrella of the J2EE framework, the J2EE platform enables the skilled Java engineer to build and deploy component-based, multitiered software applications.

I believe the J2EE platform provides the services necessary for building quality enterprise solutions, but that J2EE by itself is not sufficient to deliver systems within the tight timeframes demanded by modern businesses. Achieving this goal requires taking a broader view of the enterprise-software development process than purely focusing on the services of the J2EE Framework.

The problems J2EE developers face relate to the complexity and ever-changing nature of business software. For rapidity, we need to safeguard ourselves against the schedule-destroying impact of such changes. This book looks beyond the J2EE platform and advocates the use of techniques and practices for putting in place an *adaptive foundation* as the basis for the rapid development of J2EE enterprise solutions.

The term adaptive foundation summarizes the requirements of this broader development approach:

- The *foundation* is a set of building blocks in which a company must invest to construct a stable platform for rapid development projects.
- *Adaptive* describes the need to have practices in place that have the flexibility to accommodate change within the project's schedule.

This book introduces a range of techniques and best practices that complement the development of J2EE applications. Some of the topics we cover include iterative development, model-driven architecture, code generation, aspect-oriented programming, and test-driven development. These software engineering techniques are all candidates for inclusion in your adaptive foundation.

This opening chapter defines how investment in tools, training, and education, together with a program of continual improvement, must underpin these techniques and practices. Collectively, these elements form a solid foundation for the rapid development of enterprise systems on the J2EE platform. We look at the importance of defining this adaptive foundation as part of a wider development strategy that project teams can use as a springboard for accelerating the development process.

# The Need for Rapid Development

Developers of enterprise-level software are coming under ever-increasing pressure to deliver systems in ever-decreasing timeframes. Information technology (IT) is an enabler for business, and to compete effectively, modern companies require support from the systems that underpin their core business processes. The requirement for rapid development primarily exists because of the need to have these important systems keep pace with the fast-changing nature of today's agile businesses.

This is the yardstick for a rapid development project, not to deliver solutions in a short timeframe but to deliver business critical functionality as and when required by the business.

This presents us as professional software engineers with something of a dichotomy. While professionalism and personal pride dictate that we engineer solutions to the highest quality, business wisdom demands that the solution is both economically viable and has a short time to market. Enterprise software engineers frequently find themselves in the position aptly captured by the often-quoted adage "cost, quality and speed—pick any two"; nevertheless, the need to stay ahead of the chasing pack requires delivering on all three.

To understand why software organizations struggle to achieve these goals, let's consider some of the unique challenges involved in producing enterprise systems.

# The Enterprise Challenge

The J2EE platform is for the development of enterprise-level systems, with an enterprise system defined as an information system that supports the various business processes of an organization.

This definition caters to an extremely broad spectrum of applications and encompasses systems as large and diverse as payroll, customer billing, stock management, human resources, point-of-sale, and decision support systems, to name but a few.

Developing systems at this enterprise level presents software engineers with some very real challenges that go beyond the traditional difficulties associated with standalone shrink-wrapped software.

Here are some of the main concerns a developer must consider when designing and building enterprise-level software:

### Security.

Security is a high priority for all organizations, and security requirements consequently permeate all levels of the system. Virtually all corporate bodies have security policies in place that are mandatory across all applications.

### Operational criteria.

The operational facets of an enterprise system can encompass a wide range of requirements. Aspects such as high availability, reliability, and scalability are all prerequisites for enterprise solutions.

### Transaction support.

The transaction is a fundamental element of any business-oriented application. Many of today's database vendors have long offered support for transactions. However, for the enterprise system, the boundaries of a transaction are not constrained to the database. Rather, true global transactions can involve many databases and disparate information systems. This presents very real challenges when attempting to maintain transaction integrity across all systems in an IT infrastructure.

### Legal requirements.

Information held by most enterprise-level systems can be of a sensitive nature. Specifically, information relating to individuals is usually covered by government legislation that serves to protect the individual's privacy. Any system holding such data is therefore bound to comply with these overriding laws.

### Auditing requirements.

Auditing is closely linked with security and legal requirements. Company watchdogs monitor system access as well as the use of potentially sensitive corporate data. As such, most organizations have in place a standard set of auditing requirements for all systems.

### Quality standards.

Quality is now a business watchword, and quality standards permeate all levels of successful and highly structured organizations. IT systems are not excluded from these standards, and any vendor engaged in the development of bespoke software is expected to comply with whatever standards the customer believes are relevant.

### Enterprise resources.

A company's IT landscape is often cluttered with enterprise resources that must be carefully negotiated. Data warehouses, integration brokers, and content management systems are but a few examples of the strategic resources with which new applications are often required to interoperate.

The J2EE platform was designed to help overcome these challenges, thereby simplifying the development of enterprise systems. This next section summarizes the benefits the J2EE platform provides the enterprise software engineer.

# The J2EE Platform

The J2EE platform targets the development and deployment of distributed, multitiered software applications. J2EE achieves this by defining a rich set of services based around object distribution, transaction management, security, state management, and resource management. These services build on those already provided by the Java 2 Platform, Standard Edition (J2SE).

The features of the J2EE platform significantly reduce the overall level of effort for enterprise developers by providing a robust architectural infrastructure they would otherwise have had to implement themselves. By delegating responsibility of system concerns to the J2EE server, developers are free to focus on the implementation of distributed components that address the needs of the business.

Despite these advantages, in order to undertake the rapid development of enterprise systems, the technologies of the J2EE platform must form an integral part of a wider adaptive development approach to software engineering.

# Defining an Adaptive Foundation

Undertaking the rapid development of enterprise software requires having a strategy in place that sees the entire project team suitably equipped for the task. The techniques and practices introduced throughout this book each contribute toward developing quality software for the J2EE platform faster. However, to gain maximum advantage from the topics covered, project teams must be suitably prepared for their use.

Preparation requires underpinning the topics discussed with proper tools, training, research, and ongoing support and investment from management. Combining these critical elements, along with suitable techniques from this book, gives rise to the concept of producing an adaptive foundation as the basis for the rapid development of enterprise software. The term adaptive foundation reflects both the need to have a base in place for project teams and that the elements that make up this base must have the capacity to accommodate the changing nature of business software.

## Why a Foundation?

The term foundation cements the concept of requiring the necessary building blocks to be in place in order to perform rapid development. Arguably, the term framework would have been equally applicable. However, framework is already a well-used term within software engineering, and the intent was to avoid confusion with established frameworks such as Apache Struts or even J2EE.

Frameworks such as these form only part of the foundation for an effective rapid development strategy.

## Why Adaptive?

Perhaps the biggest schedule killers are the continual changes that bombard a development project throughout its lifecycle. These changes originate from a variety of sources, including changes in requirements, design, scope, and even in team members, customers, and management. All have the potential to adversely impact the delivery timeframe of a software business solution.

The software engineering practices we adopt must be flexible enough to absorb the impact of such changes, allowing the course of the project to change direction when required and hence generate a system that meets the needs of the customer.

The techniques and practices included in this book all fit the criterion of being able to operate within a fluid and dynamic development environment. Within these pages, you'll therefore find such practices as iterative development, active code generation, test-driven development, and aspect-oriented programming. These practices, and others like them, serve to supplement the enterprise development services already available on the J2EE platform.

# Laying the Foundations for Rapid Development

We have established that to meet the challenges of developing enterprise software, a software development company must invest in its own adaptive foundation in order to be in a state of readiness for project work. Rapid development is not possible if a team has to learn how to use new tools and techniques during the course of a project. This learn-as-you-go-approach is commonplace in the software industry but is not conducive to the delivery of on-time solutions to the customer. Instead, investment in tools and training, along with research into the most effective development practices, should all take place well ahead of the project starting up.

This same logic applies to all facets of the project. Here is a list of the concerns in which a software development company should invest if it is to build a solid foundation for conducting rapid development projects:

- People
- Tools
- Frameworks
- Practices
- Standards
- Processes and procedures
- Training
- Continuous improvement

Over the course of the next sections, we examine how each of these elements contributes to the successful outcome of an enterprise project.

## People

Developing software is a people-centric process. The success of the project revolves around the skills and experiences each member of the team brings to the development.

Endeavoring to recruit individuals with the right experience, skills, and attitude is an important factor in forming a team capable of conducting a rapid development project. A further factor is ensuring software engineers are suitably motivated and empowered to perform their work. The best method of achieving this goal is to provide a working environment that fosters personal growth through training and mentoring, and rewards and acknowledges excellence in all aspects of the software engineering discipline.

## Tools

Software development is complex, and having the correct tools in place to underpin the process can contribute greatly to the accuracy and quality of the software produced. The tools selected should improve the productivity of the team, making efficient use of the skills each member of the team possesses. An experienced team will assist in the process of identifying those tools best suited to the task ahead.

## Frameworks

In the context of this book, the J2EE platform is the core framework for the development of all enterprise software. Having staff with significant experience and knowledge of the J2EE platform available for working on a project is key for its success.

J2EE, however, is unlikely to be the only framework employed on a project, although it will be the most significant. Many frameworks exist that augment the services of J2EE, such as frameworks for Web application development or as an alternative persistence mechanism to entity beans. Additionally, a company may invest in the development of its own framework for a specialized business area.

## Practices

Adopting best practice software engineering techniques results in better software. By investing in proven practices, companies put in place the building blocks that enable software engineers to construct high-quality enterprise solutions. Some examples of best practices include adopting a test-first, or test-driven, approach to development or the use of design patterns in software architecture.

## Standards

Standards serve to unify the way we work as a team or set of teams, and provide the detail around the many and varied tasks of systems development. Examples include standards for coding, design, and documentation. They exist as a means of providing a consistent level of quality across all project artifacts.

## Processes and Procedures

Having established a working set of best practices, the step of documenting them as a set of processes and procedures pulls them together as a reference for a company's adaptive development foundation. Moreover, well-defined procedures provide a roadmap for the critical ancillary tasks that make up a complete development project. Such tasks include the use of source control, the raising and tracking of defects, and the release of software into test environments. Having procedures in place for these tasks before a project starts up is a major time saver.

Anyone embarking on a new project will have these procedures as a set of blueprints for setting up and running an effective rapid development project. Likewise, staff moving on to an existing project will have a detailed set of instructions as to how they work as part of the project team. This leaves people free to focus on the important task of developing software.

## Training

Investing in training addresses the problem of the high learning curve associated with software development. Training is a must if all members of a project team are to work productively. Training is required in all elements of the way a company develops software, not just for Java and the J2EE platform. This list of training requirements includes the use of tools, methodologies, software development practices, and internal development processes and procedures.

Training needn't be just about people sitting in classrooms and taking courses. People can learn through a variety of different mediums:

- Independent study by reading books and articles
- Collaborative learning with study groups
- Attending conferences and seminars
- Building prototypes
- Mentoring from experienced staff

The key point is to look beyond generic classroom-based training courses, as these are likely to be unavailable for all of your chosen foundation practices.

## Study Groups

One effective and enjoyable way of learning is to run a series of study groups. This approach sees everyone who is interested in learning a particular topic take part in a group discussion.

The expectation is that each member of the group will have completed background reading on the relevant topic and will be prepared to discuss his or her understanding of the subject with the other members of the group.

A moderator, who starts the discussion with an opening question for the group to consider, runs the session. The role of the moderator is then to keep the discussion flowing by asking further questions and to ensure the group remains focused on the topic.

For more information on the structure of these sessions, see http://www.industriallogic.com/papers/learning.html. This site outlines the makeup of a study group, complete with the moderator's opening questions, for learning about design patterns. However, the forum is applicable to just about any subject.

## Continuous Improvement

The software development industry does not stand still, and new tools, techniques, and practices are continually emerging. A company's adaptive foundation for development must itself be adaptive and capable of incorporating best-of-breed practices as they emerge. Likewise, existing practices already in use by project teams should undergo continual evaluation, with feedback from teams shaping the future direction of a company's development strategy.

Keeping the adaptive foundation up to date requires investing time and effort in a program of continuous improvement. Staff members need to research new techniques to determine their suitability, while information gained on the use of existing practices must be fed back into the process. Time must be set aside to write up the ongoing findings of a continuous improvement program, with the presentation of recommendations made periodically to the company's development staff.

# Foundation Investment Benefits

Establishing an adaptive foundation for rapid development requires a sizeable investment in terms of time and money. In a busy development shop or IT department, both of these commodities can be in short supply. Furthermore, the benefits of defining an adaptive development foundation can be difficult to justify in the short term, as the greatest returns are only realized after the completion of several projects. Consequently, convincing both company management and colleagues of the need for such an investment is not an easy task. Nevertheless, compelling reasons for making this investment exist:

### Competitive advantage.

This reason is also synonymous with a happy customer. The efficiencies resulting from streamlining a development process enable the production of high-quality software at a lower cost. High quality and low cost are both reasons why a customer would choose you over your competitors.

### Resource sharing.

Putting in place a companywide development foundation makes the process of moving between projects considerably easier for staff, as everyone understands how a project functions. The tools are familiar, as are the practices, processes, and procedures. Likewise, everyone should be working to a common set of principles and standards. No time is lost with an individual coming up to speed with the idiosyncrasies of a particular project.

### Return on investment (ROI).

Training budgets need to be spent wisely, and enterprise-level development tools tend to carry high price tags. Focusing money and effort on a consolidated set of development needs makes these funds go further. A consolidated approach provides a greater return than spreading scarce budgetary resources too thinly over a hotchpotch development strategy comprised of noninteroperable tools and incongruent practices.

### Consistency.

Following repeatable methods using a common framework and tools brings an element of repeatability to the software development process. This repeatability translates directly in accurate estimates, thereby enabling the objective evaluation of the risks of taking on new project work.

### Improved morale.

Finally, software developers enjoy working on projects that regard software engineering as a professional discipline. A company's willingness to invest in its staff and promote a best-practice approach to enterprise software development is an indicator of an organization that takes software engineering seriously.

Unfortunately, several barriers exist to achieving these benefits. These next sections highlight some of the factors that must be addressed in order to see a successful adaptive foundation put in place within a company.

# Critical Success Factors

There are several key factors involved in successfully adopting a companywide infrastructure for the purposes of undertaking effective, and hence rapid, software development. The establishment of a successful foundation as a base for rapid development requires meeting each of these factors, which include:

- Achieving acceptance of the various tools, techniques, and practices by all staff
- Ensuring all development staff receive education on the various elements that make up the adaptive foundation
- Gaining full support from management for the uptake of the foundation

These next sections elaborate on these points and look at options for achieving these key success points.

## Obtaining Developer Acceptance

Software engineers can be a very difficult crowd to please. As software development is a people-centric process, achieving a universal uptake of your proposed new development methods requires obtaining agreement and support from the people who develop the systems. Achieving this buy-in from fellow software engineers often requires the diplomacy skills of Henry Kissinger.

A companywide development approach is truly effective only if the developers are willing to embrace its methods and adopt its practices. Gaining acceptance from all developers builds up a critical mass of information, which sees the adopted tools, methods, and practices continually refined and evolved based on the experiences of the different project teams.

All project teams can benefit from this growing body of knowledge. However, teams that ignore the guidance of a company's proven practices and follow a different path soon find themselves isolated. If trouble strikes, the relevant expertise is unlikely to be available on other teams to assist the team with any problems that arise from the use of a divergent technology.

Admittedly, this scenario is common with development technology, because new projects often embrace the latest and greatest, if for no other reason than that the customer demands it. However, in this case, examples of breakaway groups include teams that use an alternative source-control system or decide the company's chosen development methodology is not to their liking.

tip

Adopt new techniques and practices as the project demands, but make use of a company's proven methods where they are available.

Obtaining the support of colleagues for defining this unifying development strategy is best achieved by encouraging everyone to become actively involved in its formation. You should make it possible for everyone to research new methods and contribute to the evolution of the adaptive foundation. Avoid creating a single group charged with this responsibility, since doing so will likely generate resentment among those software engineers outside of the process.

Involving everyone in the process of forming an adaptive foundation for development may present logistical problems where a large company or IT department is involved. Where a large group is concerned, you may need to resort to other tactics. Here are a few options you might want to consider.

## Seminars

Run regular seminars to advise the group on the state of play of the development strategy. Encourage questions from the floor and make sure you get back to people with answers at the next scheduled seminar. Also, be prepared to take onboard any suggestions that come out of these sessions.

Another option is to invite to people to speak at the seminars. Try to get speakers from different teams so that input is taken from all sides. You also might want to consider videoing the presentations at these seminars and making them available online.

## Groupware

The setup of a collaborative Web site, or *Wiki*, is also a good option for your hardworking colleagues who don't like leaving their desks to attend meetings and seminars.

tip

> See http://www.tikiwiki.org or http://www.plone.org for open source versions of groupware products.

Using collaborative groupware of this nature fosters an environment of teamwork and encourages everyone to contribute feedback to the development and growth of an adaptive foundation that incorporates tools and practices everyone wants to use.

These collaborative intranet sites are also a good mechanism for the distribution of documentation on the use and application of the tools and practices that make up the foundation of the development strategy. Distribution of information on the use of the adaptive foundation relates to education, which is one of the critical success factors we discuss in the next section.

## Education

When undertaking a particularly challenging software engineering task, most of us would prefer to solve the problem by taking a path we have already traveled. This usually involves falling back on the tools and techniques with which we are already familiar and consequently lie within our *comfort zone*. This attitude is understandable, as having become expert with a certain technology, few of us relish the thought of discarding all that hard-earned knowledge and starting from scratch with an alternative approach.

This reluctance to step outside of our own personal comfort zones is a primary reason why development strategies that prescribe the use of specific tools, methods, and practices struggle to gain widespread acceptance within an organization; people like to stick with what they already know, despite the benefits of alternative, and potentially superior, approaches. The key to overcoming this reluctance to embrace new approaches is education.

Education expands people's comfort zones. It gives them the confidence to work with the methods of an adaptive foundation on critical projects.

To be effective, education must encompass every aspect of the software development process and be available to all members of a project team. Seminars should be run frequently, and comprehensive documentation must be available on all facets of the foundation's methods and tools. Seminars and training courses are essential for new staff, and the makeup of projects should always include someone experienced with the adopted development process as part of the team in at least an advisory or mentoring capacity.

In my experience, failure to provide an adequate level of education on the methods of a company's chosen development foundation leads to project teams pushing their own approaches. This situation ultimately results in a fragmented development approach between teams that does not yield the same benefits as a consolidated and cohesive development strategy.

important

Adopting a companywide development strategy does not mean being dismissive of the skills and experiences people bring to the project. The formation of an effective adaptive foundation depends on input from all staff. Rather than dismissing people's ideas, evaluate them on merit to see if they warrant inclusion as part of the broader foundation approach.

## Management Support

It isn't possible to establish a foundation for rapid development without the full support of management. Management needs to support the concept and, where appropriate, enforce the concept.

To successfully build and maintain an adaptive foundation requires investment. Tools must be purchased, training organized, and time set aside for researching new technologies or trialing emerging development practices.

Management also has an active role to play in gaining global acceptance of the foundation's methods. Despite the use of seminars, collaborative Web sites, and ongoing education, certain groups or individuals may still attempt to undertake project work using methods that are tangential to those of the other teams. In this instance, if teams are unable to justify their approach adequately, then management must bring these teams into line. Failure to do so will marginalize the investment in the adaptive foundation.

On a cautionary note, management should avoid being overly heavy-handed. Software development is a creative process that is unlikely to become the factory-line-production process many people would like it to be. The drive to establish a common development strategy should be tempered with the need for software engineers to trust their own judgment and be given the leeway to build solutions to the best of their capabilities.

The intent of an adaptive rapid development foundation is to augment the skills of the project team in the pursuit of building better software solutions for the customer. A fine line exists between approaches that stifle the creative process and those that encourage it. Ensuring the adopted strategy does not cross this line requires constant refinement of the approach with feedback from project teams.

To conclude this chapter, the next section outlines the contents of this book and the topics that are introduced as potential candidates for inclusion in a company's adaptive foundation.

# Summary

Proper preparation is vital to the success of a rapid development project. Companies and project teams must ready themselves for efficient development by investing in an adaptive foundation for development that encompasses a complete software development infrastructure.

This overarching adaptive infrastructure goes beyond the choice of tools, techniques, and practices, and mandates a significant investment in education and research activities necessary to maintain these elements as a suitable platform for ongoing rapid development projects.

The concepts of the adaptive foundation pervade every chapter of this book. For each tool, technique, and practice introduced, the underlying expectation is that every element adopted as part of an adaptive foundation will receive an appropriate level of investment.

Throughout the remainder of this book, we look at techniques that expand upon the J2EE platform as a basis for conducting the rapid development of enterprise software.

The next chapter looks at the techniques that have become synonymous with the subject of rapid application development and highlights the value of prototyping as part of the development process.

## Additional Information

Although the contents of this book complement the J2EE platform, this book is not a reference manual for J2EE. If you require further information on the platform, an excellent starting point is Sun Microsystems' J2EE site, which contains a comprehensive listing of J2EE resources. The Sun Web site can be found at http://java.sun.net/j2ee.

# 2

# Rapid Application Development

If the term rapid application development (RAD) were a Java method, it would have been deprecated long ago. As of the start of the new millennium, RAD had all but disappeared from the vocabulary of most software engineers.

Though the term is slipping from popular use as the hype surrounding RAD projects fades, the demand for rapid development is still as strong now as it was when RAD first emerged on the scene in the late 1980s. Despite tremendous advancements in the field of software engineering, telling statistics indicate the IT industry still struggles to realize the fast-paced demands of the business world.

So, what happened to RAD? If the requirement for RAD is as great now as it was 20 years ago, why is the term losing favor given the advent of Internet time and the accelerating pace of technological innovation?

The answer has more to do with marketing than software engineering. The concepts behind the various RAD methods are still valid, but the terminology has changed as the techniques and practices of RAD have evolved. Instead of talking of rapidity, we now speak in terms of *agility*.

Although the terminology of RAD is disappearing, its legacy is a set of mature software engineering practices. This chapter introduces the main elements to have come out of the RAD stable and puts them within the context of the practices and techniques this book presents for the purposes of rapid J2EE development. In particular, we focus on the benefits of prototyping, a technique now commonly associated with a fast-paced development approach.

## Common Elements of RAD

RAD emerged back in the late 1980s as a response to the growing frustrations of customers who needed IT solutions delivered in shorter timeframes than were possible with the mainstream development techniques of the time. RAD methods made the promise of not only reducing time to market but also costing less than traditional methods and delivering higher quality software that better met the business requirements [Reilly, 1995].

The formation of RAD was an ad hoc process, with many IT companies promoting their own interpretations of what constituted a rapid application development approach. RAD therefore lacks a single unifying process that gives an exact definition for the term. Nevertheless, several techniques and practices are acknowledged as being common elements of a rapid development approach.

## Timebox Development

Timeboxing is a primary RAD technique that has development conducted over a fixed duration. This timeline of the project is immutable, and the functionality of the application is tailored to fit within the boundaries of the timebox. The objective for the project team is to produce a working system at the end of the timebox. Functionality is removed from the system if the team is struggling to meet this objective. Essentially, the timebox practice seeks to fit the application to the schedule rather than formulating a schedule to fit the application [McConnell, 1996].

Timebox development encourages the customer to prioritize requirements, thereby enabling the development team to focus on the early delivery of functionality critical to the application.

### Limits risk.

The customer receives a working application in a short timeframe, albeit with limited functionality. This avoids the risk common in typically mainstream development practices whereby a fully featured application is delivered in a *big-bang* approach. Such approaches risk failing to deliver any functionality come the end of the schedule.

### Avoids overengineering.

Team members are allowed no time to design for imaginary future requirements. Consequently, all design work must address only the functionality that is to be delivered at the end of the schedule.

### Energizes the development team.

An aggressive schedule focuses the attention of the team on the immediate needs of the application.

If employed correctly, the practice makes for a dynamic, pressure-cooker environment on which many development teams thrive. In the right environment, the energy and enthusiasm generated by the team for the project can result in very high productivity gains.

Chapter 3, Embracing Adaptive Methods, examines the importance of timeboxing for conducting iterative development, a software development method that sits at the heart of today's agile development processes.

## Domain-Specific Languages

In an effort to reduce the critical path during the construction phase of the project, RAD promotes the use of specialized development languages to increase productivity.

As the name implies, domain-specific languages target a distinct problem domain. They are not general-purpose programming languages like Java, but instead address a specific function. Examples of domain-specific languages include:

* Jython for ad hoc scripting purposes
* SQL for data access code
* Prolog for creating expert systems
* Tcl/Tk for prototyping user interfaces
* JSP for building HTML pages with dynamic content

> *Jython is covered in Chapter 9, Scripting*

Although the subject of alternative languages may seem moot to anyone developing for the J2EE platform, it is possible to combine the power of these domain-specific languages with Java.

Part III looks at the concepts behind a multilanguage development approach and examines how specialized languages can help augment the high-level language constructs Java already provides.

## Software Reuse

Software reuse meets two important design aims. First, it results in the development of common modules that are shareable between applications. This aspect of reuse makes possible the assembly of applications from readily available and proven software modules, thereby offering a fast and efficient method of generating systems.

Second, reuse avoids the perils of duplicating code within an application. A software architecture that has functionality duplicated throughout the code base is difficult to change due to the need to affect code changes across multiple parts of the application. This is poor design and leads to systems that are slow to develop and expensive to maintain.

Achieving both of these reuse aims in the design of systems results in substantial benefits:

* Improved productivity
* Higher quality
* Improved software reliability
* Easier maintenance
* Reduced time to market

Software architectures that take advantage of the principles of software reuse provide an increased return on investment and a reduction in the total cost of ownership for the system's owners. However, attaining these benefits requires applying strict software engineering disciplines in the area of software design.

Reuse in software design is difficult to achieve. Over the years, considerable effort has gone into the development of languages and technologies that enable the full benefits of software reuse to be realized. To date, the greatest successes in the area of reuse have come from the practice of object-oriented design. There are two main areas of interest:

* *Object-oriented programming* for implementing reusable software elements at the code level
* *Component-based architectures* for building applications from prefabricated software components

Let's briefly consider both of these methods.

## Object-Oriented Programming (OOP)

The object-oriented paradigm grew out of the desire to have languages capable of representing real-world objects and as a means of promoting software reuse. OOP languages embody the best techniques for code reuse developed to date and offer the software constructs necessary for building applications from existing software modules.

Java developers will already be familiar with the OOP reuse concepts of composition and inheritance. In addition to these, the advent of J2SE 5.0 adds another string to the Java developer's bow in the form of generics.

## Component-Based Architectures

If Java is a language for software reuse, then J2EE is a platform for component reuse. The J2EE platform makes it possible to construct enterprise systems using component-based architectures. A component-based architecture has systems built by integrating established software component.

> *Chapter 4, Designing for Rapidity, examines component-based architecture options.*

Components can span both horizontal and vertical domains in that they can provide both infrastructural and behavioral functionality. Engineers have the option of developing components inhouse or looking to other vendors to purchase shrink-wrapped offerings. In some cases, software development companies may elect to invest in the development of component libraries for a specific domain such as the government sector, financial services, or telecommunications.

Through this strategy, vendors of software development services are able to gain a sizeable competitive advantage. The construction of these component libraries is an important part of investing in an adaptive foundation for development.

## Productivity Tools

Sophisticated development tools feature prominently in many of the different approaches to RAD. Selecting the right tool can dramatically increase productivity for virtually any given project task.

In addition to increasing productivity, tools can help simplify the process of developing software, a key concern for J2EE developers. Developing solutions for the J2EE platform is a complex task. J2EE pulls together a myriad of advanced engineering concepts, which includes object-oriented programming, distributed computing, multitiered architectures, and message-oriented middleware. Selecting the right tools can help considerably in dealing with the complexities of the J2EE platform and its enterprise services. Sun's *Studio Creator* and BEA's *WebLogic Workshop* are two examples of visual development tools that seek to ease the task of developing solutions for the J2EE platform by offering graphical drag-and-drop environments.

Another item in the RAD developer's toolkit is the integrated CASE tool, or modeling tool. CASE tools were a popular choice on RAD projects, and we assess how these modeling tools can contribute to the rapid development of J2EE applications in Chapter 5, *Modeling Software*. Later in the book, Chapter 8, *Model-Driven Architecture*, takes the use of models a step further and looks at how modeling tools that support the model-driven architecture (MDA) paradigm can automatically generate early iterations of working J2EE applications from minimal domain models.

The rapid developer needs to have more than just modeling tools in his or her repertoire. The importance of a fully integrated development environment is discussed in Chapter 13, *The Integrated Development Environment*, while in Chapter 15, *Efficient Quality Assurance*, the focus is on the benefits of testing tools.

## Rapid Prototyping

Prototyping is arguable the most well known of all the RAD techniques and is ideally suited to a wide range of tasks. The practice is ideally suited for defining end-user requirements and for exploring the viability of suggested software architectures. Consequently, prototyping offers a low-risk approach to software development.

Some of the reasons to incorporate the construction of a prototype into your project schedule include:

- Addressing customer uncertainties
- Validating architectural decisions
- Resolving performance problems
- Capturing customer requirements

- Communicating ideas and intent to the customer
- Proving the choice of technology and platform
- Demonstrating user interfaces and workflows
- Driving out risk

Prototyping is a pivotal RAD technique and is referenced throughout the pages of this book. This next section looks at the different types of prototypes we can build and offers some guidelines for using them effectively.

# Working with Prototypes

Prototypes are best undertaken as self-contained units of work with clearly defined objectives. Team sizes should be small, typically numbering no more than two or three people.

As prototypes are not destined for a formal release, many of the necessary standards and procedures that cradle production-level software are not applicable, much to the delight of the development team. This level of freedom makes for an intense development environment that many teams appreciate. Productivity tends to be high as engineers are able to focus on a discrete piece of work without the burden of the usual checks and controls endemic to larger projects.

tip

Always volunteer for work on prototypes and proof-of-concepts.

Despite the benefits, the development of a prototype can sometimes appear as an unnecessary diversion when the pressure is on to deliver the real thing. For projects where time is at a premium, management often prefers to have staff focus on production code rather than diverting resources into the construction of prototypes. However, although the prototype requires upfront effort at the start of the project, its ability to drive out risk, clarify requirements, and validate the architecture enables significant time savings to be made throughout the project. Thus, by using prototyping to identify potential problems at the start of the project, these problems can be addressed early in the process before they snowball into major issues at later stages of the development.

Prototyping therefore offers a diverse range of benefits. Consequently, different types of prototype have evolved depending on their intended use.

## Prototyping Approaches and Types

Prototyping is an important concept of the IBM Rational Unified Process, which makes extensive use of the technique. The Rational Process defines several factors to consider when making use of prototyping as part of a development project [Kruchten, 2003]. The first of these factors is how prototypes fit into the overall project lifecycle. Here, there are two options:

- *Throwaway*, where the prototype is discarded once its objectives have been met
- *Evolutionary*, where the prototype is continually evolved into a production-level system

The second factor is the intended purpose of the prototype, which gives the type of the prototype. Again, there are two available options:

- *Behavioral*, which demonstrates system behavior and helps capture user requirements
- *Structural*, which validates areas of the system's architecture

Over the next sections, we look at the purposes and needs of each of the different types of prototype as well as the tools and environment necessary to support their development.

## Throwaway Prototyping

As the name implies, the throwaway prototype, also known as an exploratory prototype, does not have long for this world. Its primary objectives are to validate a solution or to clarify a problem domain. Validation could be the performance of a part of the architecture and clarification could be of the look-and-feel of the user-interface.

Regardless of the purpose of the throwaway, it will be discarded once its objectives have been realized. Because the code from which it is built is not intended to be production level, the throwaway prototype can be assembled at great speed, using whatever tools, languages, and methods prove most expedient.

## Evolutionary Prototyping

The evolutionary prototype has far loftier aspirations than does its throwaway counterpart. Here the prototype evolves throughout the life of the project, either gradually or rapidly, into the final system. In this case, the prototype is an integral part of the project lifecycle whereby the prototype is modified incrementally in response to customer feedback through a process of ongoing refactoring. This approach is closely associated with the practice of timebox development.

Since the evolutionary prototype will transform into the eventual system, greater discipline and control is necessary during its development. Unlike the throwaway, essential disciplines such as code style, code reviews, testing, and design documentation must all feature prominently in the prototype's construction.

## Behavioral Prototypes

Behavioral prototypes, as the name implies, are concerned with what the system does, not how it does it. Typically, behavioral prototypes are built as throwaways.

The behavioral prototype usually targets the user interface and provides a mechanism for discussing ideas and requirements with the customer. Feedback captured from the customer needs to be quickly reflected in the prototype, thereby providing for the rapid transformation of ideas into solid requirements. In achieving this aim, the prototype needs to be constructed using suitable high-level tools and languages in order that the customer can see a fast turn-around of ideas into demonstrable functionality.

### Structural Prototypes

The structural prototype's primary concern is proving the architecture of the system during the early stages of the project. Areas of the architecture that are identified as high risk can be proven using a small prototype before a full-scale development effort is commenced against the architecture.

Unlike behavioral prototypes, structural prototypes tend to be evolutionary instead of throwaway. Having proven a slice of the architecture, the code, rather than being discarded, is more likely to be evolved through refactoring until it is of a production level.

## Choosing Between Throwaway and Evolutionary

Throwaway and evolutionary prototypes are not incompatible on a project, as they each target different aspects of the project. You could therefore expect to use a behavioral prototype for establishing the system requirements by modeling the user interface and an evolutionary prototype to incrementally advance the architecture. Often, the question is not which prototyping approach to adopt but how best to combine the two.

Many factors impact the decision as to which approach is right for your project. The overheads of the throwaway may not be economically viable for a small project. If the project requirements are well defined, then an evolutionary prototype is probably the best option. If they are likely to be subject to constant change, then a throwaway prototype is the preferred choice in support of a requirements gathering exercise.

It is important that the type of approach be selected prior to commencing work on the final system. Starting with a throwaway and then attempting to convert to an evolutionary approach is unlikely to be successful. Likewise, the converse will result in expensive disposable code. The approach to the prototype governs the way in which the prototype is developed. Tighter quality control is required for evolutionary prototypes. Moreover, evolutionary prototypes have to be written in the language in which the final system will be implemented. In our case, this is Java. However, for the purposes of a throwaway prototype, a scripting language such as Perl, Python, or Tcl may be more applicable.

warning

Ensure the final system is capable of delivering the same functionality as the prototype.

Finally, if you are going to make use of a specialized prototyping language or toolkit to help build the prototype at high speed, be careful to ensure you are able to reproduce the full functionality demonstrated to the customer in the final system. Even slight differences in the look and feel of the user interface can result in an unhappy customer.

# Summary

Rapid application development is an approach to developing software that seeks to deliver on-time solutions that meet the needs of the customer.

Approaches to RAD vary, but the commonly accepted version of the process encompasses the key elements of:

- An adaptive development approach using timeboxed iterations
- Extensive use of prototypes
- Sophisticated development tools for improving productivity
- Domain-specific and high-level languages
- Component-based architectures for assembling robust applications from proven software components

Although the usage of the term RAD is in decline, these key elements of RAD form the basis of today's leading agile development processes. These new methods build on the promises of RAD, proclaiming to offer accelerated development times, fewer defects, increased customer satisfaction, and a solution for rapidly changing requirements [Boehm, 2003].

The next chapter examines this new breed of software methodologies and looks at the importance of adopting an adaptive approach to software development.

## Additional Information

Prototypes don't have to be developed on the computer. They can instead be constructed using a whiteboard and Post-it notes. For anyone interested in learning the techniques surrounding the use of paper-based prototypes, Carolyn Snyder has written a book on the subject, *Paper Prototyping: The Fast and Easy Way to Design and Refine User Interfaces* [Snyder, 2003].

The Robert L. Glass title, *Facts and Fallacies of Software Engineering*, observes a few home truths with regard to software reuse and the attitude of software engineers to high-end development tools [Glass, 2002]. Interestingly, Glass notes that few of us use them.

# 3

# Embracing Adaptive Methods

The number and range of books on software lifecycle methodologies is probably only eclipsed by the number of publications on weight loss. Despite the huge volume of literature and collective knowledge available on both topics, software projects still run late or fail completely to achieve their goals, and the western world still has an obesity problem.

Anyone wishing to lose weight is spoiled for a choice with an immense range of diets and dieting books from which to choose. However, the collective information in all of these works can be boiled down to a few simple facts that virtually everyone is aware of: If you eat less and exercise regularly, you will become fitter and trimmer.

I believe the same reductive analysis can be applied to software development processes and that out of all the material written on the subject, a core set of fundamental best practices exists that will help guide the majority of enterprise-level projects to a successful conclusion.

The objective of this chapter is therefore to define this distilled set of practices from the standpoint of a rapid development project. Within this chapter, we look at the rationale behind the choice of software development methodology and analyze those elements of a software engineering process that are conducive to rapid development.

We look at the classic waterfall model and see why, despite its widely recognized weaknesses, it still permeates the thinking of the majority of IT professionals. As an alternative to the waterfall model, we examine the benefits of adaptive development methods and compare two examples of this type: first, the well-established IBM Rational Unified Process (RUP), and second, the ultra-nimble process, Extreme Programming—the flagship of the agile movement.

## Why Use a Methodology?

A successful software development methodology defines how all of our tools, techniques, and practices combine into a winning formula. The techniques discussed throughout this book are meaningless in isolation unless a process is adopted to bind them into a cohesive development strategy. Indeed, the choice of methodology is a key part of defining an adaptive foundation for enterprise development.

The use of methodologies for software engineering arose out of the need to make the software development process a repeatable and quantifiable activity. Methodologies aim to place a degree of control over a software project, enabling it to be steered toward a successful conclusion through a proven series of steps and actions.

For RAD, we want a process that requires the minimum of administrative control and delivers the most productive method. The question is how much process is enough and how much is too much. Finding the correct answer has significant implications for rapid development.

## A J2EE RAD Methodology

The ideal methodology for rapid development is one that is optimal for the development underway. People tend to think of RAD methodologies as being lean and mean, carrying out only those tasks that relate directly to the success of the project.

This definition is valid but needs to be placed in context. A process that fits this criterion for a small project might be completely unsuitable for a large-scale development. Conversely, a method that has proven successful on a large project might prove completely unwieldy and inefficient when used by a smaller team.

A lean and mean approach is required, but we need to qualify the minimalist approach by being sensitive to the needs of the system under development.

In addition to being lightweight, the process adopted should exploit the strengths of the J2EE platform. J2EE solutions use distributed object-oriented technology; hence, the process followed should align with the needs of this type of solution. A process founded on procedural methods, for example, is unlikely to form a favorable complement to a J2EE project.

In order to conform with the central tenet of this book, that RAD projects require the ability to react quickly and effectively to change, the methodology selected also must offer an adaptive approach to software development. Indeed, all of the techniques in this book point toward an adaptive approach, and our choice of methodology should be no different.

Summarizing these points we get the following set of criteria for an ideal RAD methodology:

**Lightweight.**

The process must offer the minimum level of ceremony in the context of the size of system under development.

**Complementary.**

The process must work to exploit the strengths of the development tools and techniques adopted by the team. This relationship is symbiotic, as the tools and techniques should in turn support the chosen methodology.

**Adaptive.**

To be effective, the process must be able to contend with the emergent nature of business requirements, enabling the project team to change direction as and when the business dictates.

Let's consider the different types of methodologies available for enterprise developments.

## Adaptive Versus Predictive Methods

The number of different software development methodologies available is many and varied. However, after several decades of evolution, development methodologies generally fall into one of two categories: either *predictive* or *adaptive* [Fowler, 2000].

Predictive methods seek to draw upon the disciplines of established engineering principles to provide a measure of predictability to the software engineering process. They attempt to quantify the cost, duration, and resource requirements of a system up front, in the early stages of the project, by completing all work relating to requirements definition and design ahead of any actual implementation.

Predictive methods can prove very effective for systems whose requirements remain stable throughout the duration of the project. However, their rigid approach makes them resistant to change. Any refinement of the requirements downstream from the initial analysis phase can lead to costly rework. The process must backtrack in order to accommodate the change within the plan and identify the impact on the project schedule.

In contrast, adaptive methods accept that for most systems, the requirements will change during the course of the project. These methods look to put feedback mechanisms in place that enable changes to be incorporated back into the system with minimal effort and cost.

The classic *waterfall lifecycle model* personifies the predictive method, while adaptive methods rely on an *incremental development approach* for flexibility. The next sections cover the suitability of each of these lifecycle models for the rapid development of enterprise systems.

# The Waterfall Lifecycle Model

The waterfall model is the most well known of all the software lifecycles, and its basic steps have been ingrained into the heads of countless IT students. The waterfall model was one of the first attempts to bring order to the chaotic world of software development, and sought to bring predictability to software projects through the application of methods taken from the various engineering professions.

Despite its popularity, the model has some significant weaknesses that make it poorly suited to the rapid development of business software. This section reviews the waterfall approach to software development and discusses its strengths and weaknesses.

## The Classic Waterfall Model

The waterfall model offers a linear approach to software development. Practitioners of the model diligently and methodically step through its distinct phases of analysis, design, coding, and testing.

Figure 3–1 shows the steps of the classic waterfall approach.

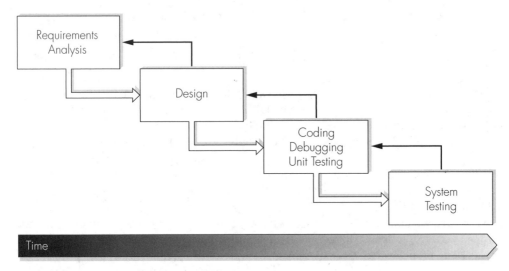

**Figure 3–1**    The waterfall lifecycle model.

The approach is document-driven, with the initial phases focusing on the creation of highly detailed requirements and design documents before any coding work commences. The phases of the waterfall model do not overlap. As the name implies, they cascade one into another.

note

> Contrary to many people's understanding of the waterfall lifecycle, the model does provide for feedback between the phases, making it possible to backtrack and undertake rework from a previous phase. However, backtracking is difficult, and essentially the waterfall model sees the project progressing in a linear fashion, with each phase building on the work of the previous phase.

## Strengths and Weaknesses

The model does offer some considerable benefits in lieu of an ad hoc approach to development. It enforces a disciplined method on the project team, ensuring that requirements are duly considered up front at the start of the project and that extensive planning is carried out before resources are committed to the development. To a degree, these are all good software engineering practices because they improve the team's understanding of the customer's needs.

Unfortunately, the waterfall lifecycle model also suffers from some inherent weaknesses:

* No system is delivered until near the end of the schedule. This is high risk, since the system may have diverged from the customer's initial expectations.

- Mistakes in the design, or missed requirements, are extremely costly to rectify in the later stages of the process, since the entire project must be backtracked to an earlier phase.

- Testing is left until the last phase of the project. Defects detected at this late stage of the development are the most expensive to fix with the waterfall model.

- Leaving testing to the end of the project also means the quality of the application being developed cannot be gauged until testing has been completed. This leaves it very late to address any quality concerns in either the design or implementation.

- The model is document-intensive and devotes considerable resources to the production of specifications for each phase.

Many of you have examples of projects conducted according to the disciplines of the waterfall model. One such project I worked on early in my career made the inefficiencies of the model abundantly clear, especially when the pressure to deliver intensified.

## A Case Study

The project team was developing a shrink-wrapped hydrographic surveying system in C++ (this was in the days before Java). The team was small, but every member was well skilled in the use of the technology and knowledgeable in the practices of object-oriented development.

The team was under considerable pressure to deliver the product. The competition had stolen a lead with the latest release of its software, and the company was in catch-up mode. The project stakeholders were in a state of constant high stress. Every passing day that we didn't deliver, the competition stole more and more of the market share. On the project, stress levels were high and tempers were short.

We were a dedicated group of developers who were well aware of the concerns of the stakeholders. We wanted to deliver quickly, but we also took pride in our work and wanted to produce a quality product.

To achieve both aims, we decided, called for a formal disciplined approach. The biggest consumer of time on the project was rework. If we could reduce the amount of rework, we could reduce our time to market.

Working on the premise that documents are cheap, while skillfully crafted object-oriented code is expensive, we put the following process in place based on our knowledge of the software engineering best practices of the day.

1. Discuss the requirements with one of the product specialists at the team's disposal.

2. Have the developer sit down and carefully document how the new functionality should operate.

3. Present the functional specification to the product specialists for approval.
   The specialists sign off the document if they are happy with the content; if not, step 1 is revisited and the document revised.

4. Once the specification has been accepted by the product specialists, the developer designs, implements, and delivers the new functionality.

5. Finally, the product specialists take on the role of testers and verify the functionality of the delivered product feature.

The approach seemed both sound and diligent. Having the product specialists accept the requirements specification meant the development team could focus on implementing the exact functionality requested. Unfortunately, things didn't progress as smoothly as anticipated.

One of my main tasks was the design and implementation of the system's real-time navigational displays. The purpose of one particular display was to provide the helmsman with a visual cue as to whether the vessel was maintaining the correct course. After creating a functional specification for the navigational display, work began on the implementation.

Weeks later, the display was complete and a new version of the software was released to the product specialists for formal testing. At this point the problems started.

The product specialists were not happy. Yes, they agreed the helmsman's display met the original requirements, and no, they could not find any defects. However, it was not what they wanted.

Seeing the display in action, they realized requirements had been missed that meant the display would prove unusable for navigation out on the water. They also didn't like the flat, two-dimensional look of the display and suggested something more three-dimensional. Why hadn't they said so at the time?

This feedback was very frustrating. I had worked extra hours to get the job done on time and to make sure the display's behavior was exactly as the product specialists had requested. From my perspective, I had achieved my goal yet had failed to deliver functionality that met their needs.

To avoid repeating the problem a second time, I took a different approach. First, I ignored the requirements document, instead taking a day to restructure the code so it roughly incorporated some of the changes. This next version was far from production quality but demonstrated some of the main new ideas. I went back to the product group with the new version, explaining that the software was not stable and was only a rough prototype. They liked the revamped display but suggested some further changes.

Over the course of the next week, I went through the cyclic process of revising and demonstrating the display. Quite soon, the display evolved to the point where the requirements were agreed and effort then went into bringing the software up to a production level.

Once the final version was ready, the product group documented the display's functionality as part of the user guide, leaving me free to get on with the next system feature.

From the experience, I learned a few things:

* In this case, writing software was quicker than writing a requirements specification.

* People like to see things working. Few of us can appreciate the nuances of the final system from reading a description in a document.

* The approach of involving the end users throughout the process, and getting their input, made for a better product. The final version of the display looked much better than my first effort.

*   If the display had been demonstrated when it was only even half complete, the problems would have been picked up much earlier, thereby saving a lot of extra work.

Despite all of this, a heroic team effort won through and the project was a success. The architecture we produced for the system proved a stable platform and served as the basis for other profitable products. In the end, we came through, but the questions arose: Is there a better way, and could we have got to market any sooner?

The answer is yes, and we could see the key to successful future projects lay in the application of an approach that allowed us to factor in feedback from the product specialists at every step of the development process. For that, we needed to ditch our waterfall variant in favor of something along adaptive lines. To do that required turning to an *iterative approach* to development.

# Iterative Development

Adaptive methods offer the ability to cope with changing requirements by adopting an iterative development approach. Iterative development is common to most forms of adaptive methods and provides some considerable advantages over conventional linear development approaches, as typified by the waterfall model. With an iterative approach, the entire project lifecycle is broken up into smaller pieces known as iterations, where each iteration is a complete "mini-waterfall" in its own right.

The approach is largely founded on the *spiral model* defined by Barry Boehm [Boehm, 1988]. The spiral model forms the basis of modern adaptive methods and is an incremental, risk-averse approach to software development. Boehm's approach was conceived in reaction to the observation that existing linear methods were discouraging more effective approaches to software engineering, such as prototyping and software reuse.

Instead of trying to digest the requirements of a system in one sitting, iterative development avoids heartburn by taking smaller, digestible bites out of the full system. These bites are known as *iterations*. A typical iteration takes a subset of the requirements through the standard phases of the waterfall model from requirements analysis through to functioning system.

Each iteration is conducted over a short, palatable timeframe, thereby providing near-term milestones for the team to achieve. At the conclusion of the iteration, a demonstrable system is available for inspection by the customer, although ideally the customer should provide input throughout the entire timeframe of the iteration.

Feedback received from the completed iteration is used for planning the objectives and scope of the next iteration. This ongoing planning effort, driven by the feedback from iterations, enables the project to adjust course as new requirements emerge and existing ones are consolidated.

Figure 3–2 shows the basic structure of an iterative development process.

Boehm described his approach as being spiral, as the model sees an iteration cycle through the phases of requirements analysis, design, implementation, and testing—although Boehm's model contained several more phases, including the important activity of risk analysis. Subse-

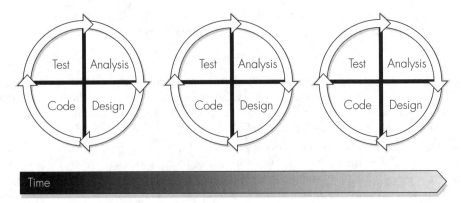

**Figure 3–2**   Iterative development lifecycle.

quent cycles follow the same path, but the system spirals gradually outward as the software grows in terms of functionality, complexity, and investment.

## The Benefits of an Iterative Approach

### Benefits of Iterative Development

- Accommodates changing requirements
- Refines system requirements
- Addresses risks early
- Produces robust architectures
- Promotes understanding and facilitates software reuse
- Provides an environment for learning
- Continually assesses software quality
- Improves the accuracy of estimates
- Continually refines the development process
- Offers an enjoyable working environment

These next sections highlight the benefits of iterative development.

### Accommodates Changing Requirements

A change in requirements can be a schedule-destroying event on a waterfall project if the change occurs downstream of the requirements phase. Iterative development projects are considerably more flexible and can be adjusted midcourse to align the project in the wake of any changes through the essential activity of iteration planning.

## Encourages Refinement of System Requirements

Customers are notorious for not knowing what they want until they have seen it in action. This isn't a criticism but an observation of basic human nature, and is something of which we are all guilty.

Having each iteration conclude in a functioning system, demonstrating a subset of the total requirements, enables the end user to build up an accurate picture of how the system will look and behave. Based on this understanding, the end user is empowered to refine the requirements until the system exhibits the required functionality.

## Addresses Major Risks Early in the Lifecycle

By continually going through each of the phases of development in each iteration, risks to the project are quickly identified. For example, integration issues can be highlighted in the first iteration when the system is still small. In comparison, the waterfall model will not uncover these same integration problems until late in the project, when the system is of such a bulk that integration problems are not easily remedied.

## Produces a Robust Software Architecture

The analysis and design activity isn't carried out just once on an iterative project; it is revisited throughout the lifetime of the development. This enables the design and architecture of the system to evolve as the system grows. Problems can be detected early, and corrections can be more easily effected. Thus, a robust architecture is the result of a process of constant refinement.

## Promotes Understanding and Facilitates Software Reuse

Iterative projects break the complexity of a system into manageable chunks. This has the advantage that initial iterations of the system are limited in scope and therefore easily understood by everyone on the team. Developers can build up an early understanding of the design and can appreciate where the system is heading in terms of a final architecture. As the system increases in functionality and consequently grows in complexity, developers can increment their understanding of the system accordingly.

This understanding of the design enables developers to make decisions as to where parts of the system can be reused or where further development is required. Conversely, waterfall projects, which have all design done up front, can leave developers ignorant of large parts of the system architecture. This runs the risk that developers will duplicate existing designs, since they may be unaware of the existence of a suitable component.

## Provides a Good Environment for Learning

People learn from their mistakes. They also learn from their experiences. With a waterfall project, having made mistakes in the design phase and gained valuable experience from the design effort, software engineers have to wait until the next project before they can apply those skills again. On an iterative project, engineers can apply the knowledge they have gained from a previous iteration into the next. Thus, the existing project gains from the skills the team is building. Moreover, the team is able to hone its skills as the project progresses.

## Software Quality Is Continually Assessed

The waterfall model leaves testing until the last phase of the project. This approach does nothing to mitigate the risk of poor-quality software being generated throughout the project. Often, with waterfall projects, good progress is made up until the point where the testing phase starts. At this time, the project team is deluged with defects, and the project schedule is immediately put in jeopardy. Iterative development has testing commencing early, enabling remedial action to be taken if the quality of the software is below expectations.

## Estimates Are More Accurate and Realistic

Long-term plans, like long-term weather forecasts, are often nothing more than a best guess. Waterfall projects suffer badly from the effects of long-term estimation practices. Estimates are built on assumptions that may prove incorrect as the project progresses. Iterative development projects avoid detailed estimation efforts until planning an individual iteration. These estimates are far more realistic because the team is estimating over a much shorter timeframe, and team members have the knowledge accumulated from previous iterations on which to found their estimates. Thus, estimates on iterative developments tend to be accurate, and they increase in accuracy as the team's understanding of the software improves.

## The Development Process Itself Can Be Evolved and Adapted

Iterations allow the continuous evolution of the development process, not just the software, as the project progresses. Shortcomings in the approach soon become apparent in early iterations, and the process can be adjusted accordingly between iterations.

## Offers a More Enjoyable Team-Working Environment

Here, the team also includes the customer. People thrive on feedback from their efforts. By ensuring a running system is available at the conclusion of each iteration, the team builds up a sense of ownership for the software it creates. Furthermore, positive feedback from the customer helps keeps the team motivated for the course of the project. Likewise, the customer gains security from seeing a working system early in the project lifecycle. Customers also feel in control as they see their ideas and changes being quickly incorporated into their system.

# Iterative Processes

The benefits of iterative development make the approach a central practice for all adaptive methods. In the next sections, we look at two types of adaptive methods. Each follows an incremental, iterative approach to software development: the IBM Rational Unified Process and the agile methodology Extreme Programming (XP).

# Introducing RUP

The RUP is a commercial method and is sold as an online resource on CD-ROM, although numerous books and articles are available on the subject.

It was developed as a complementary methodology to the Unified Modeling Language (UML) and is a use-case-driven, architecture-centric, iterative development process for producing object-oriented software. The process is the result of the combination of many software engineering best practices as well as the acquisition by Rational of several software engineering methods. Its lineage goes back to the Objectory process, created in 1987 by methodology guru Ivar Jacobson.

> *Chapter 5, Modeling Software, examines the Unified Modeling Language.*

RUP is actually a process framework rather than a methodology. It defines an extensive selection of disciplines, artifacts, activities, and roles each of which represents industry best practice for the development of object-oriented software. The best practices that underpin the RUP framework are as follows:

- Develop software iteratively.
- Manage requirements.
- Use component-based architectures.
- Visually model software.
- Continuously verify software quality.
- Control changes to software.

Due to the comprehensive nature of the framework, the process is often assumed to be high-ceremony and heavyweight. While RUP does emphasize the importance of certain key artifacts and activities that are central to the process, this assumption is largely incorrect. Instead, RUP encourages the developer to tailor the process to the needs of his or her specific project by selecting from the long list of elements RUP provides for just about every conceivable project type. By tailoring the process, RUP can take on the agility of a lightweight methodology if the needs of the project dictate. However, the reliance of the process on artifacts such as use cases and design models means it is unable to slim down to the feather-light weights of methods such as XP, which we cover later.

A second common misconception with the process is that it is based upon predictive methods rather than adaptive methods. Again, this assumption is incorrect: RUP promotes the best practice of developing software iteratively. Many adopters of the RUP have been guilty of overlaying the waterfall lifecycle model on top of the process framework, thereby turning it into a predictive method. This is counter to the best practices of the process and certainly goes against the intent of its creators.

To understand how RUP is applied on projects, over the next sections we look at two of the key drivers for the process: *use cases* and *timeboxed iterative development*. We also examine the core elements of the framework.

## A Use-Case-Driven Process

We know that a successful system meets the needs of its end users. To achieve this goal, IT staff must work closely with the business domain experts to elicit the requirements that will ultimately drive the development effort. The interaction between business representatives and members from the project team is a critical success factor for ensuring all relevant requirements are both understood and captured correctly. Achieving this objective is a challenge, since both parties approach the engagement with very different mindsets and viewpoints. The end users focus on business concerns, while the IT staff likely thinks in terms of system design and architecture.

The question becomes, "How do we capture requirements in a form that is understandable to both the business domain experts and the IT-focused software engineers?" One of the most successful methods to date of achieving this is to develop a set of *use cases*.

Use cases describe what the system should do from the end user's perspective. They are text-based documents, as opposed to diagrams, that step through the flow of a set of closely related business scenarios. Each use case represents a functional slice of the system and describes how *actors* interact with the *system* in order to execute the use case.

An actor is defined as something external to the system, usually a person, who interacts with the system. The use case itself is a series of actions a system performs for the actor.

Here is an example of the structure of a typical use case:

- *Use-case name*: A short but descriptive title based on the goal of the use case
- *Goal*: A longer description of the goal
- *Category*: Several categories are possible but are likely to be one of primary, secondary, or summary
- *Preconditions*: Conditions that must exist before starting
- *Postconditions*: Conditions present upon the successful conclusion of the use case
- *Actors*: A list of all the participating actors
- *Trigger*: The event that starts the execution of the use case
- *Flow of events*: A series of numbered steps that walks through each of the flows. You can optionally include activity diagrams for each flow:
  - Main flow
  - Alternative flows
  - Exception flows
- *Extensions*: Points at which branching to other use cases occurs within the flow of events

- *Special requirements*: Any additional processing requirements not covered by the different flows

- *Performance goals*: Measurable performance criteria the system must meet when executing the main flow

- *Outstanding issues*: Any unresolved issues that are preventing the completion of the use case

Templates for use cases vary, with publications on the subject each presenting slight variations on a common theme. The structure of the use case shown represents the elements commonly found in use-case templates. You may wish to tailor this template to suit the needs of your own project.

The most important part of a use-case document is the *flow of events* section:. This describes the interplay between actors and system for a given scenario in a concise, natural language form.

note

A scenario is a flow of events within the use case. Very often, a use case comprises additional alternative flows to the main flow. These secondary flows typically cover exception conditions or slight deviations from the main scenario.

Let's look at an example of a use case that details the flow of events for a customer who enters the office of a travel company to reserve seats on a suitable flight. Table 3–1 shows an example of the complete use case.

**Table 3–1**    Use Case Example

| | |
|---|---|
| Name | Customer flight reservation. |
| Goal | To allow a customer to reserve seats on an airline flight. |
| Category | Primary. |
| Preconditions | The Customer is in the Travel Agency office meeting with the Travel Agent. The Flight Reservation system is online, and flights are available that meet the Customer's travel needs. |
| Postconditions | The Customer has reserved a seat(s) that meets her travel requirements and is ready either to pay for the flight or to place a deposit for the reservation. |
| Actors | Customer |
| | Travel Agent |
| Trigger | The Customer requests to make a flight booking. |

**Table 3–1**   Use Case Example (continued)

| | |
|---|---|
| Main flow | 1. The use case starts when the Customer requests to make a flight reservation. |
| | 2. The Travel Agent asks the customer for the date of travel, the destinations, and the number of people traveling. |
| | 3. The Travel Agent enters the Customer's details into the Flight Reservation system. |
| | 4. The Flight Reservation system lists the available flights that match the Customer's travel requirements and displays the airfare for each option. |
| | 5. The Customer selects a flight from the list and requests to make a booking. |
| | 6. The Travel Agent asks the customer for name, address, and contact telephone number. |
| | 7. The Travel Agent enters the Customer's details into the Flight Reservation system and reserves seats on the flight. |
| | 8. The Flight Reservation system prints out the details of the booking. |
| | 9. The Travel Agent asks the Customer how she wishes to pay, at which point the use case ends. |
| Extensions | 5a. No flights match the Customer's criteria. |
| | 8a The system cannot print the flight details. |
| | 9a. Handle Customer payment (Use Case: Customer Pays Invoice). |
| Special requirements | No special requirements. |
| Performance goals | The Flight Reservation system must display the list of available flights within 10 seconds. |
| Outstanding issues | Need to identify the exact details and format of the booking information printed out by the Flight Reservation system. |

The plain language of use cases, which is both business- and technology-neutral, makes them ideal for communicating system behavior to both end users and developers. Use cases are important in RUP because they provide a common thread through many activities, particularly in the area of linking requirements to design. They also serve to focus the design, implementation, and testing efforts around a central set of requirements, which form the core of the system.

Use cases are organized by producing a *use-case model*. A use-case model is a UML diagram that graphically illustrates how the different use cases and actors interact. Models are useful for gaining an understanding of the relationships that exist between each use case and actor. However, the true value of use cases is in the text of the use case itself, not the diagram in the model.

Ivar Jacobson initially proposed the concept of use cases. As Jacobson's Objectory is one of the foundation methodologies on which the RUP framework is built, it is not surprising that use cases are one of the driving forces of the process.

Although they are an important part of the process, use cases are not confined to object-oriented development and have enjoyed widespread acceptance in all manner of projects. They are an excellent technique for capturing and understanding customer requirements and are worth considering for inclusion in any methodology.

We next examine how the RUP framework centers on the use of iterations throughout the project lifecycle.

## Iterative Development with RUP

The process prescribes an iterative approach to development with *timeboxed* iterations. Here, all iterations occur over a fixed duration but have a variable scope.

A RUP iteration focuses on a subset of the system's use cases. Within a typical iteration, the selected use cases are elaborated and a design is evolved followed by implementation and testing. The objective of each iteration is a functioning system. Should it appear that this objective will not be achieved, then the scope is reduced in preference to extending the timeboxed duration of the iteration or bringing more people on to the project.

The exact content of an iteration is dependent upon the particular *phase* of RUP within which the planned iteration is being conducted. Let's examine the different phases of a RUP project cycle.

## Phases of the Process

### RUP Phases

- Inception
- Elaboration
- Construction
- Transition

Conventional waterfall-based processes are broken down into phases according to specific software engineering activities, with phase names denoting the associated activity. We therefore commonly have requirements, analysis and design, implementation, and testing. Only a single type of activity is undertaken in each of these phases. For example, during the requirements phase, only work relating to the gathering, analysis, and documenting of requirements is performed. Absolutely no design, coding, or testing work is undertaken as part of this early phase.

RUP projects are also divided into the four discrete phases. These are *inception*, *elaboration*, *construction*, and *transition*. Unlike in the waterfall model, these phases are not aligned by activity but instead demark the achievement of a major project milestone. Phases within the process include a number of iterations, with each iteration serving to advance the project toward the phase milestone. As an iteration is a complete mini-waterfall project, we can expect to see the general activities of requirements, analysis and design, implementation, and testing being undertaken in each phase.

A common failing in implementing the RUP is to mistakenly associate these four phases with the four phases of the classic waterfall lifecycle. This is a fact Philippe Kruchten, one of the creators of RUP, went to great pains to point out with his fellow authors in the article, *How to Fail with the Rational Unified Process: Seven Steps to Pain and Suffering* [Larman, 2002].

Please note:

- Inception **does not** equal requirements
- Elaboration **does not** equal design
- Construction **does not** equal coding
- Transition **does not** equal testing

Here are the four phases of a RUP project and a brief description of the work undertaken in each phase:

### Inception.

During inception, a preliminary iteration focuses on establishing a business case for the system. A small but critical set of primary use cases are identified, and based on these, the scope of the project is estimated, architectural options explored, and key risks assessed. Findings from this phase assist in determining if the project is viable and if it should continue on to the elaboration phase.

### Elaboration.

Having made the decision to continue with the project, the elaboration phase shifts the focus of the project to iteratively constructing the architecture for the system. This exercise is conducted in parallel with a detailed investigation of the core requirements.

Iterations within the elaboration phase focus on refining these core requirements and constructing the architecture to the point where it can be demonstrated. Both requirements and the system architecture may undergo significant change during this phase because of feedback between the two tasks.

The output from this phase is a stable architecture on which the bulk of the functionality of the system can be built during the construction phase.

### Construction.

With a stable architecture in place and most of the primary requirements defined, the construction phase looks to build the remaining functionality of the system on this stable platform. The objective of the iterations for this phase is a system that is ready for deployment into a beta testing environment.

**Transition.**

Iterations in the fourth and final phase focus on producing a fully tested system, with all outstanding issues resolved, that is ready for final deployment.

Running throughout each of these phases are the different disciplines of a RUP project.

# Disciplines

A discipline represents an area of work. Disciplines are undertaken in each iteration, although the degree to which each discipline is practiced depends on the current project phase. There are nine different disciplines:

**Business modeling.**

Seeks to describe an organization's core business processes in order to assist in identifying the important requirements for the system targeted for development.

**Requirements management.**

Involves the gathering, structuring, and documenting of all requirements.

**Analysis and design.**

Involves the conception and demonstration of an architecture for the system that is capable of supporting the requirements of the system.

**Implementation.**

Writing, testing, building, and debugging the source code for the system.

**Test.**

Performing quality-assurance tests, such as functional, performance, and system testing.

**Deployment.**

Undertaking all the necessary tasks to ensure the system is deliverable into the environment of the end users.

**Project management.**

Planning and monitoring of the project.

**Configuration and change management.**

Associated with all tasks that relate to change control, versioning, and release management.

**Environment.**

Tailoring the process to a specific project and selecting and supporting the project infrastructure and associated development tools.

The amount of effort required in each discipline varies as the project traverses through the four different phases over time. Iterations in inception and elaboration phases will be heavy on the business modeling and requirements management disciplines. Later in the project, during the transition phase, effort in these disciplines will have trailed off but may still play a minor part in later iterations.

# The Elements of RUP

## RUP Elements

- Roles: Who?
- Activities: How?
- Artifacts: What?
- Workflows: When?

The RUP framework provides all the elements necessary for building a comprehensive project around the different disciplines. For each discipline, RUP defines a set of *roles, activities, artifacts,* and *workflows* that represent the core elements of the lifecycle model. Each of these elements is an answer to the questions of *who, how, what,* and *when.*

## Artifacts: The What

An artifact is a work product used to capture and convey project-related information. Artifacts can be documents, models, model elements, source code, or executables. Complete artifact sets are defined that align to each discipline; for example, artifacts from the *analysis and design* discipline include a *software architecture document* (SAD) and a *design model.*

## Activities: The How

Producing an artifact requires undertaking an activity. The RUP views an activity as a unit of work carried out by a member of the team with a specific role. Examples of activities for the analysis and design discipline include those of *architectural analysis* and *database design.* Artifacts resulting from these two activities include a software architecture document and a data model respectively.

## Roles: The Who

RUP allocates responsibilities to members of the team by handing out roles. Roles are associated with a set of performed activities and owned artifacts. From the activities and artifacts mentioned so far, the *software architect* is responsible for undertaking the architectural analysis activity and producing the software architecture document artifact, while the *database designer* produces a database model as an artifact resulting from the database design activity.

Team members are not assigned a single role but instead take on a range of roles as and when the project dictates. On smaller projects, a member of the team may hold several roles if he is undertaking a range of activities, whereas large projects may require a single person to be dedicated to a particular role.

## Workflow: The When

To work with the different artifacts, activities, and roles, we need more information than merely a list of each element. It is necessary to understand how each different element interacts as part of the process. This is the purpose of workflows.

A workflow is represented in RUP as a modified activity diagram illustrating how a particular set of activities is organized. Workflows equate to the disciplines we have already covered. In fact, a discipline is a type of high-level workflow, as disciplines represent a logical grouping of a set of artifacts, activities, and roles. A discipline is therefore one type of workflow. A second type of workflow is the *workflow detail*, which breaks disciplines down into finer levels of granularity.

Within RUP, we therefore have phases, iterations, disciplines, roles, activities, and artifacts. The question is how you go about combining all of these elements into a coherent project plan.

# Planning

Planning is a key part of RUP, which encourages the production of two types of plan: a coarse-grained *phase plan* and a series of detailed *iteration plans*.

The phase plan is a single plan that spans the duration of the entire project from inception to transition. This high-level plan defines the anticipated dates for the major project milestones, the required project resources, and scheduled dates for each of the planned iterations.

The phase plan is created early in the project during the inception phase. Detailed planning is reserved for the iteration plan, which, like traditional management plans, allocates tasks to individuals and specifies minor milestone dates and project review points. Milestone dates within the iteration plan are made with an expectation of accuracy, as the estimates are made for near-term deadlines as opposed to the long-term forecasts of the phase plan. Toward the end of the iteration, the plan is concluded and work on the plan for the next iteration commences. Thus, in RUP it is common to have two iteration plans: one plan for tracking progress to schedule in the current iteration and a second plan that is under construction for the upcoming iteration.

Two of the most frequently asked questions regarding planning for iterative processes relate to how iterations should be structured throughout the project and what should be the length of an individual iteration.

For structuring the iterations within the project, Philippe Kruchten gives some guidance in an article on planning iterative projects [Kruchten, 2002]. For very simple projects, Kruchten suggests a single iteration for each of the four phases:

- Inception: A single iteration to produce a user-interface prototype or mock up
- Elaboration: One iteration to build a stable architectural prototype
- Construction: One iteration to advance the software to the beta release stage
- Transition: A last iteration to complete the final system

Where a large project with many unknowns in terms of both problem domain and technology is under development, Kruchten advises the following structure between the phases:

- Inception: Two iterations to enable suitable prototyping activities
- Elaboration: Three iterations to explore different solutions and technical options
- Construction: Three iterations, or as many are required, to build in all the called-for functionality
- Transition: Two iterations to incorporate operational feedback

The length of a timebox for a single iteration is governed by the size of the project team. Extremely large projects with hundreds of people involved require careful coordination in order to maintain momentum for the project. This coordination effort soaks up time and tends to lead to longer iterations. Smaller teams can work to iterations with shorter durations.

Ideally, iterations should be short and focused, running to weeks rather than months. Iterations of two to five weeks work well if the team size allows it. Where longer iterations are unavoidable, then consider setting minor milestones within the timeframe of the iteration. This helps keep the team focused on delivery and prevents risks from creeping back into the project. These minor milestones also help in tracking longer iteration plans.

## Supporting Enterprise Projects

Enterprise J2EE developments and RUP fit well together. The way in which enterprise projects are conducted can vary greatly based on both the customer and the development team involved. Thanks to the extensive range of elements RUP provides, the process can tailor to suit most situations.

The size and scope of enterprise developments varies immensely, ranging from teams with only a handful of developers to projects comprised of hundreds of people spread across geographically distant locations. The RUP framework supports both extremes and can meet the needs of small, adaptive style projects while also providing the high-ceremony artifacts necessary for developments conducted on a much grander scale.

Although RUP supports a lightweight adaptive approach, this is not the nature of the majority of enterprise-level developments. Traditionally, such projects are highly contractual, requiring upfront fixed-price quotes for agreed-upon levels of functionality. This type of engagement is the forte of RUP. Placing great importance on early prototype and investigation work helps to drive out the risks involved in this type of project.

Another factor in adopting RUP is the current trend for offshore development. Regardless of whether you favor this contentious practice, it has become a part of the IT industry. The extensive range of artifacts RUP defines makes it possible to conduct large projects with distributed development teams spread across the world. Here, elements of the process provide a common technical vocabulary between teams of different cultures and backgrounds, allowing them to work effectively and collaboratively on a system.

Furthermore, practitioners of best practice processes such as RUP are also able to convey a high degree of professionalism. When organizations are selecting software vendors, an important criterion is often their adopted development methodology. Companies with development teams who demonstrate a knowledge and investment in an established lifecycle model are more likely to win business than those companies who see little value in such methods.

## Disadvantages of RUP

RUP is not without its downsides. A major issue is the amount of time and effort that must be invested in knowledge and education of the process framework. The extensive nature of the framework means this investment is often considerable, as becoming expert in the use of the process requires both training and practical experience. Ensuring all team members receive sufficient upfront training before embarking on any project is an important part of developing an adaptive foundation within a company in order to facilitate rapid development methods.

If taking RUP on board is viewed as being too expensive, an alternative is to adopt the practices of a lightweight agile methodology. We look at the benefits of these methods next.

### Key Points of RUP

- Can be scaled according to project size
- Employs best practice software engineering methods
- Is use-case-driven and architecture-centric
- Complements the use of UML diagrams for modeling
- Provides a comprehensive range of artifacts, activities, and roles
- Is suited to large-scale enterprise-level developments
- Requires a substantial investment in training and education

# Agile Methods

While the RUP framework allows for the adoption of either a lightweight or a heavyweight approach, RUP tends toward a high-ceremony, heavyweight process due to the emphasis it places on project artifacts.

In recent years, the software development community has invested significant effort in establishing overtly lightweight processes that rely on a minimum level of ceremony to deliver quality software solutions for systems with emergent or rapidly evolving requirements. Efforts in this area by the leading methodologists have given rise to a number of new development processes, collectively known as *agile methods*.

Processes of this type are based on incremental development with timeboxed iterations. They differ from process frameworks such as RUP in that they emphasize the importance of performing a particular activity rather than producing a specific artifact. Such processes lay claim to being *people-centric* as opposed to *document-centric*.

The software engineer has a number of these methods from which to choose, including SCRUM, Crystal, and feature-driven development (FDD). However, by far the most well known of the agile methodologies is XP, and it is this process that we cover next.

# Introducing XP

XP is a lightweight, agile process whose creation is attributed to Kent Beck, Ward Cunningham, and Ron Jefferies. XP was first put into practice back in 1996 by Kent Beck, who applied the process on the now famous C3 project at DaimlerChrysler. The process personifies the current crop of agile methods and targets small to medium projects with vague or rapidly changing requirements.

XP has created a huge buzz within the software development community, and much discussion still rages about the true benefits of its ultra-lightweight approach to development. Unlike most methodologies that stress the importance of upfront design and meticulous documentation, XP throws away the old rulebook and instead concentrates on the act of coding rather than documenting.

This standpoint has made the process immensely popular with hardcore developers, who have welcomed XP with open arms. To most software engineers, it was as if someone had announced that cigarettes, chocolate, and alcohol were all good for your health.

Unfortunately, the minimalist approach of XP has been interpreted by some engineers as being an excuse to discard many of the disciplines of software development and jump straight into the activity of coding. As we shall discover, this is not the intent of XP, and instead the method promotes a deliberate and highly disciplined approach to software development. Arguably, XP requires more discipline than RUP, which gives the engineer the option to omit many parts of the process. Instead, XP demands that you embrace all of its practices.

## The XP Practices

### Extreme Programming Practices

- Planning game
- Small releases
- Metaphor
- Simple design
- Testing
- Refactoring
- Pair programming
- Collective ownership
- Continuous integration
- Forty-hour week
- Onsite customer
- Coding standards

The RUP framework comes with an abundance of disciplines, activities, artifacts, and roles, any of which you may choose to incorporate in your project. XP is more concise and is essentially comprised of 12 basic *practices*, each of which you must follow in order to exploit the full benefits of the process.

These practices, or rules, of XP align with the key activities of *planning*, *designing*, *coding*, and *testing*. Each practice is undertaken in accordance with the XP values of *simplicity*, *communication*, *feedback*, and *courage*, which permeate the entire process.

Let's begin with the 12 practices that make up XP:

### Planning game.

Plan regularly and involve all members of the team in the planning activity, including the customer. Plans are devised based on business priorities supplied by the customer and technical estimates from the development team.

### Small releases.

In line with the value of simplicity, first put a simple system quickly into production, and then release new versions over a number of short iterations.

### Metaphor.

Have a simple shared story of how the system operates to guide all development effort.

### Simple design.

Keep the design simple and avoid designing for unspecified requirements. Refactor out complexity as soon as it is discovered.

### Testing.

Write unit tests continually and ensure they execute flawlessly. Automated unit tests are written ahead of the implementation of a class. Suspend development until a failed test has been rectified. Customers write tests to validate new features.

### Refactoring.

Developers continually restructure the code base without changing its behavior to maintain simplicity, remove duplication, improve communication, and add flexibility.

### Pair programming.

All production code is written by two developers working at a single machine.

### Collective ownership.

Any developer can change any system code at any time.

### Continuous integration.

Integrate all code as soon as any task is complete. Look to integrate all code several times a day.

### Forty-hour week.

Stick to a 40-hour week. Never work overtime two weeks in a row.

### Onsite customer.

Have an empowered representative from the customer working with the development team and available any time to answer questions or discuss requirements.

### Coding standards.

All developers write code in accordance with a common set of coding standards, thereby emphasizing communication throughout the code base.

The 12 practices complement one another to the extent that to omit a single practice could cause the whole process to unravel. For example, *simple design* requires *refactoring* to remove unnecessary complexity; refactoring relies on the *testing* practice to guard against unintended changes in system behavior. XP therefore requires discipline from the team in ensuring all practices are employed on the project.

The practices of XP lay down the rules for how developers work on an XP project. To understand how an XP project is conducted, we need to look at the activities of XP.

## Planning

Planning is a critical activity on any project, more so if the project is following an adaptive method. These methods require decisions on the direction of the project to be made at every step, and in close consultation with the customer, if the project is to be carefully steered toward a successful conclusion.

Planning on an XP project is a continuous activity driven by the feedback from both customers and developers. Like RUP, planning in XP occurs on two levels. The first level is the broad project plan, or release plan using XP terminology. This defines the overall structure for the project and gauges the number of iterations necessary to complete the system.

The second level of planning is the detailed iteration plan. This covers just a single iteration. Iterations in XP run for approximately two weeks, and the content of an iteration is decided upon based on the customer's prioritized requirements and estimates from the developers for each requirement. A release is made at the conclusion of an iteration, as dictated by the practice of *small releases*.

Throughout the iteration, teams should look to integrate their work on a regular basis, as specified by the *continuous integration* practice. This avoids the danger of costly integration problems caused by last-minute integration efforts.

XP iterations are timeboxed, so discussion is required with the customer to determine which requirements must be included within the allocated timeframe. The need to collaborate closely with the customer in all aspects of the project, including its planning, gives rise to the XP practice of having an onsite customer.

Where RUP iterations are driven by use cases, XP iterations are planned around *user stories*. The function of an XP user story is similar to that of a use case but is considerably simpler and shorter, usually running to just a few sentences. The iteration evolves the story, but the "written" story remains in its original terse form. Like use cases, user stories also drive other project tasks, with acceptance tests being written for the stories provided.

> Acceptance testing is described in Chapter 15, Efficient Quality Assurance, along with tools for supporting the testing activity.

Figure 3–3 illustrates how user stories drive iterations within XP.

In addition to release and iteration planning, XP teams look to hold short, standup meetings at the start of each day to lay out the tasks for the day, arrange pair-programming teams, and discuss any issues that may have arisen since the last meeting.

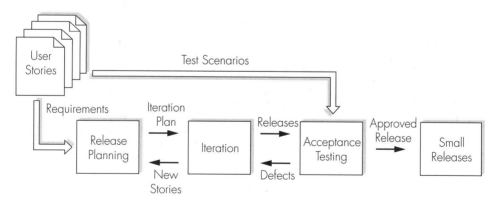

**Figure 3–3**     User stories and the XP iteration lifecycle.

# Designing

Design is one of the most contentious areas of XP, as according to the main practices, followers of XP do not appear to do any design work. In contrast, RUP capitalizes on its links with the UML and uses modeling as the main design activity.

XP has no place for models, stating only that design should be kept simple, as per the *simple design* practice. This is enforced by the *refactoring* practice, which looks to remove complexity at every opportunity. Furthermore, all members of the team should have a common understanding, or *metaphor*, as to what the system is and how it works.

As for formal design processes, the original C3 project used Class, Responsibilities, and Collaboration (CRC) cards for running design sessions, and this technique has proven popular with some XP teams.

## Designing with CRC Cards

CRC cards offer a simple but effective approach to design that involves several people from the team. As XP encourages collaborative development, any method able to effectively engage a number of people in the design process is a good candidate for an XP project.

Start the design session by getting hold of a stack of blank cards. If you can't find any of these, the back of a business card will just about do, but you'll need to reduce the size of your handwriting.

Each card represents an object in the system. Write the name of the object at the top of the card, the responsibilities down the left-hand side, and the collaborating classes to the right of each responsibility.

The session starts with a particular functional scenario, or user story, and each member of the group holding a number of cards. The group talks through the scenario, with the conversation passing to the holder of the card whose class is responsible for that part of the story. The details on the cards change as a result of the discussion until a set of classes, responsibilities, and associated collaborations have been identified that will execute the required scenario.

In an XP CRC session, no formal design is produced, but the group takes away an understanding of how the system will implement the required functionality.

# Coding

If the subject of design on XP projects is contentious, then the practice of *pair programming*, whereby two developers share a single machine, is positively explosive.

The arguments against pair programming are twofold. First, management becomes nervous about the productivity implications of having two developers constrained by the bottleneck of just one machine. Second, developers become almost territorial over a task they have taken responsibility for, and they have a tendency to feel threatened at the thought of having anyone closely scrutinizing their work. Frequently, developers cite the need for quiet time in order to fully focus on a problem, claiming the need to be *"in the zone"* in order to overcome technical development challenges.

Resistance to pair programming can be quite extreme, with developers vehemently denouncing the need for the practice. It is well worth reading the article *The Case Against XP*, by Matt Stephens, on the subject of pair programming and XP in general. This amusing article provides an opposing viewpoint to the practices of XP and can be found on the Software Reality site at http://www.softwarereality.com/lifecycle/xp.

If you have tried pair programming, you likely found it mentally exhausting. Having a second developer working with you on a piece of code seems to keep you constantly alert. Common distractions, such as getting up and making coffee or surfing the Web, get pushed to one side with a second pair of eyes on the screen. The excessive mental effort pair programming imposes is probably one of the reasons why XP recommends sticking to a 40-hour week.

The pair-programming practice came into being as an *extreme* reaction to code reviews. While they may sound like a good practice, code reviews, as they are commonly practiced, are a flawed quality-control process.

Code reviews are often left to the last minute on a project, by which time it is often too late to fix any of the problems identified by the review. Moreover, conducting a thorough review takes time, as the reviewer must form a clear understanding of the developer's intent and approach. Seldom is enough time set aside to conduct a proper review. Likewise, reviewers often have their own tasks to complete and so frequently fail to invest the necessary effort in the review process.

The XP solution to the problems surrounding code reviews is to have them occurring all the time. Pair programming achieves this, since the developer pair is continually checking the code against both the requirements and the project's *coding standards*. Mixing up pairs regularly ensures that no developer flaunts the project standards unnoticed. Furthermore, the practice also links in with *collective ownership*, as knowledge of the code is spread around the entire team.

Pair programming is making in-roads into mainstream development as more and more companies discover that two heads really are better than one. Some novel approaches are being formed that enable people to more easily work together in pairs. One group at HP undertook a distributed XP project and gave all developers hands-free headsets and desktop sharing software in order that team members could pair program remotely.

Pair programming does have its limitations and is not suitable for all programming tasks. A classic example is research or investigative work. Here, people really do need some quiet time to explore and read. However, if programmers are writing *production* code, then under XP rules, they should be doing so in pairs.

## Testing

XP has single-handedly breathed new life into the concept of test-driven development, whereby tests are written ahead of any implementation.

Under XP, all classes in the project should have supporting unit tests. This practice enables refactoring of the code base without the danger of system behavior being impacted.

Unit tests also support the practice of *collective ownership* of the code. If a programming pair is changing code developed by other members of the team, the supporting unit tests will ensure they can do so without inadvertently destabilizing existing system behavior. The test suite should identify this situation if it occurs.

Upon identifying a defect, the programmer must write a unit test for the problem. This approach guards against the defect creeping back into the system.

> *The test-first development approach is examined further in Chapter 14, Test-Driven Development.*

## XP Roles

Agile methods have gone to great lengths to reaffirm the importance of the individual worker. Early methodologies looked to downplay the role of the individual, seeking to make software development a production-like process, with IT staff undertaking factory-type roles.

Job descriptions in XP are sparse compared to the comprehensive list included under RUP. Nevertheless, this serves to underline the importance of the individual on the project and the significant contribution he or she makes.

True to the nature of the profession, software engineers on an XP project must be multi-skilled. They are expected to take part in the planning, designing, coding, and testing of the system. Thus, XP breaks away from the standard convention of defining specific roles for architects, designers, managers, coders, testers, and the like. XP places greater emphasis on generalists rather than on specialists, so if you're working on an XP project, expect to get your hands dirty.

Unfortunately, J2EE developments often have a need for specialist skills due to the diverse range of Java-based technologies involved. It is not atypical to find developers who are expert in JSP but have never written an Enterprise JavaBean. Even fewer developers will have been near a J2EE Connector Architecture (JCA) adapter. This can be an issue, especially with the *collective ownership* practice. Attempting to get the entire development team through the learning curve associated with the intricacies of JCA technology in many cases just isn't practical. Pair programming is one way of spreading the knowledge, but on complex J2EE systems, it is hard to avoid the need for specialization in a particular J2EE technology. XP does advocate the consultant role, which can help in this area.

The following list provides a brief description of the roles for an XP project, as defined by Kent Beck:

### Programmer

The programmer is a fully fledged software engineer and represents the heart of the process. The programmer is involved in almost every aspect of the development, contributing to the planning, designing, programming, and testing of the system.

### Customer

The business skills of the customer complement the technical skills of the programmer. A customer on an XP project is a decision maker, and by writing user stories and ongoing involvement in the project, steers the direction of the development. An XP customer is also a tester and takes on the responsibility for writing the functional tests that ultimately become the acceptance tests for the finished system.

### Tester

As both the programmer and customer roles take on the responsibility for writing tests in XP, the role of the tester switches to focusing on the customer. The tester takes charge of ensuring all tests are incorporated into an automated build process and communicates the results of test runs to the team.

### Tracker

A key to successful planning is the ability to compare actual task completion times to estimates. Iterative development benefits from this ability, as the estimation process can be refined between iterations. The tracker role is responsible for collating the actual times and providing these figures as feedback to the developers. The tracker also gauges the progress of the team against the overall goals of the project and uses this information for planning purposes.

### Coach

The coach is the XP process expert and advises the team on all matters relating to the implementation of an XP project. This role diminishes as the project progresses, as collectively, the whole team begins to pick up responsibility for the process.

### Consultant

The role of the consultant is to inject technical knowledge into the team as and when it is required. Consultants tend to be transient members of the group who pass on their valuable technical skills by mentoring the team in a particular problem area.

### Big Boss

The final role is for the individual who is ultimately responsible for the project. The role involves helping to guide and assist the team through problems, acquiring additional resources as required, and making some of the hard decisions around delivery in consultation with the team.

Now that we've covered the main points of an XP development, let's consider how well suited the process is for the development of a J2EE solution.

## Adopting XP for Enterprise J2EE Projects

XP will be not be a perfect fit for all projects, since certain conditions must be present in order to get maximum benefit from the method. First, a business domain expert is required from the customer to work closely with the development team. This individual must be empowered to make key decisions about the direction and behavior of the system being developed.

The customer is not the only one who must commit to an XP development. Management must also back the approach and be prepared to embark on a project that may have uncertain requirements and no clear deliverables from the outset. This presents the manager with all manner of contractual challenges around price and delivery commitments.

For XP to work, the software engineers assigned to the project must be prepared to adopt its practices faithfully. XP is a disciplined process and requires teams to adhere to all of its practices in order for the process to operate effectively. Developers who don't want to work in pairs and resent other developers changing their code would be better off placed on other projects—preferably with another company.

Even if all of these conditions are in place, XP is still not a good match for all project types. To quote from Kent Beck's *Extreme Programming Explained* [Beck, 1999]:

> There are times and places and people and customers that would explode an XP project like a cheap balloon.

So, how well does XP gel with a J2EE-based project? Well, XP is technology-neutral. The original C3 project was an object-oriented project developed in Smalltalk, and XP has been used effectively with other programming platforms since then, so the use of the J2EE platform should not be a barrier to adopting XP.

When J2EE projects do find themselves hitting the limitations of XP has more to do with the nature of enterprise development than with the J2EE platform itself. Enterprise developments tend toward large teams, with a current trend toward having split-site development using off-shore resources.

XP works best with small teams averaging around 10 people, and with the team members in close proximity. Big team sizes are definitely an issue for XP, as the lightweight process lacks the necessary ceremony to coordinate large numbers of developers. Nevertheless, XP as a process is still evolving, and work is currently ongoing to determine how XP can scale for larger projects.

Another major barrier to the use of XP on enterprise projects is the contractual nature of these developments. A fixed-price quote with clearly defined scope is the norm for an enterprise system. Working to these contractual constraints requires a level of predictability that does not sit well with the low-ceremony approach of XP.

Instead, XP in its current form favors inhouse, collaborative projects. Projects of this type fit the profile for an XP project extremely well. Onsite domain experts are often easily arranged, and as the customer and development team all work for the same company, the contractual requirements are not so stringent. It is possible to operate an XP project with an external customer, but a good relationship must be in place for the process to prove workable.

To conclude, XP and J2EE can work well together, but pick your projects with care. Don't opt for an excessively lightweight process when the conditions call for something more substantial.

## Key Points of XP

- Offers a deliberate and disciplined approach to software development
- Freely available and documented by numerous books and articles
- Lightweight and low ceremony
- Easy to learn and understand
- People-centric as opposed to document-centric
- Targets small- to medium-sized projects
- Less well suited to enterprise-sized projects

# Summary

The characteristics of a software lifecycle methodology that uniquely qualify a process as being suitable for rapid development include the following:

- *Lightweight,* by requiring the minimum level of procedure for the size and scope of the system under development
- *Complementary,* to the techniques and tools you adopt as part of your adaptive foundation for rapid software development
- *Adaptive,* so system changes can be easily accommodated by the process

Adaptive methods are preferable to conventional predictive approaches, as they offer the necessary techniques to accommodate changing requirements. The key to adaptive methods is their iterative approach to development, the benefits of which are:

- Low risk, as early iterations are used to target identified areas of high risk early in the process

- Well suited to projects with emergent requirements, as iterations refine the requirements over time
- High quality, with testing being a continuous activity undertaken from the outset of the project
- Improved customer satisfaction, as the customer plays an active role in guiding the evolution of the system

Two examples of popular methodologies offering iterative approaches are the IBM Rational Unified Process and the agile methodology, Extreme Programming.

Of these two, RUP provides an extensive process framework from which a tailored process can be designed for a particular project type. Due to its comprehensive list of activities and artifacts, RUP scales well and so is applicable for both small and extremely large projects. The ability of RUP to contend with large development projects, potentially with distributed development teams, makes it an ideal candidate for enterprise-level J2EE systems.

In comparison, XP offers a highly disciplined, ultra-lightweight process that has been proven to work well for small teams developing projects with the vaguest of requirements. It is easy to learn and is proving popular with the software engineers who have so far embraced its values and practices.

Now that we have covered some of the key concepts around the choice of a development process for rapid development, we can move on to the business of designing, building, and testing our J2EE solutions.

## Additional Information

Philippe Kruchten, one the founding fathers of RUP, has openly criticized publications that misrepresent the practices of his process, particularly those that present it as a waterfall model. I'm confident I've done his creation justice, but if you want to hear about the process framework from the horse's mouth, as well as learn more about RUP, then you should read his excellent book, *The Rational Unified Process: An Introduction* [Kruchten, 2003].

Numerous resources exist for XP, with volumes of material being published on the process. A good starting point is Kent Beck's original text on the subject, *Extreme Programming Explained* [Beck, 1999]. A detailed online reference is also available for XP at http://www.extremeprogramming.org.

From my exposure to XP, I was always of the opinion that XP would be unsuitable for split-site development, especially for projects with the bulk of the development work taking place offshore. I may need to revise my opinion, as Martin Fowler has written a thought-provoking article on his experiences using XP with an offshore development shop in Bangalore. The article is available from http://martinfowler.com/articles/agileOffshore.html.

For more information on use cases, Alistair Cockburn has written a number of articles on the subject, which can found at his Web site at http://alistair.cockburn.us. His site also contains an example of a use-case template on which the example in this chapter is based. See http://alistair.cockburn.us/usecases/uctempla.htm.

The site also includes information on Alistair's agile methodology framework, Crystal.

# Part II: Agile Architectures

The ability to react quickly to change is an important aspect of rapid development and a theme that is reiterated throughout this book. Changes to customer requirements have the potential to snowball all the way through the software development process, with catastrophic implications for the project schedule. If the effects of changes can be minimized, then the likelihood of finishing the project on time and within budget is greatly increased. Successfully handling change all comes down to a project's agility.

Part II looks at what steps can be taken to make a project agile from the perspective of architecture and design. We cover the importance of designing solutions conducive to rapidity from the outset and consider ways to apply J2EE technology that produces practical, workable application designs.

To support the design process we examine the roles of modeling and modeling tools, and assess how models offer an effective and inexpensive means of assessing the impact of any change. Coupled with this information is the use of code generators, used to insulate the project from the ravages of rapidly changing requirements.

Part II concludes with a discussion on Model-Driven Architecture, a development paradigm that brings together design, modeling, and code generation.

# 4

# Designing for Rapidity

Designing an enterprise-level system is a difficult and challenging task. Business requirements are typically both complex and diverse, while concerns such as security, integration, operational management, scalability, performance, internationalization, and standards compliance all contribute to making the job of the architect a hard one.

Consequently, any architecture that meets all of the expectations that surround enterprise-level software is an achievement. Unfortunately, where rapid development is concerned, meeting all requirements is only part of the story. For a RAD project, the architect must also design for timeliness of delivery.

This chapter looks at the importance of design for rapid development and examines how decisions made during the definition of a system's architecture can have a significant impact on the ability to complete systems in a reduced timeframe.

Guidelines for design decisions that help to decrease the development timeframe of a project are explored, and we take an impartial view of the merits of the J2EE platform and outline practical J2EE-based architectures that are complementary to rapid development.

## Architecture and Design Objectives

Before delving into the details of architectures that can help with rapid development, let's establish exactly what is meant by the terms *architecture* and *design*.

Asking this question often stirs up considerable debate among IT professionals, especially architects. Many working hours have been lost as software engineers split hairs over the differences between the roles of the architect and designer. In the interests of productivity, and for the purposes of this discussion, architecture can thought of as the *big picture*.

It's helpful to think of architecture as the blueprint for building the system. In this way, architecture forms an overarching set of principles, standards, protocols, frameworks, and directives that orchestrate the various design elements of the overall application.

Architecture differs from design in terms of scope. Architecture takes the wider view; design has a much narrower focus. Put simply, architecture has breadth and design has depth. The architect paints with a wide brush; the designer is more focused and concentrates on adding detail to the picture.

## The Architect

> The ideal architect should be a person of letters, a mathematician, familiar with historical studies, a diligent student of philosophy, acquainted with music, not ignorant of medicine, learned in the responses of jurisconsults, familiar with astronomy and astronomical calculations.
>
> From Vitruvius, circa 25 BC

Architecture is important for rapid development because it forms the basis for large-scale software reuse. Considering the wider picture enables the identification of readily reusable components for quickly assembling a system. System architectures are themselves a reusable commodity, as architectures tailored to specific problem domains can form part of a company's adaptive foundation.

The following list is not exhaustive but identifies those system traits the architecture would typically include:

### Performance.

For a given load, will the application meet the performance levels detailed by the system's technical requirements? For example, will the system provide a two-second response time for a specific user action under maximum load?

### Scalability.

Can the capacity of the system to undertake higher loads be increased without the need to change the code?

### Robustness.

Is the system fault-tolerant and able to comply with the levels of availability defined in the customer's technical requirements?

### Maintainability.

Is it easy for developers to correct any defects that surface or to add new functionality?

### Manageability.

How easy is it for IT operators to manage the operational needs of the system in a production environment?

### Security.

Given the nature of the information maintained by the system, is the level of security sufficient?

### Customer standards.

Does the system conform to the customer's own architectural standards and principles?

### Timeliness.

Can the solution be delivered in the timeframe available?

The timeframe available in which to deliver the system is an important factor when defining the system's architecture and warrants equal consideration with other architectural concerns, such as system performance, scalability, robustness, security, and maintainability.

The priority timeliness is given should be set by the customers, and that priority must be respected by architect and designer alike. A common failing in the IT industry is to overengineer solutions, thereby risking missed delivery dates. The time to develop a solution can be of paramount importance to the customer. A drop-dead date for a system could be just that—any later and the customer might be out of business.

Warning

> Though the architect must consider all customer requirements, the architect also has a responsibility to advise the customer on the potential implications for the system if architectural compromises prove necessary to achieve a short-term delivery date.

# RAD Architecture and Design

A RAD architecture is one that upholds timeliness of delivery as a central overarching principle. A RAD architecture both meets the needs of your customers and expedites the delivery of the system. In short, it is about defining an architecture that is implemented easily and efficiently by the development team and hence completed in a timeframe acceptable to the customer.

The following are some options for achieving this goal.

# Work to the Strengths of the Team

Contrary to what many project managers would like to believe, software engineers are not faceless drones who spend all their spare time reading technical reference material on Java. The members of any given project team have acquired a diverse and varied range of skills and knowledge during their time in the software development industry. Knowing the strengths of the team is an important consideration when designing the system: the architecture should take advantage of these strengths.

Some people may find this a contentious statement, arguing that architecture must be based on the technology that best fits the system requirements. This is a valid argument. If the choice of technology was always based on the knowledge of the team, most IT applications would still be implemented in COBOL. Nevertheless, the team's collective technical background should be taken into consideration when time is a critical factor for the project.

## Important

> The same rule applies when looking to the job market for skills for the project. If members of the team leave, or a new project team has to be formed, filling vacant job roles could prove problematic if skills in an uncommon technology are required.

As an example, consider the choice of which scripting language to adopt on a new project. Both Jython and Groovy are excellent choices as scripting languages. Both are each compatible with Java and offer highly expressive language constructs. Nevertheless, if the team has a large base of experience with Perl, then neither Jython nor Groovy may be the best option. Where possible, you may wish to stick to what the team knows well and work to your strengths. Without doubt, there is value in learning new technologies—just be cautious of learning on time-critical projects.

> *Chapter 9 looks at Jython and Groovy.*

# Use Best-of-Breed Frameworks

J2EE is all about frameworks, yet extensive as the J2EE platform is, it does not cater to every scenario. Enter the application framework to plug the gaps.

A suitable software framework can significantly reduce the amount of code we need to write and improve the quality of the design. Thanks to the groundswell of support for all things Java, J2EE developers are spoiled for choice when it comes to the availability of software frameworks.

Frameworks are available for just about every conceivable application, including Web development, security, build environments, test environments, and GUI development. Table 4–1 lists a selection of the popular offerings from the Java community and highlights the diversity of the frameworks available.

**Table 4–1**   Open Source Frameworks

| Name | Description | Reference |
|------|-------------|-----------|
| **Web** | | |
| Apache Struts | Struts is a popular Web application framework based on the model-view-controller (MVC) design paradigm. | http://jakarta.apache.org/struts/index.html |
| JavaServer Faces | A technology for developing user interfaces for Web applications using an industry-standard set of APIs. JavaServer Faces technology was developed under the Java Community Process as JSR-127. | http://java.sun.com/j2ee/javaserverfaces |
| Apache Tapestry | Dynamic Web application development framework that centers on a component model in preference to a scripting approach. | http://jakarta.apache.org/tapestry |
| Persistence | Powerful, high-performance, object/relational persistence framework for Java objects. | http://www.hibernate.org |
| **Hibernate** | | |
| ObjectRelational-Bridge | OBJ is an object/relational mapping tool from Apache Software Foundation. | http://db.apache.org/ojb |
| **Logging** | | |
| Apache Log4J | Log4J provides an externally configurable logging framework. | http://logging.apache.org/log4j/docs/index.html |
| **Application** | | |
| Spring | Spring provides a layered framework for producing Java and J2EE applications. The Spring framework can either augment the services of the J2EE platform or be used standalone for developing highly flexible component-based systems. | http://www.springframework.org |
| **Build Environment** | | |
| Apache Ant | Popular Java-based build utility that uses an XML-based syntax for creating build scripts. | http://ant.apache.org |
| CruiseControl | Framework for supporting the practice of a continuous-integration build environment. | http://cruisecontrol.sourceforge.net/index.html |

**Table 4–1**    Open Source Frameworks

| Name | Description | Reference |
| --- | --- | --- |
| Apache Maven | Maven describes itself as a project management and project comprehension tool, and takes responsibility for managing and orchestrating the various artifacts that the project comprises. | http://maven.apache.org |
| **Testing** | | |
| JUnit | An almost ubiquitous xUnit-based testing framework for Java developers. | http://junit.source-forge.net |
| Apache Cactus | Cactus extends JUnit and focuses on the challenges of testing server-side components. | http://jakarta.apache.org/cactus/index.html |

The choice of which framework to use on a project is an important decision that can be critical to the success of the project. The following guidelines should help you through the decision-making process:

### Team knowledge.

Look to work with products that have proven successful on other projects, and consider frameworks with which the team already has experience.

### Maturity.

How long has the framework been used in commercial software development? Is it an open source project maintained by Apache, or is it the result of someone's PhD? A mature software product has all the rough edges knocked off. Be prepared for problems if the software has yet to be used on a commercial development.

### Fit for purpose.

Pick a framework that meets the specific needs of the system. Where an acceptable match cannot be found, longer term benefits maybe realized by investing in the development of your own framework for a specific business area.

### Tool support.

Tool support is a significant criterion in the selection of a suitable framework, because the combination of framework and development tool can offer significant productivity gains.

### Longevity.

Try to select frameworks that will remain supported for the predicted lifetime of the system. A framework that disappears from view once a system reaches production presents ongoing maintenance and support problems.

Picking the best framework for your project reduces the development timeframe and should contribute to the quality of the final application. Here are some metrics to use as a guide when assessing a framework in terms of its maturity and longevity:

- Availability of mailing lists and discussion forums
- Level of activity on these forums
- Response time for users getting questions answered and quality of the answers
- Frequency of new releases of the framework
- Community feedback in terms of perceived quality and usability
- Number of open defects
- Quality of documentation

Choosing a framework is an important decision, so be sure to do your homework before making it.

# Think Ahead

By thinking ahead during the design process, you can make the lives of developers and testers alike a lot easier. The need to think ahead is especially relevant in the area of testing.

Sadly, testing is often unfairly seen as the poor relation to development. This perception is unwarranted, as testing is an integral part of the software development lifecycle. As a rough rule of thumb, testing hours on a project will likely equal that of development—any less, and the system is probably undertested.

Any actions you can take as an architect to make testing easier will not only result in a higher quality system, but also reduce the total testing effort. Exactly how the architect can design with testing in mind is largely dependent on the application.

> *Testing is a key part of RAD and is covered in some detail in Chapters 14 and 15.*

Outlined below are some points for consideration when working on the system design.

## Include Test Stubs and Unit Tests as Part of the Design

Considerable effort is often wasted on projects when developers produce their own ad hoc testing harnesses. These test harnesses sprout like weeds throughout the project's code base. They burst into existence as developers find themselves unable to test new components or modules due to a dependency on a piece of software that hasn't yet been written. The solution is often to quickly implement a test stub in place of the missing software. Unfortunately, this task consumes time, and on a large project, this practice can quickly get out of hand with engineers duplicating the same test stubs.

These test stubs seldom find their way into source control and are often of dubious quality because no time has been set aside to the developer for this task on the project plan. To avoid this problem, the architect must think strategically and incorporate all necessary test stubs into the design. The designer must work in conjunction with the project manager to ensure software components are built in a logical sequence to avoid the need for ad hoc test stubs. Where this is not possible, the test stub should be included as part of the object model and time set aside on the plan for the development of the stub.

With this approach, all test harnesses and stubs become part of the project's build cycle and are available to the entire team. They can also be made available to the test team for early testing of delivered components. The test team in turn can give feedback on the quality of the test stubs.

Therefore, the rule is, think about your testing needs early on, and design testing into the system. Your developers and your testers will thank you for it.

## Be Wary of Weakly Typed Interfaces

Due to the surge in popularity of XML as a format for data transfer, the interfaces on distributed components the world over are taking on a very similar appearance. Thus, many methods now have the signature

```
void update(String document);
```

The parameter document in this case carries an XML document as the payload. Using XML in this way has largely taken over from the conventional approach of defining each argument as a typed parameter on the method as it provides an effective approach for ensuring loose coupling between components. The structure of the XML document can be modified without the need to change the interface, allowing for a design that is very resilient to change.

The downside to this approach is that the compiler cannot perform any type checking of the data on our behalf. Type checking, or validation of the document against a schema, must now take place at runtime. With XML, Java becomes a type-less language.

This presents the test team with something of a headache. Errors are harder to catch at runtime than at compile time, and the testing effort must now be exhaustive.

If you intend to use XML in this manner to achieve a highly decoupled system, then ensure the necessary safeguards are in place to replace the compiler's type safety. Where practical, validate against an XML schema and always log any errors caught at runtime in a manner that makes them immediately apparent.

## Be Wary of Designing for Reuse

Software reuse is a key element of RAD, but reuse is a double-edged sword. Making the reuse of software components part of your strategy for rapid development is not an easy task, even with the benefits of Java as an OOP language and J2EE as a container for housing prefabricated components.

Designing code for reuse is a difficult and time-consuming task. The developer must consider all reasonable future scenarios for a component and accommodate them accordingly within the software architecture. This adds excessive complexity to the component's design and implementation. On a project with a tight timeframe, you should avoid overengineering the architecture for future reuse purposes. Rapid development project teams should design only to have the software meet the current known requirements, not possible future ones.

This fits in with the fundamental XP principle of keeping the design simple—a principle aptly described by the XP expression, "*You ain't gonna need it*," or YAGNI. Remember, less code means fewer defects.

> *Chapter 3 covers the practices of XP.*

**warning**

> Rapid development requires designing *with* reuse as opposed to designing *for* reuse.

Designing for reuse adds considerable complexity to the project and hence consumes additional resources and time. Instead, develop reusable components as a separate research and development project aimed at building your company's adaptive development foundation.

Have the components built, tested, and documented before rapid development project teams use them. A suite of suitably designed prefabricated components provides a development company with a competitive advantage, but this is an investment that needs to be made as part of a company's preparation effort for rapid development. Don't build the components of your adaptive foundation on time-critical customer projects.

## Apply Orthogonal Design

Orthogonality is a term taken from geometry that applies to two lines that intersect at right angles. As vectors, these lines are said to be orthogonal and therefore independent. Thus, move along one of the lines, and your position projected on the other line remains unchanged.

Despite its origins in geometry, orthogonality is becoming a watchword in development circles after being popularized as a software engineering concept by Andrew Hunt and David Thomas in their book *The Pragmatic Programmer* [Hunt, 1999].

For software engineering, the term neatly summarizes those elements of design that are synonymous with well-constructed software; that is, they exhibit the admirable characteristics of loose coupling and high cohesion.

Orthogonal components are independent, self-contained, and have a clearly stated responsibility. Changes to the internals of an orthogonal component do not impact other components within the system.

This independence between components is vital to rapid development. A loosely coupled system can more easily accommodate change than one that is tightly coupled. A change in the database should not require a change in the code responsible for the application's user interface, and vice versa.

An orthogonal design safeguards against change, and a design that can absorb the impact of change supports rapid development. Moreover, components that exhibit orthogonality are easier to code, test, and maintain due to their self-contained nature. Again, these are all attributes that help make a team productive and greatly benefit a RAD project.

Object-oriented development practices, if applied correctly, result in orthogonal designs. A staple of object-oriented design is the use of interfaces. By designing our components around interfaces, we can use interfaces as shields against implementation changes.

One successful approach for achieving an orthogonal design is to base your design upon the use of layers.

## Adopt a Layered Architecture

In software engineering, separating the application code into layers is good design practice and enables the construction of robust applications. In the layered approach, each layer provides its services to the layer immediately above through a series of well-defined interfaces.

Each layer should rely only on the services of the layer immediately beneath it. This ensures higher layers in the design hierarchy are insulated from changes in the lower layers.

Here are the layers commonly found in business software:

* *Presentation*, for user-interface components
* *Application*, where the system's business logic resides
* *Data*, for providing business components with access to external resources such as persistent data stores or other enterprise systems

Layers are abstract and represent a logical boundary within the software, not a physical one. Distributed computing makes it possible to achieve a physical separation of a system's logical layers into *tiers*. The tiers of a multitier architecture are physically remote from one another, typically located on different servers or executing in a separate process. This physical division of the layers into tiers gives rise to a *multitier* architecture.

The architecture of a J2EE application comprises three tiers.

### Client Tier

The client tier is the "final front-tier." It should contain code specific only to the user interface and rely upon the middle tier for all business knowledge. J2EE clients run on anything from desktops to handheld devices and access the middle tier remotely, using an appropriate network infrastructure such as a LAN or via the Internet.

## Middle/Business Tier

On the J2EE platform, this middle tier is the J2EE server, which provides services for addressing the concerns of both Web clients and application business logic. The middle tier of the J2EE platform divides into two tiers for each of these concerns:

- The Web tier provides services for orchestrating the interaction between Web-based clients and the system's business logic
- The EJB tier manages the system's business components deployed within the tier as Enterprise JavaBeans

The J2EE server manages access to resources required by the business components. These resources reside within the enterprise information system (EIS) tier.

## Enterprise Information System Tier

The EIS tier, or back-end tier, is the lowermost tier in J2EE and houses the enterprise resources upon which a J2EE application relies. Examples of enterprise resources include relational databases and existing legacy systems. The resources of the EIS tier do not fall under the control of the J2EE server. Instead, the J2EE server offers a set of standard services for integrating with EIS tier resources. These services include

- The JDBC API for relational database access
- Java Naming and Directory Interface (JNDI) for access to directory servers
- The J2EE Connector Architecture (JCA) for integration with existing information systems
- Java Messaging Service (JMS) for asynchronous communications with other application resources

The J2EE server undertakes the responsibility of managing and pooling connections to the various resources of the EIS tier as well as the management of transactions that span enterprise resources.

The J2EE platform makes possible the design of orthogonal systems using multitier architectures. The next section considers the strengths and weaknesses of using multiple tiers and explores some design options for J2EE architectures.

# Approaches to J2EE Architecture

Building applications with multitier architectures involves the use of *distributed computing*, a complex area of software engineering. Although the J2EE platform does much to simplify the development of three-tier systems, distributed computing makes designs of this nature inherently more complex than systems comprised of only one or two tiers. This added complexity means architects should carefully consider whether the requirements of the system justify a distributed solution.

In the past, the prominence of Enterprise JavaBeans (EJBs), the flagship technology of the J2EE platform, has lead some architects to produce complex multitier architectures for systems whose requirements would have been met with a simpler model.

Although EJB technology has possibly the highest profile of all the J2EE services, Enterprise JavaBeans form only part of the J2EE specification, and their use is not mandatory in all J2EE applications. Furthermore, EJB architectures are possible that do not rely on the remote-method invocation services of the J2EE container.

If you can avoid the use of a distributed architecture for systems that do not require it, then simpler designs result. Avoiding complexity in this way is important for rapid development projects, as complex designs can wreak havoc on tight schedules.

Complexity makes:

* Designs and code difficult to understand

* Timeframes longer due to steep learning curves

* Software maintenance expensive

* Changes difficult to assess and apply

* Mistakes easy to make

Over the course of the next sections, we examine the strengths and weaknesses of distributed systems and consider possible architectures that do not rely upon the services of distributed components.

## Two-Tier Versus Multitier Architectures

Prior to the emergence of distributed computing technologies like J2EE and CORBA, enterprise information systems typically adopted a two-tier, or *client/server* architecture. Under the client/server model, business logic was implemented as an integral part of a rich, or *fat*, client application that accessed data housed in a central database server.

The client/server model enjoyed considerable success. It was easy to understand, simple to test, and well supported by numerous high-level visual development tools. These benefits made the client/server architecture ideal for rapid development. Sadly, two-tier architectures do have some key shortcomings:

### Deployment.

The client/server model sees all functionality built as a monolithic, standalone application and deployed directly to the client machine. Large organizations requiring widespread deployments to thousands of desktops face a huge, logistical challenge. Often, deployments of this nature can only be made out of hours, or in some extreme cases, over the course of a weekend. Consequently, while the two-tier model enables software changes to be applied quickly, it has inherent weaknesses when it comes to releasing new, business-critical, functionality in a timely manner.

### Sharing of services.

The monolithic structure of client/server applications presents some very difficult problems when it comes to sharing services between applications across the enterprise. Increasingly, organizations require their core IT systems to share information or services. The lack of a centralized business or services tier in the client/server model makes this all but impossible. One option is to share common code modules, or components, between systems. However, this again presents deployment problems.

### Poor separation of presentation and business logic.

Placing business and presentation logic within the same tier can lead to a commingling of these two concerns. Arguably, this is an indication of poor design rather than a true weakness of a client/server architecture. A well-designed application would see the two layers cleanly decoupled using well-founded object-oriented design practices. Unfortunately, often over the course of the lifetime of the system, software entropy sees the two layers merge without the benefit of physically separate tiers to keep the layers logically distinct.

In searching for a solution to the shortcomings in the client/server model, developers concluded that you can never have too much of a good thing. If splitting systems into two physical tiers proved effective, then the addition of a further tier would also be a good thing. Experience proved them mostly right, and so the middle tier was born.

The use of a middle business tier offers many benefits beyond that of the client server model:

### Centralized business intelligence.

The middle tier enables business components to be located in a central location and accessed remotely by disparate systems. Here, the middle tier addresses the problem of core business functionality being effectively locked away within the heavyweight clients of the client/server model.

### Ease of deployment.

Thanks to the middle tier, gone is the headache of deploying business components to thousands of desktop machines over the corporate network. With all business components centrally located, changes can be deployed quickly and easily with minimal impact on the system's user base.

### Redundancy.

The deployment of business components into a *clustered* middle tier provides built-in redundancy for systems. Thus, the use of multiple machines to replicate the middle tier sees important business components maintained in a high-availability environment.

**Scalability.**

Clustering components of the middle tier over multiple server nodes also allows for scalability. As system usage increases, so too can the number of machines in the architecture.

These benefits have pushed the multitier model to the forefront as the architecture of choice for enterprise software. The technology of the J2EE platform provides a distributed component model for developing systems with multitier architectures, with Enterprise JavaBeans a key technology for developing business components for deployment to the middle tier.

# Enterprise JavaBeans

Enterprise JavaBeans helps realize the RAD concept of developing software using component-based architectures. The EJB architecture defines components that encapsulate functionality into deployable modules with clearly defined interfaces known as *enterprise beans*.

The J2EE platform supports three types of enterprise bean objects:

- *Session beans*, for encapsulating business logic
- *Entity beans*, as a mechanism for presenting an object-based view of entities within a persistent data store
- *Message-driven beans*, for consuming messages delivered to the server via the JMS API

The remainder of this discussion focuses on the use of session beans for building distributed enterprise solutions.

An EJB architecture provides substantial benefits when building an enterprise system:

- Improves productivity by managing transaction and security concerns on behalf of the developer based on information specified in the enterprise bean's deployment descriptor
- Provides scalability by intelligently managing the allocation of resources and transparent state management of stateful components
- Supports and mediates access to business components by multiple client types, including fat clients and thin browser-based Web applications
- Insulates the client from networking issues by providing location transparency, whereby methods on a component can be invoked regardless of the physical location of the client or the component

The final point concerning location transparency is of specific interest, as this EJB technology makes possible the development of distributed architectures with the J2EE component model.

# Remote and Local Client Views

Clients of session bean objects can view methods on a bean's interface either *remotely* or *locally*. With a remote method invocation, a client running in a separately executing Java Virtual Machine (JVM) accesses the bean instance. With local access, the client resides within the same JVM as the bean object. Alternatively, as of the EJB 2.1 specification, clients may access session bean objects through a bean's Web Service. This is essentially another form of remote access.

Clients obtain remote access to a session bean object through the enterprise bean's *remote interface* and *remote home interface*. These interfaces ultimately extend the java.rmi.Remote interface, part of standard Java Remote Method Invocation (RMI). By building on RMI, clients can access bean functionality across machines and process boundaries. The complexities surrounding network connection issues are all handled by RMI on behalf of the developer.

An enterprise bean may also expose a *local interface*. Local interfaces do not offer location transparency, meaning that clients can access a bean only if it is executing in the same JVM through its local interface.

We look at the benefits of local interfaces shortly, but first let's consider some of the implications surrounding the development of enterprise beans that expose remote interfaces to their clients.

# Distributed Components

Providing enterprise beans with remote interfaces makes possible the development of systems with distributed architectures. The J2EE platform does a very creditable job of reducing the difficulties associated with building complex architectures of this type. Nevertheless, adding remote interfaces to business components results in certain issues of which the architect must be aware before deciding upon a distributed solution.

Rod Johnson eloquently raised awareness of these issues within the Java community in his book *Expert One-on-One J2EE Design and Programming* [Johnson, 2002]. These issues include performance overheads, complexity, and object-oriented impedance.

## Performance

EJB technology relies on standard Java RMI for its distributed capabilities, which provides the client of the enterprise bean with location transparency when accessing the bean through its remote interface. However, the process involved in making a method invocation across a JVM or machine boundary, makes RMI calls several orders of magnitude more expensive than the equivalent calls on a local object.

To understand why remote calls incur a performance penalty, let's review the steps involved in an RMI method call.

In making the call, RMI creates a *stub* object on the client responsible for sending method parameters and receiving return values across the network. This packaging of method calls for transmission across the wire is called *marshaling* and is a common approach to remote method calls. RMI uses Java object serialization to convert parameters into a stream of bytes for sending across a network.

The client stub does not talk directly to the object on the server but to an RMI *skeleton* object, which is the server-side equivalent of the client stub, and retrieves all calls sent across the network before forwarding them to the real object. This server-side skeleton object makes the call on the remote object on the client's behalf.

This same process is followed every time a method on a session bean object's remote interface is called. The overheads of remote method calls means careful design is necessary to ensure the benefits of location transparency do not come at the cost of system performance.

tip

Passing large objects as parameters in remote method calls further reduces performance. If an object contains references to other objects, then these member objects are also serialized as part of the call. To reduce the size of some objects, you can exclude unnecessary objects by marking them with the transient keyword.

Since RMI uses Java serialization for marshaling, for very large objects you should consider overriding writeObject() on java.lang.Serializable and implementing some form of compression algorithm. Don't forget to implement a corresponding decompression algorithm for readObject().

## Complexity

Although RMI can make the calling of remote enterprise beans a seamless process, distributed computing still introduces additional complexities for the developer.

The first issue is the need for developers using RMI technology to be aware of the subtle but important differences between making remote calls and calling a local Java object.

Parameters in a remote call are *passed by value*, due to the need for RMI to copy the parameter in order to send it across the network. If the remote object modifies the state of an object passed to it by value, then the object referenced by the caller *does not reflect* these changes.

With a call on a local object, parameters are *passed by reference*. Consequently, if the called method modifies the state of an object passed as a parameter, then the object referenced by the caller *does reflect* these changes. This is a subtle difference in the semantics of the call, but it can cause frustration for developers unaware that Java's calling conventions have suddenly changed.

Remote clients must also guard against the prospect that networking issues could cause a remote call to fail. Trapping these network errors isn't an onerous task, as you only need to catch thrown java.rmi.RemoteException exceptions. However, complexities arise with the need to handle these exceptions, because they are orthogonal to the standard exceptions a business method would normally throw. The architect must have a strategy in place for satisfactorily handling these remote exceptions and translating them into meaningful error messages for the presentation layer. Avoiding the need to deal with remote exceptions therefore has positive implications for rapid development.

## Object-Oriented Impedance

Employing the distributed capabilities of EJB technology requires a change in the way we apply object-oriented design practices.

In a nondistributed architecture, developers work directly with objects from the domain model. Here, domain objects represent business entities and expose interfaces with fine-grained methods, such as get and set methods.

The performance overheads of a distributed application preclude the use of objects with fine-grained methods, as they increase the number of network roundtrips when a client interacts with a remote object.

To keep the number of roundtrips to a minimum, remote interfaces have to be coarse-grained, whereby methods combine the functionality of several fine-grained methods into a single call.

To provide guidance when building distributed architectures, Sun Microsystems published a collection of J2EE design patterns [Deepak, 2003]. These patterns are essential reading for anyone building distributed applications. The Session Façade and Transfer Object patterns both offer effective strategies for managing the performance overheads of remote calls.

Despite the existence of these patterns, they still impose on the architect's object-oriented thinking process. The architect must be aware of the constraints of the implementing technology and reflect this in all designs. Having the implementing technology dictate the makeup of a component's interface is counter to the practice of good object-oriented design.

## Choosing the Appropriate Design

Distributed components are not a prerequisite for all enterprise architectures. Unless the requirements of the system dictate a distributed architecture, a simpler application is possible by avoiding the need to employ the remote method invocation capabilities of the J2EE platform. The architectural decision as to whether to use distributed components therefore has a significant impact on rapid development projects.

In this section, we look at two possible J2EE architectures, Web-centric and EJB-centric, although numerous permutations of the two designs presented are possible. The next two sections evaluate the merits of each design from the standpoint of a system whose main architectural driver is the delivery timeframe.

## Web-Centric Architecture

One trend in enterprise systems that has become very apparent is the move away from fat user interfaces to lightweight clients. In fact, thanks to the popularity of the browser, user interfaces have become positively anorexic.

The Web application is emerging as the de facto standard for enterprise applications, a trend that has the potential to make the task of developing enterprise software far simpler.

Let's consider a basic J2EE architecture to support an enterprise Web application that does not make use of the services of EJB technology. Figure 4–1 illustrates a Web-centric design.

Does anything in Figure 4–1 look familiar? The presentation tier is gone. In its place is the Web container (or Web tier), acting as a consolidated presentation and business tier. The browser-based interface enables us to return to a model similar in structure to the classic client/server architecture. Thus, the Web-centric model sees a single JVM housing presentation and business logic in a common *Web tier*. This design swaps a multitude of client machines for a single server and removes the deployment problems associated with the client/server model.

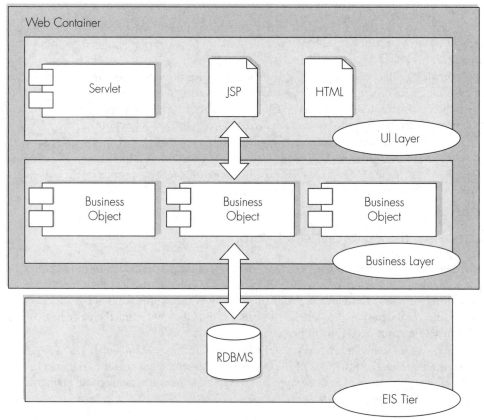

**Figure 4–1**    Web-centric enterprise architecture.

The Web-centric design shown has just two tiers (or two-and-a-half with the browser): the Web tier, and the EIS tier. The use of layers within the Web tier separates user interface code from business logic.

note

> For clarity, the architecture depicted in Figure 4–1 does not show all of the layers required in an enterprise system. For example, a production system would put in place layers to split business objects from lower-level data access objects.

Business objects are implemented as Plain Old Java Objects, or POJOs, in preference to heavier weight enterprise beans. The term POJO refers to a *vanilla* Java class that exposes no specialized interfaces.

The nondistributed Web-centric architecture shown in Figure 4–1 has several key benefits:

* User-interface and business components both execute within the same JVM, providing high performance

* Using plain Java objects instead of enterprise beans for encapsulating business logic removes the additional configuration and deployment complexities associated with EJB technology

* Unit testing of the business objects is simpler because, unlike session bean objects, they can be tested without being deployed to the J2EE server

* No RMI calls are involved, so standard Java pass-by-reference calling conventions remain unchanged

* Business objects can expose fine-grained interfaces

A prerequisite for most enterprise architectures is scalability. The Web-centric design scales across application servers, although suitable load-balancing hardware or software is required to manage the allocation of requests between server nodes.

Like any solution, the Web-centric architecture has its limitations, including the following:

### Supporting Web-interfaces only.

The Web-centric architecture supports only browser-based interfaces. If the system requirements mandate fat clients accessing the business layer remotely, then an EJB architecture is more appropriate. Alternatively, the use of a framework such as Apache's Axis enables business object interfaces to be exposed to heterogeneous remote clients as Web Services.

### Security.

While it is possible to secure Web applications, plain Java business objects do not offer the same declarative security model as is available for enterprise beans. Securing business objects within the Web-centric architecture to the same method level allowed by EJB technology requires the time-consuming task of writing application-specific security code.

### Transaction support.

To support transactions, business objects must implement their own transaction management. The transaction management services of the J2EE server can be invoked programmatically, but this approach involves considerably more effort than the declarative transaction model EJB technology provides.

### Threading issues.

The EJB container manages concurrent threads of execution on behalf of the developer. In the Web-centric model shown, the developer is responsible for addressing threading issues. The development of multithreaded systems is notoriously error prone and time consuming.

The next section introduces enterprise beans that expose local interfaces into the Web-centric architecture.

## EJB-Centric Architecture

To counter some of the shortcomings in the Web-centric architecture presented previously, this next solution modifies the architecture to incorporate enterprise beans that provide a *local view* of their interfaces to clients.

Figure 4–2 illustrates a possible EJB-centric architecture for our Web application.

The architecture shown Figure 4–2 turns the business objects into session beans and deploys them into the J2EE server's EJB container. The session bean objects that represent the system's business components do not expose remote interfaces. Instead, they each make available a *local interface* to clients.

The EJB 2.0 specification introduced local interfaces for enterprise beans in response to industry concerns surrounding performance issues with EJB architectures. Placing a local interface on an enterprise bean enables a client resident within the same JVM to invoke the methods on the bean instance using standard Java pass-by-reference calling conventions, avoiding the overheads incurred in a remote call.

In the architecture shown in Figure 4–2, both the J2EE server's Web container and EJB container exist within the same JVM, making the components of the Web application local client's of the session bean objects. The EJB-centric architecture still has the same two-and-a-half tiers as the Web-centric version, with the Web container and EJB container acting as layers within the middle tier.

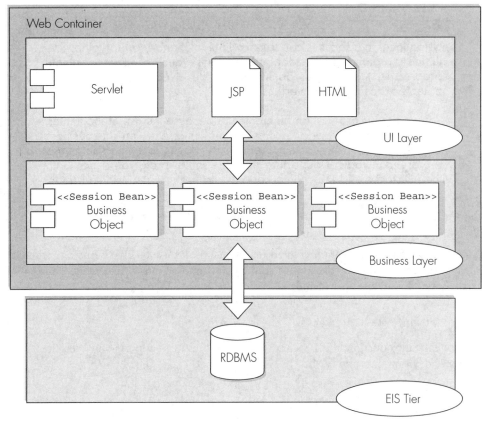

**Figure 4–2** EJB-centric enterprise architecture.

The benefits of an enterprise architecture built using enterprise beans with local interfaces include the following:

- Performance is excellent as in-process method invocation does not carry the over-heads of Java RMI
- The declarative model of EJB technology is available for addressing security, trans-action management, and thread safety
- Remote exceptions are not thrown and so do not have to be handled
- Enterprise beans can expose fine-grained business interfaces

## Architecture Prototyping

> Using local interfaces is congruent with evolutionary prototyping. Preliminary prototypes can adopt a Web-centric design. As development progresses, the business objects can be evolved into session bean objects exposing local interfaces.
>
> This change is gradual and incremental because the use of local interfaces preserves the original fine-grained interfaces on the business objects. Alternatively, adding remote interfaces to enterprise beans represents a radical departure from the initial prototype, since both the interfaces and the calling code would require a substantial refactoring effort.

The EJB-centric architecture presented represents a valid use of EJB technology where the system requirements call for declarative security and transaction management. Some of the weaknesses of this architecture include:

### Supports only Web interfaces.

Despite the introduction of EJB technology, the architecture supports only Web clients colocated within the same JVM.

### Physical separation of layers.

It is not possible to split Web components and business components into separate tiers for deployment to different servers.

### Configuration overheads.

The EJB architecture introduces configuration overheads for the business components. You should ensure these overheads warrant the benefits EJB technology brings to the architecture.

### Container-bound testing.

As enterprise beans, the business components now require the services of the EJB container for unit testing purposes.

The architecture examples discussed are just two possible approaches to building enterprise systems. Simple architectures are faster and easier to implement than complex ones. Distributed architectures introduce complexity. Ensure the requirements of the system justify this additional level of complexity before embracing a distributed component model.

# Summary

Designing for rapidity requires making decisions during the definition of a system's architecture. These decisions impact the ability of the project team to deliver an IT solution within the customer's timeframe.

Some of the factors we discussed in this chapter when timeliness of delivery was a key concern of the customer included the following:

* Delivery timeframe is a contributing factor to the definition of the system's architecture
* Build software that is orthogonal using a layered architecture
* Design the system for testing from the outset
* Work to the strengths of the team
* Adopt proven frameworks
* Keep designs simple and be wary of designing for future reuse
* Avoid building of unnecessarily complex system architectures by using only the J2EE technologies that help solve the business problem

In the next chapter, we examine the benefits of modeling tools for rapid development and explore how the process of modeling can help the software engineer in the task of building enterprise applications.

## Additional Information

The collection of J2EE patterns published by Sun Microsystems is available online as part of Sun's *Java BluePrints* program, a developer resource aimed at defining a set of best practices for building Java applications. The Java BluePrints program, along with the core J2EE patterns, resides at http://java.sun.com/blueprints.

The two J2EE architectures presented in this chapter were based upon some of the architectures presented by Rod Johnson in his excellent book *Expert One-on-One J2EE Design and Programming* [Johnson, 2002]. This title offers guidance and advice for applying J2EE technologies to real-world business problems.

Patterns in architecture are becoming increasingly important. Martin Fowler's book, *Patterns of Enterprise Application Architecture* [Fowler, 2002], introduces a range of patterns for building enterprise architectures.

# 5

# Modeling Software

A picture is worth a thousand words, and from this common adage, the integrated computer-aided software engineering (CASE) tool was born.

CASE, or *modeling tools*, emerged in the 1980s and were promoted as the silver bullet for rapid development, claiming to increase productivity and yield higher quality software. Consequently, they became one of the mainstay technologies of the RAD paradigm.

This chapter covers the use of models and modeling tools in the software development process. The Unified Modeling Language (UML) for defining software models is introduced, and we cover the advantages models bring to the task of developing component-based applications. Specifically, we shall see how UML models:

- Communicate the software architecture to members of the team
- Help validate the design and assess the impact of requirements and design changes
- Assist in the process of exploring and understanding the structure and dynamics of applications and components

The chapter also examines the benefits of using modeling tools for constructing and maintaining models and provides guidelines for selecting a suitable modeling tool. We also cover how making models the center of the development process can improve developer productivity, yield higher quality software, and reduce timeframes.

## Why Model?

In the context of software engineering, a model is an abstract diagrammatic representation of the form, structure, and intent of a software application using a standard notation. Typically, this standard notation is the UML.

It is not mandatory to use the UML for defining a model. However, the UML has become firmly established as the de facto standard for software modeling since it was first formalized by the famous trio of Booch, Rumbaugh, and Jacobson, collectively known as the three amigos.

Models make it possible to describe the pertinent aspects of a system's architecture clearly and accurately, and serve as a rich communication medium. Here are some of the things you can represent with a model:

- Understanding and describing the problem domain
- Software structure, organization, and constraints
- Object and component collaboration
- Information flow
- System state
- Database structure, organization, and constraints
- Packaging and deployment of the application components

Models offer a mechanism for communicating the system design to all members of the project and help build a common understanding of the system. They also assist in the process of validating the ability of the design to meet the customer's requirements.

## Communication

Most people are familiar with models of one form or another. I'm not referring to software models but to the type more commonly built by children with a little help from a responsible adult, usually to prevent any serious damage with the modeling knife or to stop tiny fingers from becoming glued together.

Children build models because it is fun and educational. Moreover, they lack the skills and resources necessary build the real thing. My first such model was a reconstruction of a World War II Spitfire, constructed using a plastic modeling kit, a sharp knife, and some glue.

The finished model could be shown to school friends to explain how a real Spitfire worked. The model perfectly illustrated where the pilot sat, the location of the guns in the wings, and how the propeller spun and pulled the aircraft through the air.

When it comes to modeling software as opposed to toy aircraft, the same benefits apply. UML diagrams help construct low-cost models of the software and enable the communication of system design and behavior quickly, accurately, and succinctly.

### Communication with the Customer

By modeling the system requirements, an analyst can convey to the customer his or her understanding of the business functionality the application must exhibit. A carefully constructed software model highlights any areas of ambiguity, thereby allowing them to be addressed during the initial stages of the development process with input from the customer.

## Communication with the Project Team

When modeling the design of the application, the same benefits apply. A low-cost model of the design provides an excellent mechanism for communicating all aspects of the design to both customers and colleagues. With the UML, ideas and possible design solutions can be sketched out on a whiteboard where they can be readily discussed and refined among the design team.

## A Common Vocabulary

In this manner, the UML serves as a common vocabulary for the effective communication of solutions. Representing designs in this format is a significantly faster process than producing reams of written documentation and is less ambiguous.

The benefits of the UML as a common vocabulary that can span language and cultural barriers should not be understated. Given the business practice of moving development work offshore, software engineers are finding themselves in the position of having to work as part of *virtual teams*, where team members are geographically remote. In order for this project structure to work successfully, accurate communication of technical information between team members and a common understanding of the system is imperative.

# Validation

Children and software engineers are not the only people who build models. The practice is commonplace in the engineering profession. Going back to the example of the model aircraft, real aircraft designers employ a similar technique as part of the design process and build a mockup of the final aircraft.

The aircraft designer's model is made from a malleable material like clay and is built to prove the viability of a new plane's design. By placing the clay model in a wind tunnel, metrics can be obtained as to how the real plane will perform once it leaves the drawing board. In this way, the designer can get an early indication of whether the design meets the specifications for the plane in terms of speed, stability, and load-bearing qualities.

Software models provide the same benefits. UML *interaction diagrams* enable the software engineer to determine if the various components that make up the design are capable of collaborating in order to execute each of the system's use cases.

Design validation has two main benefits: it helps drive out risk, and it enables change on the project to be measured and controlled.

## Driving Out Risk

Models are inexpensive to build. By being able to test a model early in the development process, the risk of a design failing to meet a significant customer requirement is drastically reduced.

Finding shortcomings in the software architecture later rather than sooner can be an expensive and time-consuming business. Though *refactoring* tools for making sweeping changes to the code are of considerable value, time savings can be made if the number of refactorings an application must undergo are kept to a minimum.

## Controlling Change

Change is endemic to the software development process. A model is an effective mechanism for assessing the impact of any change on the design and hence the final system.

Like the clay models of the aircraft designer, software models are also malleable. We can update our model in light of the change and then revalidate the model. If it transpires that one of the use cases is no longer supported by the original design, then we can go back to the model and refine it further. Thus, the model can be used to experiment without the need to write lines and lines of code.

## Models and Prototypes

Models are complementary to the development of prototypes on projects. Models can highlight areas of the system that require further investigation, thereby promoting the development of prototypes that target the major design risks to the system.

# Multiple Views of Architecture

UML diagrams help capture both the static and dynamic structure of software architecture. Unfortunately, architecture defines a diverse range of system concerns, making it very difficult to represent even the simplest of systems with a single diagram.

Rather than trying to think of architecture as one giant picture, it is easier to break this picture into smaller chunks, or views. In his paper "The 4 + 1 View Model of Architecture" [Kruchten, 1995], Philippe Kruchten defined five concurrent interlocking views of architecture. Using this multiple view approach, each of the four views models a separate set of architectural concerns. Architects use the fifth view for the illustration and validation of the other views.

Since Philippe Kruchten's paper first came out, the view names have undergone a few changes. Here are the generally accepted 4 + 1 views of architecture:

**Logical view.**

The logical view defines the structure and organization of the software in terms of packages, classes, subsystems, and layers.

**Implementation view.**

The perspective of this view focuses on the various files and components that constitute a deliverable release of the software. Unlike the logical view, this is a physical view of the makeup of the system.

**Process view.**

The process view describes the concurrency concerns of the system and models the interaction of runtime aspects such as tasks, processes, and threads.

**Deployment view.**

The deployment view defines the different hardware nodes of the system and describes the location of software components within the runtime environment.

**Use-case view.**

This final view is a special view that helps shape the architecture and is taken from the perspective of the customer, analysts, and testers.

There are two wider perspectives of architecture: logical and physical. These two perspectives represent the view's type. Logical views focus on software constructs such as packages and classes. Physical views model hardware nodes and files.

Table 5–1 depicts the types of each of the four views.

**Table 5–1**    Architectural View Types

| View | Type |
| --- | --- |
| Logical | Logical |
| Implementation | Physical |
| Process | Logical |
| Deployment | Physical |

Architects can use the different UML diagrams to build up these concurrent views of the software architecture. The overall architectural picture is a mosaic of all the UML diagrams used to depict each of the various views.

We examine the main UML diagrams next, with respect to the 4 + 1 view model of architecture.

# The Unified Modeling Language

Building a model requires a suitable modeling material. For software models, this modeling material is the UML, which enables analysts, designers, and developers to describe the static and dynamic structure of all aspects of the system. The UML diagrams most commonly used in software development are

- *Use-case* diagrams for defining the organization of a system's use cases
- *Activity* diagrams for representing process flow
- *Class* diagrams to show the static structure of software
- *Interaction* diagrams to show the dynamic structure of software

- *State* diagrams for depicting an object's possible states
- *Component* diagrams for defining the relationships between system components
- *Deployment* diagrams for illustrating the physical configuration of software and hardware

Let's examine these diagrams in more detail.

## Use-Case Diagrams

If you are employing use cases to drive the development approach, then a use-case diagram will form part of the analysis model of the functional requirements of the system. The use-case diagram provides a pictorial representation of the various relationships between the use cases and actors that make up the system. A member of the team wearing the analyst's hat generally produces use-case diagrams in consultation with business representatives.

> *Use cases are discussed in Chapter 3.*

The notation of the use-case diagram is very simple and generally easily understood by non-technical staff. This makes use-case diagrams an ideal mechanism for discussing system requirements with the customer. Figure 5–1 illustrates a basic use-case model.

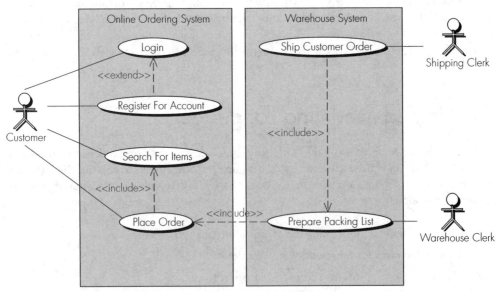

**Figure 5–1**   Use-case diagram.

The use-case diagram depicts the following elements:

- Actors, represented as stick men

- Use cases, shown as ellipses

- The communication association between an actor and a use case, as defined by a solid line

- The relationship between use cases, depicted by a dashed line with an arrow for indicating the direction of the relationship

- The system responsible for executing a use case, identified as an enclosing rectangle

The use-case diagram in Figure 5–1 shows the three main *actors* of Customer, Shipping Clerk, and Warehouse Clerk. The Customer actor *communicates* with the Login, Register for Account, Search for Items, and Place Order use cases. Each use case resides in the Online Ordering *system*. A *relationship* is shown between the Login and Register for Account use cases.

note

> Use-case diagrams might suggest that use cases are graphical rather than text-based, detailed requirements documents. You may find the use-case model is a nicety rather than an essential modeling element. UML diagrams are not a prerequisite for working effectively with use cases.
>
> It is more important that the use cases themselves correctly detail the system requirements than that a use-case diagram exists. If you are running short on time, you may wish to ignore the initial use-case diagram and concentrate your efforts on accurately defining the content of each use case.

For the architect, a use-case model serves as the *use-case view* of the software architecture. This is the special fifth view of the architecture, and it defines the key system use cases as being *architecturally significant*.

These use cases are a subset of the total that make up the complete system and form the basis for ongoing modeling and prototyping efforts during the inception and construction phases. During later stages of the project, they offer a baseline against which system changes that impact the software architecture can be measured. These use cases are also known as *primary* use cases.

Care should be taken when selecting the primary use cases that shape the system's architecture. Be sure to pick a diverse cross-section of use cases to model for the initial architecture rather than focus exclusively on one functional area. Avoid the obvious high-profile candidates that concentrate on screen inputs and outputs, and instead look to functionality that defines integration requirements, security concerns, exception handling, and batch processes. These all assist in addressing technical risk early in the project.

# Activity Diagrams

Activity diagrams are similar to flow charts and describe process flow, representing both conditional and parallel behavior. Consequently, activity diagrams model the system's dynamic behavior. Figure 5–2 shows an activity diagram.

The notation of the activity diagram defines a process flow for a specific scenario:

- Activities performed at each step of the process flow are shown as rounded rectangles
- Transitions between activities are denoted using arrows
- A fork, where a transition splits into two or more parallel activities, is shown as a black bar with one transition entering and several leaving
- A join, where two or more parallel activities converge into a single activity, is shown as a black bar with several transitions entering and one leaving
- The object, actor, or system responsible for a particular activity is represented by an enclosing rectangle known as a swim lane

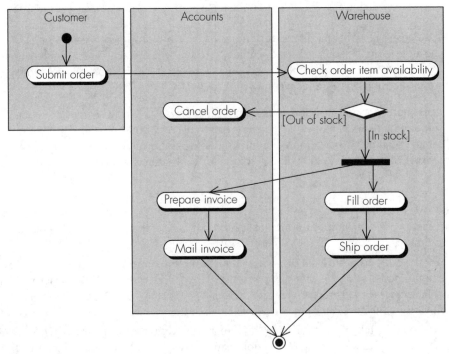

**Figure 5–2**   Activity diagram.

Activity diagrams are applicable to all five architectural views. One of the most effective uses of the activity diagram is to include it within a use-case document to illustrate the use case's different flows.

# Class Diagrams

The class diagram is probably the most widely known UML notation and defines the static organization and structure of the software. Class diagrams receive the most attention from software engineers because they offer a convenient notation for conveying software structure. They are commonly used in the definition of the logical and process views.

Figure 5–3 depicts the basic notation of a class diagram and shows the classes involved in the system, modeling the relationships between classes of type Customer, Account, Corporate, Personal, Order, and Item:

- Classes are shown as rectangles with the name of the class at the top of the rectangle

- Attributes and operations are shown inside of the class element

- Associations between classes are represented by solid lines

- Adornments on associations further describe the relationships that exist between classes, such as generalization and aggregation

- Role navigability is represented by arrows on association relationships

- Associations with no arrowheads are bidirectional

- Multiplicity is shown by numbers on the association

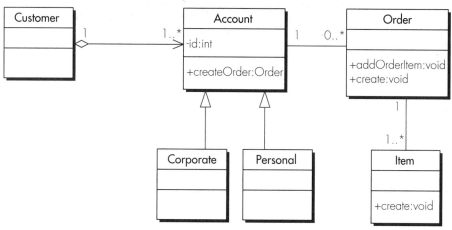

**Figure 5–3**   Class diagram.

From the UML diagram, an association exists between the classes of Customer and Account. The multiplicity for the association specifies a Customer may have one or more instances of the Account class. The association between these two classes is unidirectional, meaning Account objects are visible to objects of type Customer, but not vice versa.

The empty diamond states that the relationship between the two classes is one of simple *aggregation*. A solid diamond denotes an association by *composition*, which links the lifetimes of the two objects in the relationship.

## composition and aggregation

Composition and aggregation are both forms of containment whereby one object holds a reference to another object. The semantics of aggregation and composition relationships define how the lifetime of the contained object is managed.

With composition, the containing class is responsible for creating and removing the internal object. The contained object cannot exist after its parent has been removed.

In an aggregation relationship, the lifetime of the contained object is independent of the containing object, and so it is free to live a life of its own.

Looking at other parts of the diagram, we can see that classes Corporate and Personal are both specialized forms of Account, thanks to the generalization relationship depicted in the diagram.

## tip

Class diagrams can describe the organization of a system's design elements in fine detail. However, many architects find detailed class diagrams become cluttered and difficult to read. Consequently, basic class diagrams that describe the software at a high level are often more informative than those containing a highly detailed view.

The class diagram can also be used in a high-level form as a package diagram. Here, the package diagram shows the organization of the software into packages and defines the dependencies that exist between them.

## Interaction Diagrams

Whereas class diagrams give a static view of the software, interaction diagrams are dynamic. Interactions diagrams are found in all five of the view models of architecture.

Interaction diagrams come in two types: *sequence* and *collaboration*. They both demonstrate the dynamics of the software system and illustrate how objects defined in the class diagram collaborate to execute each of the system's use cases. In this way, interaction diagrams are a means of demonstrating that the model can meet all the business requirements detailed in each use case.

Sequence and collaboration diagrams model essentially the same information, but each has a slightly different emphasis.

- Sequence diagrams are organized on time, with events occurring in chronological order as you progress down the page
- Collaboration diagrams emphasize object organization and message flow

Models can be built using either or both types of interaction diagram, depending on preference. Most modeling tools automatically generate the alternate diagram type for you.

The sequence diagram in Figure 5–4 depicts the following information:

- The object or actor who initiates the scenario is located at the left edge of the diagram
- Objects are shown at the top of the diagram as rectangles
- The lifetime of each object is represented by a vertical dotted line
- Messages passed between objects are defined by solid arrows
- The activation bar, a thin vertical rectangle drawn over the object's lifetime, illustrates the duration of a message

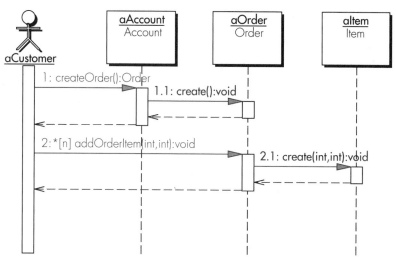

**Figure 5–4**   Sequence diagram.

The example is for a very simple scenario and models the passing of messages between objects for associating an order with a Customer account and adding items to the Order.

Sequence diagrams enjoy greater popularity than collaboration diagrams, but the choice of interaction diagram type is purely one of preference. For comparison, Figure 5–5 depicts the collaboration diagram equivalent of the sequence diagram represented in Figure 5–4.

Message flow in a collaboration diagram uses a different notation than that of the sequence diagram:

- Associations between objects are shown with solid lines
- Small arrows on the associations show the passing of messages
- Message sequencing is defined by numbering each message

Be sure to define interaction diagrams for the primary use cases that form the use-case view of the architecture; otherwise, validation of the static model is not possible. The interaction diagram proves the objects in the system can collaborate to execute the flows specified in each architecturally significant use case. Furthermore, interaction diagrams help members of the project understand how objects in the system should interact.

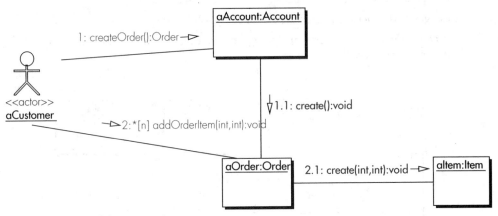

**Figure 5–5**   Collaboration diagram.

## Statechart Diagrams

Objects in a system have both state and behavior. Statechart diagrams map the different states of objects within the system and identify the actions that trigger an object's change in state. Like interaction and activity diagrams, statechart diagrams model the dynamic aspects of the system and apply to all five views.

Figure 5–6 shows a UML statechart diagram.

The statechart diagram conveys the following information:

* The different states of an object, shown as rounded rectangles

* The actions resulting from a change in state, defined in the lower part of the state's rectangle

* Transitions between states, represented by arrows

* The event that triggers a state transition, shown as text on the transition arrow

Figure 5–6 shows the basic states in sending out a customer invoice. The Preparing Invoice state is entered by the event account outstanding.

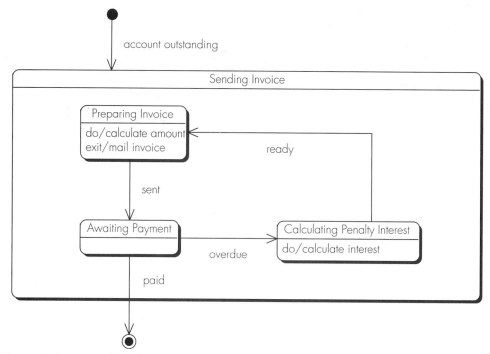

**Figure 5–6**    Statechart diagram.

Within the Preparing Invoice state, the action of calculating the invoice is undertaken. On leaving the state, the action is to mail the invoice to the customer.

Statechart diagram are excellent for modeling any part of the system considered state-driven.

## Deployment and Component Diagrams

Component and deployment are two different diagram types that are often merged into a single diagram. They fall into the category of a physical diagram, showing the packaging and deployment structure of system components.

Component diagrams show static structure and are incorporated into the implementation view if created as a single diagram. Deployment diagrams also describe static structure and form part of the deployment view.

Figure 5–7 depicts a combined component and deployment diagram.

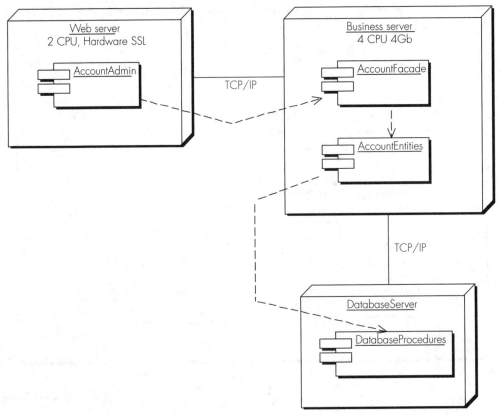

**Figure 5–7**    Combined deployment and component diagram.

Architectural elements defined in the diagram shown in Figure 5–7 include:

- Hardware nodes, represented by the rectangular boxes
- Physical software components, shown by the rectangles with two large tabs on the left edge
- The relationships between components, shown as dashed arrows
- The communications protocol between hardware nodes—for example, TCP/IP

The diagram depicts the three server nodes of a multitier distributed architecture, with software components deployed to each tier. Communication between the tiers is over TCP/IP.

# Common Failings

To recap, adopting modeling techniques as part of the development process gives very distinct advantages to the project:

- Improves customer communication
- Improves team communication
- Reduces design risks
- Measures and helps control requirement changes

These are all valid reasons for employing modeling techniques on the project. However, not all software development organizations use modeling for the betterment of the software but for other, less laudable reasons:

- Internal quality procedures mandate the production of UML design artifacts for documentation purposes.
- Having sought funding for a modeling tool, the project team feels honor-bound to justify the expenditure.
- The customer has specified a model as a project deliverable.

Using only these reasons for adopting modeling on a project is a sure sign of the development team *going through the motions* of software modeling. Here, the application of modeling is construed as just another task on the project plan instead of as being central to the development process.

If development teams are not confident of the real reasons for using modeling methods, they risk engaging in *cargo cult* software development. In this situation, modeling becomes a time-waster rather than a time saver.

## Cargo Cult Software

Stephen McConnell coined this novel phrase in an editorial for *IEEE Software* magazine [McConnell, 2000]. The term *cargo cult* comes from a description by theoretical physicist Richard Feynman [Hutchings, 1997] of a South Seas people who, during World War II, enjoyed the benefits of regular visits from Allied planes bringing supplies for the soldiers stationed there. The island nation prospered on the inflow of goods and materials delivered by the planes. When the war was over, the planes stopped coming and the good times ended.

Determined to have the planes return, the island people mimicked the actions of the Allied servicemen. They built runways and used fires for runway lighting; they constructed a hut to use as a control tower and staffed it with a controller who wore pieces of wood on his head as imitation headphones. Despite this careful attention to detail, the planes did not return.

The islanders' mistake was in associating the actions of the servicemen with the reasons for the arrival of the planes. Thus, they'd missed a fundamental piece of the puzzle.

In his article, Steve McConnell drew the same comparisons between software development companies who mimic the actions of their more successful competitors and expect the same results. They too are missing something fundamental, a basic understanding of the reasons for employing the process.

Although McConnell's article was on software processes, the same criticisms can be made of many software development teams who adopt model-centric development practices. All too often, UML diagrams are generated without fully appreciating their true value.

# Modeling Tools

Applying modeling techniques on a project can save significant time and effort through improved communication within the team. Using a modeling tool in conjunction with those modeling techniques can turbo-charge the entire process.

A modeling tool can be an invaluable asset for supporting the software engineer throughout the design process. Although a modeling tool will not turn an inexperienced object-oriented designer into an expert, it will increase the productivity of those software engineers who are already proficient in model-based development methods.

Modeling tools have enjoyed a revival in recent years, with many newer commercial products establishing a market for themselves. The tools available range from simple drawing packages to fully integrated design and development environments.

This section looks at the required feature set of a modeling tool and covers how each feature of the tool can save the software engineer time and effort.

## Choosing a Modeling Tool

Selecting a modeling tool that best fits your development needs depends essentially on what you intend to use the tool for and how much you wish to pay. Many companies are guilty of using high-end modeling tools as nothing more than expensive drawing packages, while others struggle to gain the full benefits of model-based development due to the limitations of a low-cost modeling product.

It is advisable to decide on the exact level of functionality you want from the tool before purchasing. Remember that some of the more expensive tools are very sophisticated, so don't forget to factor training into the total cost.

Table 5–2 lists some of the popular modeling tools. For those wishing to try their hand at modeling, most product vendors provide either limited-functionality community editions or fully featured evaluation versions. All of the tools included are Java-based and so should be available for most platforms.

**Table 5–2**   Modeling Tools

| Name | Availability | Reference |
| --- | --- | --- |
| ArgoUML | ArgoUML is open source and available under the BSD license. | http://argouml.tigris.org/ |
| EclipseUML | EclipseUML from Omondo is the leading UML tool plug-in for the vastly popular open source Eclipse IDE. Both free and commercial editions are available from the Omondo site. | http://www.omondo.com/ |
| Poseidon | Poseidon from Gentleware is a commercial extension to ArgoUML as is permitted under the BSD license. Poseidon is a popular modeling tool with a freely available community edition that offers a lot of features. | http://www.gentle-ware.com/ |
| Together | The Together range of modeling products is a highly regarded, fully featured offering from Borland. A reduced functionality community edition is available from the Borland site. | http://www.borland.com |

Most of the UML diagrams in this book were produced using Borland's Together range of modeling tools.

In choosing the right tool for your needs, you must appreciate the different features modeling tools offer and how these features can be of benefit during the modeling process. Here are some of the main features to look for in a modeling tool:

- UML support
- Model validation
- Forward and reverse engineering
- Design pattern support

# UML Support

Like all languages, the UML has its own particular syntax and semantics. A modeling tool should be able to validate the UML to ensure correct use of the language. A UML diagram communicates a huge volume of information, and using the UML incorrectly can result in serious misinterpretations of the design. The language-checking ability of the modeling tool can help prevent this confusion.

Most tools support all of the main UML diagrams to a lesser or greater degree. You should take into account the level of support a tool provides for each diagram type based upon your expected usage of a particular diagram. For example, if you intend only to model during the analysis phase of the project, then strong support for deployment and component diagrams is of less value than if planning to model throughout the entire software development lifecycle.

The version of the UML supported by the tool is also a factor. The UML is an evolving language, and the standard is governed by the Object Management Group (OMG). As the language changes, tool vendors must rush to keep their products in step with the new versions. The need to have the latest version of the UML would therefore be a reason for choosing one tool over another.

# Model Validation

An interaction diagram provides proof that the components of the system can execute a specific use case. Removing a component from the model or changing a component's interface affects the flow of messages involved in executing a particular use case.

Unlike the basic drawing tools that can only reproduce UML notation, a modeling tool should detect inconsistencies between the object model and any of the interaction diagrams.

When defining interaction diagrams, modeling tools enforce the passing of messages between objects. If the appropriate method has not been defined on a class, then it is impossible to pass that particular message to an instance of the class. The modeling tool's governance of message passing helps to highlight omissions in the design model and prevents objects being organized in a manner that will fail to execute a particular use case.

Validation of the model's interaction diagrams is beneficial for projects following an iterative development process, since the system's design is continually evolved over the course of several iterations. Early detection of design errors prevents these inadvertent but time-wasting mistakes from being implemented in the application.

# Forward and Reverse Engineering

Building a model requires nothing more than a pen and paper, but this can be very limiting for large-scale projects. If we are to use a model to drive the development process, then it is essential that the model be kept updated—a tedious chore if the model is paper-based.

The ability to both generate Java source from the model and import Java code back into the model is therefore an important consideration when selecting a modeling tool. The process of exporting and importing is called *forward* and *reverse* engineering:

- Forward engineering generates code from the model

- Reverse engineering builds the model from an existing code base

Not all of the UML diagrams make good candidates for the code- and model-generation process. Most tools forward- and reverse-engineer to and from class diagrams. Some tools also support the forward and reverse engineering of interaction diagrams.

A *roundtrip* is the process of continually jumping between model and code. This process enables changes made in the code to be reflected in the model and vice versa. Figure 5–8 illustrates the roundtrip process as a UML activity diagram.

These are the main advantages of roundtrip support in a modeling tool:

- Time saving as model is used to generate the code

- Helps ensure both model and code remain in sync

- Enables code changes to be validated against the model

> *The process of performing a roundtrip with a modeling tool is demonstrated in Chapter 7.*

The ability to roundtrip safeguards against one of the worst fates that can befall a model—it becomes out-of-date.

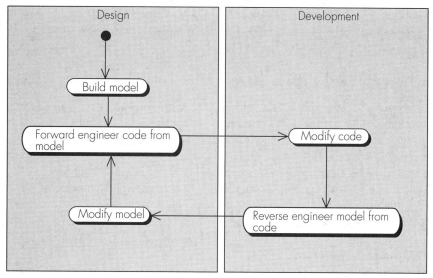

**Figure 5–8**    Activity diagram showing the roundtrip process.

To be of real use, the life of the model should extend beyond the design phase. As has been covered, the model enables change to be assessed throughout the entire software development lifecycle, including when the project has been delivered and has transitioned into a maintenance phase.

One of the biggest project failings is that the model ceases to be maintained after the initial design work is completed. Without the ability to update the model from the code, the two quickly diverge, leaving the code as the only true representation of the design.

If the model is perceived as being out of date, developers cease to trust the information held in the model and turn instead to the code for answers. Unfortunately, code does not give up its design secrets in as easily a digestible form as a UML diagram. Consequently, developers must hunt through the source code to determine the workings of the system.

It is therefore imperative that model and source code are kept synchronized as the project progresses. Roundtrip support enables this to be achieved relatively painlessly. Someone still has to take on the responsibility of reverse engineering the code back into the model, but this is a far less arduous a task than updating the model manually.

note

> Roundtrip support is important when undertaking an iterative development process. As the model is revisited as part of the design process at the start of each iteration, the model must reflect changes in the code made during the previous iteration's implementation effort.

The ability of any modeling tool to synchronize model and code cannot be understated. As soon as the model falls behind the code, the project team will discard it. Tools that offer good roundtrip support help instill in the developers faith that the model is accurate and reliable. Getting developer buy-in to the model ensures it can continue to drive the development process.

## Design Pattern Support

Design patterns are a powerful tool for software reuse, and software reuse is an essential ingredient for rapid development. Design patterns form the basic building blocks of architecture, and with their application, the designer can construct an architecture based on proven, best-practice designs.

Patterns enable high-quality solutions to be arrived at quickly and easily. A good modeling tool should facilitate the designer in the application of design patterns, making it easy to incorporate best-of-breed design constructs into any solution.

Modeling tools can support design patterns by providing pattern templates or pattern wizards for automatically generating standard patterns. Figure 5–9 shows a screenshot of a pattern-selection dialog from Together ControlCenter.

Here, the designer chooses from a list of patterns. In this example, the *Business Delegate* pattern, as defined in the book *Core J2EE Patterns* [Deepak, 2003], has been selected. Via the dialog,

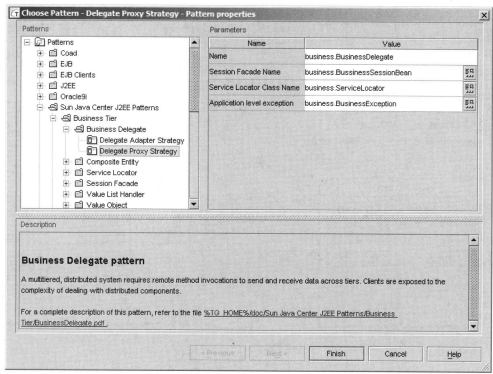

**Figure 5–9**    Together ControlCenter pattern template.

the designer can specify the class names generated from the template. A link to reference documentation for the pattern appears in the lower pane of the dialog window.

From this template, the classes defined by the pattern are created and added to the active diagram with the relationships between the classes correctly modeled.

Figure 5–10 displays the classes that resulted from the pattern template. As Figure 5–10 illustrates, the classes have been created in strict compliance with the pattern. Together ControlCenter has also generated much of the boilerplate code involved in the pattern, leaving the software engineer free to concentrate on the implementation detail.

Working with patterns using a template-driven approach has some distinct advantages over simply building the pattern a class at a time:

- The classes are generated in accordance with the guidelines of the design pattern
- Templates make patterns easy to apply, which encourages their use

First, the modeling tool ensures the pattern is laid down in compliance with the original specification of the pattern. Like the UML, design patterns are an example of a common vocabulary for software engineers, who can use patterns to describe application designs as well as build with them. Incorrect interpretation of a design pattern negates the advantages of this

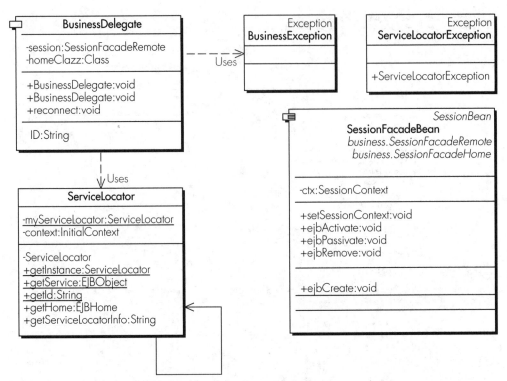

**Figure 5–10**    Classes generated from the Business Delegate template.

common vocabulary and can cause confusion, making ongoing maintenance of the application difficult. The use of a pattern template ensures each pattern is applied correctly, thereby removing the opportunity for the designer to misinterpret them in the design.

Having patterns so easily accessible also encourages extensive use of patterns in the design process. A traditional approach would see the designer referring to a pattern's specification and then tediously defining each class and all the relationships. With a modeling tool, a comprehensive list of patterns is only a few keystrokes away. The designer not only can apply patterns quickly to a design but also can experiment with different patterns and pattern combinations as part of the model.

note

Template use is analogous to painting a room in a house. Painting a wall with a narrow, fine brush would get the job done but would take all day. A far more practical tool than the small brush for this task would be a wide paint roller, which would see the job completed in considerably less time. Pattern templates are therefore our software equivalent of a paint roller.

In addition to providing templates for the established design patterns, the modeling tool should allow designers to create their own pattern templates. This feature enables designers to build the experience of quality designs gained from other projects into the modeling tool. If the modeling tool is used as part of a team environment, these patterns become available to the rest of the team, thereby sharing valuable design knowledge among the group.

# Why Modeling Tools Fail

This chapter has extolled the virtues of modeling techniques and modeling tools. The use of models in software development offers significant advantages to the software engineer. Modeling tools underpin the development of software models and enable a model-centric approach to software development.

Despite the benefits of modeling tools, their use is far from commonplace on development projects. These next sections examine some of the reasons projects are seemingly unable to make effective use of modeling tools.

## Christmas Puppy Syndrome

Animal rights campaigners spread the message that a dog is for life, not just for Christmas. Anyone buying a modeling tool would do well to heed this advice. Research has shown that like the Christmas puppy, modeling tools in general do not enjoy a lot of use once the wrapping has been removed and the novelty of the new toy has worn off.

This is an expensive white elephant to leave sitting on the shelf. Modeling tools are sophisticated pieces of software, targeted at the enterprise developer, and as such, they often carry enterprise-sized price tags.

The reason many modeling tools fail to win popularity with developers is not because of any shortcomings with the tools themselves; instead it is often because of the purchaser's unrealistic expectations.

Here are some of the common misconceptions surrounding the capabilities of modeling tools:

* Complex code can be replaced with simple diagrams.
* Object-oriented design knowledge is not required.
* Modeling tools provide an ease-of-use layer on top of J2EE.
* They ensure a proper development methodology is followed.
* They are easy to use, so no training is needed.

The next sections address each misconception in turn.

## Replacing Code with Diagrams

A well-thought-out picture can convey a great deal of information succinctly and accurately. The use of diagrams to convey design detail is a central tenet of software modeling. One of the major misconceptions, however, is that the information in a UML diagram can be translated directly into fully functional code and that the UML offers a superior substitute to Java as a programming language.

Modeling tools can generate source code from UML artifacts such as class and interaction diagrams, and yes, the code they generate does save the developer effort. However, this level of code generation falls far short of the concept of *executable UML,* whereby the entire system is maintained purely in model form. The UML is simply not expressive enough to describe a system to the level at which it can be executed directly.

Models and modeling tools are not a replacement for developers, and the concept of fully executable UML is still more of a research project than a viable commercial reality.

## Modeling Tools as a Replacement for OO Skills

Buying a state-of-the-art modeling tool will not make you a skilled object-oriented designer. If you cannot exhibit artistic flair with a box of colored crayons, then you are equally unlikely to prove a talented artist with the latest computer graphics package.

warning

> Applying modeling techniques without staff skilled in object-oriented design will cost time, not save it.

Modeling tools support designers in developing object-oriented software. They enable designers to use their hard-earned object-oriented design skills productively. Consequently, modeling tools are best used by designers already conversant with object-oriented development practices. They are not a tool for novices, nor are they a teaching aid.

## Ease-of-Use Layer

Modeling tools do not provide an abstraction layer upon the underlying platform for which the software is targeted. For our purposes, the underlying platform is J2EE. While some modeling tools cater to the development of J2EE components, these tools do not remove the need for the software engineer to understand the intricacies of J2EE. It is the architect's responsibility to apply his or her knowledge of J2EE when designing with the tool; the tool will not do this for the architect.

Interestingly, much work is ongoing in this area to make models platform-neutral. In this way, code can be generated directly from the model for any given platform. This approach is known as Model-Driven Architecture (MDA), and the technology is still in its infancy. If the goals of MDA can be realized, a significant step forward in terms of software development productivity can be made.

> *Model-Driven Architecture is discussed*
> *in Chapter 8.*

## No Inbuilt Methodology

Modeling tools are process-agnostic in that they do not support any particular software development methodology. Instead, it is left to the project team to use the modeling tool as part of the chosen development process.

Perhaps the confusion that modeling tools come with a ready-made methodology has come about because of the association with the UML and the IBM Rational Unified Process. Booch, Rumbaugh, and Jacobson, who formulated the UML, also combined their own respective development methodologies to create the Unified Process that later became the IBM Rational Unified Process. The UML and the RUP, while quite distinct in their uses, are synonymous in the minds of many developers. Because the UML is common to virtually all modeling tools, the leap is often made that by using a modeling tool, a RUP-like process is intrinsically followed. This is certainly not the case. Models are complementary to the development methodology, not a replacement.

## Training Is Not Required

Getting the most out of a modeling tool involves being aware of all the tool's features and understanding how to use those features on a development project. A common failing is to introduce project teams to new tools with no supporting information on how those tools can assist the team in the process of developing quality software.

Training on the use of the tool, possibly in conjunction with general training on UML notation, helps to educate the development team on the benefits the chosen modeling tool brings to the software development process. Training also helps teams buy in to the concept of working with models.

# Succeeding with Modeling Tools

Given that modeling tools are not always successfully utilized on development projects, this section examines what steps can be taken to ensure that any investment in such tools generates a respectable return.

Here are several guidelines that take the risk out of adopting modeling methods and modeling tools, and enable the benefits of a model-driven approach to be fully appreciated by the development team.

## Key Points for Adopting Models

- Start small.
- Learn modeling before buying a tool.
- Make the tools available to the entire team.
- Allow time for the team to learn.
- Remember that models are about communication.

## Start Small

Moving to a model-based development approach need not involve purchasing the most expensive and extensively featured modeling tool on the market. A simple paper-based approach is one method for gradually introducing modeling methods to the team. Encourage your peers to discuss designs using the UML diagrams introduced in this chapter. Consider using a freely available community-edition modeling tool in your early modeling efforts.

Information and experience gained from these reduced feature-set tools can be used in preparing a business case to management for upgrading to a more sophisticated product. The knowledge gained from the low-end product should provide valuable ammunition for your cause.

## Learn Modeling First

If you are new to modeling, don't let a modeling tool be your first introduction to the practice. Make sure you understand the basics of the UML and the rationale behind modeling methods before you start grappling with the idiosyncrasies of a particular modeling tool. A modeling tool will make you a more productive modeler; however, despite what the marketing material may claim, it is not a teaching aid.

## Make the Tools Available to the Team

Be wary of purchasing a modeling tool for just one person on the team. Design is a team effort, and having only a single license for a modeling product means designs cannot be worked on collectively. Models are an effective mechanism for communication, and good communication is essential for a successful project. Give everyone on the design team the means to communicate.

## Allow Time to Learn

Do not introduce modeling methods into the pressure-cooker environment of a new project and expect to see spectacular results. Be realistic. Allow yourself and the team time to become familiar with both the methods and the modeling tool before putting them into practice on a project with a tight timeframe. Learning modeling skills takes time and must be accounted for on any project plan. A good strategy is to bring in a mentor to help accelerate the learning process.

## Remember to Communicate

Finally, although accuracy in UML design artifacts is important, remember that the UML is all about communication. Take the time to learn the UML, but do not become so obsessive with the correct use of the UML notation that you fail to communicate your designs.

# Summary

Making models part of the development process offers significant benefits. Models help to

- Improve communication of the system design among the project team
- Explore system requirements and behavior with the customer
- Improve the entire team's understanding of how the system operates
- Validate the design against the primary use-case scenarios

Using modeling tools to construct UML diagrams further enhances the benefits of a model-based approach to development:

- Roundtrip support keeps models current on iterative development projects.
- Checking of UML syntax helps ensure the accurate communication of designs.
- Validation of the design using interaction diagrams provides an early alert of design issues.

The next chapter looks at code generation techniques and investigates how code generators provide an effective mechanism for incorporating change on a project.

# Additional Information

Martin Fowler's book *UML Distilled* [Fowler, 2003] covers the different UML models and the associated UML notation.

The designers of the UML have also written a comprehensive guide to their creation, *The Unified Modeling Language User Guide* [Booch, 1998].

Scott Ambler is a keen advocate of modeling techniques and devised his own development process based on models. Information on his *Agile Modeling* process can be found at http://www.agilemodeling.com.

# 6

# Code Generation

Developing enterprise software requires a mixture of two mindsets: the creative and the mundane. The creative mindset calls for software engineers to apply their expertise to the task of building reliable, scaleable solutions. For the mundane, however, software engineers must resign themselves to the drudgery of the many repetitive tasks that are an all too common part of enterprise software development.

Code generation methods offer a means of delivering enterprise solutions extremely rapidly by reducing the mundane, repetitive tasks developers face. Consequently, code generators have tremendous potential for rapid development projects, and if used correctly, they can both shorten development timeframes and improve software quality and accuracy. Moreover, code generation can also make the software development process a far more enjoyable experience by freeing developers of routine tasks, enabling them to focus their attention on building better solutions.

This chapter discusses the different approaches to code generation and looks at best practices for applying code generation techniques to the development of enterprise software for the J2EE platform. Specifically, we cover a new programming paradigm, attribute-oriented programming, and explore how this and other code generation techniques can deliver higher developer productivity and more accurate software, and can help make the project team significantly more agile.

To achieve this aim, this chapter covers the following areas:

- The different types of code generators and the benefits they provide
- Apache's Velocity template engine for building custom code wizards
- Attribute-oriented programming for simplifying the development of J2EE components using XDoclet
- The issues involved in making code generation techniques part of the development process

Collectively, we'll see how the many facets of code generation can facilitate an adaptive approach to software development.

# What Is Code Generation?

Code generators are software constructs that write software. It is code-writing code.

Code generation is a technique already common on development projects. The code wizards offered by most integrated development environments (IDE) are a form of template-driven code generation with which most of us are familiar. Other examples include the forward-engineering capabilities of modeling tools and the use of the Java decompiler (JAD) to reverse-engineer Java source from bytecode.

The use of code generation techniques is wide and varied, but code generators can be loosely categorized as either *passive* or *active* [Hunt, 1999].

### Passive code generators.

These code generators are run once to provide the developer with a flying start. They produce code that the developer then modifies. Code wizards are an example of passive generators.

### Active code generators.

Code generators that fall into the active category produce code that is continually regenerated throughout the project. The code produced is not modified by the developer and is overwritten each time the generator is run.

The distinction between active and passive code generation is a subtle one and essentially comes down to how the generated code is maintained over the course of the project. If the code generator is made part of the build process and generates fresh source each time a build is instigated, then we are using active generation. If the output from the same generator is taken by the software engineer, modified, and placed under source control, then we have passive code generation.

Both techniques can save time and effort, although the two techniques are applied quite differently. These next sections examine the uses of each type of code generation.

# Passive Code Generators

The advantages of passive code generators are well known to developers thanks to the popularity of code wizards used by virtually all IDEs. Such are the benefits of passive code generators that few developers would consider using an IDE that did not number code wizards among its features.

Passive code generators are typically template driven. The template is a parameterized blueprint of the code to be produced. The generator is supplied with the necessary parameters, and the code generator undertakes a basic parameter-substitution process on the template in order to generate the required output.

Passive code generators are simple and therefore easily written. Open source tools are available that make the task of developing passive code generators all but trivial. One such offering is *Velocity* from the Apache Software Foundation.

Velocity is a powerful Java-based template engine. Although its use is primarily aimed at the generation of dynamic content at runtime, it is also an effective tool for writing your own code generators. Full details of the Velocity template engine can be obtained from http://jakarta.apache.org/velocity.

Velocity can be used to write all manner of specialized code generators for your project, including supplementing the code wizards already provided by your favorite IDE.

Here is an example of a rudimentary code wizard written using Velocity. This simple generator accepts a series of parameters, such as class name and author, and outputs a Java file as the result.

## Code Generation with Apache Velocity

Velocity is a template-driven engine, so the first task is to define a template for our class wizard. Listing 6–1 shows the basic template on which our newly generated classes are based.

### Listing 6–1    Velocity Template

wizard_template.vm

```
/*
 * Created by: $author
 *
 */

public class $class extends $base {

  #if ($add_ctor == true)
  public $class() {
  }
  #end

  #if ($add_main == true)
  public static void main(String[] args) {
  }
  #end

} // $class
```

The template is defined using the Velocity Template Language (VTL), a special markup language specifically designed for working with templates. The example illustrates the use of the two parts of VTL, *references* and *directives*.

VTL references are the parameterized part of the template and are substituted for actual data when the Velocity engine is run. A VTL reference is any string commencing with the $ character. The example includes five references: $class, $base, $author, $add_ctor, and $add_main.

VTL directives are used for controlling the generation of output. The VTL notation specifies that directives start with the # character. From the template shown in Listing 6–1, VTL directives have been used to determine if either a constructor or a main method is required for the generated class. This is accomplished using the #if directive combined with the references $add_ctor and $add_main.

Table 6–1 lists the available VTL directives.

**Table 6–1**    VTL Directives

| Directive | Description | Example |
|---|---|---|
| #foreach | Iterates through a list of objects. | #foreach ($item in $list)<br>  $item.Name<br>#end |
| #set | Assigns a value to a reference. | #set ($myRef = $yourRef) |
| #if<br>#else<br>#elseif | For constructing conditional statements. | #if ($expenditure > $income)<br>  Save<br>#end |
| #parse | Renders another Velocity template. | #parse ("mail.vm") |
| #include | Renders the named files without parsing. | #include ("footer.txt") |
| #macro | Defines a new VTL directive based on existing directives known as a Velocimacro (VM). | #macro (vmmacro $arg1 $argn)<br>  #if ($arg1 > $argn )<br>    Show $arg1<br>  #end<br>#end |
| #stop | Stops execution of the template engine. | #if ($condition) #stop #end |
| ##<br>#+<br>+# | Comments. | ## Single<br>#*<br>Multi line<br>*# |

With our template defined, the next task is to map actual data to the references in the template. Listing 6–2 shows the implementation for the code generator.

## Listing 6–2   The ClassWizard Code Generator

```java
// ClassWizard.java

import java.io.FileWriter;

import org.apache.velocity.Template;
import org.apache.velocity.VelocityContext;
import org.apache.velocity.app.VelocityEngine;

public class ClassWizard {

  public static void main(String[] args) {

    // Set the name for the new class
    //
    String className = "MyNewClass";

    try {
      // Rev up the velocity engine
      //
      VelocityEngine engine = new VelocityEngine();
      engine.init();

      // Get the template from the engine
      //
      Template template =
        engine.getTemplate("wizard_template.vm");

      // Create context and add data
      //
      VelocityContext context = new VelocityContext();
      context.put("class", className);
      context.put("author", "John Smith");
      context.put("base", "MyBaseClass");
      context.put("add_ctor", new Boolean(false));
      context.put("add_main", new Boolean(true));

      // Generate output from the template
      //
      FileWriter writer = new FileWriter(className + ".java");

      template.merge(context, writer);

      writer.flush();
    } catch (Exception ex) {
      System.err.println(ex);
    }
  }

} // ClassWizard
```

The code generator initializes an instance of the Velocity engine and loads in the template. Data is mapped to each VTL reference defined in the template using a `VelocityContext`. Once all references have been bound to data, the `VelocityContext` is merged with the `Template` instance to produce the output file.

The output generated after compiling and running the code is shown in Listing 6–3.

### Listing 6–3   Generated File

```
MyNewClass.java
/*
 * Created by: John Smith
 *
 */

public class MyNewClass extends MyBaseClass {

  public static void main(String[] args) {
  }

} // MyNewClass
```

So as not to obscure the example, the parameters supplied to the Velocity context were hard-wired in the code. This is less than ideal for a generic code wizard. I will leave it as an exercise for you to supply the code generator with data for binding with the template at runtime. Parameters could be supplied as command-line arguments, from a file, or from a swing-based user interface.

## Benefits of Passive Code Generation

Passive code generators are a productive tool for getting the developer off to a good start. They can provide an extensive head start, and they range from generating small classes, as shown in the example, to generating entire object hierarchies.

When generating from a template that embodies software engineering best practices, the code they generate is consistently of a high quality. Where the code generator is developed inhouse, it is expected that the resulting code will always comply with company standards, assuming of course that this holds true for the template.

As a final note, not all passive code generators are code wizards. Another possible use of a passive generator is for migrating systems between platforms. One company I encountered used a code generator extensively for converting Oracle Forms applications to Java. The company initially began as part of a larger IT department, when the development team was first charged with the task of porting a large Oracle Forms application to Java. The application to be ported was extensive, and the conversion effort was expected to tie up a large team over a long time-frame. Due to the high costs of a manual approach, the company instead decided to invest its energy into the development of a code generator to automate the initial conversion effort.

The generator they produced was unable to convert every line of code. However, it was able to convert enough of the application that only a small development team was needed to fix up those areas too complex to convert automatically.

The project was completed successfully, and the development team went on to offer its services to other organizations undertaking similar conversion exercises. Thanks to the code generator developed from the previous project, the company was able to leverage this for considerable competitive advantage when competing for Oracle Forms conversion work. From a sales perspective, it could tick all the right boxes: do the job quicker, to a high standard, and at a lower cost.

# Active Code Generators

Active code generators have the power to deliver extremely high productivity gains. Unlike passive generators, the active code generator does not rely upon the services of a software engineer to modify the code generated. Instead, the active code generator is able to inject code directly into the application as and when needed.

Active code generators typically comprise three different parts: metadata, a pattern template, and the code generator itself:

### Metadata.

Metadata is data that describes other data, thereby giving data shape and form. Metadata is available from many sources, including databases, XML schemas, and UML models.

### Pattern template.

The pattern template is used by the code generator to render the data described by the metadata in a new form.

### Code generator.

The code generator binds the metadata with the pattern template to produce the desired output. The code generator can also embody code generation rules that further define the form of the generated code.

Figure 6–1 illustrates how metadata, templates, and code generator combine to produce source code.

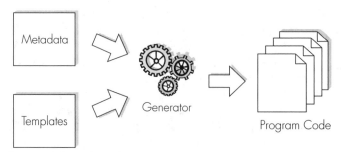

**Figure 6–1**    Elements of active code generation.

# Benefits of Active Code Generation

The benefits of code generation are best conveyed by example. One such example comes from a project I was involved with in which a developer on the team was able to apply an active code generator very successfully.

A requirement of the system was to transmit information across a system boundary via a messaging service to the client's enterprise information system (EIS). The payload of the message was an XML document, and the project plan called for the development of a suitable XML schema to define the contents of the message for validation purposes.

The customer stipulated that the structure of the XML document must be driven by the schema of the database being used as a staging area for holding requests ready for sending. The physical design of the database was not under the control of the project but was instead designed and maintained by the customer's own enterprise data group.

One of the first tasks on the project plan called for the specification of the XML schema for the messages, using the design of the customer-supplied database as a model. On the surface, this appeared to be one of those mundane tasks common to enterprise development projects. However, instead of taking the traditional approach and handcrafting a first cut of the XML schema, the developer charged with the task opted to build a code generator.

The code generator was written in Java and used a JDBC connection to query the metadata held in the database. The metadata from the database provided all the information necessary from which to generate a schema.

The code generation approach was successful for the following reasons:

### Increased speed.

The time taken to write the code generator and produce the first version of the XML schema was less than the time estimated to produce the XML schema by hand.

### Improved accuracy.

The code generator removed the opportunity for human error, which is a serious flaw of the handcrafting approach. Once the code generator had been adequately tested, a repeatable, accurate result was possible each time the generator was run.

**Better agility.**

The underlying database was prone to change. Changes in the database design were easily accommodated by simply rerunning the code generator. By incorporating the code generator into the project's daily build process, it was possible to guarantee that database and XML schema remained in sync.

This ability to rerun the code generator to produce a new XML schema at virtually no cost made the project highly agile. The customer's database was covered contractually by change-control procedures. Thus, any change by the customer to the database that resulted in an impact on the project team was a chargeable piece of work. The database did indeed change throughout the life of the project, but the code generator made it possible to turn these changes around with minimal cost to the customer and a high degree of accuracy. For this reason, the project team established a reputation with the customer as a group capable of working very productively and delivering changes quickly.

## Active Code Generators and Boilerplate Code

The ability of active code generators to turn around change very quickly and at low cost makes them a powerful tool for rapid development. The more of an application's code that can be generated, the less code has to be written by the development team. In this way, the use of active code generators increases the productivity of the language, thereby making the team agile. We code only what is needed, and the code generator and the compiler do the rest

Active code generators are especially well suited to J2EE projects, as they offer a solution to the large amounts of *boilerplate* code that must be written when developing a J2EE application. Boilerplate code is code that has to be implemented for software to comply with the demands of a particular framework. This type of code is extraneous from a business perspective because it implements no business functionality and exists solely for the purposes of the hosting platform.

For the J2EE platform, one of the worst offenders in this regard is the Enterprise JavaBean (EJB). An enterprise bean is a heavyweight component that requires a considerable amount of framework-dependent code to be written in order to be able to interact with the EJB container.

Some of the additional program artifacts associated with EJB technology include the following:

**Configuration information.**

J2EE applications require extensive configuration in order to operate. For an enterprise bean, it is necessary to produce both the standard configuration information for the EJB deployment descriptor and vendor-specific deployment information for the target J2EE application server.

**Required interfaces.**

Each enterprise bean deployed into the container must provide home and remote interfaces. The list grows if local interfaces are also to be supported on the enterprise bean.

**Design pattern artifacts.**

Though not strictly classed as boilerplate code, the architecture of a system employing EJB technology relies upon the application of best-practice J2EE design patterns. The use of patterns such as *Transfer Object* and *Business Delegate* results in standard classes being developed to support the enterprise bean in its environment. Although these additional classes are not mandated by the J2EE platform, good architectural design necessitates their development.

These additional program artifacts make for a code-intensive development process that is not conducive to the needs of rapid development. Thankfully, active code generation addresses this issue by generating much of the boilerplate code on our behalf.

A programming paradigm has been conceived that seeks to employ active code generation techniques to overcome the problem of developing heavyweight components for code-intensive platforms like J2EE. This paradigm is known as *attribute-oriented programming* and is discussed next.

# Attribute-Oriented Programming

Active code generators can work effectively given well-defined metadata and a suitable pattern against which to generate the required code. Attribute-oriented programming leverages the benefits of active code generation by augmenting the code with special metadata tags known as *attributes*.

## What Are Attributes?

Attribute-oriented programming languages enable special declarative tags, or attributes, to be embedded within the body of the code. During compilation, these attributes are extracted by the compiler and passed to an attribute provider, responsible for generating code based on the properties of the attribute and the nature of the code within which it is embedded.

The purpose of attributes is to enable the base language to be extended through the provision of custom-attribute providers. The attribute providers are essentially active code generators that inspect the code surrounding the attribute and produce further code.

## Attributes Versus Preprocessor Directives

For those familiar with languages such as C and C++, attribute-oriented programming might sound very similar to *preprocessor directives*, a language construct not available in Java. Preprocessor directives are special instructions within the code that are handled by a preprocessor prior to compilation. Typically, these directives take the form of macros that are expanded within the body of the code before the source is compiled.

Preprocessor macros are a simple, but powerful, form of code generation and are used extensively within C and C++. Such is the power of the preprocessor that early C++ compilers were essentially preprocessors that expanded macros to generate straight C programming language code that was then compiled.

Though macros are powerful, if used incorrectly, they can result in some very ugly code that is extremely difficult to read and maintain. Macros can considerably alter the appearance of the language, making it very difficult for anything other than the C++ preprocessor to parse. In the past, complex macros have stopped the reverse-engineering features of some high-end modeling tools dead in their tracks. This might be why James Gosling decided to stay well clear of preprocessor directives with Java, presumably preferring instead to keep the language clean and uncluttered.

Attributes differ from preprocessor directives in that the generated code is not expanded within the body of the main code, but rather is written to a separate source file that is later compiled. This approach has the advantage that the original code is not changed behind the scenes, as is the case with macros. Instead, the newly generated file can be both viewed and debugged.

Attributes also serve to annotate the code, whereas macros are embedded into the control flow of the program. This difference makes attributed code much easier to read and understand than code that is plagued with the overzealous use of macros.

## J2SE 5.0 Annotations and Attributes

Microsoft has augmented its C++ compiler to support attributes embedded within the C++ language to simplify the development of COM objects for the Microsoft platform. The .NET platform also supports the use of attributes, although these are used more to direct the behavior of a component at runtime rather than at compile time.

The release of J2SE 5.0 brings *annotations* to Java, a new language construct synonymous with the concept of attributes for declaring metadata within the body of a program. The new annotations construct that now forms part of J2SE 5.0 was defined under the Java Community Process as JSR-175, *A Metadata Facility for the Java Programming Language.*

J2SE 5.0 annotations realize the attribute concept, enabling existing program elements, such as classes, methods, and fields, to be annotated with additional metadata information. This information embedded within the code can then be used by development tools to generate additional program artifacts.

The compiler is also able to store some annotations as class-file attributes, making them accessible at runtime via a new reflection API. The existence of runtime attributes presents application frameworks with the opportunity to inject bytecode at runtime instead of generating code as part of a precompilation step.

Work is already underway on a number of different technologies that leverage the power of Java's new metadata facility. As an example of how annotations are used within the body of a program, here is a code snippet that uses annotations defined by JSR-181, *Web Services Metadata for the Java Platform.*

```
@WebService
public class BusinessService
{
  @WebMethod
  public string myBusinessMethod() {

    .

    .

    .

  }
}
```

The annotations in the code are identified by the @ symbol, a notation commonly found inside comment blocks for use with Java's Doclet API. One of the objectives of JSR-181 is to allow the developer to convert a plain Java class into a Web Service simply by adding predefined annotation types.

From the example code snippet, the annotation types of @WebService and @WebMethod instruct a JSR-181-aware precompilation tool to generate the Web Services Definition Language (WSDL), schema, and other program artifacts necessary to expose the class as a Web Service.

The Java community has awaited the implementation of JSR-175 as part of J2SE 5.0 with some considerable excitement. During the wait, the open source community stepped in to fill the void by bringing the benefits of attributes to the Java platform using another approach.

## Attributes and J2SE 5.0 Annotations

The availability of annotations in J2SE 5.0 puts the Java community in a state of transition. During the time it takes for developers to move to J2SE 5.0, we can expect to see tools like XDoclet that rely upon metadata switching from attributes as Javadoc comments to true J2SE 5.0 annotations.

The concepts behind attribute-oriented programming remain unchanged. Instead, annotations provide a formal language construct to support declarative programming paradigms.

# Introducing XDoclet

*XDoclet* is an open source product that makes the power of attribute-oriented programming available to Java developers. As XDoclet precedes J2SE 5.0 annotations, it does so by enabling custom attributes to be specified within Java code as innocuous, compiler-friendly, Javadoc tags.

XDoclet began life as *EJBDoclet* and was the brainchild of leading open source contributor Rickard Öberg. The original EJBDoclet was built as a Javadoc plug-in that used the Doclet API to create custom Javadoc tags. With this ingenious approach, Öberg used his newly defined tags to generate Java files rather than the HTML pages commonly associated with Javadoc output.

As the name implies, EJBDoclet was primarily concerned with code generation for EJB support. However, since its inception, EJBDoclet has extended its portfolio to include software components other than enterprise beans. In line with this wider scope, the product name was changed to XDoclet, and it was launched as an active open source project. For the purposes of this discussion, we focus on the enterprise-bean-generation capabilities of XDoclet.

The custom Javadoc tags of XDoclet make it possible to generate much of the boilerplate code necessary for enterprise bean development.

The best way to appreciate the time XDoclet can save on a project is to look at an example. The next sections do just this, putting XDoclet through its paces by seeing just how much boilerplate code can be generated from the skeleton of a simple session bean.

The first step is to install the XDoclet software.

## Installing XDoclet

XDoclet is maintained as a Source Forge project and can be downloaded from `http://xdoclet.sourceforge.net`. Full installation and setup instructions, along with information on the open source license, are provided as part of the download.

XDoclet is run using the Jakarta Ant build utility from Apache. Ant has proven extremely popular among the Java community and has overtaken build tools such as *make* as the de facto standard for building Java applications. A copy of Ant can be freely downloaded from the Apache site, see `http://ant.apache.org`.

If you are unfamiliar with Ant, you may wish to read the documentation that comes with the installation before continuing with this chapter. However, the Ant syntax is relatively straightforward, and the examples covered are explained in detail. We start by covering the Ant build file necessary to run XDoclet over our source files.

## Setting Up the Ant Build File

The XDoclet installation comes with a number of Ant tasks that are used for invoking the doclet engine from Ant build files. The two main Ant tasks XDoclet provides are `<ejbdoclet>` for EJB support and `<webdoclet>` for Web applications. Since we are generating the code for an enterprise bean, the example covers the use of the `<ejbdoclet>` Ant task.

*Ant is covered in Chapter 12.*

Listing 6–4 shows the relevant extracts from the Ant build file.

## Listing 6–4    Ant Build File

```xml
<!-- Setup xdoclet classpath -->
<path id="project.class.path">
    <fileset dir="${libs.dir}/xdoclet-1.2">
        <include name="*.jar"/>
    </fileset>
    <pathelement location="${j2ee.lib}"/>
</path>

<!-- Define the ejbdoclet task -->
<taskdef name="ejbdoclet"
            classname="xdoclet.modules.ejb.EjbDocletTask">
    <classpath refid="project.class.path"/>
</taskdef>

<!-- Invoke xdoclet compilation -->
<target name="generate">
    <ejbdoclet destdir="gen-src"
                ejbspec="2.0">

        <!-- Source files to be processed by xdoclet -->
        <fileset dir="src">
            <include name="**/*Bean.java"/>
        </fileset>

        <!-- Code generation options -->
        <remoteinterface pattern="{0}Remote"/>
        <homeinterface/>
        <localinterface/>
        <localhomeinterface/>
        <utilobject cacheHomes="true"
                    includeGUID="true"
                    kind="physical"/>

        <!-- Generated deployment descriptors location -->
        <deploymentdescriptor destdir="${ejb.dd.dir}"/>

        <!-- Container specific -->
        <weblogic destdir="${ejb.dd.dir}"
                    xmlencoding="UTF-8"
                    validatexml="true"/>
    </ejbdoclet>
</target>
```

The comments in the build file highlight the various steps necessary for setting up and running the doclet engine. Next, we go over each step in more detail.

## Setup the XDoclet Classpath

As with any Java program, the classpath must be configured to point to all the libraries the running application requires. The `<path>` tag builds up a classpath that includes all of the XDoclet libraries and the EJB library:

```
<path id="project.class.path">
    <fileset dir="${libs.dir}/xdoclet-1.2">
        <include name="*.jar"/>
    </fileset>
    <pathelement location="${j2ee.lib}"/>
</path>
```

The `<fileset>` tag provides a convenient shorthand for adding all of the libraries in the XDoclet directory to the classpath without having to specify each individual library. The locations of the various libraries are defined with Ant properties, which are set up elsewhere in the build file. The use of properties is considered good practice for Ant build files because it allows the build file to be tailored for different environments.

## Define the XDoclet EJB Task

Ant needs to know what to do when it encounters the `<ejbdoclet>` tag. The `<taskdef>` task tells Ant where it can locate the class that will handle the `<ejbdoclet>` tag on behalf of Ant:

```
<taskdef name="ejbdoclet"
            classname="xdoclet.modules.ejb.EjbDocletTask">
    <classpath refid="project.class.path"/>
</taskdef>
```

Attributes for the task specify the name of the new tag and the implementing XDoclet class. The classpath established earlier gives directions to the libraries required by the `<ejbdoclet>` task.

## Invoke XDoclet from Ant

The `<ejbdoclet>` task initiates XDoclet, providing all the configuration details the doclet engine requires in order to generate code from the Java source files.

We use this task to tell XDoclet the location of the destination directory for all generated code and the EJB version to be supported. Taken from the example, we have the following:

```
<ejbdoclet destdir="gen-src"
            ejbspec="2.0">
```

The `destdir` attribute specifies the location for all source generated by XDoclet, while the EJB version is specified with the `ejbspec` attribute.

The next step is to supply XDoclet with the location of all source code to be parsed. This is achieved with the <fileset> task, as shown below:

```
<fileset dir="src">
    <include name="**/*Bean.java"/>
</fileset>
```

The <fileset> task submits a list of all files for processing to XDoclet. For the example, all source resides in the src directory, and we've further informed XDoclet we are only interested in files with a filename that matches the *Bean.java pattern.

## warning

> Do not use the same directory for handwritten and generated code. Keep the two separate to avoid the risk of inadvertently modifying generated program artifacts.

The ability to specify different directories for source and generated output is critical to good housekeeping, as it keeps the source that is produced by XDoclet distinct from code managed by hand. This separation lessens the likelihood of a developer inadvertently changing generated code, which would result in any changes being lost once the build process was rerun. Moreover, the separation of the two code types also enables *clean* operations to be implemented more easily, as all code under the gen-src directory can safely be deleted.

The next elements determine just what the <ejbdoclet> task is to generate from the source it parses. In this case, we produce remote, home, and local interfaces as well as a deployment descriptor and helper class for the enterprise bean. This is achieved with elements nested inside the <ejbdoclet> task as follows:

```
<remoteinterface pattern="{0}Remote"/>
<homeinterface/>
<localinterface/>
<localhomeinterface/>
<utilobject cacheHomes="true"
            includeGUID="true"
            kind="physical"/>
<deploymentdescriptor destdir="${ejb.dd.dir}"/>
```

Additional instructions can be passed to the doclet engine by specifying attributes for the nested elements. For example, with the <remoteinterface> tag, we specify that the word *Remote* be appended to the end of the remote interface name.

For the deployment descriptor, we request that it be generated to a different directory than that of the other generated code. Typically, deployment descriptors are generated directly into the target build directory to simplify the packaging of the enterprise bean later in the build process.

The final element in the example is vendor-specific and generates a deployment descriptor proprietary to BEA WebLogic Server:

```
<weblogic destdir="${ejb.dd.dir}"
          xmlencoding="UTF-8"
          validatexml="true"/>
```

XDoclet is not shackled to a single J2EE vendor and provides support for generating deployment descriptors for many of the different application servers currently available. The use of these elements makes it easy to target multiple vendor application servers by including elements for each server within the `<ejbdoclet>` task. Refer to the XDoclet documentation for a complete list of all the application servers supported.

With the build file created, we are nearly all set to start generating code for our session bean. All that is needed is a Java file complete with attributes.

## Creating a Session Bean

To begin building our enterprise bean, we must first write the implementation for the session bean and add the various XDoclet attributes as Javadoc tags. Listing 6–5 shows the source for a basic Customer session bean, complete with XDoclet attributes.

### Listing 6–5   Session Bean with XDoclet Attributes

```
// CustomerServiceBean.java

package customer;

import java.rmi.RemoteException;

import javax.ejb.EJBException;
import javax.ejb.SessionBean;
import javax.ejb.SessionContext;

/**
 * @ejb.bean
 *   name="CustomerService"
 *   jndi-name="CustomerServiceBean"
 *   type="Stateless"
 *
 * @ejb.resource-ref
 *   res-ref-name="jdbc/CustomerDataSource"
 *   res-type="javax.sql.Datasource"
 *   res-auth="Container"
 *
 * @weblogic.resource-description
 *   res-ref-name="jdbc/CustomerDataSource"
 *   jndi-name="CustomerDS"
```

```
 *
**/
public abstract class CustomerServiceBean
  implements SessionBean {

  /**
   * @ejb.interface-method tview-type="both"
   */
  public void createCustomer(CustomerVO customer) {
  }

  /**
   * @ejb.interface-method tview-type="both"
   */
  public void updateCustomer(CustomerVO customer) {
  }

  /**
   * @ejb.interface-method tview-type="both"
   */
  public CustomerVO getCustomer(int customerID) {
    return new CustomerVO();
  }

} // CustomerServiceBean
```

The code in Listing 6–5 is a very minimal implementation of a session bean. However, from this one source file, all the code necessary to assemble a complete enterprise bean can be generated. From this example, the following file types are produced:

- `ejb-jar.xml` deployment descriptor
- `weblogic-ejb-jar.xml` proprietary deployment descriptor
- Home, remote, and local interfaces for the enterprise bean
- Helper class for accessing the enterprise bean

Producing all of these files by hand is a slow, tedious, and error-prone process. XDoclet does all of the grunt work for us with the help of a few carefully placed attributes in the bean class.

## Declaring XDoclet Attributes

The XDoclet attributes masquerade as Javadoc tags. They take the form of a namespace followed by a tag name located within the namespace scope. Properties of the tag are passed in as named arguments. Here is the format of an XDoclet tag:

```
@namespace.tag name="value" name2="value"
```

Within the code of the bean, XDoclet tags are embedded at the class and method levels. Each tag augments the information already defined in the Java. The doclet engine does not simply parse the file, looking for tags and ignoring the code. Instead, where XDoclet encounters a tag, it uses the Java Doclet API to retrieve information on the code annotated by the tag. All of this information, both tag and source, is used in the code generation process.

## Class-Level Tags

The class-level `@ejb.bean` tag gives the bean a name, the JNDI lookup name, an optional display name, and a type. For the example, a type of `stateless` has been defined for a stateless session bean. Here is how this information is expressed with XDoclet tags:

```
@ejb.bean name="CustomerService"
  jndi-name="CustomerServiceBean"
  type="Stateless"
```

The example also has two further tags at the class level: `@ejb.resource-ref` and `@weblogic.resource-description`. Each of these tags defines a resource; in the example, a data source has been defined. The output from each tag is output directly to the deployment descriptors. The tag with the namespace `@weblogic` is a proprietary tag and results in the details of the data source being written to the `weblogic-ejb.xml` deployment descriptor. Equally, other proprietary tags can be used here to support alternative J2EE vendors.

XDoclet supports a comprehensive range of tags and allows a complete deployment descriptor to be specified entirely within the code as attributes. For the full list of tags, refer to the XDoclet documentation.

## Method-Level Tags

Method-level tags give fine-grained control for each method. The example illustrates the use of the `@ejb.interface-method` to tell the doclet engine whether the method is to be part of the bean's remote or local interface. The options available are `remote`, `local`, or `both`. Wanting to generate as much code as possible from the example, I have specified `both`, which as the name implies sees the method added to each interface type.

With the build file created and source file suitably adorned with attributes, all that remains is to execute the build file and examine the output.

## Inspecting the Output

Issuing `ant generate` from the command line unleashes XDoclet upon the source, and the result is all the files necessary to assemble a complete session bean. Table 6–2 lists the files created by XDoclet.

**Table 6–2**   XDoclet Generated Files for the **CustomerService** Session Bean

| Name | Description |
|---|---|
| `ejb-jar.xml` | EJB deployment descriptor |
| `weblogic-ejb-jar.xml` | Deployment descriptor for BEA WebLogic Server |
| `CustomerServiceHome.java` | Home interface |
| `CustomerServiceLocal.java` | Local interface |
| `CustomerServiceLocalHome.java` | Home for local interface |
| `CustomerServiceRemote.java` | Remote interface |
| `CustomerServiceUtil.java` | Helper class for accessing the session bean |

The list in Table 6–2 illustrates the amount of baggage associated with a single enterprise bean. Each file is related to and must be kept in sync with the originating bean class. A change in the bean class must be reflected across all of the different interfaces and deployment descriptors. Performing this task manually is monotonous, time consuming, and subject to error.

The tag-like attributes of the XDoclet engine enable all of these files to be generated from a single source. A change to the bean class can be replicated out to all files associated with the enterprise bean by running the XDoclet engine.

XDoclet is an active code generator, and consequently, the output of the doclet engine can be considered disposable. The generation of all source files by XDoclet should be made part of the build process. In this way, the bean class, deployment descriptors, and EJB interfaces are kept in sync.

Discrepancies in these files can often be hard to detect. The relationship between a remote interface and the implementing bean class is not enforced by the compiler. This relationship is defined by configuration parameters in the enterprise bean's deployment descriptor. Errors in configuration-based relationships are difficult to detect, as they require runtime tests to determine any fault. The use of a code generator in this instance removes the possibility of such time-consuming errors occurring.

Let's examine what has been generated from our solitary bean class. Listing 6–6 shows an extract from the `ejb-jar.xml` for the session bean. As can be seen, all the pertinent information from the bean class has been extracted by the doclet engine and defined in the EJB deployment descriptor.

## Listing 6–6    Generated ejb-jar.xml

```
<!-- Session Beans -->
<session >
  <description><![CDATA[]]></description>

  <ejb-name>CustomerService</ejb-name>

  <home>customer.CustomerServiceHome</home>
  <remote>customer.CustomerServiceRemote</remote>
  <local-home>customer.CustomerServiceLocalHome</local-home>
  <local>customer.CustomerServiceLocal</local>
  <ejb-class>customer.CustomerServiceBean</ejb-class>
  <session-type>Stateless</session-type>
  <transaction-type>Container</transaction-type>

  <resource-ref >
    <res-ref-name>jdbc/CustomerDataSource</res-ref-name>
    <res-type>javax.sql.Datasource</res-type>
    <res-auth>Container</res-auth>
  </resource-ref>

</session>
```

The bean class defines the vendor-specific tag, @weblogic.resource-description at the class level. Output from this tag is proprietary to WebLogic Server and is written to the WebLogic deployment descriptor, weblogic-ejb-jar.xml. Listing 6–7 contains an extract from the deployment descriptor. The information generated by the @weblogic.resource-description tag is represented in the deployment descriptor by the element <resource-description/>.

## Listing 6–7    Generated weblogic-ejb-jar.xml

```
<weblogic-enterprise-bean>
  <ejb-name>CustomerService</ejb-name>
  <stateless-session-descriptor>
  </stateless-session-descriptor>
  <reference-descriptor>
    <resource-description>
      <res-ref-name>jdbc/CustomerDataSource</res-ref-name>
      <jndi-name>CustomerDS</jndi-name>
    </resource-description>
  </reference-descriptor>
  <jndi-name>CustomerServiceBean</jndi-name>
  <local-jndi-name>CustomerServiceLocal</local-jndi-name>
</weblogic-enterprise-bean>
```

A useful tool for viewing the different Java classes and interfaces generated by XDoclet, and indeed any code generator, is a modeling tool with reverse-engineering capabilities.

> *Reverse engineering code into model*
> *form is covered in Chapter 5.*

Figure 6–2 illustrates a class diagram produced using Borland's Together ControlCenter and displays all the classes generated for the enterprise bean that are contained by the customer package. The diagram emphasizes the absence of any relationships between the originating bean class and the generated classes. These relationships are defined within the EJB deployment descriptors and so are not covered by the UML notation.

You may find reverse engineering very helpful when working with generated code. After running the code generator, the modeling tool can display what new classes have been injected into the model by the generator and how they impact the existing design model.

Our example has reached the point where it can be compiled and packaged as an enterprise bean. In getting to this point, a sizeable amount of code was generated for what is a very simple session bean with a minimum set of XDoclet tags. Now that we know how to generate the code, the next question is how we manage the code generated.

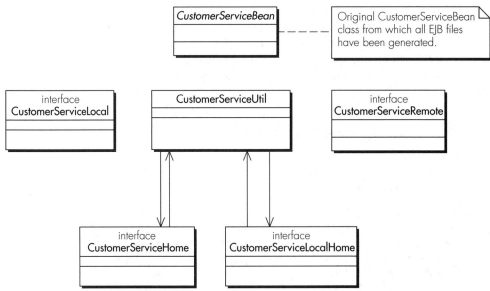

**Figure 6–2**   Class diagram for the `CustomerServiceBean`-generated class.

# Working with Actively Generated Code

So far, we have covered the reasons why code generators are a valuable tool for the rapid developer and how code generation techniques can be applied to the development of J2EE solutions. In this section, we examine a set of guidelines for working with actively generated code.

## Guidelines for Code Generation

Although active code generators such as XDoclet increase productivity on a project, the code generated must be carefully managed as part of the project build process. Failure to achieve this aim can result in confusion among developers as to which code can be modified and which code is the responsibility of the generator. Confusion of this nature negates the rapid development advantages code generators offer.

The guidelines look to avoid this confusion, enabling the full benefits of code generation techniques to be achieved.

### Key Points for Code Generation

- Generate code as part of the build process.
- Keep generated code separate from other source.
- Do not place actively generated code under source control.
- Be wary when using refactoring tools.
- Avoid mixing active and passive code generation.

### Generate Code as Part of the Build Process

Actively generated code is a disposable commodity. It can be quickly reproduced at near zero cost. Consequently, making the code generator part of the build process offers an effective method for ensuring all built code is an accurate reflection of the metadata upon which it is based.

Executing the code generator only when it is believed the underlying metadata has changed presents the risk of the code becoming out of sync with the source metadata. This risk can be easily mitigated by ensuring all code is generated afresh as part of a regular build process.

### Keep Generated Code Separate from Other Source

To safeguard against the problem of a developer accidentally modifying generated code, it is good practice to have the build process generate the code in a directory separate from that of other source. In this way, the generated code is treated as if it were a compiled binary.

Alternate source directories are useful in this scenario. They enable the generated source to be cleanly separated from handwritten code and allow an IDE to correctly recognize the code as part of the application.

## Do Not Place Actively Generated Code Under Source Control

Placing code that is actively generated under source control invites developers to mistakenly modify code that will be overwritten the next time the code generator is run. This practice also makes the build process complex, because it must integrate with the source control system.

To avoid these problems, generated code should not be placed under source control. Instead, place the metadata used by the code generator under source control if this is possible. Likewise, if the code generator has been produced inhouse, it should also reside under source control. With this approach, the build process gains an additional step:

1. Compile the code generator.
2. Run the code generator against the metadata.
3. Build the application from all sources.

It is possible to forego building the inhouse code generator, instead relying on previously built binaries. However, this approach risks failing to pick up on rule or pattern changes within the generator, which might otherwise impact the code generated. While compiling the generator may slow down the build process, it has the advantage that all generated source is guaranteed current.

## Be Wary When Using Refactoring Tools

Refactoring tools have become a popular feature in many IDEs. They allow the software engineer to make sweeping changes to the code structure across the entire code base. They are a powerful development aid and are used extensively on projects adopting an agile development process.

Refactoring tools, however, show little respect for the distinction between generated code and handwritten code. The impact of a refactoring exercise can easily result in generated code being modified inadvertently by the tool. This is a problem, because the amended code will be overwritten when the code generator is next run.

Where an inhouse code generator is used, the responsibility falls to the developer to ensure the code produced by the generator reflects the changes applied by the refactoring tool.

Attribute-oriented programming tags, as used by XDoclet, are also vulnerable to this practice. As XDoclet tags are embedded within comments, they are usually overlooked by refactoring tools. Consequently, the generated code becomes out of step with the rest of the code base once the doclet engine is run.

Fortunately, the Java compiler can help to detect such problems, as can a rigorous testing schedule. Nevertheless, caution must be exercised if refactoring tools are to be used in conjunction with active code generators.

## Avoid Mixing Active and Passive Code Generation

The guidelines outlined so far have focused on ways to avoid actively generated code from being inadvertently modified by developers. Unfortunately, the need to modify actively generated code is sometimes inescapable.

When this situation arises, several options are available to protect the modified source from being overwritten:

### Modify the code generator.

In preference to updating the code, if an inhouse generator is used, modify the code generated to reflect the required code changes.

### Extend the generated code.

The object-oriented paradigm offers many ways to extend the functionality of software components, including inheritance and composition. In some cases, the *Decorator* pattern may also prove effective. Consider these software engineering approaches before modifying any generated code.

### Use merge tools.

A suitable merge tool, as is commonly used with merge-based source control systems such as CVS, enables modified code to be integrated with generated code. However, unless a *trivial merge* is the result of the union of the two code versions, a manual merge with the tool is required. Such an automated build system would be extremely cumbersome to implement.

### Don't do it.

Finally, modifying actively generated code is problematic at best, regardless of what methods are used to manage the result. Think hard before taking this step, and proceed only if all other options have been exhausted.

The last point cannot be overemphasized. Having to guard against accidental code loss in the modified code adversely affects the productivity gains offered by active code generators. Keep it simple, and leave the generated code alone.

## Summary

Code generation is one of the cornerstone techniques of rapid development. Through the application of both passive and active code generators, we saw how it is possible to speed up the development process and simplify the task of creating complex J2EE components, such as enterprise beans, with attribute-oriented programming.

Now J2SE annotations make program-level metadata available at both compilation and runtime. This new language feature is expected to herald a new wave of development tools that simplify the development of Java applications. Already, the draft EJB 3.0 specification is looking to use annotations to enable developers to define enterprise beans as lightweight classes. We can therefore expect annotations to feature prominently in future versions of J2EE servers.

Code generation delegates the boring, humdrum tasks to the code generator, leaving us free to work creatively and imaginatively on the problem of building better solutions for the customer. After all, it is the application of the creative mindset that makes software engineering such an engaging profession.

Chapter 7 continues with the theme of code generation and focuses on one of the richest sources of metadata available, the database.

## Additional Information

Another form of programming based on the principles of code generation is *generative programming*. This term was first coined by Krzysztof Czarnecki and Ulrich Eisenecker in their book, *Generative Programming: Methods, Tools, and Applications* [Czarnecki, 2000]. Generative programming involves using active code generators to solve families of software engineering problems rather than using custom solutions to solve individual problems.

The *Code Generation Network* site, found at `http://www.codegeneration.net`, provides links to various code generation resources, including a wide range of code generators for Java developers.

# 7

# Rapidity and the Database

Although there is a perverse sense of pleasure to be had from writing carefully optimized data access code, the repetitive and error-prone nature of the task soon reduces it to a menial chore.

The J2EE platform offers a sophisticated set of services for accessing relational database management systems (RDBMS), yet despite these services, many developers find the task of writing data access code for enterprise systems a time-consuming and laborious process.

This chapter examines the problems relational databases present for the rapid developer. By applying the techniques covered in the previous chapters, we look at how the right development tools and code generation techniques can help to alleviate the issues identified with writing data access code.

Specifically, we focus on the open source tools *Hibernate* and *Middlegen*; two products that can ease the frustrations often associated with implementing a persistence layer by both simplifying data access technology and reducing the amount of code we must write.

First, let's examine the problems relational databases present the enterprise specialist.

## The Database Dilemma

Enterprise-scale database servers are highly sophisticated software products capable of storing enormous amounts of data in a format that is fully optimized for blisteringly fast data access and retrieval. Given this level of sophistication, why do databases cause such frustration for the J2EE developer?

A number of factors, both cultural and technical, combine to make life harder for the developer:

- Enterprise data is a valuable corporate asset, and its access and management is often carefully controlled.

- Databases use relational rather than object technology, resulting in an object–relational impedance mismatch.
- Databases are sensitive to change, with database schema modifications having the potential to impact significantly any dependent systems.

To understand why databases present such barriers to producing solutions rapidly and agilely, let's consider each of these factors in turn.

# Enterprise Data Is Valuable

Enterprise data is a valuable company asset that is strategic to an organization's ability to conduct its core business. Consequently, companies go to great lengths to safeguard the integrity and security of such vital corporate resources. Having enterprise data prized so highly and treated so carefully has its implications for development teams:

- In many organizations, development teams and database teams are operated as separate groups.
- Enterprise databases are unlikely to be used exclusively by a single application but by other systems and reporting tools as well.
- As new systems replace old systems, applications must deal with legacy data structures.
- Access to information may be restricted if the data is commercially sensitive.

It is worth considering these points in more detail, as each has an impact on how a development project is conducted.

## Separate Development and Database Teams

Due to the importance of company data, it is common for companies to run a dedicated team of database administrators (DBAs) and data architects charged with safeguarding and administering all enterprise-level data repositories. This enterprise data team is often independent of the application development project team, but typically advise the project team on database design issues.

The implications of this distinction between application and data teams mean software architects do not have complete freedom to structure the data used by the application as they see fit. Instead, it is likely the data architect, whose role is to ensure the application needs of a single development project are not in conflict with corporate data standards and policies, must approve all database designs in some capacity.

This constraint may prevent the development team from adopting certain data access technologies that require data structure to be laid down according to a specific format. Moreover, the development team architects may find themselves having to work with a database structure that is not to their liking and may preclude the use of some data access technologies.

Although many architects might feel aggrieved not to have total control over the design of an application, it is reasonable that someone with specialized database design skills should be involved in the database design. The skill set for designing and maintaining a database is vastly different than that of designing J2EE applications.

This issue points to a cultural difference between teams using object-oriented methods to develop software and those charged with the integrity of corporate data. In his book *Agile Database Techniques* [Ambler, 2003], Scott Ambler suggests appointing someone to the role of mediator between the development and database groups. Ambler defines this role as the *Agile DBA*.

The role of the Agile DBA is to bridge the gap between the J2EE development team working with object-based techniques and the database group whose focus is on data modeling. By mediating between the two groups, the Agile DBA should ensure both teams are working toward the same goal, regardless of paradigm.

## Shared Data Between Systems

Data that is truly enterprise-level is unlikely to be the sole preserve of a single system. Such data is usually accessed, and possibly even updated, by other applications within the organization.

Shared access is likely to come from multiple directions. Batch processes running reconciliation or data-fix jobs are common. Most organizations use commercial software tools for accessing data in order to generate reports. Consequently, a J2EE application is likely to share a database with batch processes and commercial reporting tools.

Shared database access between applications has implications for the data architect and the J2EE architect. The data architect must design the schema of the database according to the best practices of database design to ensure efficient use of the database for all systems, not just those using object-oriented technologies. Thus, the data architect is reluctant to violate the principles of good database design to meet the needs of a single application unless the application in question is of significant strategic importance to the business.

For the J2EE architect, sharing a database with other systems presents design issues, especially if considering the use of EJB-caching technology, as is offered by entity beans for addressing performance concerns.

## Legacy Data Structures

Many new enterprise systems are either replacing older systems or being integrated with existing systems. Corporate data also tends to have a longer life span than software systems, so existing data must be migrated to newer systems as they come online.

Project teams therefore find themselves working with legacy data structures that are a hangover from an older system. In this situation, the team has no control of the structure of the data and must work with the design in place. Given the tendency for software to atrophy over time, legacy data structures often bear the scars of numerous enhancements, design changes, and emergency *quick fixes*. Such legacy data structures can result in data access code that is extremely difficult to write due to the convoluted nature of the data design upon which it must be based.

## Data Security and Confidentiality

Where data is considered especially commercial sensitive or of a personal nature, access to data that is a copy of a production version may not be possible for the development team. This situation is most likely to arise when an existing database is being built upon.

A project team might be denied access to the very data it is expected to work with for a variety of reasons, including government laws regarding personal data.

This issue is of particular relevance where an organization employs the services of a separate software development company to undertake application development on its behalf. With this scenario, the commercially sensitive nature of the data may prevent the external development team from accessing any data representative of the production version. If this situation arises, additional tasks must be added to the project plan to cover the creation of suitable test data for the development and testing teams.

note

> Some companies have policies that mandate that all sensitive customer data, such as names, addresses, and phone numbers, be either stripped or obfuscated before being made available to development teams.

In addition, not being able to work with actual data and realistic data volumes presents some significant risks to the project. These risks relate to performance, since exploratory prototypes cannot be used to validate that the design will meet the performance criteria required of the system. Subtle differences between test data and actual data may also present problems when the system is released into a live environment.

All of the issues discussed so far take time to manage and thus may extend the timeframe of the project.

# The Object-Relational Impedance Mismatch

Object-oriented and relational database technologies represent separate and distinct conceptual paradigms. The term *object-relational impedance mismatch*, or impedance mismatch, was coined in the early 1990s to formalize the problems endemic to moving between the object and the relational worlds.

The impedance mismatch problem occurs because object and relational techniques each work toward different objectives. Databases rely on the mathematical precision of relational algebra to structure business data in an efficient *normalized* form. Object-oriented design methods go beyond pure data modeling to define business processes as a collection of collaborating business components that have both state and behavior.

Given the impedance mismatch problem, the question arises, Why are object and relational technologies so frequently used together for the development of enterprise systems? An alternative to the relational database does exist in the form of the object database management system

(ODBMS). However, ODBMS technology is taking time to mature and has yet to prove itself at the enterprise level. For this reason, almost all enterprise software uses a relational database.

Relational databases are a mature and proven technology and can trace their origins back to the 1970s when Dr. E. F. Codd, the father of the relational database, was working on defining his famous twelve rules.

Contrast this history with object-oriented technologies such as J2EE, which have only emerged into the mainstream in the past decade. Despite the frustrations the impedance mismatch causes object-oriented practitioners, relational databases are likely to be the standard form of database technology for enterprise software for the foreseeable future. Therefore, it is important to understand the constraints imposed by impedance mismatch and why the problem causes such headaches.

To appreciate the problems, consider the ideal behavior a J2EE architect would like to see from a persistence mechanism. Most well-designed object-oriented systems are constructed around a domain model. The domain model describes the various relationships between each object involved in the problem domain. Typically, the objects and the relationships between them are represented using a UML class diagram.

Ideally, the architect would like object instances from this domain model to be *transparently* persisted to and from the underlying database, although a good design would see a persistence layer residing between the business objects of the domain and the data store for decoupling purposes.

> *The importance of layers in software architecture is covered in Chapter 4.*

The keyword here is that of transparency. True persistence transparency enables objects to be transferred between the database and the application without concern for the intricacies of how the state of an object is persisted to the data store.

Unfortunately, impedance mismatch problems make true transparency difficult to achieve if a relational database is the target. Let's consider some of the reasons this should be the case.

## Mapping Database Types to Java Types

The first problem is relatively straightforward. The properties of a persistent Java class must be mapped to columns in a database table. The Java language and relational databases support subtly different basic types. For persistence to occur, the types must be mapped correctly to ensure no loss of data results from, for example, long Java strings being truncated in VAR-CHAR(20) columns. The mapping of types is relatively easy to manage. Mapping relationships, however, is considerably more complex.

## Mapping Relationships

On the surface, the differences between object and relational technologies appear to be only superficial. After all, relational databases enable relationships to be specified between entities, while the object-oriented model defines relationships between classes.

Database designers use entity-relationship (ER) diagrams to describe relationships between database entities. ER diagrams are not part of the UML but are a recognized modeling notation. Relationships between entities in a database are modeled based on cardinality and enforced using foreign keys. Three possible relationship types can be modeled with relational technology:

- One-to-one
- One-to-many
- Many-to-many

note

> The many-to-many relationship, although it may be modeled, is not supported by relational databases. Common practice in this case is to use a link, or association table, to split the many-to-many relationship.

The object-oriented designer has a richer set of relationships to draw upon. Information that can be both modeled in the UML class diagram and implemented in the Java code includes:

- Relationship cardinality
- Association by both composition and aggregation
- Inheritance
- Unidirectional and bidirectional relationships

Coercing these relationships to fit those of the relational database model is not a trivial task, and a direct mapping of object model to database schema can result in a suboptimal database design. This gives rise to the argument as to which technology, object-oriented or relational, should be driving the design of the data model.

## Data Models Driving the Object Model

For the majority of enterprise systems, the data model drives the design of a system's object model. The reasons for taking this approach are as follows:

- Object models tend to translate into inefficient database schemas.
- Databases are often accessed by other enterprise systems not using object-oriented technology.
- Database schemas are more rigid and harder to change than the object models, which are in the hands of the development teams.

Despite these reasons, life is considerably simpler for the development team if the object model translates directly into the underlying data architecture. This approach removes many of the headaches associated with mapping between the two paradigms and enables systems to be constructed swiftly.

Nevertheless, for the development of enterprise software, such arguments are likely to prove moot. As we discussed previously, enterprise data is a valuable commodity, and no data architect is likely to accept a data model from an object-oriented designer that does not comply with the best practices of data modeling techniques.

# Data Access Options

When it comes to implementing a persistence layer, J2EE application developers seem to be spoiled for choice, with an almost bewildering range of data access technologies available. This section provides an overview of some of the more common mechanisms employed on projects for implementing one of the most important layers in the application:

- The JDBC API
- Object/Relational mapping tools
- Entity beans
- Java Data Objects

The foundation of all these technologies is the JDBC API, which we discuss first.

## Java Database Connectivity (JDBC)

The ability to write code for data access using the JDBC API is a skill most Java developers possess. JDBC enables us to communicate directly with the database, pushing and pulling information to and from the relational world into that of the object-oriented, forming a bridge between the two paradigms.

The strengths of JDBC lie in its popularity, as it is perhaps the most common method of database access for Java applications. By coding to the JDBC API, developers can

- Establish database connections
- Execute SQL statements
- Invoke database-stored procedures
- Process database results
- Achieve a degree of portability between different database products

Here are some of the main advantages of using a JDBC driver for database access:

- Most Java developers are familiar with the JDBC API.

- Developers skilled in SQL and relational database technology can construct highly optimized SQL statements.
- JDBC drivers are available for all major DBMS products.
- JDBC resources are managed by the J2EE server.

JDBC enables the use of SQL as a domain-specific language for simplifying data manipulation with convenient and easily understandable language constructs. With a suitable database driver, the developer has the option of constructing SQL statements within the code and executing them against the database at runtime.

This approach, in addition to being time consuming and error prone, is very sensitive to database change. Changes to table names, column names, or the order of columns within a table require the data access code to be updated. Worse still, differences between data access code and the database schema are only detected at runtime, as embedded SQL statements are not validated at compile time. The careful use of stored procedures is one method of alleviating the impact of the runtime detection issue.

Some of the problems associated with the use of the JDBC API for object persistence include the following:

- The process of writing code to map objects to a relational database is time consuming and error prone.
- Embedding SQL within Java code results in a brittle data access layer that is easily broken by database schema changes.
- The writing of highly optimized SQL statements is a skill not all Java developers possess.
- Poorly written SQL statements can have a catastrophic effect on database performance.
- Although the JDBC API is common between DBMS products, SQL syntaxes vary to the degree that JDBC data access code is not portable between databases.

The next sections look at database access technologies that use JDBC as a base but attempt to avoid some of these pitfalls.

## Object/Relational Mapping Tools

One technology that has grown in maturity and sophistication in recent years is object/relational (O/R) mapping. Mapping tools offer a method of storing an object-oriented domain model transparently to the database without the need to write a line of JDBC data access code or SQL.

The task of persisting an object's state is handled by the O/R mapping product, which generates the JDBC calls on our behalf. All that is required of the developer is to specify, usually via an XML-based configuration document, the mapping rules for a particular class. Based on the rules in the configuration document, the O/R mapping tool undertakes all data access, leaving the developer free to concentrate on implementing critical business functionality within the application instead of writing boilerplate data access code. Defining the mapping rules can be done by hand but is more commonly generated by the O/R mapping tool.

The benefits of O/R mapping technology include these:

- Increased developer productivity, as the O/R mapping tool generates the JDBC calls necessary for object persistence

- A flexible persistence layer, as database changes can be reflected in the application by regenerating all data access code

- Simpler software architectures, as the persistence concern is handled by the O/R mapping tool

- Better system performance, as the generated data access code is optimized for the target DBMS

- The ability to operate both outside or inside the confines of a J2EE server, applicable to both the EJB and Web containers

- Portability, as the SQL generated by the O/R mapping tool can target a specific DBMS

tip

> The ability to operate O/R mapping tools outside of the J2EE server has excellent implications for evolutionary prototyping.
>
> For example, a persistence layer can be used either as part of a prototype built as a Web application, using only the Web container, or as part of a two-tier application developed using Swing for the GUI.
>
> The persistence layer for either prototype scenario can then be evolved to an EJB architecture by having session beans make use of the O/R mapping tool.

During this chapter, we look at an example of an open source O/R mapping tool. First, let's look at two Java technologies that build on the services of the JDBC API, but with an O/R mapping approach to object persistence.

## Entity Beans

Entity beans are a form of O/R mapping technology and are a member of the Enterprise Java-Beans family. Entity beans provide an object-oriented view of business domain model entities held in persistent storage, where persistent storage can be either a database or an existing application. By providing a wrapper around the underlying data, entity beans attempt to simplify the process of data access and retrieval. Entity beans are a core part of the EJB specification and so can be considered the *official* persistence layer for J2EE applications.

An entity bean is a shareable, in-memory representation of a row in a database table. The combination of being both shareable and in-memory allows entity beans to operate as a caching mechanism for application data. The responsibility of controlling concurrent access to the cached data in the bean and refreshing or writing the cache when needed is the responsibility of the EJB container. The EJB container also safeguards the state of an entity by ensuring it can survive a server crash.

While the EJB container manages the state of an entity bean and ensures support for concurrent access, the mechanism by which the underlying row in the database is accessed and updated is the responsibility of the developer. The decision as to how data access is managed is dictated by two different flavors of entity bean:

### Bean-Managed Persistence (BMP).

BMP entity beans rely on the developer implementing framework methods on the bean, such as `ejbLoad()` and `ejbStore()`, for managing data access. Typically, data access code takes the form of calls to the JDBC API.

### Container-Managed Persistence (CMP).

CMP is a form of rudimentary O/R mapping that sees the EJB container take on the responsibility for access to the data source. CMP was introduced as part of the EJB 1.1 specification, but unfortunately, the technology was not adequately specified to a workable level until version 2.0 of the EJB specification was released. It is now recommended that entity beans developed for the EJB 2.0 and 2.1 specifications use CMP in preference to BMP.

Here is a list of some of the main benefits entity beans offer as an object-persistence mechanism:

- They are a mandatory part of the EJB specification and are supported by all compliant J2EE servers.
- Entity beans are well supported by development tools.
- They provide higher performance through instance pooling.
- Management of the lifetime of an entity bean instance is the responsibility of the J2EE server.
- Entity beans can survive a server crash.
- The J2EE server manages access to shared entity bean instances from multiple threads.
- As Enterprise JavaBeans, entity beans offer declarative support for security and transactions.

Although the inclusion of entity beans within the EJB specification would seem to make them the persistence technology of choice, the reaction of developers to the merits of entity beans has been less than favorable. Some of the complaints raised regarding entity beans include these:

- The CMP O/R mapping functionality offered by entity beans is limited when compared to mature O/R mapping tools such as TopLink and CocoBase.

- It is not possible to model the inheritance relationship.

- Entity beans, like all enterprise beans, are heavyweight components and require considerable amounts of framework code (boilerplate).

- Components are more suited to business objects than persistent domain model objects.

- Entity beans are complex to develop and do not align with the domain model, especially if inheritance is involved.

- Entity beans cannot be tested outside of the container.

- Developers have found enterprise beans difficult to work with.

The hostile reaction of the Java community to entity beans has seen other technologies spring to the fore. One such technology is Java Data Objects.

## Java Data Objects

Somewhat confusingly, Java also has a second O/R mapping technology that competes with entity beans. Java Data Objects (JDO) is a specification defined under the Java Community Process by JSR-012, *Java Data Objects*. A second iteration of the JDO technology is currently under review, which is covered by JSR-243.

note

Find the JDO specifications for JSR-012 and JSR-243 at `http://jcp.org/en/jsr/detail?id=012` and `http://jcp.org/aboutJava/communityprocess/edr/jsr243/index.html` respectively.

The JDO specification has a set of objectives similar to O/R mapping products in that the stated aim of the technology is to provide Java developers with a transparent Java-centric view of persistent information residing in a variety of data sources.

The scope of JDO is wider than providing a purely object/relational mapping technology. JDO implementations cover a range of data storage mediums, including object databases and enterprise information systems. In this way, JDO provides an object view of persistent storage regardless of the underlying persistence technology, whether relational, object-based, or otherwise.

Here are some of the main features and benefits JDO technology brings to the Java platform:

- It provides a standard Java-centric API for true transparent object persistence.
- JDO implementations support the inheritance relationship.
- JDO persistent classes run both inside and outside of a J2EE server.
- A JDO *enhancer* can add data access code for persistence to standard Java objects (or plain old Java objects, POJOs) at the bytecode level.
- JDO implementations offer access to EIS persistence resources via the J2EE Connector Architecture on the J2EE platform.

Unfortunately, the JDO specification has failed to strike a chord with O/R mapping tools vendors, presumably because products such as *CocoBase* from Thought Inc. and *TopLink* from Oracle have already carved themselves a sizeable market niche.

The JDO architecture also faces an uncertain future. The first draft release of the EJB 3.0 specification under JSR-220 announced that the next incarnation of the EJB architecture would provide yet another standard for a Java O/R mapping technology.

Since that time, Sun Microsystems has announced that as both the EJB and JDO specifications are undergoing further revision under the Java Community Process, members of both the JSR-220 and JSR-243 Expert Groups will collaborate to define a single specification for providing transparent Java object persistence. Only time will tell what this move means for the future of JDO and entity beans.

# Code Generation and O/R Mapping

The database is a rich source of metadata, making the writing of data access code a prime candidate for code generation techniques. As we learned in Chapter 6, *Code Generation*, active code generation can help increase developer productivity and promote project agility.

The next sections cover by example how O/R mapping tools can combine with code generation techniques to automate the generation of all data access code for a project. The example covers the use of code generation and O/R mapping tools from the perspective of the data model driving the process, as this is the typical scenario for enterprise software.

Two open source tools are used in the example: *Hibernate* and *Middlegen*. Hibernate offers O/R mapping, while Middlegen is a database-driven code generation tool, able to generate mapping files for a variety of O/R mapping technologies, including entity beans, JDO, and Hibernate.

note

Using code generation for producing data access code is not exclusive to O/R mapping products. Entity beans and standard JDBC calls can both benefit from code generation techniques.

The example has a number of steps that demonstrate an end-to-end generation process from entity model to database and then back to an object models:

1. Create a database.

2. Define the entities of a data model using a modeling tool.

3. Use the modeling tool to forward-engineer the script to create a database schema.

4. Create the database schema.

5. Use Middlegen to construct Hibernate mapping files by reverse engineering from the database schema.

6. Use the Hibernate tool, `hbm2java`, to create plain Java classes from the mapping files.

7. With the modeling tool, reverse-engineer the generated Java code to view the object model.

8. Compare the original data model against the generated object model.

First, we look at the two main products used in the example.

## Introducing Hibernate

Hibernate is an open source O/R mapping product. Unlike entity beans, which are heavyweight components, Hibernate allows standard Java objects, or POJOs, to be transparently written and retrieved to and from the underlying data store.

As with commercial O/R mapping tools, Hibernate supports enterprise-level capabilities, including transactions, connection pooling, a powerful SQL-like query language, and the ability to declaratively define entity relationships. The tool also integrates with J2EE, making it suitable for both J2SE-based and J2EE-based applications.

Hibernate uses configuration files to hold metadata describing mapping settings and entity relationship information. The Hibernate configuration files are one of the tool's key strengths. They offer extensive configuration options, making it possible to precisely define the behavior of the persistence framework. Such configuration precision ensures Hibernate can be tuned to deliver a high-performance persistence solution.

Hibernate supports the definition of inheritance, association, and composition relationships types, in addition to the specification of relationships based on Java collections. Hibernate supports most of the leading RDBMS products.

Although Hibernate is open source, it is nevertheless a proprietary API. Unlike JDO, it has not gone through the JSR process and consequent community review. Despite this, the Hibernate development team has arguably eclipsed JDO by providing a robust implementation with a highly detailed level of documentation. Consequently, Hibernate has enjoyed good word of mouth regarding the quality of the product, and developers have been quick to embrace Hibernate as the open source mapping tool of choice. The Hibernate team claims the product is the leading O/R mapping toolkit for Java.

The Hibernate binaries, source, documentation, and examples can be downloaded from `http://www.hibernate.org`. Hibernate is available under the LGPL license, which allows commercial use. As usual, check with the site for full licensing details.

## Introducing Middlegen

Over the years, various code generators have emerged that use database metadata to drive the code generation process. Middlegen is one such open source product that has proven popular with developers and complements Hibernate's persistence capabilities by taking on the chore of generating Hibernate mapping files.

Middlegen uses JDBC to access database metadata and the Velocity engine for code generation. The use of JDBC enables Middlegen to support most of the major RDBMS vendors. Like XDoclet, Middlegen uses an Ant build file for launching the product.

> *The Velocity template engine and*
> *XDoclet are discussed in Chapter 6.*

Middlegen uses a plug-in approach for code generation. After Middlegen has determined the database structure, the task of generating code is handed over to those plug-in generators that have been configured with the `<middlegen>` Ant build task. At the time of writing, plug-ins are available for generating entity beans, JDO classes, and Hibernate mapping files.

The example focuses on generating Hibernate mapping files; however, Middlegen is not constrained to this one persistence technology. The ability to produce code for more than one type of persistence mechanism is vital, as either the architecture or customer requirements may mandate the persistence technology used. The plug-in architecture of Middlegen provides the ability to accommodate such changes.

To download the latest version of Middlegen, along with full documentation and a comprehensive sample application, visit `http://boss.bekk.no/boss/middlegen/`.

note

As with all successful software technologies, ongoing development work continues to refine and improve the product. This is certainly the case with Middlegen and Hibernate. At the time of writing, I am using versions 2.x of both Middlegen and Hibernate. Middlegen currently has a version 3.0 in the pipeline, while Hibernate is producing a new version of its Middlegen plug-in for version 3.0. The release strategy is to make all of these betas final at the same time.

So as not to be totally out of date, the example uses a preview of the new Hibernate plug-in, which is available for download from the Hibernate site.

With all the necessary software installed, we can move on to generating the persistence layer. However, before we can look at how code generation techniques can combine with O/R mapping tools to save us time and effort, we need a RDBMS installed and an operational database established with a suitable schema.

The next section covers the setup of the RDBMS and creation of the database schema required for the example.

# Setting Up the Database

To illustrate the virtues of Hibernate and Middlegen, we first install a suitable RDBMS and create a database for which a persistence layer can be generated.

The first step is to install an RDBMS, and in this case, we use the services of *MySQL*.

## Introducing MySQL

MySQL is a small, efficient database and is freely available for most platforms. MySQL offers several types of the product, including *MySQL Pro*, a commercial version intended for use in production systems, and *MySQL Standard*, which is available free under the GNU Public License (GPL). Both versions of MySQL offer identical functionality, the only differences being in the terms and conditions of the license.

The upcoming example uses version 4.0 of MySQL Standard. MySQL binaries are available for download from `http://dev.mysql.com/downloads/mysql/4.0.html`.

Comprehensive installation instructions, along with the MySQL manual, can be found at `http://dev.mysql.com/doc/mysql/en/Installing.html`.

Access to a MySQL database from Java requires the MySQL *Connector/J* JDBC driver. This is a Type 4 driver, and like MySQL Standard, is free to download. The latest version can be pulled down from `http://www.mysql.com/products/connector/j`.

From this download, we get `mysql-connector-java-3.0.11-stable-bin.jar`, which must be placed on the classpath of any Java application requiring access to a MySQL database.

For any additional information regarding MySQL, refer to the main product Web site at `http://www.mysql.com`.

Once the database has been installed, the next step is to build up a suitable database schema for use in the example.

## Creating a Database Schema

To generate the persistence layer from the database, we need a suitable schema from which to work. For the example, I have put together an entity-relationship (ER) diagram containing four entities: `Customer`, `Account`, `Purchase_Order`, and `Item`.

The ER diagram in Figure 7–1 defines the relationships between the entities.

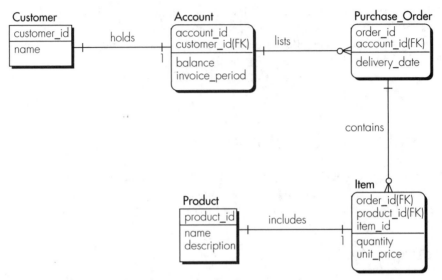

**Figure 7–1**    Entity-relationship diagram for the Customer schema.

From the ER diagram, the following relationships are apparent:

* Each Customer entity can have exactly one Account.
* Each Account can have many Purchase_Order entities.
* A Purchase_Order is comprised of many Item entities.
* A one-to-one relationship has been defined between Item and Product.

To save time creating the schema from the diagram, the data modeling features of a modeling tool were used to generate the data definition language (DDL) statements from the ER diagram. The example uses Borland's Together ControlCenter to produce the DDL.

note

> Unfortunately, the generated scripts weren't exactly what I was after, making it necessary to tinker with the output. I therefore claim this to be an example of passive, not active, code generation.

The final version of the database script is shown in Listing 7–1.

## Listing 7–1    Database Script customer-mysql.sql

```sql
DROP TABLE IF EXISTS Customer;
DROP TABLE IF EXISTS Account;
DROP TABLE IF EXISTS Purchase_Order;
DROP TABLE IF EXISTS Item;
DROP TABLE IF EXISTS Product;

CREATE TABLE Customer
(
  customer_id mediumint(7) NOT NULL,
  name varchar(127),
  PRIMARY KEY (customer_id)
) TYPE=INNODB;

CREATE TABLE Account
(
  account_id mediumint(7) NOT NULL,
  customer_id mediumint(7) NOT NULL,
  balance mediumint(7),
  invoice_period mediumint(7),
  PRIMARY KEY (account_id),
  INDEX customer_idx(customer_id),
  FOREIGN KEY (customer_id) REFERENCES Customer(customer_id)
) TYPE=INNODB;

CREATE TABLE Purchase_Order
(
  order_id mediumint(7) NOT NULL,
  account_id mediumint(7) NOT NULL,
  delivery_date date,
  PRIMARY KEY (order_id),
  INDEX account_idx(account_id),
  FOREIGN KEY (account_id) REFERENCES Account(account_id),
) TYPE=INNODB;

CREATE TABLE Product
(
  product_id mediumint(7) NOT NULL,
  name varchar(127),
  description text,
  PRIMARY KEY (product_id)
) TYPE=INNODB;

CREATE TABLE Item
(
  item_id mediumint(7) NOT NULL,
  order_id mediumint(7) NOT NULL,
  product_id mediumint(7) NOT NULL,
  quantity mediumint(7),
  unit_price mediumint(7),
  PRIMARY KEY (item_id, order_id),
```

```
     INDEX order_idx(order_id),
     INDEX product_idx(product_id),
     FOREIGN KEY (order_id) REFERENCES Purchase_Order(order_id),
     FOREIGN KEY (product_id) REFERENCES Product(product_id)
) TYPE=INNODB;
```

The changes made were around declaring the type of the tables to be *InnoDB* by adding the line TYPE=INNODB. Without this specification, MySQL discards the relationship information imposed by the foreign key constraints. Another option to changing the scripts would have been to configure MySQL to use InnoDB table types by default.

Looking at the Account table, a relationship is expressed through the customer_id foreign key to the Customer table. It is a MySQL condition that to be able to define a foreign key, an index must exist for the key. Hence, the script declares INDEX customer_idx (customer_id). This creates the index necessary to allow the relationship to be defined between the Account and Customer entities.

## Running the Database Script

To create the database schema, we must first create a database and run the script. Start MySQL using the instructions appropriate for your particular platform—for example, mysqld --console.

MySQL comes with a command-line application for interacting with the database engine. Issue mysql from a command shell to start the application, enter the following commands to create a database called customer, and run the script.

```
mysql> create database customer;
mysql> use customer
mysql> source customer-mysql.sql
```

Issuing show tables at the mysql prompt lists the newly created tables for the schema.

With the database established and the schema created, we can now put both Hibernate and Middlegen through their paces.

# Generating the Persistence Layer

The example takes the Customer data model directly from the database and generates a persistence layer of POJOs. Once the persistence layer has been generated, we reverse-engineer the Java into a UML class diagram and compare the result with the original ER diagram.

The code generation process involves several steps:

1. Produce an Ant build file for running Middlegen.
2. Run Middlegen against the database and fine-tune the code generation options using the GUI.

3. Generate Hibernate mapping documents.

4. Use the Hibernate tool hbm2java to generate Java classes from the Hibernate documents.

Listing 7–2 shows the relevant extracts from the build.xml file required to run Middlegen.

## Listing 7–2   Database-Generated Ant Build File

```xml
<?xml version="1.0" encoding="UTF-8"?>
   .
   .
   .


<!-- Use Middlegen to create hibernate files from DB -->
<target name="generate"
        description="Run Middlegen">

   <taskdef name="middlegen"
            classname="middlegen.MiddlegenTask"
            classpathref="project.class.path"/>

   <middlegen appname="${name}"
              prefsdir="${gen.dir}"
              gui="true"
              databaseurl="${database.url}"
              driver="${database.driver}"
              username="${database.userid}"
              password="${database.password}"
              schema="${database.schema}"
              catalog="${database.catalog}">

     <hibernate destination="${gen.dir}"
                package="${name}.hibernate"
                genXDocletTags="true"
                genIntergratedCompositeKeys="false"/>

   </middlegen>
</target>

<!-- Generate Java from mapping files -->
<target name="hbm2java"
        depends="generate"
        description="Creates Java classes from hbm files">

   <taskdef name="hbm2java"
            classname="net.sf.hibernate.tool.hbm2java.Hbm2JavaTask"
            classpathref="project.class.path" />

   <hbm2java output="${gen.dir}">
     <fileset dir="${gen.dir}">
```

```
        <include name="**/*.hbm.xml"/>
      </fileset>
    </hbm2java>
  </target>

</project>
```

The build file controls the entire code generation process. These next sections cover each step.

## Running Middlegen from Ant

The Middlegen tool does the hard work of creating the Hibernate mapping documents for us. The Middlegen tool is invoked from an Ant build file, and the <middlegen> task is provided for this purpose. From the example build.xml, we have the following:

```
<middlegen appname="customer"
           prefsdir="gen_src"
           gui="true"
           databaseurl="jdbc:mysql://localhost/customer"
           driver="org.gjt.mm.mysql.Driver"
           username=""
           password=""
           schema=""
           catalog="">
```

This task provides Middlegen with the information it requires to use the MySQL JDBC driver to connect to the Customer database through the attributes of databaseurl and driver. The attributes username, password, schema, and catalog provide further connection detail. These attributes are not needed if MySQL is running locally on a Windows platform.

The use of the gui attribute becomes clear shortly but basically tells Middlegen to open its visual configuration tool.

The next step is to tell Middlegen what to generate. Middlegen uses plug-ins for controlling code generation, and we use the Hibernate plug-in, which requires the nested element <hibernate> for configuration:

```
<hibernate destination="gen_src"
           package="customer.hibernate"
           genXDocletTags="true"
           genIntergratedCompositeKeys="false"/>
```

The package attribute provides the Hibernate plug-in with Java package information. The next two attributes require a little more description. The genXDocletTags tells the plug-in to generate XDoclet tags in the XML mapping documents. The XDoclet tags are ignored by the mapping documents. However, the Java generation tool later in the process picks up this additional metadata.

Where we have a composite primary key, Hibernate provides the option to generate an external primary key class. The choice of either an external or an internal primary key class is specified with the `genIntegratedCompositeKeys` attribute. We generate our own keys externally and set this attribute to `false`.

With this minimal Middlegen configuration complete, we can now invoke the build file and start the tool.

## The Middlegen GUI

By setting the `gui` attribute to `true`, we have informed Middlegen we wish to use the GUI tool to configure the output from the plug-ins. Running the example build file brings up the screen shown in Figure 7–2.

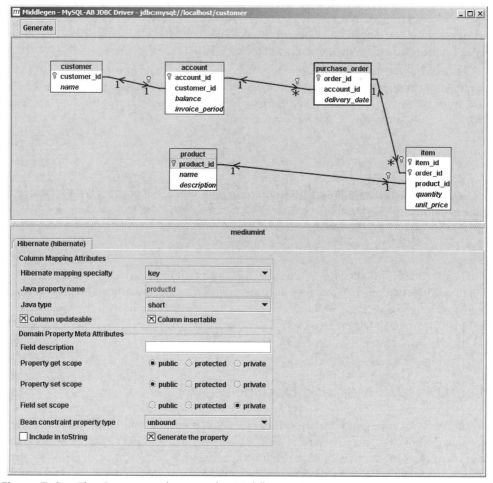

**Figure 7–2**   The Customer schema in the Middlegen GUI.

The GUI allows us to assist Middlegen in correctly determining the relationships between entities. From the metadata available in the database, Middlegen is unable to infer the type of relationships established by a foreign key constraint.

> In preference to running the GUI, it is possible to define relationship information within the build script.

With the configuration used in our minimal build file, Middlegen assumes all foreign key constraints are modeling one-to-many relationships. Thus, on first opening the GUI, one-to-many relationships are defined between entities where a one-to-one relationship was expected—for example, Customer and Account, Product and Item. Thankfully, the GUI allows this initial interpretation to be corrected. By pressing the <ctrl> key and clicking with the mouse on the relationship, the cardinality of the association can be corrected.

The GUI also enables the output from the Hibernate plug-in to be further fine-tuned. Selecting either an entity or property in the ER diagram displays a configuration dialog for the element in focus. In this way, we can control exactly what is to be generated for the persistence layer. This dialog is shown in the lower pane of Figure 7–2.

> By default, all configuration settings made with the GUI tool are stored in the generated source directory. Cleaning all files from this directory results in these configuration settings being lost.

When satisfied with all settings, pressing the *Generate* button on the toolbar causes the Hibernate plug-in to generate mapping documents for each database entity. This process is visible in the console from which Middlegen was launched and provides a visual cue when the generation process has completed.

Let's assess what Middlegen has produced.

# Hibernate O/R Mapping Documents

As stated earlier, the output from the <middlegen> task is not Java source but Hibernate XML mapping documents. These documents instruct Hibernate how the mapping between a Java class and a database entity is to be orchestrated. A mapping document is produced for each entity in the Customer schema. Listing 7–3 shows the XML mapping document generated for the Purchase_Order database entity.

## Listing 7–3    Middlegen-Generated PurchaseOrder.hbm.xml

```xml
<?xml version="1.0"?>
<!DOCTYPE hibernate-mapping PUBLIC
    "-//Hibernate/Hibernate Mapping DTD 2.0//EN"
    "http://hibernate.sourceforge.net/hibernate-mapping-2.0.dtd" >

<hibernate-mapping>
<!--
    Created by the Middlegen Hibernate plugin

    http://boss.bekk.no/boss/middlegen/
    http://hibernate.sourceforge.net/
-->

<class
    name="customer.hibernate.PurchaseOrder"
    table="purchase_order"
>
    <meta attribute="class-description" inherit="false">
        @hibernate.class
          table="purchase_order"
    </meta>

    <id
        name="orderId"
        type="short"
        column="order_id"
    >
        <meta attribute="field-description">
            @hibernate.id
              generator-class="assigned"
              type="short"
              column="order_id"

        </meta>
        <generator class="assigned" />
    </id>

    <property
        name="deliveryDate"
        type="java.sql.Date"
        column="delivery_date"
        length="10"
    >
        <meta attribute="field-description">
            @hibernate.property
              column="delivery_date"
              length="10"
        </meta>
    </property>
```

```
<!-- associations -->
<!-- bi-directional many-to-one association to Account -->
<many-to-one
    name="account"
    class="customer.hibernate.Account"
    not-null="true"
>
    <meta attribute="field-description">
        @hibernate.many-to-one
          not-null="true"
        @hibernate.column name="account_id"
    </meta>
    <column name="account_id" />
</many-to-one>
<!-- bi-directional one-to-many association to Item -->
<set
    name="items"
    lazy="true"
    inverse="true"
>
    <meta attribute="field-description">
        @hibernate.set
          lazy="true"
          inverse="true"

     @hibernate.collection-key
       column="order_id"

        @hibernate.collection-one-to-many
          class="customer.hibernate.Item"
    </meta>
    <key>
        <column name="order_id" />
    </key>
    <one-to-many
        class="customer.hibernate.Item"
    />
</set>

</class>
</hibernate-mapping>
```

In Listing 7–3, it is evident how the configuration is used to map Java types to database types. This ease-of-use configuration is one reason why Hibernate is proving a favorite with developers. Many of the attributes are self-explanatory. For example, the mapping of a class to a table is achieved with the <class> element:

```
<class name="customer.hibernate.PurchaseOrder"
      table="purchase_order">
```

Likewise, the <property> element maps properties to columns:

```
<property
  name="deliveryDate"
  type="java.sql.Date"
  column="delivery_date"
  length="10"/>
```

The `<id>` element is similar to that of the `<property>` element but identifies the property as being a primary key:

```
<id
  name="orderId"
  type="short"
  column="order_id">
  <generator class="assigned" />
</id>
```

The `<generator>` element specifies how the primary key will be produced. A value of `assigned` indicates that we will supply Hibernate with the key. Alternatively, Hibernate can generate the key on our behalf from a variety of unique key-generation algorithms it provides.

Not all configuration settings are quite so easily understood, and some elements warrant further description. The `<meta>` element looks a little out of place: it appears to be using Javadoc notation and repeats configuration detail that is already specified in other tags. For example,

```
<meta attribute="field-description">
  @hibernate.many-to-one
    not-null="true"
  @hibernate.column name="account_id"
</meta>
```

These are XDoclet tags and are parsed by the XDoclet Hibernate plug-in when encountered in Java source. These tags exist because the `genXDocletTags` attribute was set for the nested `<hibernate>` element in the Ant build file. This information is picked up in the next step when Java source is generated from the Hibernate mapping documents. These XDoclet tags are written out to the Java classes that are mapped by the Hibernate XML mapping documents. Using XDoclet, should we wish, we can regenerate the mapping documents from the Java instead of from the database. XDoclet provides developers with the option to adopt an object-driven rather than data-driven generation approach.

Once the Hibernate mapping documents have been produced, we can move to the next stage of the process: generating Java from the mapping information.

## From Mapping Documents to Java

Closing the GUI causes the Ant build file to run to completion. Hibernate comes with the *hbm2java* tool, used to generate Java from mapping documents, and the build file invokes this tool once Middlegen has completed its part of the process. The relevant section of the `build.xml` file is the `<hbm2java>` task:

```
<hbm2java output="gen_src">
  <fileset dir="gen_src">
    <include name="**/*.hbm.xml"/>
  </fileset>
</hbm2java>
```

This task generates a Java class for each Hibernate mapping document. Listing 7–4 shows an extract from the PurchaseOrder class produced from the PurchaseOrder.hbm.xml mapping file.

## Listing 7–4   PurchaseOrder.java Extract Generated from PurchaseOrder.hbm.xml

```java
/**
 *          @hibernate.class
 *            table="purchase_order"
 *
 */
public class PurchaseOrder implements Serializable {

  /** identifier field */
  private Short orderId;

  /** persistent field */
  private customer.hibernate.Account account;

  /** persistent field */
  private Set items;

  /** full constructor */
  public PurchaseOrder(Short orderId,
                       Date deliveryDate,
                       customer.hibernate.Account account,
                       Set items) {
    this.orderId = orderId;
    this.deliveryDate = deliveryDate;
    this.account = account;
    this.items = items;
  }

  /**
   *            @hibernate.many-to-one
   *              not-null="true"
   *            @hibernate.column name="account_id"
   *
   */
  public customer.hibernate.Account getAccount() {
    return this.account;
  }

  public void setAccount(customer.hibernate.Account account) {
```

```
      this.account = account;
  }

  /**
   *              @hibernate.set
   *               lazy="true"
   *               inverse="true"
   *             @hibernate.collection-key
   *              column="order_id"
   *               @hibernate.collection-one-to-many
   *                class="customer.hibernate.Item"
   *
   */
  public Set getItems() {
    return this.items;
  }

  public void setItems(Set items) {
    this.items = items;
  }
    .
    .
    .


}
```

Comparing the Hibernate mapping documents with generated Java gives an insight into how O/R mapping is handled by Hibernate. Of note are the embedded XDoclet tags, denoted with the @hibernate namespace. The XDoclet Ant task <hibernatedoclet> can be used to drive the generation of the mapping documents from the Java source if required.

## Completing the Round Trip

The generation of the persistence layer was initiated from an ER diagram. Despite a few manual changes to the DDL for producing the database schema, the entire persistence layer was constructed by code generators. The result is a set of lightweight Java objects that provide an object view of the database entities.

Reverse engineering the generated Java code into a UML class diagram enables the object relationships to be compared with the original ER diagram. Figure 7–3 shows the UML class diagram for the persistence layer.

**Figure 7–3**   UML class diagram mapping to Customer database schema.

note

Adornments have been added to the diagram to show multiplicity between classes that have not been detected as part of the reverse-engineering process. However, these are only small refinements that describe what is already expressed in the generated code.

At the conclusion of the code generation process, we now have a transparent, object-based persistence layer with which to work. Best of all, other than an Ant build file, it wasn't necessary to write a line of code to produce it.

## Reverse-Engineering Fallibilities

If you try to reverse-engineer the output from Hibernate using a modeling tool, you will not see the same UML class diagram as is shown in Figure 7–3. Some of the relationships will be missing.

This is not a shortcoming in the reverse-engineering capabilities of the modeling tool, but rather one of the common problems inherent in reverse engineering, even from languages as clean and elegant as Java.

The problem is that Java simply does not contain enough information for the modeling tool to be able to establish the relationship. Examining the PurchaseOrder class, we can guess that a relationship exists between PurchaseOrder and Item from the property Set items.

While we can make the assumption this attribute will house a collection of Item objects, it could contain any object type. Consequently, the modeling tool failed to show any relationship between the two classes, and the relationship had to be added manually.

This problem should be solved with the support for generics in J2SE 5.0. Thus, we can now write

```
Set<Item> items;
```

This will give modeling tools the hint they need to correctly identify the relationship between the two classes.

# Summary

We've established that the production of data access code for enterprise-level software can be a laborious, time-consuming task. Thankfully, due to the metadata maintained by the database on the information it holds, data access code is ideally suited to code generation techniques.

To demonstrate this, we examined how the code generation tool Middlegen can be combined with the O/R mapping tool Hibernate to offer a powerful framework for generating an object-based view of a system's relational database entities.

One area of database development highlighted is the importance that organizations attach to enterprise data. Databases often contain critical and sensitive information, so they are carefully controlled corporate resources. Sensitivities surrounding access to this type of data can be detrimental to rapid development. This issue is a political consideration for the project and one that is best addressed through careful project management.

The next chapter focuses on Model-Driven Architecture, an approach to systems development that combines design, modeling tools, and code generation. If the protagonists of MDA are to be believed, this technology is the proverbial silver bullet for rapid development.

## Additional Information

For more information on entity beans, visit Sun Microsystems' J2EE site at `http://java.sun.com/j2ee`.

The latest news and developer information on JDO can be accessed at `http://www.jdocentral.com`.

For a side-by-side comparison of O/R mapping products, see `http://c2.com/cgi-bin/wiki?ObjectRelationalToolComparison`.

# 8

# Model-Driven Architecture

ince Chapter 4, *Designing for Rapidity*, we have progressed from design concerns to modeling tools to code generation techniques. This chapter looks at Model-Driven Architecture (MDA), a model-centric software development approach that combines the practices of modeling and code generation into a single paradigm. MDA pushes both technologies to the extreme, using models as the basis for generating a substantial amount of the code for the entire application.

Vendors of MDA tools are promoting the paradigm as the next generation in software development, promising unprecedented levels of developer productivity and software quality.

This chapter examines the merits of these claims and assesses the benefits MDA offers the rapid developer. The chapter covers the concepts underpinning the paradigm and demonstrates the use of *AndroMDA,* an open source MDA product.

## The Promise of MDA

Throughout the history of the software industry, many new development tools and methodologies have emerged onto the IT landscape proclaiming to revolutionize software development. Sadly, many of these hoped-for revolutions in IT have failed to bring about improvements in the status quo, further supporting the argument of Frederick Brook that there is no silver bullet [Brooks, 1995].

MDA is the new kid on the block, and its advocates are not shy about proclaiming the virtues of the MDA paradigm. Only time will tell if MDA can succeed where so many other development approaches have failed.

The software engineering industry's thought leaders are divided on the likely future for MDA, with some quarters dismissing the paradigm as unworkable. Nevertheless, the reasons for adopting MDA are compelling, and those advocating the uptake of MDA are pointing to an ever-increasing number of success stories as proof the paradigm is effective.

MDA encourages a business-centric approach to development and uses modeling as a means of allowing the architect to focus on business-critical system functionality without the distraction of technical implementation constraints. From these early models, MDA-compliant tools generate executable code, thereby reducing dramatically the effort involved in producing a functioning system.

This use of models and code generation means some of the touted benefits of MDA will sound familiar from our discussions in previous chapters:

### Reduced development timeframes.

The focus of MDA is on models, not code. Models are produced at the business level and translated into code using sophisticated code generation tools. This ability to jump from business model to implementation cuts out much of the coding effort and enables a running system to be available early in the project lifecycle.

### Consistent quality of software.

MDA puts the automated process of transforming models into a working implementation under the control of the architect. The architect can produce best-practice transformation rules for converting models to code. This transformation process can then be applied to every applicable development project, resulting in software that is of a consistent quality and standard.

### Platform portability.

The models that initiate the MDA process are platform-neutral. By using code generators tailored to a specific platform type, MDA promises platform independence that enables systems to target any technology or framework for which a suitable code generator exists.

These are some of the promises; but what exactly is MDA, and how does it differ from the traditional use of models within the software development process? Moreover, how can MDA help us write quality J2EE solutions in a reduced timeframe?

> *Models and the Unified Modeling Language are covered in Chapter 5.*

To answer these questions, the next section walks through some of the main concepts underpinning MDA.

# MDA Explained

MDA is a model-based approach to software development defined by the Object Management Group (OMG), the same body responsible for administering the UML and CORBA. The aim of the paradigm is to enable a system to be fully specified using software models, independent of any supporting technology platform. This architectural separation of concerns between system and platform is an overarching principle for realizing the three primary goals of MDA:

- Portability
- Interoperability
- Reusability

To this list, we could also add the development concerns of agility and rapidity.

The MDA approach defines a process whereby a working application can be generated from a business domain model, known as a *platform-independent model* (PIM). This leap from conceptual model to working application is achieved by the refinement of a series of models, with each model being generated at ever-decreasing levels of abstraction. The final model in the process is tightly coupled to the target platform, and from this, a substantial percentage of the code for a working application can be generated.

Let's consider some of the core concepts that make up the MDA paradigm.

## Platform

MDA uses the term *platform* to embody all the technical aspects of a system relating to its implementation. The MDA standard provides the following definition for the term:

platform definition

> Technological and engineering details that are irrelevant to the fundamental functionality of a software component.

This definition covers such technical aspects as the choice of middleware, such as J2EE, or .NET, as well as such pressing technical design decisions as which design patterns to apply and what model-view-controller framework to adopt for the Web application.

As we shall see, MDA places great emphasis on *platform neutrality* and separates invariant business functionality from the design requirements of the target platform.

## Models

The MDA paradigm uses models for all of the benefits associated with modeling. Models are an extremely good means of communication, both with the customer and among members of the development team. They also provide a means to validate the design against any requirement changes throughout the project lifecycle using UML interaction diagrams.

Models can assist in the development of quality software, even if not supported by sophisticated modeling tools. Models drawn on the whiteboard or scribbled down on notepaper all contribute toward clearly articulating aspects of the system to the members of the project team.

MDA maximizes the benefits of modeling by making the model central to the development process and incorporates the strengths of automated application generation.

## code generation with modeling tools versus MDA

> The forward-engineering approach of modeling tools is fundamentally different than that of MDA.
>
> Modeling tools generate code at the class and method levels; MDA tools generate nearly complete applications.

With MDA, models are transformed at ever-decreasing levels of abstraction until a functioning application is arrived at. The relationship between models that provide a view of the same system at different levels of abstraction is often called a *refinement*. This concept is pivotal to MDA, which sees models refined throughout the development process.

Two types of model form the backbone of the MDA paradigm: the PIM mentioned earlier and the specialized *platform-specific models* (PSM).

To this list could also be added the code model, or *implementation*. The OMG defines an implementation as a specification capable of providing all the information necessary to put it into operation. The source code produced for a particular implementation is considered a model by MDA, as it is executable by a machine.

Figure 8–1 depicts the lifecycle of the MDA models.

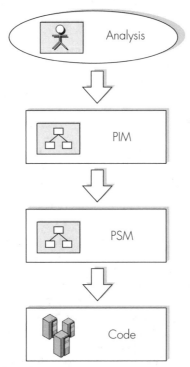

**Figure 8–1**   MDA model lifecycle.

Let's look at these two model types and the purpose each serves in the MDA lifecycle.

## Platform-Independent Model

The PIM results from an intensive analysis phase and focuses on the core business functionality required by the customer. As the name suggests, the PIM gives a view of the system that is not constrained to any particular platform. Instead, the PIM embodies pure business behavior.

Not surprisingly, given the involvement of the OMG, the MDA approach recommends the use of UML notation for constructing the PIM, with class diagrams commonly used to describe the business domain. The UML is ideally suited to this type of model due to its rich and expressive syntax. Moreover, because the PIM is constructed in collaboration with the customer, UML diagrams are an effective mechanism for communicating system intent and behavior.

What the PIM does not show is the use of platform-specific technologies required to realize a working application. The next MDA model type provides this view.

## Platform-Specific Model

The PSM is a refinement of a PIM for a particular platform, where the platform represents an actual operating system, framework, middleware, database product, or any of a number of system-implementation technologies. The PSM is therefore closely aligned with application code and is at a level where code can be directly generated from the structure the model defines.

The PSM is equivalent to the type of model produced with a modeling tool such as Together ControlCenter. It is at a low level of abstraction that sits just above the final implementation. Using a suitable transformation process, the PSM is further refined into executable application code.

The process of transformation between model types is known as *mapping* and is another core MDA concept.

# Mapping

The crux of the MDA paradigm is the method by which models are transformed on the journey from PIM to working application. Mapping is therefore one of the most fundamental MDA concepts, and the success of the paradigm hinges on how effectively this task can be automated.

Essentially, a mapping is a set of rules and techniques that enable one model type to be converted into another form, for example, mapping from a PIM to a PSM.

note

> Mappings can be defined between any of the MDA models. For example, it is valid to map directly from the PIM to the code model.

The task of generating code from a PSM is well-known technology and is already demonstrated by established modeling tools such as Together ControlCenter and IBM's Rational

Rose. The greatest challenge for MDA-compliant tool vendors lies in the transformation of PIM to PSM.

In conventional development without MDA, the architect instructs the project team on how a PIM is to be rendered as an executable design. The architect may decide to implement the system's Web application component using the Apache Struts framework instead of Java Server-Faces. Likewise, the architect may make the call to construct the persistence layer using Hibernate rather than entity beans.

> *Hibernate and entity beans are discussed in Chapter 7.*

The architect's decisions are not simply a list of frameworks and technologies. The architect may elect to access the persistence layer via the use of the *Data Access Object* pattern, with *Values Objects* returned to the client application through a *Session Façade*.

These architectural directions, and many more, must all be applied by the design team in order to take a PIM to the point where it can be built as a working solution. For the MDA tool to go from PIM to PSM, it too must follow the same directions. This is a highly complex task with which even the best architects and designers still struggle.

The MDA approach states the transformation process can be manual, but the true benefits of MDA are only realized if this process can be automated by the use of software tools. In this regard, an MDA tool could be regarded as a form of expert system, because the process is one of applying the knowledge and skill of the experienced architect to the mapping problem.

> *An overview of expert systems is provided in Chapter 10.*

MDA tool vendors find themselves in the position of not only developing products capable of accurately performing this mapping, but also having to convince skeptical developers that such an approach is feasible. They must sell the concepts as well as the benefits of MDA against those of existing model-centric processes.

# MDA Versus Traditional Modeling

Modeling tools such as Together ControlCenter and Gentleware's Poseidon enable the software engineer to use UML models to develop software applications. A question that commonly arises is how development processes centered on the use of tools such as these differ from an MDA development approach.

The similarities between the two approaches are not immediately apparent. Both look to leverage the power of modeling techniques to drive the development process, and the toolsets of each approach take time to learn. Moreover, neither claims to be an ease-of-use layer on top of J2EE. For each approach, strong technical knowledge and design skills are still a prerequisite as they are with traditional approaches.

Nevertheless, differences between MDA and other model-driven development methods do exist. The next sections highlight these differences by looking at the strengths and weaknesses of MDA for software development.

# Strengths

The defining difference between the two approaches comes down to the level of abstraction employed. MDA leverages the power of high-level PIMs to drive the development process. This higher level of working gives MDA fundamental advantages over conventional, technology-specific modeling processes.

## Business Focused

The construction of a platform-independent domain model is not exclusive to the MDA paradigm. Domain models are commonly constructed at the outset of any model-centric approach.

Traditional modeling methods rely on the business model to establish an understanding of the problem domain with the customer. The architect uses the requirements captured in this early model to build a PSM, which can be readily converted into code by most modeling tools.

The construction of the PSM is a skilled and time-consuming task. Before the modeling tool can generate a functioning system, the design team must have defined a detailed PSM.

The modeling tool generates a system from the PSM, but it does not assist in the transformation of business requirements into a functioning system. Consequently, the architect finds his or her attention diverted away from the critical business needs of the customer, and instead becomes focused on the technical challenges of implementing a solution for a specific platform.

The need for the architect to design a PSM is a distraction that can result in the initial business model being neglected. Using conventional modeling tools, the PSM becomes the main focal point of the development effort.

MDA forces the architect to concentrate on the domain model, or PIM, first and regards the PSM as a stepping-stone on the way to a working application. The use of the PIM to drive the development process keeps the focus on the customer requirements and not on the implementation platform.

## Supports an Incremental Development Process

An MDA-compliant tool can convert a business model into a functioning application at the click of a button, with mapping rules filling in the gaps for the missing infrastructure required by the target platform. Admittedly, the generated system will be very raw and most likely lacking in critical business functionality. However, the generated application provides a solid foundation on which to build further functionality.

This ability to jump from business model to demonstrable application is perfectly suited to development processes founded upon short, incremental, iterative cycles. In this way, a working prototype can be constructed from a minimal model in an incredibly short timeframe. This type of development process has proven benefits, not just for rapidity but also for building systems that accurately meet the needs of the customer.

## Leveraging Change

Traditional modeling tools provide a one-to-one mapping with the application code. Change a property on a class in a UML class diagram, and a single Java class is affected. Some model changes have no effect on the generated code. Switching an association between composition and aggregation, for example, is unlikely to result in any change to Java source.

With an MDA-compliant tool, a change in the PIM results in widespread change in the generated application. An update to a business entity in a PIM ripples through all layers of the architecture. The DDL generated for creating database tables changes; objects in the persistence layer change; business components change; and any corresponding Web application components change.

This ability to make sweeping and consistent application changes with a small modification to a conceptual model is a powerful feature of MDA tools, enabling customer requirement changes to be effected extremely rapidly.

## Fewer Application Defects

A high percentage of defects found in application code are a result of code errors as opposed to incorrectly specified requirements. By using best-practice software generation methods in the mapping from PIM to PSM, the overall risk of code errors being introduced is significantly reduced.

## Technology portability

Java is a crossplatform development language, which raises the question, Why would a paradigm whose focus is on platform independence be of relevance to anyone building J2EE solutions? The answer lies in the interpretation of the term *platform*.

J2EE is a constantly evolving platform. A search of the Java Community Process site at http://jcp.org is testament to the rapid rate of change Java technologies continually undergo.

A high-profile example is the EJB 3.0 specification, as defined by JSR-220, which has switched the focus of Enterprise JavaBeans from heavyweight components to lightweight POJOs, requiring minimal boilerplate code for deployment into the EJB container. Keeping pace with this change, and thereby keeping a system current, is an ongoing battle.

MDA, with its use of models to describe systems using platform-neutral semantics, can help extend the life of a system by ensuring the long-lived business functionality endures beyond the shorter-lived platform technology.

The MDA paradigm can make us more adaptive in relation to these fast-paced technology changes. For software engineers, MDA reduces the cost of change, making it possible to adopt emerging Java-based technologies without requiring prohibitively expensive application upgrades.

This is a good thing for any system, as it helps ward off the unwanted label *legacy application*.

## Weaknesses

Powerful as the MDA paradigm appears to be, it is not without an Achilles' heel. Some of the weaknesses in the paradigm are as follows.

### Working with Legacy Systems

One area where MDA tools fall behind their conventional modeling counterparts is in working with existing applications and data structures. Modeling tools can reverse-engineer applications into model form. However, as code is a representation of the system implemented on a specific platform, the models these tools build are all platform-specific. They do not reverse-engineer to the level of the PIM.

Mapping from PSM to PIM is complex and hard to automate. Most MDA tools focus their efforts on mapping from PIM to PSM. Consequently, anyone looking to reverse-engineer to a PIM in order to use an MDA approach has a hard task. The MDA standard specifies a mapping from PSM to PIM; currently, however, few tools can satisfactorily demonstrate this particular mapping.

Even if a PIM is produced for an existing system, problems still face the MDA practitioner. The power of an MDA tool to effect sweeping changes in the application code by a small change to the PIM is likely to prove too intrusive on the underlying application. It is akin to using a chainsaw where a scalpel is required.

Due to the technical challenges involved in mapping back to a PIM, traditional modeling methods are likely to prove more effective when extending or working with existing applications and data structures. Although an MDA approach should not be ruled out, a modeling tool is likely to prove the more effective software tool in this scenario, because it enables the architect to make small, strategic changes to what might be a fragile architecture.

### Viability

In theory, MDA is the ultimate solution for rapid development. Produce an accurate, high-level model of the system requirements, press a button, and generate the system. In practice, though, the million-dollar question is, does it work?

The approach sounds both simple and obvious, but then, you could also state that the obvious method to reduce the traveling time between New York and London is to use technology that supports instantaneous teleportation. While the idea may sound good on paper, and it is possible to produce a long list of benefits for using teleportation technology over a commercial airline, making the concept a reality is another matter entirely.

Mapping from PIM to PSM is a difficult task. Ordinarily, this is a challenging task for a skilled design team; successfully automating the process has to be harder still.

It is in this critical area that opponents of MDA claim the paradigm falls down. MDA opponents argue the current state of the technology is not yet at a stage where a quality application can be produced without intervention from a skilled software engineer.

Despite this claim, tools are available that claim to be MDA-compliant. Moreover, the OMG proudly lists a growing number of MDA success stories on its Web site at `http://www.omg.org/mda/products_success.htm`.

The best way to establish the truth is to judge for ourselves by looking at a current MDA tool and analyzing how it addresses the problems inherent in mapping between models.

# MDA Compliant Tools

The list of commercially available MDA-compliant tools is a short but growing list. Two of the market leaders are *OptimalJ* from Compuware Corporation and *ArcStyler* from Interactive Objects Software. Both products are sophisticated, enterprise-level MDA offerings pursuing the MDA vision for the next generation of software development tools.

A trial version of OptimalJ Professional Edition is available from the Compuware Web site at `http://www.compuware.com`. A community edition of ArcStyler can be downloaded from `http://www.io-software.com`.

Although both tools support platforms other than J2EE, it is interesting that both have a Java bias. This is a common trend: Java is supported by more code generators than any other language. It would be nice to believe this fact is a result of the willingness of the Java community to embrace cutting-edge software engineering methods, though skeptics might argue it is a sign of serious shortcomings in both Java and J2EE.

In keeping with the stated preference for using software that is freely available to demonstrate the concepts discussed within this book, we use the services of an open source MDA tool.

## Introducing AndroMDA

It is perhaps an indication of the growing acceptance of the viability of MDA that an open source MDA product has emerged. *AndroMDA*, pronounced *Andromeda*, is the product of considerable hard work by its founder, Matthias Bohlen, and his dedicated team of contributors.

Matthias's first release of the tool went under the name of *UML2EJB* and focused on generating EJB from UML models. The success of the tool prompted a widening of scope, and the development team moved away from pure EJB generation toward an MDA-compliant tool. The result of their efforts was a revamped UML2EJB, subsequently renamed AndroMDA to reflect its MDA approach.

AndroMDA is freely available for download from the product's Web site: `http://www.andromda.org`. Full instructions for installing and running AndroMDA come with the software.

The AndroMDA distribution also includes a complete example that can be deployed into the *JBoss* application server. Rather than walk through a similar example, we look under the hood of AndroMDA to see how the product transforms models into code. This information will help familiarize you with the product and provide an insight into how AndoMDA can be customized to perform your own PIM-to-PSM mappings.

# MDA with AndroMDA

Compared to the slick commercial MDA products, AndroMDA offers a *nuts-and-bolts* approach to practicing MDA. It provides no form of visual development environment, instead initiating the entire MDA process using an Ant build file.

It may seem strange that a tool proclaiming to support MDA should have no means of visually building a PIM. This is in stark contrast to products like OptimalJ that offer a complete integrated MDA development environment with support for building the initial model through to editing, deploying, and debugging the generated application. In this regard, OptimalJ rates as a complete MDA implementation.

Due to the wide scope of the MDA domain, the MDA standard states MDA can be practiced using a federated collection of tools, each supporting a specific aspect of the process. For example, a tool may focus on support for mapping from PIM to PSM, while another generates code from the PSM. MDA makes this approach possible by ensuring models are shareable between tools.

AndroMDA relies on a suitable modeling tool to first generate the PIM from which it can start the code generation process. AndroMDA generates a working application with the template engine Velocity and the attribute-oriented programming product XDoclet.

> *Chapter 6 covers both Velocity and XDoclet.*

Figure 8–2 provides an overview of MDA with AndroMDA.

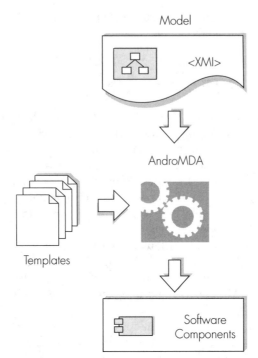

Model

<XMI>

AndroMDA

Templates

Software
Components

**Figure 8–2**    Code generation with AndroMDA.

Moving from PIM to working application with AndroMDA involves a number of steps:

1. A PIM is generated using a modeling tool capable of exporting the model in XML Metadata Interchange (*XMI*) *format*.

2. AndroMDA imports the PIM and builds an in-memory representation of the model.

3. Configurations settings in the Ant build file used to invoke AndroMDA define pluggable *MDA cartridges* that provide a mapping between the PIM and the working application.

4. The MDA cartridges associate special identifiers in the object model, known as *marks*, with *templates* that generate code from the model.

5. Depending on the MDA cartridges installed, where necessary, AndroMDA may generate customizable implementation classes that can be modified by the developer to add functionality to the generated application.

6. To conclude the process, all generated code is compiled and deployed into the target environment.

note

> Notice in Figure 8–2 that AndroMDA foregoes the mapping to a PSM and instead goes directly to the implementation model. This direct transformation from PIM to code is a valid MDA approach and complies with the MDA standard.

Commercial MDA tools such as OptimalJ support the generation of a PSM. Generating a PSM allows the architect to further refine the PSM and so gives greater control over the application generated. AndroMDA users must rely on the pluggable MDA cartridges to produce suitable output. However, refinement of the model is possible under AndroMDA by modifying the templates used by the relevant MDA cartridges.

The steps outlined introduce several new MDA concepts, such as *marks* and *cartridges*, which warrant further explanation.

## Model Interchange with XMI

AndroMDA uses the XMI specification for importing models built with a modeling tool. XMI is another OMG standard that, along with standards such as UML and MOF, has been bundled under the MDA umbrella.

Unfortunately, while XMI is a standard for model interchange, like ice cream, it comes in many different flavors. In practice, these different flavors, or dialects, virtually negate the benefits of the XMI standard, because different dialects raise compatibility issues between modeling tools. This situation is at odds with the MDA concept of sharing models between tools.

Due to this confusion over the XMI format, you may find you cannot use your favorite modeling tool for generating a model that can be imported into AndroMDA. To avoid this problem, you can use a modeling tool the AndroMDA team states is compliant with an XMI dialect AndroMDA expects. One such product that has close ties with AndroMDA is *Poseidon* from Gentleware, a commercial spinoff from the open source modeling tool *ArgoUML*. A community edition of this product is available from the Gentleware Web site at http://www.gentleware.com. The community edition offers a good feature set and supports the exporting of models as XMI.

An AndroMDA plug-in has been developed for Poseidon that integrates the two products and enables AndroMDA to access a Poseidon model in its native format. Full details of this plug-in are available from the Gentleware and AndroMDA sites.

If Poseidon is not to your liking, *MagicDraw* from No Magic is also recommended. A community edition of MagicDraw is obtainable from http://www.magicdraw.com.

## PIM Marks

Despite the richness of information conveyable by a UML model, tools that perform the mapping between PIM and PSM often require some direction as to how a mapping should be performed. The MDA standard provides several guidelines for the mapping process, one of which is the use of *marks*.

Marks identify those elements within a PIM that must be transformed with a predetermined set of transformation rules. The marks themselves can be from a variety of UML-compliant sources, including:

* Type information for model elements such as classes or associations
* Specific roles within the model
* Stereotypes

The use of stereotypes is one of the more common approaches to marking the PIM, and this is the method used by AndroMDA.

Stereotypes, a concept from the UML, are a means of extending the UML. They enable model elements to be embellished with additional values, constraints, and if required, a new graphical representation. Essentially, they serve as metaclasses within the UML. Declaring a model element to be of a particular stereotype causes the element to take on the full list of characteristics associated with the stereotype.

The UML notation has the name of the stereotype enclosed within *guillemets*, or chevrons. Perhaps the stereotype with which most people are familiar is the <<interface>> stereotype. Although Java supports the use of interfaces through a reserved keyword, other languages do not, and the UML relies on a specialized form of the `class` type to represent elements with this behavior. The <<interface>> stereotype expresses the constraint that all methods of the class are abstract. The stereotype further allows UML tools to render classes of this type using a circle for the notation instead of the classic rectangle.

The <<interface>> stereotype is already well used by the code generation facilities of most modeling tools. Such tools know how to generate Java interfaces from elements expressing this stereotype instead of generating Java classes.

We can declare stereotypes for our models as we wish and have the MDA tool map them accordingly. Figure 8–3, drawn using MagicDraw, depicts a simple class diagram showing stereotypes known to AndroMDA. Table 8–1 summarizes the stereotypes used in the example model. These stereotypes are used during code generation to direct output.

The PIM shown in Figure 8–3 has a stereotype for each class. Adding the stereotype <<Service>> to `CustomerService` marks the class as being a provider of some form of business service. In a PIM, we are unconcerned with how the customer service is represented in the final system. Likely, implementation options include a Web Service, an enterprise bean, or even an RMI object.

A stereotype of <<Entity>>, as shown on the `Customer` class, indicates some form of domain model object, which requires persistence. Again, how this persistence is implemented is the concern of the transformation process. The modeler defers the decision as to whether technologies such as entity beans, JDO, or an O/R mapping product like Hibernate will be used. Although this model is supposed to be platform-neutral, admittedly the operation `findByCustomerID()` has distinct EJB architecture overtones.

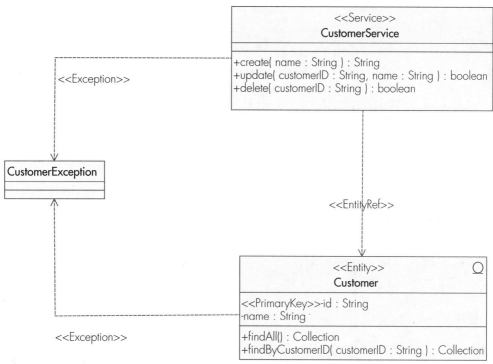

**Figure 8-3**   PIM with AndroMDA-compliant stereotype marks.

Not only the classes but also the associations and operations in the diagram have been marked. The dependency association between CustomerService and Customer carries a stereotype of <<EntityRef>>. Likewise, the attribute id has been stereotyped with <<PrimaryKey>>. All of this metainformation is used by AndroMDA to determine the architecture of the application generated.

**Table 8-1**   AndroMDA Stereotypes

| Stereotype | Description |
| --- | --- |
| <<Entity>> | Denotes an object in the business domain. |
| <<Service>> | Identifies a class that acts on domain objects. |
| <<PrimaryKey>> | Unique identifier for persistent domain object. |
| <<FinderMethod>> | Method to query for domain object from persistent store. |
| <<EntityRef>><br><<ServiceRef>> | Identifies relationship between classes that MDA cartridge must be aware of. |

**Table 8–1**    AndroMDA Stereotypes (continued)

| Stereotype | Description |
|---|---|
| <<Exception>> | Denotes an exception that must be thrown by all business methods of a dependent class. |
| <<WebAction>> | Maps to the *controller* part of a Web application using the model-view-controller paradigm. |
| <<WebAppConfig>> | Web application configuration object. |
| <<WebForm>> | Maps to the *model* part of a Web application using the model-view-controller paradigm. |
| <<WebPage>> | Maps to the *view* part of a Web application using the model-view-controller paradigm. |

Next, we examine how AndroMDA transforms model elements into code based on their stereotype.

## MDA Cartridges

AndroMDA code generation is driven by stereotypes. Stereotyped elements in a PIM are mapped to code using pluggable code generation *cartridges,* with cartridges existing to specify the transformation rules for each AndroMDA stereotype.

We saw a similar approach used with Middlegen, albeit without the use of stereotypes. Middlegen allows different persistence mechanisms to be supported with plug-ins. Our example used the Hibernate plug-in to generate Hibernate configuration files based on metadata retrieved from the database. Other Middlegen plug-ins exist for entity beans and JDO. Middlegen delegates the task of generating code to its plug-ins. Middlegen itself takes responsibility for interrogating the database for the necessary metadata, supplying this information to all plug-ins configured from the Ant build file.

> *Middlegen is covered in Chapter 7.*

AndroMDA plays a similar role to Middlegen, except AndroMDA obtains its metadata from a UML model instead of the database. An AndroMDA cartridge is similar to a Middlegen plug-in insofar as they both generate code from metadata.

Four cartridges come complete with the AndroMDA distribution:

**andromda-ejb.**

This cartridge generates a persistence layer using entity beans with session beans acting as a *Session Façade* over the persistence layer.

### andromda-hibernate.

Like Middlegen, AndroMDA provides a cartridge for building a persistence layer using the Hibernate O/R mapping tool. With the Hibernate cartridge, Java classes are generated with embedded Hibernate XDoclet tags. Session beans are also laid down over the Hibernate based persistence layer.

### andromda-java.

This is the simplest of the four cartridges and generates *Value/Transfer Objects.*

### andromda-struts.

No system is complete without a Web front end. The `andromda-struts` cartridge generates all the files necessary for a Web application based on the Apache Struts framework.

The AndroMDA core searches the classpath to locate any installed cartridges. Model elements that have a known AndroMDA stereotype are passed to each cartridge discovered on the classpath.

Cartridges are configured under the <andromda> Ant task. This task points AndroMDA at a PIM and specifies those cartridges used for generating the application. Listing 8–1 shows a section taken from an Ant build file of a build configuration using the `andromda-struts` cartridge.

## Listing 8–1   AndroMDA Build File

```
<andromda basedir="."
          modelURL="${model}.xmi"
          lastModifiedCheck="true"
          typeMappings="${andromda}/src/xml/TypeMapping.xml">

  <userProperty name="foreignKeySuffix" value="_FK" />

  <outlet cartridge="java"
          outlet="value-objects"
          dir="${gen.dir}" />

  <outlet cartridge="hibernate"
          outlet="entities"
          dir="${gen.dir}" />

  <outlet cartridge="hibernate"
          outlet="entity-impls"
          dir="${impl.dir}" />

  <outlet cartridge="hibernate"
          outlet="session-beans"
          dir="${gen.dir}" />

  <outlet cartridge="hibernate"
          outlet="session-impls"
          dir="${impl.dir}" />

</andromda>
```

The nested element `<outlet>` configures the location of all source generated by each cartridge's outlet. An outlet is essentially a template defined within the MDA cartridge. We look at the function of outlets in the next section. Each cartridge is referred to by its name, as specified using the `cartridge` attribute, with the `outlet` attribute identifying the outlet within the cartridge.

The ability to direct generated source to different locations is important, as some generated classes are intended to be modified by the developer. This fits in with the code generation guideline of separating actively generated code from code maintained by hand.

In the next section, we deconstruct the anatomy of an AndroMDA cartridge to determine how it generates code from a UML model.

## Anatomy of a Cartridge

Cartridges enable a stereotype to be married to a template. AndroMDA uses the Apache Velocity as its template engine, making the task of building a cartridge simple for anyone familiar with the Velocity Template Language (VTL).

> *For a summary of VTL commands, see Chapter 6.*

The MDA standard states a mapping may include templates, which it describes as parameterized models for specifying a particular transformation. Templates offer a very powerful mapping mechanism and enable entire design patterns to be generated from a single mark in the PIM.

The secret to how a cartridge associates a stereotype with a Velocity template lies in the cartridge's deployment descriptor. Each AndroMDA cartridge must provide a deployment descriptor named `andromda-cartridge.xml` that resides under the META-INF directory in the jar file.

Listing 8–2 shows the deployment descriptor for the `andromda-hibernate` cartridge.

**Listing 8–2    AndroMDA Hibernate Cartridge Deployment Descriptor**

```
<cartridge name="hibernate">
  <property name="persistence" value="hibernate" />

  <stereotype name="Entity" />
  <stereotype name="Service" />

  <outlet name="entities" />
  <outlet name="entity-impls" />
  <outlet name="session-beans" />
  <outlet name="session-impls" />

  <template
    stereotype="Entity"
    sheet="templates/HibernateEntity.vsl"
```

```
    outputPattern="{0}/{1}.java"
    outlet="entities"
    overWrite="true"
  />

  <template
    stereotype="Entity"
    sheet="templates/HibernateEntityImpl.vsl"
    outputPattern="{0}/{1}Impl.java"
    outlet="entity-impls"
    overWrite="false"
  />

  <template
    stereotype="Entity"
    sheet="templates/HibernateEntityFactory.vsl"
    outputPattern="{0}/{1}Factory.java"
    outlet="entities"
    overWrite="true"
  />

  <template
    stereotype="Service"
    sheet="templates/HibernateSessionBean.vsl"
    outputPattern="{0}/{1}Bean.java"
    outlet="session-beans"
    overWrite="true"
  />

  <template
    stereotype="Service"
    sheet="templates/HibernateSessionBeanImpl.vsl"
    outputPattern="{0}/{1}BeanImpl.java"
    outlet="session-impls"
    overWrite="false"
  />

</cartridge>
```

The first clue to how the AndroMDA core triggers a cartridge is with the `<stereotype>` elements:

```
<stereotype name="Entity" />
<stereotype name="Service" />
```

These two lines associate the cartridge with model elements bearing the stereotypes of <<Entity>> and <<Service>>. The cartridge generates code for model elements based on either of these two stereotypes using a template. AndroMDA allows multiple template types to be associated with a single stereotype, thus several templates can be used in generating the code for a single model element.

The `<template>` element maps stereotypes to templates:

```
<template
    stereotype="Entity"
    sheet="templates/HibernateEntity.vsl"
    outputPattern="{0}/{1}.java"
    outlet="entities"
    overWrite="true"
/>
```

The `stereotype` attribute declares the stereotype being mapped, while the `sheet` attribute points AndroMDA at the Velocity template for code generation. Templates are bundled as part of the cartridge jar file, and along with the deployment descriptor, are all that is required for a valid cartridge.

The `outlet` attribute links the template to the `<outlet>` custom Ant task specified under the `<andromda>` task in the Ant build file. This setting informs the Velocity engine of the location of all output generated with the template.

The `overWrite` attribute enables AndroMDA to differentiate between code that is actively generated and code that is modified by the developer. For classes where the developer adds business functionality, setting the `overWrite` attribute to false ensures modified code will not be overwritten each time AndroMDA is run.

## Cartridge Templates

The final part of a cartridge is the Velocity templates referenced in the deployment descriptor. These templates perform the mapping from the UML model to code. The AndroMDA core makes available information on model elements to the template. This information can then be rendered as required with the VTL.

Table 8–2 lists the objects supplied by AndroMDA for use in the Velocity templates.

**Table 8–2**    AndroMDA VTL Scripting Objects

| Object | Description |
| --- | --- |
| `$model` | Holds the model imported via the XMI file in the form of a UML 1.4 model. |
| `$class` | Represents the UML model element from which code will be generated. |
| `$transform` | Helper object for transforming model objects into a printable form, thereby making them easier to use from VTL. |
| `$str` | Helper object for performing string formatting operations. |
| `$date` | The current date as a `java.util.Date`. |

To appreciate how these objects can be used from within a template, an extract of a template from the andromda-java cartridge is shown in Listing 8–3.

## Listing 8–3   Cartridge Template Extract from ValueObject.vsl

```
public class ${class.name} implements java.io.Serializable
{

#foreach ( $att in $class.attributes )
#set ($atttypename = $transform.findFullyQualifiedName($att.type))
    private $atttypename ${att.name};
#end
...

#foreach ( $att in $class.attributes )
#set ($atttypename =
    $transform.findFullyQualifiedName($att.type))
#if ( ($atttypename == "boolean") ||
    ($atttypename == "java.lang.Boolean") )
  /**
#generateDocumentation ($att "     ")
   *
   */
  public $atttypename
    is${str.upperCaseFirstLetter(${att.name})}()
  {
      return this.${att.name};
  }
#else
  /**
#generateDocumentation ($att "     ")
   *
   */
  public $atttypename
    get${str.upperCaseFirstLetter(${att.name})}()
  {
      return this.${att.name};
  }
#end

  public void
    set${str.upperCaseFirstLetter(
      ${att.name})}(${atttypename} newValue)
  {
      this.${att.name} = newValue;
  }

#end
}
```

The template example in Listing 8–3 illustrates the use of AndroMDA scripting objects to define the attributes in a Java class, complete with getter and setter methods. The template illustrates how easily information can be pulled from the model and transformed with a Velocity template.

By building your own cartridges or manipulating the cartridges AndroMDA supplies, all manner of transformations are possible from the model. Existing templates can be modified to meet your own coding standards, or you may add a template to the cartridge to generate unit tests for certain model elements.

AndroMDA makes it easy to create cartridges that can be tailored to the needs of your project. This extensibility makes AndroMDA a powerful model-driven code generation framework.

# AndroMDA Applied

The powerful and versatile code generation features of AndroMDA make it ideal for rapid development. As do most MDA-compliant tools, it has excellent potential for prototyping, since a nearly complete framework for the application can be generated very quickly. Furthermore, requirements changes can be readily reflected in the application by updating the model and regenerating.

As is the case with most MDA tools, the downsides of the paradigm also apply to AndroMDA; specifically, difficulties can arise when working with legacy systems.

Two questions are often asked concerning AndroMDA: Can the tool perform roundtrip engineering from source to model, and how does AndroMDA guard against overwriting hand-written code?

## Reverse Engineering the Model

You cannot reverse-engineer from code back to the model. Although this feature is expected of any high-end modeling tools, the MDA-compliant tools take a different approach to model-driven development than do modeling tools like Together ControlCenter.

Reverse engineering is a problem for MDA-compliant tools due to the difficulties inherent in transforming from a PSM to a PIM. To avoid the need to undertake this difficult mapping, MDA tools instead look to protect code modified by the developer, allowing the PIM to be changed and new code generated without overwriting any business logic added by the developer.

This brings us to the next question: If we are updating the PIM and regenerating each time, how are the business rules implemented in the code preserved between build cycles?

## Managing Handwritten Code

No matter how sophisticated the UML model, all MDA-generated applications of any real complexity will require further modification by a developer. Such modifications are required in order to add the all-important business rules to the application. It is therefore vital the MDA tool treats all handwritten code as sacrosanct and preserves the state of modified code between generation cycles.

The methods of safeguarding handwritten code vary between MDA tools. High-end tools such as OptimalJ have the concept of guard blocks, areas of code that the developer must not modify. By using the OptimalJ development environment, the OptimalJ code editor ensures this rule is followed. Any code modified outside of these guarded areas is preserved.

Tools like AndroMDA, which do not control the editing of Java source, must resort to other means. AndroMDA generates special implementation classes that are updated with application-specific behavior by the developer. When an AndroMDA build is next initiated, AndroMDA detects the presence of these classes and ensures they are not overwritten.

The implementation classes typically extend generated classes. A change to the UML model, which results in a change to the superclass of an implementation class, should be flagged as an error by the compiler. Although this approach leaves the developer with work to do in the event of a domain model change, no handwritten code is lost.

## AndroMDA 3.0

The information in this section applies to version 2.0 of AndroMDA. At the time of writing, Matthias and his team are hard at work on version 3.0. This new version looks to increase the sophistication of the transformation process and introduces several new features:

* A `bpm4struts` cartridge capable of generating Web-based workflows from UML activity diagrams
* Model validation at the time of code generation
* Pluggable template engines, giving options other than Velocity
* A new EJB cartridge able to support Java inheritance of abstract enterprise beans

Developers are invited to look in on the progress of the new version at `http://team.andromda.org`.

This site for version 3.0 looks very professional. If the quality of the site is backed up by the quality of the software, then the next version of AndroMDA will be worth waiting for.

Keep your eye on the AndroMDA Web site for all breaking news.

# Summary

MDA is touted as a potential revolution of the software development process, claiming improved developer productivity, reduced development timeframes, and higher quality software. All of these points make MDA worthy of consideration for anyone undertaking a rapid development project.

MDA technology is still improving, and the dream of fully executable UML models is still unrealized. Despite this, the current crop of MDA tools are well suited to the development of new applications and the generation of prototypes, making MDA products ideal for incremental development processes.

Where MDA tools are less effective is when working with existing systems or legacy data. In this scenario, conventional modeling tools are likely to prove a more productive option.

Regardless of whether you consider MDA a viable technology for software development, the use of AndroMDA to leverage the power of model-based software generation makes it a valuable tool to add to the enterprise software engineer's repertoire, even if it is used purely for prototype generation.

The next chapter moves on to domain-specific languages and looks at how languages other than Java can be applied to the development of enterprise systems.

## Additional Information

All of the OMG standards documents on MDA and its associated standards can be freely downloaded from the OMG Web site at http://www.omg.org. Current information on MDA is available from the same site at http://www.omg.org/mda.

The OMG also has a guide available to the MDA paradigm, at http://www.omg.org/docs/omg/03-06-01.pdf.

The AndroMDA team operates a mailing list for all discussions relating to the practice of MDA with AndroMDA. For help and advice on using AndroMDA, see http://sourceforge.net/mail/?group_id=73047 or try the newer "Tiki" at http://team.andromda.org/tiki/tiki-index.php.

# Part III: Rapid Languages

Programming languages are a software engineer's main building material. Java is the programming language for the J2EE platform, but alternative programming languages and paradigms exist that can complement Java's object-oriented semantics. In Part III, we examine some of these alternatives from the perspective of the advantages they provide for rapid development.

The topics covered include the use of scripting languages for undertaking the many and varied tasks that make up an enterprise project; rule-based languages for defining complex and dynamic business logic; and the benefits of aspect-oriented programming for producing highly maintainable software and as a means of effecting rapid changes to an application's entire code base.

# 9

# Scripting

Scripting languages are the software engineering equivalent of duct tape. Their powerful and expressive syntax makes them ideal for all of those extraneous ad hoc tasks associated with software development. Batch jobs, small utility tools, automated build processes, and throwaway prototypes are all suitable candidates for the use of a scripting language.

This chapter examines the benefits of using scripting languages on enterprise projects and introduces Jython, a Java implementation of the popular scripting language Python, which is tightly integrated with the Java platform.

## Why Use a Scripting Language?

A computer language is akin to a tool in the toolbox of any tradesman. Each tool is designed for a specific task, be it a hammer, a screwdriver, or wrench. Tools are an aid to productivity, but you only get the benefits of the tool by using it for the right task; hammers bang in nails and screwdrivers are for screws.

The same toolbox concept applies to software engineering. The choice of programming language for undertaking a specific task has a bearing on the developer's productivity.

Java is obviously the main language on any J2EE project. Nevertheless, introducing concepts and language constructs from other programming paradigms can help when tackling areas of functionality to which Java is not ideally suited.

Java is a strongly and statically typed programming language. By contrast, scripting languages tend to be weakly typed and highly dynamic.

Strong typing is important for production systems, as the compiler scrupulously checks for any unintended type conversions, raising them as an error before the system is even run.

Mission-critical systems, such as military software and air-traffic-control systems tend to use *Ada*, a language developed by the Department of Defense that is considerably more stringent on type safety than Java. For these systems, the presence of an undetected defect could have lethal consequences.

Type safety is therefore a mechanism for assisting in the development of reliable and robust software, and it is an important language feature for any software that requires high levels of reliability.

However, not all software developed on an enterprise project falls into this category, and there are many extraneous tasks surrounding the development of the main application for which less scrupulous languages are better suited. This is where scripting languages enter the picture.

Here are some examples of these additional project tasks that can benefit from the use of a scripting language:

- Exploratory prototyping of user interfaces
- Writing code generators
- Writing automated test scripts
- Controlling batch jobs
- Generating ad hoc reports
- Automating build and release procedures

The next section considers the features of a language that make it well suited for scripting purposes.

# Features of a Scripting Language

Scripting languages lack the formal semantics of conventional languages like Java. They are loosely typed and highly dynamic, two features which make them ideal for noncritical project tasks.

The main features of a scripting language include

- High level and informal language constructs
- Expressive syntax
- Loose typing
- Interpreted as opposed to compiled

Over the years, the software industry has spawned a large number of languages that exhibit these features, a testimony to the benefits of scripting languages. There are many well-known and highly regarded examples:

- Python
- Perl
- Ruby
- Tcl

The biggest question facing a J2EE project team is which language to choose. The following lists some points to consider when making the choice. Does the language

- Complement the experience of the project team?
- Offer crossplatform support?
- Integrate with Java, allowing access to existing Java classes?

In addition to these points, characteristics such as the language's maturity, performance, and quality must also be considered.

## Team Experience

With a number of languages to choose from, looking to assess the expertise of members of the team with a particular scripting language is an important consideration. Although offering powerful language constructs and informal semantics, scripting languages are not easy to learn. They employ many concepts that are not available in Java, meaning training time must be set aside to bring a developer up to speed.

tip

> If the team is skilled in a language such as Python, then adopting Jython, the Java equivalent, is one way of leveraging that previous Python experience.

Investment in the education of a team in a particular scripting language should be part of a company's wider adaptive foundation for rapid development. Standardization on a common scripting language across project teams allows the sharing of scripts and modules between groups. Staff will also be available in a mentoring role for projects using the scripting language for the first time.

## Crossplatform

Not all of the main scripting languages are crossplatform. Scripts can be migrated between machines with different operating systems and architectures only if an interpreter for the language exists for the target platform.

Java offers crossplatform support, and it would be preferable if a scripting language were available that offered the same capability. Language builders have addressed this problem by developing scripting languages that execute under a Java Virtual Machine (JVM). Thus, the language is supported on any platform that can host a JVM.

Several languages are available that fall into this category. Table 9–1 lists some of the open source offerings.

**Table 9-1**    Scripting Languages for the Java Platform

| Name | Description | Reference |
| --- | --- | --- |
| Groovy | New language that combines many popular features from languages such as Smalltalk, Python, and Ruby | http://groovy.codehaus.org/ |
| Jacl | Jacl (pronounced *Jackal*), or the Java Command Language, is a Java implementation of the Tcl scripting language | http://www.scriptics.com/software/java/ |
| JRuby | Java implementation of the popular Ruby scripting language | http://sourceforge.net/projects/jruby |
| Jython | Java version of the object-oriented scripting language Python | http://www.jython.org |
| Rhino | A JavaScript interpreter written entirely in Java | http://www.mozilla.org/rhino/ |

Several of the JVM scripting languages are implementations of popular scripting languages; for example, *Jython* brings Python to the Java platform, and *JRuby* is a Ruby implementation. Other languages, such as *Groovy*, have been created specifically for the Java platform.

## Integration with Java Classes

For tasks such as writing ad hoc reports, producing automated test cases, or building user-interface prototypes, the scripting language must have the ability to work directly with Java objects.

This is the main reason for choosing a Java-based scripting language over one of the established languages. Without Java integration, many common scripting tasks are far more cumbersome, thereby negating the use of the scripting language.

To appreciate the relationship between scripting language and Java, the next section introduces Jython, a scripting language that is tightly integrated with the Java platform.

# Introducing Jython

Jython is a pure Java implementation of the popular scripting language Python. Implemented entirely in Java, Jython runs under any compliant JVM. For its part, Python is a high-level, dynamic, object-oriented scripting language that has enjoyed considerable popularity with developers from all disciplines of software engineering.

The features of the Python language enable the writing of scripts that are far shorter than the equivalent code implemented in Java. The features of the Python language include the following:

- Support for high-level data types, making it possible to express complex operations in a single statement
- Loose typing, so variables do not have to be declared before they are used
- A syntax that does not rely on curly braces or semicolons, instead using indentation to group statements and newline characters for delineating statements

This melding of the J2SE platform and Python has resulted in an exciting symbiosis. Jython harnesses the strength of the Python scripting language and offers crossplatform capabilities by virtue of the JVM under which it runs. Jython is also designed to integrate with Java, making it possible to access Java classes from within a script. Consequently, developers have the best of both worlds: access to the full services of the J2SE platform as well as the extensive set of libraries Python encompasses.

Jython's features include the following:

### Portability.

Jython code executes on any platform that supports a compliant JVM.

### 100% Java.

Anything you can do with Java, you can do with Jython. This includes the development of applets, GUIs, and J2EE components such as servlets. The only difference is that in Jython you'll do it with fewer lines of code, albeit at the expense of type safety. You can also mix and match classes between the two languages. This includes being able to subclass classes defined in Java from Jython, and vice versa.

### Interpreted and compiled.

As with most scripting languages, Jython code is interpreted. Although interpreting a language does incur a cost in terms of performance, the approach allows for changes to the code to be quickly applied and tested, thus avoiding the overhead of lengthy build cycles. Despite the decreased runtime performance, interpreting code offers better productivity gains over that of compilation. However, in this regard, Jython provides a bytecode compiler for converting certain Jython classes into *.class* files.

### Embedded.

As well as being able to share classes with Java, Jython code can be embedded within Java programs. In this way, it is possible to have Jython code execute from within a Java application in much the same way as embedded SQL.

### Object-oriented.

The Python language supports object-oriented language constructs such as classes and inheritance. The language is actually multiparadigm and provides procedural language semantics, including functions and global variables.

In the next sections, we cover the major points regarding Jython and the Jython scripting language:

- Installing and running the Jython interpreter
- The basics of the Jython language
- Using a Java class from within a Jython module
- Building a user interface using Swing components
- Writing and deploying a servlet written as a Jython script

The first step is to download and install Jython.

## Installing Jython

Jython, along with a comprehensive set of documentation, is available for download from `http://www.jython.org`. The site details the installation steps and provides a few basic tutorials.

Note that Jython initially started out in life as *JPython*. The *P* has since been dropped in order to sidestep some tricky licensing issues. Jython is open source and available for free download and use. Nevertheless, as is the case with all software used within this book, you should carefully read the licensing terms before using any of the software covered.

### documentation

> The Jython site contains information that specifically relates to Jython, and not the Python language. For extensive documentation on the Python syntax, including a library reference and complete tutorial, visit the Python Web site at `http://www.python.org`.

## Running Scripts

There are several ways to execute Jython scripts. Starting the Jython interpreter in *interactive mode* allows Jython statements to be entered and executed directly from the Jython shell.

Launch the Jython interpreter using the appropriate command file found in the `bin` directory of the Jython installation. On a Windows platform, this is `jython.bat`.

Entering `jython.bat` at a command prompt starts Jython in interactive mode.

```
Jython 2.1 on java1.4.1_02 (JIT: null)
Type "copyright", "credits" or "license" for more information.
>>> x = 1
>>> if x:
...    print 'Hello World'
...
Hello World
>>>
```

The interpreter accepts commands at the *primary prompt*, identified by the three greater-than signs: >>>. The *secondary prompt* accepts continuation commands and is identified by three dots: . . . .

Jython also executes Jython statements as scripts and exits the interpreter on completion. Jython script files typically have an extension of *.py*, and are submitted to the Jython interpreter for execution from the command line:

```
jython myscript.py
```

Now that we know how to run Jython programs and execute Jython statements, let's examine the rudimentary elements of the Jython language.

## The Jython Language

To appreciate the brevity of the Jython syntax, we look at a complete example that demonstrates reading from a file. Manipulating files and file contents is a common use for scripting languages, so it is a good place to start. Here, the code opens a text file and displays the length of each word within the file.

```
f=open('sample.txt')

for word in f.read().split():
  print word, len(word)

f.close()
```

The code shown isn't a code snippet; it is a complete example. Firing up the Jython interpreter and entering the above statements gives the following output:

```
Monty 5
Python's 8
Flying 6
Circus 6
```

Notice that it isn't necessary to define a class or even a main method. Furthermore, Jython's type-less syntax means the example is devoid of any type declarations, keeping the code very succinct. Statements are also grouped by indentation and not by curly braces, as in Java, thereby keeping the script short and concise.

note

Python isn't named after a snake but after the famous BBC comedy *Monty Python's Flying Circus.*

The file parsing example relies on Jython's intrinsic support for *compound data types* such as lists and maps. The `strip()` function in the example transforms the contents of the file from a string to a list. The `for` statement then iterates over the elements of the list.

List processing is a powerful concept in Jython, making for a highly expressive syntax. Defining both lists and maps in Jython is very easy. Note Jython uses the term *dictionary* for lists that hold key/value pairs.

```
list = ['The', 'Life', 'of', 'Brian']
map = {10: 'The', 20:'Meaning', 30:'of', 40:'Life'}
```

The same declarations in Java are slightly more verbose:

```
List list = new LinkedList();
list.add("The");
list.add("Life");
list.add("of");
list.add("Brian");

Map map = new HashMap();
map.put(new Integer(10), "The");
map.put(new Integer(20), "Meaning");
map.put(new Integer(30), "of");
map.put(new Integer(40), "Life");
```

Jython wouldn't be object-oriented without the ability to define classes. Here is a class declaration of type `Customer`, with methods `update()` and `total()`.

```
# Customer class declaration
#
class Customer:

  def update(self, value):
    self.amount = value

  def total(self):
    return self.amount
```

The `def` keyword defines a function or method. The `self` parameter is important because it represents the equivalent of the `this` reference in Java. Jython implicitly passes this reference each time a method on an instance of the object is called.

note

> Jython is not tied to the object-oriented paradigm, and unlike Java, allows the declaration of functions outside of the scope of a class.

Instantiating the `Customer` class uses another terse piece of syntax. Here is how to create an object and invoke its methods:

```
obj = Customer()    # Create Customer instance
obj.update(10)
print obj.total()
```

The first line creates an instance of the `Customer` class. Note that there is no requirement in Jython to use Java's equivalent of the `new` keyword or to define the type of the object being referenced by the `obj` variable. Jython only discovers whether the `update()` and `total()` methods actually exist on the `obj` reference when the interpreter attempts to execute those lines of code.

## Integration with Java

Now that you have been introduced to some of the basics of the Jython syntax, it's time to move onto something more interesting. Up until this point, all the examples could have been completed using Python, the scripting language on which Jython is based.

The advantage of choosing Jython over Python, or over alternative scripting languages such as Perl or Ruby, is the ability of Jython to integrate seamlessly with existing Java classes.

To demonstrate this integration capability, we create a standard Java class and use it from a Jython script. Listing 9–1 shows the `Person` class.

### Listing 9–1  Person Java Class Declaration

```java
public class Person {

  private String name;
  private int age;

  /**
   * Default constructor
   */
  public void Person() {
  }

  /*
   * Getter and setter methods for class properties
   */

  public int getAge() {
    return age;
  }
  public void setAge(int age) {
    this.age = age;
  }

  public String getName() {
```

```
    return name;
  }

  public void setName(String name) {
    this.name = name;
  }
}
```

Before the `Person` class can be accessed from within a Jython script, you must set the CLASS-PATH environment variable so Jython can find the new classes to load. Optionally, you may write an alternate Jython startup file that sets the classpath for the interpreter accordingly.

The following is a three-line script that creates and initializes an instance of the `Person` class and prints out its properties.

```
import Person

obj = Person(name = 'Bill', age = 20)

print obj.name, obj.age
```

The `import` statement pulls the `Person` module into the script's namespace. If the classpath is set incorrectly, Jython will report an error at this point.

Once the class is loaded into the script, an instance of the class is created. The syntax used to initialize the object is a shorthand form. On loading the class, Jython scans the class for common patterns and can recognize JavaBean-compliant getters and setters. Jython represents these methods as properties and allows them to be set through the constructor using the notation

```
Person(name = 'Bill', age = 20)
```

With an instance of the `Person` class created, the final line prints out the two properties name and age. Again, note the convenience of being able to use property notation rather than formal method semantics.

Like Java, Jython supports inheritance, making it possible for classes to derive from both other Jython classes and Java classes. Jython supports inheritance through the syntax

```
Class DerivedClass(BaseClass1, BaseClass2, BaseClassN):
```

From the syntax, you can see that Jython goes beyond Java's single inheritance and supports multiple inheritance. However, when Jython classes inherit from Java classes, only a single Java class can be included in the inheritance hierarchy of a Jython class.

Listing 9–2 shows a Jython script that has the `Customer` class extend the `Person` Java class. The integration between the two class types is seamless, with the `main` function accessing methods from both the superclass and the deriving `Customer` class.

## Listing 9–2    Script PersonDemo.py

```
# Import Person Java class
#
import Person

# Customer class declaration
#
class Customer(Person):

  def update(self, value):
    self.amount = value

  def total(self):
    return self.amount

# Main function
#
def main():
  # Create instance of Customer
  #
  obj = Customer(name = 'Bill', age = 20)

  # Using Customer properties
  #
  print obj.name, obj.age

  # Using Person methods
  #
  obj.update(99);
  print obj.total()


# Entry point for script
#
if __name__ == '__main__':
  main()
```

Now that we have introduced Jython's syntax and integration support for Java, the next sections provide examples of some uses for Jython scripts.

# User-Interface Prototyping

Scripting languages are ideal candidates for constructing exploratory prototypes of user interfaces. Using Jython's integration capabilities with Java enables the development of user-interface prototypes with familiar Java class libraries, such as AWT and Swing. Listing 9–3 illustrates a simple user interface written in Jython and using Swing classes.

### Listing 9–3   User-Interface Script listbox.py

```
import java.lang as lang
import javax.swing as swing
import java.awt as awt

def exit(event):
  lang.System.exit(0)

win = swing.JFrame("Jython Example", windowClosing=exit)
win.contentPane.layout = awt.GridLayout(2, 1)

win.contentPane.add(swing.JList(['Rapid','J2EE','Development']))
win.contentPane.add(swing.JButton('Close',actionPerformed=exit))

win.pack()
win.show()
```

The source file listbox.py can be executed directly from the command prompt by invoking jython listbox.py.

Figure 9–1 displays the output from the script.

Jython also makes a very good *glue* language. If server-side business components are already in place, Jython can serve as a rapid development language for building user interfaces that expose the underlying business services to the end users.

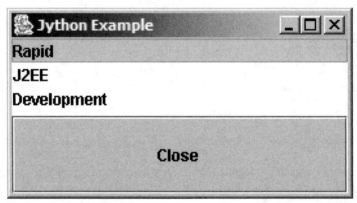

**Figure 9–1**   Output from listbox.py.

# Creating a Jython Servlet

The Jython installation provides a special servlet that loads and executes Jython scripts within a Web server's servlet engine. This handy utility allows servlets to be written and deployed as Jython scripts.

Servlets are ideal candidates for use in rapid prototyping. They are easily built and deployed, and can operate independently of the server's EJB container. Using Java, however, servlets still need to be compiled, deployed, and configured. This is not so for the Jython servlet script; it only needs to be deployed.

Listing 9–4 provides an example of a servlet implemented in Jython.

## Listing 9–4    Jython Servlet Script params.py

```
# params.py
import java, javax, sys

class params(http.HttpServlet):
  def doGet(self, request, response):
    response.setContentType("text/html")
    out = response.getWriter()

    out.println("<HTML>")
    out.println("<HEAD><TITLE>Jython Servlet Example</TITLE></HEAD>")
    out.println("<BODY>")

    out.println("<TABLE  BORDER=\"1\" WIDTH=\"100%\">")
    for name in request.headerNames:
      out.println("<TR><TD>" + name + "</TD>");
      out.println("<TD>" + request.getHeader(name) + "</TD></TR>")

    out.println("</TABLE>")
    out.println("</BODY></HTML>")
```

Running the servlet first requires configuring and deploying Jython's PyServlet. This servlet is responsible for loading and executing Jython scripts on the fly. The servlet is configured in the Web application's web.xml deployment descriptor, as shown in Listing 9–5.

## Listing 9–5    PyServlet Configuration in web.xml

```
<servlet>
  <servlet-name>pyservlet</servlet-name>
  <servlet-class>org.python.util.PyServlet</servlet-class>
</servlet>

<servlet-mapping>
  <servlet-name>pyservlet</servlet-name>
  <url-pattern>*.py</url-pattern>
</servlet-mapping>
```

You can test out the Jython servlet with a suitable servlet container such as Apache's Tomcat. First, create a new directory structure for the servlet under the `webapps` directory: `<TOMCAT_HOME>/webapps/<context>`. If necessary, copy one of the example Web applications that come with the Tomcat installation.

Modify the `web.xml` deployment descriptor so it contains an entry for `PyServlet`, as shown in Listing 9–5. You also need to copy `jython.jar` to the `lib` directory of the Web application: `<context>/WEB-INF/lib`. The `jython.jar` is needed to load the Jython interpreter. Alternatively, the servlet parameter `python.home` can be set, which specifies the location of the `jython.jar`. If this parameter is not defined in the deployment descriptor, `PyServlet` assumes `<context>/WEB-INF/lib` by default.

The final step is to copy the Jython script, in this case, `params.py`, into the newly created `<context>` directory structure. Start Tomcat and test the servlet by accessing

```
http://<host_name>:8080/<context>/params.py
```

Figure 9–2 shows the output from the servlet.

Jython is not the only scripting language to provide such good support for Java. Another scripting language worthy of consideration is Groovy, a Java-centric scripting language that is rapidly growing in popularity.

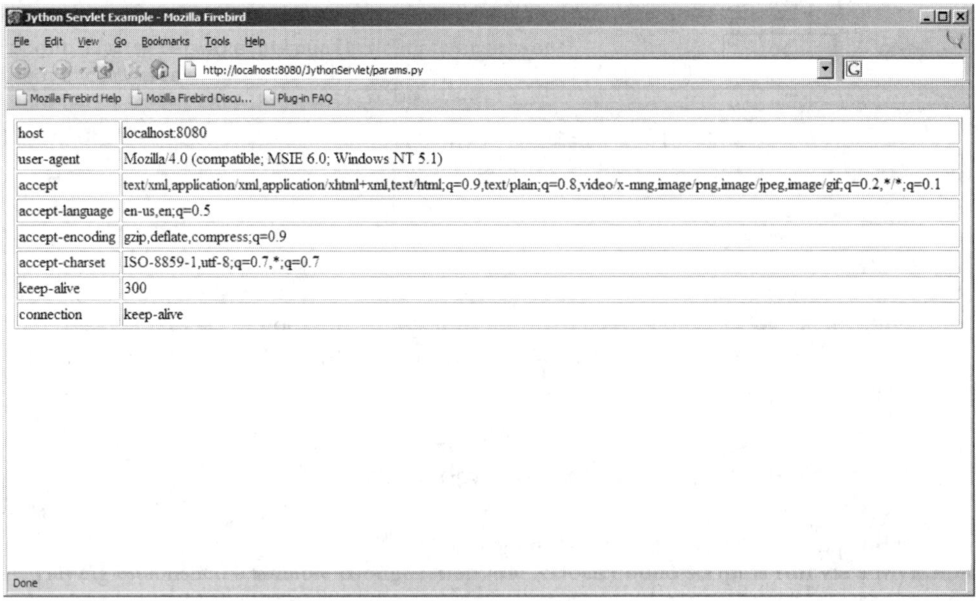

**Figure 9–2**    Output from servlet `params.py`.

# A Groovy Alternative

Jython is a mature Java implementation of the well-established scripting language Python. Groovy is a relative newcomer to the scripting scene, but it is gaining such interest that it threatens to eclipse Jython as the Java developer's preferred scripting language.

Like Jython, Groovy is 100% Java and offers the same seamless integration with the Java platform. Unlike Jython, Groovy is not a Java implementation of an existing scripting language but is designed from the ground up for use by Java developers, although it does borrow some of the best features from languages such as Python, Ruby, and Smalltalk.

Groovy's creators, Bob McWhirter and James Strachan, intended the language to feel immediately familiar to Java developers and stayed with the curly braces. You can even use semicolons, but they are optional, presumably for those of us who can't get out of the habit.

Functionality wise, there is little difference between Jython and Groovy, although Groovy may look a little slicker in the tools it provides. Groovy even has the equivalent of Jython's servlet, known as a *Groovlet*.

What makes Groovy so interesting is its acceptance under the Java Community Process as JSR-241, *The Groovy Programming Language*. When finalized, this will make Groovy the second official language for the J2SE platform. This is an exciting prospect, as a second language confirms J2SE as a true development platform and more than just the Java language. In this regard, it is possible Groovy is blazing a trail for other languages to follow.

Groovy resides under the Codehaus at `http://groovy.codehaus.org`. The language is well advanced but as of this writing is available only as a beta. The latest Groovy installation is available from the site. The site also provides extensive documentation with plenty of examples.

If you are keen to try Groovy, you might like to implement the Jython examples shown in this chapter using the Groovy language as an exercise. This exercise will help you determine which of the two scripting languages best suits your needs. Choosing between the two might be a dilemma, but it's nice to have such a good choice.

# Summary

Jython offers the developer a powerful scripting language. Jython's major strength is as a glue language working with existing Java classes. Thus, it is ideal for developing throwaway prototypes, either behavioral to show the customer or structural to validate part of the architecture. You'll find it has a thousand and one uses, and you will find yourself applying it to tasks you'd never before contemplated with languages like Java.

If Jython isn't for you, then there are plenty of alternatives to consider. Groovy is proving very popular, and Java implementations of high-profile scripting languages like Ruby and Tcl are also available.

Above all, do not be put off by the learning curve of a dynamic, type-less scripting language. Once you master it, you'll wonder how you ever got by without it.

New languages are being designed all the time. Admittedly, many have a lifespan similar to that of the fruit fly. Nevertheless, the good ones do tend to stick around. As developers, we should have an open mind about what new languages may offer. Who knows—the next template-based, object-oriented, pattern-centric, scripting language may have something to offer that makes all of our jobs a little easier.

For the next chapter, we move on to a different paradigm and examine how rule-based languages are well suited to expressing business logic in enterprise applications.

## Additional Information

If you'd like to learn more about Jython, several books are available in addition to the online resources mentioned in this chapter. *Jython Essentials* [Pedroni, 2002] by Samuele Pedroni and Noel Rappin is an informative text, as is *Jython for Java Programmers* [Bill, 2001] by Robert W. Bill.

To keep track of the progress of the Groovy JSR, see the Java Community Process site at `http://jcp.org/en/jsr/detail?id=241`.

# 10

# Working to Rule

Arecurring theme of this book is that rapid development is achievable by being able to quickly and effectively accommodate change. One area of most applications that is subject to continual change throughout the life of the system is the business rule.

This chapter examines the benefits of applying rule-based languages and rule-engine technology to the problem of constantly mutating business logic. Specifically, this chapter covers how rule engines can assist in rapid application development by:

- Enabling the description of rules in a language appropriate for expressing complex business knowledge.
- Improving system maintainability by cleanly separating business logic from application logic.
- Allowing the definition of business-rule sets as an enterprise resource, thereby enabling business rule changes to be swiftly effected across all corporate systems.
- Providing sophisticated end-user tools for visually specifying business logic.

We cover some of the main concepts behind rule-based programming by introducing the expert system shell language Jess, a rule engine specifically designed for writing rule-based systems for the Java platform.

## Business Rules

Business rules are the core of any enterprise system. Collectively, they define how an organization functions. A correctly modeled set of business rules captures the various aspects of the organization in terms of policy, strategy, and procedure. By implementing these business rules, an IT system ensures a company's strategic initiatives are fully realized.

## What Is a Business Rule?

A business rule is a statement or directive that defines, constrains, or controls some aspect of the business. It both asserts business structure and dictates business behavior.

The rules themselves are domain specific and range from the mundane to the exotic. Some examples include the following:

1. Stock items must be replenished when levels drop below 5 percent.
2. All creditors paying invoices within 30 days of billing will receive a 10 percent discount.
3. Jet aircraft are not permitted to land on grass runways.

Let's take a closer look at the structure of the common business rule.

## Structure of a Business Rule

Most business rules can be specified using a syntax that is familiar to all developers. The structure of the business rule is one of a condition, followed by an action to be acted upon if the condition is met. Thus, business rules can be defined in terms of an "`if ... then ...`" style of construct.

The previous examples can be rewritten using this syntax:

1. If stock levels fall below 5 percent, **then** replenish the stock.
2. If an invoice is paid within 30 days of billing, **then** the price is discounted by 10 percent.
3. If you are flying a jet aircraft **and** the airport runway has a grass surface, **then** divert to another airport.

Though business rules have a simple structure, they are liable to change, making them dynamic in nature.

## Dynamic Nature of Business Rules

Companies today face relentless market competition, and consequently many organizations are finding that agility is an essential survival trait. An agile company is one that can respond quickly to changes in the marketplace by making changes to core policy, strategy, and operational procedures. As the business rules define all of these behaviors, the rules themselves cannot be static. Instead, such rules are dynamic by their very nature and must be maintained in a format whereby they can be readily changed.

Consider the example of the rule that specifies a discount is to be given to all customers paying their bills within 30 days. In this example, the company instigating the rule may wish to reward customers with air points with a nominated airline instead of a cash discount. Alternatively, the company may offer a 10% discount to all customers who pay their account using direct debit.

# Business Rules in Software

As business rules direct how an organization engages with the market, the ability to change focus as market forces dictate is of paramount importance to any company wishing to remain successful. Organizations are therefore seeking architectures for their enterprise systems capable of supporting an adaptive business model in which business rules are truly dynamic.

Unfortunately, traditional systems suffer a number of limitations when it comes to supporting dynamic business rules:

- Business rules are commonly hardcoded in enterprise systems.
- Traditional languages like Java do not offer the most appropriate semantics for expressing dynamic business logic.
- Business and system concerns, although orthogonal, are interleaved within the code.
- Rules are often duplicated across a company's IT systems.

It is worth considering each of these points in further detail.

## Hardcoded Rules

Business rules are a dynamic attribute of any enterprise system, yet traditional development methods hardcode business logic using general-purpose, third-generation languages, of which Java is an example.

This approach fails to meet the adaptive model businesses are demanding, because hardcoded rules are immutable, and changes can be effected only by rebuilding all or part of the system. Defining rules in this way does not reflect the dynamic nature of the rules themselves. Moreover, the use of a language like Java requires the services of a software engineer to apply all of the necessary changes. Potentially, the business expert could make such changes.

## Rule Definition Languages

Although the `if ... then ...` structure of the business rule at first appears well suited to languages such as Java, this is unfortunately not the case. Java necessitates the services of skilled software engineers for implementing and changing business logic. Such changes are arguably best applied by those most skilled in the logic being defined: the domain experts. It can therefore be argued that business rules should be defined using a specialized natural-language syntax that enables business experts, as opposed to software experts, to build and maintain the rules.

Addressing the language issue from a different tangent, Java, as we know, is an object-oriented language. However, languages from a very different paradigm exist that are constructed specifically for the implementation of rule-based systems. These languages employ a declarative paradigm, as opposed to an imperative one, and originate from research projects into artificial intelligence (AI)–based systems. In upcoming sections, we look at the application of these specialized languages for the definition of business logic.

## Tight Coupling of System and Business Logic

In traditional systems, the software that enables the application to operate and the software responsible for implementing the business logic become intertwined. This scenario further exacerbates the difficulties inherent in enabling domain experts to maintain the all-important business logic. The business expert must understand the operation of the entire application in order to accurately separate business functionality from application functionality.

The reverse is also true of the software engineer, who is required to be expert not only in the architecture of the system but also in the business domain itself. An architecture that supports the clean separation of the two concerns of business and system would enable the responsibilities for the development and maintenance of the system to be divided between the business and the software experts.

## Rule Duplication

A company may find that as part of its wider IT portfolio, business rules are repeated several times in numerous different systems. This situation is not uncommon in large organizations and often occurs where systems overlap in terms of functionality. This situation can also arise during the transition phase as new systems are introduced to replace legacy systems.

Rule duplication significantly increases the total cost of ownership for an organization and adversely affects its propensity for agility. Changes to business processes must be effected across several different systems, thus incurring additional expense in terms of cost and time.

To address these issues with defining business rules, software vendors are turning to *rule engines*, a technology that was previously the preserve of academia and the computer scientist.

# Rule Engines

The rule engine originates from an area of computer science that has long battled with the issues surrounding the embedding of human logic and expertise into computer software. Research into AI, and the offshoot from that research in the form of *expert systems*, led to the development of rule engines as a means of organizing and managing large and complex rule sets.

An expert system, also known as a *production system*, is an AI-derived application that employs a knowledge base of human expertise for the purposes of problem solving in a well-defined problem domain, such as medical diagnosis or hardware fault-finding. Achieving this aim requires defining potentially thousands of complex, interrelated rules, which capture the knowledge of a human expert.

Developers of expert systems use rule engines within their products because they offer several benefits over conventional software engineering approaches: Specifically, they:

- Allow the dynamic addition of rules and data.
- Enable the definition of rules using specialized rule-based languages.
- Make rules easier to manage by centralizing them in one location.
- Reduce the complexity involved in modeling extremely complex sets of rules.

Rule engines enable developers to employ declarative programming techniques on software systems using rule-based languages. Conventional approaches to software development rely on programming languages that use the *imperative* computational model. Imperative languages like Java provide the computer with a list of commands to execute in a specific order. *Declarative* programming languages instead state a set of conditions and then leave it to the computer to determine how the conditions should be satisfied.

Declarative programming techniques help facilitate the development of rule-based systems and have proven extremely effective in the field of expert systems.

## Rule-Based Systems

A rule-based system relies upon the services of rule engines as means of inferring which rules to apply when solving a particular problem. The architecture of a rule-based system generally comprises three main elements:

- Rules in the form of if ... then ... statements
- A *knowledge base* of facts, or data
- A rule engine

A rule-based system, such as an expert system, defines rules using the familiar construct of the if ... then ... clause, introduced earlier for business rules. Within an expert system, a rule represents a *heuristic*. The heuristic is an attempt to express the guidelines, or *rules of thumb,* a human expert applies when solving a particular problem.

note

Rule engines are sometimes referred to as *inference engines.*

Data is represented within the system as *facts*, which are typically maintained within a knowledge base.

The rule engine is responsible for matching facts to rules—matching facts against the if part of the rule. If a match is found, then the rule engine executes the actions defined for the rule's then statement.

note

Not all rule-based systems use this approach. Systems built using the logic programming language *Prolog* define both facts and rules as predicates and so do not differentiate between the two.

Execution of the rule engine ceases when all facts have been matched. Since rules are able to modify the knowledge base as part of their actions, the rule engine can go on to fire further rules as a result of the actions of each rule.

## Rules Engines in Enterprise Systems

Rule-based systems have previously been the domain of computer science rather than business systems. Nevertheless, the areas of business rules and rule-based systems do overlap, and the research into the development of expert systems can be applied directly to the definition of business rules within enterprise systems. After all, a system designed to model complex human reasoning should have no trouble with the humble business rule.

You should consider using a rule engine if:

* Your business rules are subject to frequent change.
* Other systems implement the same rules.
* The business rules are highly complex and difficult to represent using conventional programming languages.

Rule engines, like databases, are enterprise resources. Where a database manages an organization's data, correspondingly, a rule engine manages a company's business knowledge. This makes rule engines complementary to the multitier architecture of the J2EE platform, which accesses the business knowledge managed by a rule engine in the same manner as corporate data assets held in a database are accessed.

In the next section, we examine how Java applications can employ the capabilities of a rule engine using Jess, a Java Expert System Shell.

# Introducing Jess

The Java Expert System Shell, or Jess, is a Java implementation of the popular CLIPS expert system shell. CLIPS, the C Language Integrated Production System, is a public domain software tool for developing and delivering rule-based systems.

NASA initially developed the CLIPS environment in the mid-1980s to provide NASA software engineers with a portable, high-performance implementation of an expert system shell. The CLIPS language was modeled on OPS5, one of the leading expert system languages. The OPS5 language was originally developed by Charles Forgy at Carnegie-Mellon University, and the language continues to be synonymous with expert system projects.

Jess is a Java implementation of CLIPS and is to CLIPS what Jython is to Python. Although CLIPS can integrate with Java through a well-defined API, Jess provides the same level of seamless integration with Java as was witnessed with Jython. Jess is compliant with CLIPS to the extent that software written for Jess will run largely unaltered under CLIPS.

> *Jython is covered in Chapter 9*

Dr. Ernest J. Friedman-Hill at Sandia National Laboratory created Jess to support the development of expert systems in Java. Since its inception, many have realized the potential of Jess for adding the power of the rule engine to any Java application. This interest has gone well beyond the scope of expert system development, and Jess is being used effectively in enterprise systems.

In addition to being rule-based, Jess is a general-purpose programming language and provides the developer with a dynamic scripting language with which to access Java class libraries.

## Installing Jess

Unlike its predecessor CLIPS, Jess is not public domain software. However, a trial version is available for evaluation purposes, and those in academia may apply for a free license.

Jess can be downloaded from `http://herzberg.ca.sandia.gov/jess/index.shtml`.

The documentation provided with the installation is comprehensive and includes a reference guide for the Jess language and the Java API along with example code.

note

> If you have obtained a trial version of Jess, it will expire after 30 days, so don't leave it too long before you start your research.

## Jess Example

To help understand how Jess defines rules, we look at a simple example of a Jess program and then examine each section of the code in turn. Listing 10–1 implements one of the business rules listed earlier, which states that jet aircraft are not allowed to land on grass runways.

## Listing 10–1    airplane.clp

```
; Fact templates
;
(deftemplate airplane (slot name))
(deftemplate jet extends airplane)
(deftemplate prop extends airplane)

; Rules
;
(defrule can-use-grass-runway
  "Planes that can use a grass runway"
  (prop (name ?n))
  =>
  (printout t "Aircraft can use grass - " ?n crlf))

(defrule can-use-asphalt-runway
  "Planes that can use asphalt"
  (airplane (name ?n))
  =>
  (printout t "Aircraft can use asphalt - " ?n crlf))

; Add some facts
;
(deffacts aircraft-facts "Aircraft type facts"
  (prop (name "Cessna 172"))
  (prop (name "Tiger Moth"))
  (jet (name "Boeing 737")))

; Start the rule engine
;
(reset)
(run)
```

The airplane.clp example is run directly from the command line:

```
java -cp jess.jar jess.Main airplane.clp
```

Running the code for the example displays the types of runway surface an aircraft can use.

```
Jess, the Java Expert System Shell
Copyright (C) 2001 E.J. Friedman-Hill and the Sandia Corporation
Jess Version 6.1p6 11/21/2003

Aircraft can use asphalt - Boeing 737
Aircraft can use asphalt - Tiger Moth
Aircraft can use grass - Tiger Moth
Aircraft can use grass - Cessna 172
Aircraft can use asphalt - Cessna 172
```

So, what does this example do? Well, the code states a few rules about the landing capabilities of jet aircraft as opposed to those powered by a propeller. Within the example, jet aircraft are only allowed to land on sealed runways, in this case, runways with an asphalt surface. Propeller-driven aircraft aren't quite so fussy and can land on all runway surfaces. Note this is a sweeping generalization about the capabilities of jet and prop-driven aircraft types.

The first part of the program defines a data structure for the different runway types using the deftemplate construct. These data structures hold the data for the facts declared later in the code.

```
(deftemplate airplane (slot name))
(deftemplate jet extends airplane)
(deftemplate prop extends airplane)
```

This declares an airplane structure with a single slot, name. The data structures jet and prop inherit from airplane.

It won't be a rule-based program without any rules, so the next part of the code uses the defrule statement to declare a few rules about the different types of aircraft.

Jess rules are similar in form to the classic if ... then ... structure of business rules. In Jess, the if statement equates to the left-hand side (LHS) term of the rule. The LHS term details the pattern the rule engine matches against facts in the knowledge base. Where a match is found, the Jess rule engine fires the actions defined in the rule's right-hand side (RHS) term. Thus, rules are expressed as

If LHS then RHS

The Jess notation is terser, so we get

LHS => RHS

Here is the rule that states only propeller-powered aircraft can land on grass runways.

```
(defrule can-use-grass-runway
   "Planes that can use a grass runway"
   (prop (name ?n))
   =>
   (printout t "Aircraft can use grass - " ?n crlf))
```

Adding, or *asserting*, facts of type prop causes the can-use-grass-runway rule to fire. The second rule in the example stipulates which aircraft can use a sealed runway. For the purposes of the example, all aircraft can use an asphalt runway, regardless of whether they are jet or propeller powered. This second rule is defined as

```
(defrule can-use-asphalt-runway
   "Planes that can use asphalt"
   (airplane (name ?n))
   =>
   (printout t "Aircraft can use asphalt - " ?n crlf))
```

Rules are no good without facts upon which to act. The example uses the `deffacts` statement as shorthand to assert a number of named facts into the rule engine's knowledge base.

```
(deffacts aircraft-facts "Aircraft type facts"
  (prop (name "Cessna 172"))
  (prop (name "Tiger Moth"))
  (jet (name "Boeing 737")))
```

The `deffacts` construct sets up the program's data, adding each aircraft to the knowledge base according to its type, either a `prop` or a `jet`.

The `deffacts` statement is not the only way to add facts to our knowledge base. We could have used a rule to achieve the same result and instead written

```
(defrule start-up
  "Rule to be executed first"
  =>
  (assert (prop (name "Cessna 172")))
  (assert (prop (name "Tiger Moth")))
  (assert (jet (name "Boeing 737"))))
```

Rules with no LHS terms are always executed first by the Jess rule engine. Thus, the `start-up` rule is fired when the program is reset and the facts asserted. This in turn fires the remaining rules, and the output of the program is generated. However, before this can happen, we need to reset the program and start the rule engine. The final two lines of code complete the example:

```
(reset)
(run)
```

The rule engine runs until all rules eligible for execution have been fired, after which the program exits.

## The Rete Algorithm

Like CLIPS, Jess uses an optimized algorithm for determining which rules are eligible for firing in the form of the Rete algorithm. The efficiency of this algorithm enables rule-based systems to offer superior performance to that of their procedural counterparts that must rely on a multitude of conditional statements for defining rules.

## Forward and Backward Chaining

Rule engines like Jess that start by matching the LHS terms of a rule are called *forward chaining* systems. These systems are data-driven: they start from the facts. Once running, the execution cycle of one rule can update the facts in the knowledge base, causing the condition of another rule to be met, thus firing the rule.

Alternatively, rule engines that operate by commencing with a stated goal that is matched to the RHS terms are known as *backward chaining* systems. Jess uses predominantly forward chaining but has the flexibility to use the backward chaining approach. The logic programming language *Prolog* is a classic example of a backward chaining system.

## Jess and Java

Running Jess programs through the Jess interpreter is one thing, but how can Jess be put to work in a Java or J2EE application? Thankfully, Jess provides a Java API for this very purpose.

Mixing Jess with Java combines the object-oriented and rule-based paradigms. This allows the definition of business rules using the Jess language, while Java is used to assert facts into the rule engine and retrieve the results.

The next example demonstrates the hybrid approach. For convenience, the initial rules and data structures from the first example have been retained. Listing 10–2 shows the rules the example Java program will be loading.

### Listing 10–2    airplane_rules.clp

```
; Fact templates
;
(deftemplate airplane (slot name))
(deftemplate jet extends airplane)
(deftemplate prop extends airplane)

; Rules
;
(defrule can-use-grass-runway
  "Planes that can use a grass runway"
  (prop (name ?n))
  =>
  (printout t "Aircraft can use grass - " ?n crlf))

(defrule can-use-asphalt-runway
  "Planes that can use asphalt"
  (airplane (name ?n))
  =>
  (printout t "Aircraft can use asphalt - " ?n crlf))
```

The rules and structures in `airplane_rules.clp` are loaded into working memory by the `Airplane.java` example, as shown in Listing 10–3.

## Listing 10–3    Airplane.java

```java
import java.util.Iterator;

import jess.Fact;
import jess.RU;
import jess.Rete;
import jess.Value;

public class Airplane {

  public static void main(String[] args) {

    try {
      // Create an instance of the rule engine
      //
      Rete rete = new Rete();

      // Load in the rules
      //
      rete.executeCommand("(batch src/airplane_rules.clp)");

      rete.reset();

      // Add 4 facts
      // First 3 facts are added to rule engine using Java
      //
      Fact f1 = new Fact("jet", rete);
      f1.setSlotValue("name",
                   new Value("Boeing 737", RU.STRING));
      rete.assertFact(f1);

      Fact f2 = new Fact("prop", rete);
      f2.setSlotValue("name",
                   new Value("Cessna 172", RU.STRING));
      rete.assertFact(f2);

      Fact f3 = new Fact("prop", rete);
      f3.setSlotValue("name",
                   new Value("Tiger Moth", RU.STRING));
      rete.assertFact(f3);

      // Fourth fact is added by executing Jess statement
      //
      rete.executeCommand(
        "(assert (jet (name \"Airbus 320\")))");

      // Kick the rule engine into life
      //
      rete.run();

      // Facts can be listed programmatically
```

```
      //
      System.out.println("\nAsserted facts");

      Iterator iter = rete.listFacts();
      while (iter.hasNext()) {
        System.out.println("Fact: " + iter.next());
      }

      // Alternatively Jess can do the job for us
      //
      System.out.println("\nFacts as told by Jess");
      rete.executeCommand("(facts)");
    }
    catch (Exception e) {
      System.err.println(e);
    }
  }
}
```

Embedding Jess within a Java application first requires instantiating an instance of the `Rete` class. This is the Jess rule engine and provides an interface that allows the calling Java code to perform common Jess tasks such as asserting facts and defining rules. The `Rete` class also provides the method `executeCommand()` for parsing and running Jess statements.

The example uses the `executeCommand()` method to load the rules from `airplane_rules.clp` into the rule engine.

```
rete.executeCommand("(batch src/airplane_rules.clp)");
```

The ability to execute a Jess command provides a convenient shortcut. Running the `batch` command to load the rules avoids the need for construction of both a `FileReader` and a `Jesp` class to parse the input file. Executing the `batch` command saves a few lines of code.

Facts are asserted into the rule engine by instantiating a new `Fact` instance and adding it to the `Rete` object. Here is the declaration of a fact for the `jet` data structure.

```
Fact f1 = new Fact("jet", rete);
f1.setSlotValue("name",
                new Value("Boeing 737", RU.STRING));
rete.assertFact(f1);
```

Alternatively, facts can be asserted using a Jess command:

```
rete.executeCommand("(assert (jet (name \"Airbus 320\")))");
```

With the rules loaded and all facts asserted, the rule engine is ready to run:

```
rete.run();
```

Listing 10–4 shows the output from the complete program.

## Listing 10–4   Output from Airplane.java

```
Aircraft can use asphalt - Airbus 320
Aircraft can use asphalt - Tiger Moth
Aircraft can use grass - Tiger Moth
Aircraft can use asphalt - Cessna 172
Aircraft can use grass - Cessna 172
Aircraft can use asphalt - Boeing 737

Asserted facts
Fact: (MAIN::initial-fact)
Fact: (MAIN::jet (name "Boeing 737"))
Fact: (MAIN::prop (name "Cessna 172"))
Fact: (MAIN::prop (name "Tiger Moth"))
Fact: (MAIN::jet (name "Airbus 320"))

Facts as told by Jess
f-0   (MAIN::initial-fact)
f-1   (MAIN::jet (name "Boeing 737"))
f-2   (MAIN::prop (name "Cessna 172"))
f-3   (MAIN::prop (name "Tiger Moth"))
f-4   (MAIN::jet (name "Airbus 320"))
For a total of 5 facts.
```

The Java API provided by Jess is proprietary to the Jess rule engine. Other rule-engine implementations, like *JRules* from ILOG, offer their own proprietary interfaces for accessing the services of the rule engine from a Java application.

To standardize on rule-engine access from the Java platform, a Java Specification Request (JSR) has been approved under the Java Community Process that defines a common API for rule engines.

# The Java Rule-Engine API

Considering that rule-based programming offers such benefits for enterprise systems development, it should be no surprise that the Java Community Process instigated a JSR on the subject. JSR-94 covers the integration of rule-engine technology into the J2SE platform, and its existence highlights that rule-engine technology is more than just an academic exercise where commercial systems are concerned.

The need for JSR-94 arose from the proprietary nature of rule-engine vendor APIs. Currently, rule-engine vendors each offer their own proprietary interfaces for integrating their particular rule engines into Java applications. Due to the lack of a suitable standard, a diverse range of rule-engine interfaces has resulted. Software engineers must learn each vendor's API and rewrite application code should they wish to migrate between different rule-engine products.

In order to address this problem, JSR-94 defines `javax.rules`, a lightweight API that looks to standardize access to rule engines from Java. Although the JSR specifies the J2SE platform, it is relevant for use in the J2EE environment.

The `javax.rules` API detailed in the JSR employs an approach similar to that of the JDBC API, whereby the client communicates via a standard interface with a vendor-supplied rule-service provider. The following code snippet is taken from JSR-94 and illustrates this approach:

```
Class.forName("org.jcp.jsr94.ri.RuleServiceProvider");
RuleServiceProvider serviceProvider =
    RuleServiceProviderManager.getRuleServiceProvider(
        "org.jcp.jsr94.ri.RuleServiceProvider");
```

The use of the `javax.rules` API is intended to provide compile-time compatibility between rule engines. Runtime compatibility, however, is not accommodated because the JSR does not encompass the definition of the rule language's semantics. Consequently, while code written with `javax.rules` compiles against any rule-engine provider compliant with the JSR, the implementation of the rules themselves likely will need to be migrated according to each rule engine's language.

JSR-94 has been approved and is available for download from

```
http://www.jcp.org/en/jsr/detail?id=094
```

The reference implementation bundled with the JSR is implemented as a wrapper over Jess, which operates as the driver for the rule-service provider. An example application comes with the JSR but requires the installation of a current `jess.jar`. The full details for building and running the example are provided with the JSR.

# Enterprise-Level Rule Engines

The benefits of applying rule-engine technology to the problem of defining and managing business rules within enterprise-level systems have not gone unnoticed by solution vendors. With organizations demanding highly dynamic systems capable of supporting an agile business model, the rule engine has come to the fore as one solution for delivering on these demands.

Consequently, software vendors are developing and marketing enterprise-centric versions of the rule engine that specifically target the enterprise-level computing market.

Such products offer the developer the benefits of a rule-based programming language for defining business logic, combined with powerful development tools for building, compiling, and orchestrating rules. Two notable examples of these types of product include *Fair Isaac Blaze Advisor* from Fair Isaac Corporation and ILOG's *Business Rule Management System* (BRMS).

## Enterprise Rule-Engine Features

The next sections focus on what rule-engine products can offer the enterprise system. As we shall see, rule engines such as Blaze Advisor and ILOG JRules not only provide the developer with the tools to build and deploy business rules, but also make it possible for business users to define their own rules.

## Externalized Business Rules

Rule engines make the clean decoupling of business logic from application code possible. Using such an approach, business rules can be maintained and managed independently of the application.

Extracting the business logic from the application and placing business rules in a central rules repository where they can be accessed remotely offers a number of architectural advantages that are worth reiterating.

First, the business logic is not owned by any one application but is instead accessible by any system across the enterprise. This eliminates the problem of business logic being replicated between systems and thus removes the associated support overheads incurred when maintaining duplicate business logic across systems.

Second, rules can be defined independently of the technology of the systems that use them. Therefore, productive rule-based languages can be used for the definition of rules and rule sets as opposed to the general-purpose languages used to implement the systems themselves.

## Rule-Based Language Support

Rule-engine vendors enable a variety of languages to be used in the development of working rule sets. Languages range from the fully declarative, including OPS5-style syntax, to languages more suited to the business end user. Moreover, with all the hype surrounding XML, it should come as no surprise that vendors are also turning to XML for representing rules. This approach has advantages in that standard XML tools can be used for managing rules in this format.

For its part, Jess offers a very powerful language for defining rules but is inarguably a developer's language and is not intended for use by the business user. Indeed, the creator of Jess describes the Jess language as being for *real* programmers.

Unlike Jess, which is specifically aimed at the software engineer, other commercial rule engines cater to business users wishing to maintain their own rule sets by providing a natural-language-type business-rule syntax. Although potentially not as expressive as a true programming language, these business rule languages enable business domain experts to control their own business logic, thereby enabling business-rule changes to be applied without the need for involvement from software developers.

Many software engineers will find the concept of end users managing complex business logic in this manner unrealistic, even threatening, especially as the need to undertake extensive testing on any changes that impact a production system cannot be overlooked. The thought of business users releasing new business functionality on an unsuspecting organization will have many software engineers shaking their heads in dismay. Nevertheless, end-user programming languages are a major selling point for rule-engine vendors, albeit the use of such languages must be carefully controlled and managed. The majority of business users are technically competent, and products like Blaze Advisor and ILOG JRules have been developed to meet the expectations of an increasingly sophisticated end user.

## Rule Management Tools

Enterprise-level rule engines offer more than just the rule engine and rule definition language. In order for rules to be easily defined, managed, and tested, products provide visual development tools that can be readily employed by both the software developer and the skilled business user.

As software engineers, we should expect sophisticated development and debugging tools for any languages we use. The same holds true for rule-based languages, and indeed the best examples of these products provide the developer with powerful visual development environments for building, compiling, and optimizing business rules.

note

> Version 7 of Jess, codenamed *Charlemagne*, will include a development environment in the form of a plug-in for the Eclipse platform. Charlemagne is in alpha release at the time of writing.

## Rule-Engine Evaluation Criteria

Following are factors to be considered when evaluating rule-engine products:

### Performance.

Most organizations rely on thousands of business rules to operate. The ability of a rule engine to accommodate rule sets of this size and return an acceptable level of performance is of paramount importance. Most forward-chaining rule engines employ the Rete algorithm, which is ideally suited to this task. Some vendor products also enable rules to be precompiled for additional performance gains.

### Cost.

All development projects work to a budget. Rule-engine price is typically based on feature set, so an application whose rules will only be defined by developers may not justify the additional costs of a rule engine that supports business-user development tools.

### Scalability.

This factor is critical where enterprise-level systems are concerned. A rule engine that cannot work effectively in a scaleable J2EE environment is likely to preclude its selection.

### Rule management tools.

Business-user-oriented languages might not be an important criteria for your particular project. Nevertheless, even if end-user interface tools are not required, rapid application development still demands the use of productive development and debugging tools for any language, rule-based or otherwise.

### Integration.

For a J2EE system, it must be possible to invoke the rule engine from J2EE components. Some rule engines are available as EJB components and are easily integrated into a J2EE solution. In addition to supporting the J2EE platform, the rule engine may also need to be accessible from other systems across the enterprise. The ability of the rule engine to support calls from heterogeneous systems is therefore an important factor if systems other than J2EE are required to make use of the services of the rule engine.

### Rule language(s).

Most rule engines support the `if ... then ...` rule construct. Some rule engines offer a choice of languages, ranging from developer-level rule-based languages to natural-language syntax for the business user.

### API.

In addition to the features offered by the rule language, the API provided by the rule engine is of particular interest to developers. Compliance of the rule engine with JSR-94 is also a consideration.

To find out more about the capabilities of commercial rule engines, visit the sites of Fair Isaac Blaze Advisor and ILOG JRules to review their whitepapers and product documentation. Blaze Advisor resides at `http://www.fairisaac.com`, and ILOG JRules can be found at `http://www.ilog.com`.

## Summary

As with scripting languages, knowledge of a rule-based language is a valuable skill that software engineers should have at their disposal. Rule-based programming is no longer considered purely the domain of the computer scientist but is finding an application in the development of business systems.

Business rules represent one of the greatest areas of complexity within enterprise systems, and the rule engine offers an effective mechanism for managing their sophisticated and dynamic nature. Rule engines are therefore well suited to rapid application development, offering the following benefits:

- Rules can be externalized from all applications to a centralized repository where they can be managed using specialized rule management tools.

- Rule-based programming languages are more suited to defining business rules than are languages such as Java.

- Business rules can be defined and managed by domain experts rather than by skilled IT professionals.

* The rules themselves are dynamic, enabling business-rule changes to be effected across the enterprise without the need to rebuild system components.

The next and final chapter on rapid development languages covers *aspect-oriented programming*, one of the software industry's most exciting new paradigms.

## Additional Information

The CLIPS software, along with examples and tutorials, is available from the site `http://www.ghg.net/clips/CLIPS.html`.

Jess is not public domain software. However, numerous Java implementations of rule engines exist that are. Table 10–1 lists some of them.

**Table 10–1**  Open Source Java Rule Engines

| Name | Reference |
| --- | --- |
| Drools | http://drools.org/ |
| OFBiz Rule Engine | http://www.ofbiz.org/docs/rules.html |
| Algernon | http://algernon-j.sourceforge.net/ |
| TyRuBa | http://tyruba.sourceforge.net/ |
| JTP Java Theorem Prover | http://www.ksl.stanford.edu/software/JTP/ |
| JEOPS, Java Embedded Object Production System | http://www.di.ufpe.br/~jeops/ |
| InfoSapient | http://info-sapient.sourceforge.net/ |
| JShop | http://www.cs.umd.edu/projects/shop/description.html |
| RDFExpert | http://public.research.mimesweeper.com/RDF/RDFExpert/Intro.html |
| Jena 2 | http://www.hpl.hp.com/semweb/jena2.htm |

For more information on the intricacies of the Rete algorithm, refer to the paper in which it was first defined, *Rete: A Fast Algorithm for the Many Pattern/Many Object Pattern Match Problem* by Charles L. Forgy [Forgy, 1982].

# 11

# Aspect-Oriented Programming

D omain-specific languages offer the benefits of specialized language constructs for undertaking work in a particular problem domain. We've looked at examples such as Jython for scripting and the rule-based language Jess for defining business logic. This chapter focuses on the use of aspect-oriented programming (AOP), a programming paradigm that offers the ability to effect rapid change across a system's entire code base with surgical precision.

The AOP paradigm brings an extra dimension to the design activity, making it possible to produce highly maintainable and extensible systems. Moreover, AOP introduces a dynamic element to the static nature of conventional software architecture, enabling the swift evolution of applications to accommodate emerging business concerns.

In the last few years, AOP has started to make its way into mainstream development, with J2EE vendors finding AOP ideally suited to the development of enterprise software. A new concept has been born, *aspect-oriented middleware*, and application server designers are rushing to adopt the lightweight, dynamic model AOP brings to the middle tier. Consequently, J2EE is on the cusp of a completely new approach to developing enterprise software.

This chapter introduces the major concepts of AOP and introduces two popular open source AOP products: *AspectJ* and *AspectWerkz*. AspectJ extends the Java language to include AOP constructs, while AspectWerkz adopts a framework-based approach. This chapter examines the merits of both approaches to implementing AOP and looks at how AOP languages and frameworks can complement the services offered by the J2EE platform.

The chapter concludes with some low-risk options for adopting AOP as part of your development toolkit.

First, we cover just why the world needs yet another programming paradigm.

## Why AOP?

AOP grew out of the research labs of the famous Xerox Palo Alto Research Center (PARC). The paradigm resulted from work undertaken by a number of teams on several different areas of software engineering including reflection and alternative variants of object-orient programming (OOP). A team led by Gregor Kiczales identified a key shortcoming in conventional programming paradigms, the ability of these languages to contend with *crosscutting concerns*, and AOP was the result of research into addressing these shortcomings.

To understand how the AOP paradigm can benefit the software development process, it is necessary understand the nature of the crosscutting concern issue that AOP addresses.

## Crosscutting Concerns

Object-oriented design focuses on the clean separation of *concerns* within a system. A concern is a concept, objective, or functional area that is of interest to the system. For example, a core concern of a stock-control system would be tracking stock items held at the warehouse.

Object-oriented languages provide the constructs necessary to localize the different concerns of a system into discrete modules. This is a fundamental approach to good software design and was practiced long before OOP came on the scene. Procedural languages put the rudimentary building blocks in place to enable the functional decomposition of concerns into modules. OOP built on the structures offered by procedural languages for modularization, introducing concepts such as information hiding and abstraction to facilitate the separation of concerns within a software system.

The problem with concerns is that they don't all fit neatly into little boxes. Some concerns freely cross module boundaries and intersect with other concerns. These are known as *crosscutting concerns* and are generally associated with *system-level concerns* such as logging, threading, security, transactions, and performance. Such concerns are *orthogonal* to the core business concerns.

> *Chapter 4 discusses the concept of orthogonal design in software architectures.*

Crosscutting concerns are a dilemma for the software engineer, as OOP languages fail to offer a convenient mechanism for protecting the code base from the unwanted complexity they introduce into even the cleanest of software designs.

## Code Tangling and Scattering

Crosscutting concerns are damaging to the design of software systems. They introduce the two unwanted side effects of *code tangling* and *code scattering* into the software architecture. Code tangling and scattering adversely affect the readability and maintainability of the application:

### Code tangling.

Tangling occurs when different concerns coexist within the same module. For example, a module that implements a specific business concern may also contain code that relates to logging, persistence, and performance. Tangling occurs when the implementation of the business logic becomes intertwined with the code for these other requirements within the body of the module.

### Code scattering.

Scattering occurs when the implementation of a crosscutting concern spreads over many modules. Logging is a classic example, as logging code exists in many of the application's classes. Changes to logging therefore require visiting numerous parts of the system.

The impacts of crosscutting concerns on enterprise software are detrimental to the objectives of producing applications that are both readable and maintainable. Software that is hard to understand is difficult to maintain; code that is difficult to maintain cannot undergo rapid change in response to the evolving requirements of the business.

Fortunately, OOP is not completely defenseless against the ravages of crosscutting concerns, and various strategies are available to keep their impact to a minimum. These strategies essentially include the use of frameworks, design patterns, domain-specific languages, and mix-in classes. We briefly cover each of these techniques before examining how AOP addresses the issue.

## Traditional Approaches to Crosscutting Concerns

The next sections look at the main techniques available for managing crosscutting concerns within the confines of a single paradigm OOP language such as Java.

### Frameworks

Frameworks offer an effective means of separating core and system-level concerns, and the J2EE platform is an excellent example of this.

The J2EE platform frees the software engineer of many of the major system-level concerns that, by their very nature, tend to fall into the category of crosscutting concerns; threading and security are just two examples of system-level concerns that J2EE makes transparent to the developer. Each of these concerns is imperative for a high-performance, secure system, yet J2EE technology enables the developer to focus on implementing business knowledge and delegates the task of managing threads and authenticating and authorizing users to the J2EE server.

Having the J2EE server take responsibility for some of the major crosscutting system-level concerns significantly reduces the level of code tangling and scattering throughout the code base. Thread synchronization code does not appear in any of the application's components because threading is entirely handled by the J2EE container, although the developer must still be wary of certain design decisions, such as the use of the Singleton pattern. Likewise, security in J2EE is effectively modularized by regulating security concerns to the deployment descriptor.

Despite the inarguable effectiveness of the J2EE platform in dealing with many system-level concerns, not all crosscutting concerns are system-level concerns. The J2EE platform cannot manage application-specific *business crosscutting concerns,* nor can the platform easily accommodate additional ad hoc system-level concerns not catered for by the platform. We therefore have only a partial solution to the crosscutting problem.

Fortunately, J2EE and AOP are not mutually exclusive, and AOP can build on the services of the J2EE platform.

## Design Patterns

With careful design, it is possible to devise solutions with OOP techniques that can modularize crosscutting concerns, separating them from the system's core concerns. The *Visitor pattern* is a good example of such a design and is applicable where objects within a hierarchy perform a number of unrelated operations [Gamma, 1995].

The authors of the Visitor pattern saw a need to prevent unrelated operations from *polluting* the classes within the hierarchy. Pollution of classes relates directly to the crosscutting concerns we are attempting to manage.

A Visitor pulls together the different and diverse operations performed on a particular class. The main class then *accepts* the Visitor, requesting it to perform these unrelated, crosscutting operations on its behalf.

Visitor gathers related operations together and separates unrelated ones, thereby promoting an application architecture that sees an object model aligned along concern boundaries.

The disadvantage of the Visitor pattern is that the main classes in the object hierarchy must be aware of Visitor objects and be prepared to invoke their behavior. Arguably, this is a crosscutting concern in itself, as framework code for the implementation of the pattern now must become part of the application. Code tangling is still evident within the code, albeit at a reduced level.

## Mix-in Classes

The concept of mix-in classes is more appropriate for OOP implementations that support multiple inheritance than for single-inheritance languages like Java.

With this technique, functionality resides in discrete, loosely coupled and highly cohesive classes. Each class defines a specific behavior or trait. Fully featured classes result by mixing the different classes available from the object hierarchy. This approach enables the various concerns of a system to be assembled using multiple inheritance. The mix-in approach is workable, but very careful design of the class hierarchy is required to achieve a breakdown of functionality at the correct level of granularity.

Although Java does not support multiple inheritance per se, it can simulate the technique using interfaces and composition. The mix-in class design is more cumbersome to implement using these constructs than with true multiple inheritance. However, if Java were to ever support multiple inheritance, the complexities associated with its use, such as object construction order, shared-data member instances, and the need for virtual inheritance, would all outweigh the benefits the mix-in technique offers. Moreover, even with this technique, the main class still must orchestrate the calling of the different methods.

## Domain-Specific Languages

To contend with crosscutting concerns, it is possible to look to other paradigms than OOP for help—for example, using a rule-based language for implementing business logic.

> *Chapter 10 introduces rule-based languages.*

Here, a rule-based language implements business concerns, while the services of the J2EE platform handle system-level concerns. Java serves as the glue between J2EE services and the rule-based language.

This is an effective approach because rule-based languages offer an excellent vocabulary for defining business logic. However, J2EE components still need to know the point at which to fire the business rules, and again, this represents a mixing of concerns.

The ideal solution for crosscutting concerns would see core concerns implemented in ignorance of orthogonal crosscutting concerns, thereby avoiding code tangling. Moreover, a language should offer the ability to modularize crosscutting concerns in the same way as is currently possible with core concerns in OOP languages. This would prevent code scattering.

The AOP paradigm provides the language constructs necessary to achieve these aims and is examined in the next sections.

# AOP Explained

The primary goal of the AOP paradigm is to provide a mechanism for modularizing crosscutting concerns. The creators of AOP wanted a programming approach that could abstract and encapsulate crosscutting concerns, thereby facilitating software reuse.

Through the modularization of crosscutting concerns, AOP makes it possible to avoid code scattering and code tangling. Moreover, AOP implementations go beyond this primary goal and bring a dynamic element to the static nature of object-oriented applications. The static model of OOP designs is sensitive to change, with a change in requirements having the potential to wreak havoc upon the conventional static model. As we shall see, the dynamic capabilities of AOP implementations are of significant interest for rapid development because they offer the flexibility to accommodate change within the system.

To understand AOP, we must understand the concepts and terminology the paradigm introduces to the software engineering discipline.

## Concepts and Terminology

OOP adds numerous new terms to the software engineer's vocabulary, such as *inheritance, composition, overloading, overriding*, and everyone's favorite—*polymorphism*. Learning the practices of OOP requires familiarity with these alien concepts.

Like OOP, AOP also comes complete with its own nomenclature, requiring our vocabulary to expand once again to encompass the paradigm's concepts of *crosscutting concerns*, *join points*, *pointcuts*, *advice*, *aspects*, and *weaving*.

Here is an explanation of the AOP terminology:

### Join points.

A join point represents the point at which a crosscutting concern intersects with a main concern. Join points are well-defined locations in a program's execution path, and examples include method invocation, conditional statements, and object instantiation. Essentially, a join point can be any point in an application's execution.

### Pointcuts.

If a join point is a well-defined point in an application's execution, then a pointcut is a language construct that identifies specific join points within the program. A pointcut defines a collection of join points, with a pointcut designator picking out specific join points and values at these points. The pointcut also provides a context for the join point.

### Advice.

Advice is the code executed upon reaching a particular pointcut within the program. Advice is therefore an implementation of a crosscutting concern.

### Aspects.

Aspects encapsulate join points, pointcuts, and advice into a unit of modularity for crosscutting concerns and offer reuse mechanisms for crosscutting concerns equivalent to that of a Java class for core concerns.

### Weaving.

Having separated the different concerns, to complete the system, it is necessary to recombine them to form the executing program. This process of interleaving aspects with the main application is known as *weaving*. The AOP weaver composes the different implementation aspects into a cohesive system in accordance with specific weaving rules.

AOP is therefore a process of weaving aspects that define crosscutting concerns into an application implemented in a conventional language that defines the core concerns. The result of the weaving process is a combination of concern types that make up the final system.

Classes and aspects are independent of one another, with only the pointcut declaration serving to bind the two paradigms. Classes are therefore unaware of the presence of aspects, and this is an important AOP concept.

This relationship between aspects and classes is very well described in an excellent early paper on AOP, *Aspect-Oriented Programming: A Critical Analysis of a New Programming Paradigm* [Highley, 1999]. The paper's authors illustrate the relationship between OOP classes and AOP aspects by describing a mythical world inhabited by *hunchbacks* and *dragons*.

# Hunchbacks and Dragons

Taken from the paper, the hunchbacks of the mythical world all worked in houses with glass ceilings. Dragons flew around the skies, observing the behavior of the hunchbacks in the houses below. The hunchbacks couldn't look up and so were unaware of the existence of the dragons.

The hunchbacks communicated with hunchbacks in other houses by sending each other mail. The mail they received from other hunchbacks helped direct the work they completed for the day. The dragons, being inquisitive creatures, kept a close eye on the hunchbacks, including reading the hunchbacks' mail—however, the dragons never stole or interfered with the mail.

At a given point, the dragons would suddenly leap into action. They might, for example, paint one of the houses red. The hunchbacks would notice their house had magically changed color, but they wouldn't do anything about it. They would continue with their everyday tasks, still oblivious to the existence of the dragons.

This allegory perfectly captures the relationship between classes and aspects. From the story, the classes relate to the hunchbacks while the flying dragons represent aspects. An OOP application is self-contained, but aspects allow the augmentation of the application's behavior without the need to change the underlying static object model. Aspects therefore offer the ability to inject new behavior into an existing system dynamically and transparently.

The task of mixing the two worlds of OOP and AOP is achieved using a weaver.

# Weaving Methods

The process of weaving is critical to AOP. As the AOP paradigm has evolved, various approaches to the process of weaving have emerged. The following lists the different methods for injecting advice into a Java application:

**Compile-time.**

This approach produces a woven application during the stages of the compilation process. First, aspects and classes are compiled to standard Java bytecode. Weaving then takes place as a postcompilation step using bytecode manipulation to add advice at the designated join points within the program.

**Load-time.**

Load-time weaving defers the weaving process until the application is in a running state. Weaving then occurs at the bytecode level at class-load time. This method is known as *code injection*.

**Runtime.**

Here, the process is similar to that of load-time weaving, except weaving at the bytecode level occurs as join points are reached in the executing application. This approach is also known as *interception* or *call-time* weaving.

Load-time and runtime weaving methods have the advantage of being highly dynamic, enabling on-the-fly changes to a running system. On the downside, such changes can adversely affect system stability and performance. In contrast, compile-time weaving offers superior performance, but requires the rebuilding and deployment of the application in order to effect a change.

Having set the scene, it is now time to go over an AOP example to illustrate how the various AOP concepts are applied. We first look at an example of AOP using AspectJ, an AOP language implementation, and then compare it to AspectWerkz, a framework for adding aspects to Java applications.

# Introducing AspectJ

AspectJ was the first implementation of the AOP paradigm to come out of the research work undertaken at Xerox PARC and is the most mature and complete AOP implementation currently available. The Xerox team, led by Gregor Kiczales, produced AspectJ both as a first cut at a language specification for AOP and an AOP implementation. The Xerox AspectJ team chose to extend the Java language to support aspect-oriented concepts in addition to developing compilation and debugging tools for their new Java variant.

AspectJ represents a language-based AOP implementation, bringing new constructs and semantics to Java with additional keywords. These additions turn Java from a single-paradigm to a multiparadigm language, able to exploit the benefits of both OOP and AOP. Historically, this approach follows the same route as taken by C++, which extended the C programming language to incorporate OOP constructs.

When AspectJ reached a level of stability, it was relocated from the research labs of Xerox PARC into the arms of the open source community. AspectJ is now maintained as an Eclipse Technology project and can be found at `http://eclipse.org/aspectj`.

## AspectJ and Eclipse

The Eclipse platform is a generic development environment that offers a powerful collection of Java development tools (JDT), including a Java source editor, compiler, and debugger.

> *Chapter 13 describes the Eclipse platform and the JDT in detail.*

AspectJ builds on the services of the JDT to provide the AspectJ Development Tool (AJDT), a fully featured Eclipse plug-in that brings the capabilities of the Eclipse platform to the AspectJ language, including content assist on keywords, aspect browsing, compilation error tracing, and the debugging of aspects.

Despite its links with Eclipse, AspectJ is not bound to the Eclipse platform. The primary focus of the project is the AspectJ compiler, which is available as a standalone executable. As a standalone release, independent of the AJDT, AspectJ supports the compilation and execution of applications. A structure browser is also available for interrogating AOP constructs within the code.

AspectJ also integrates with other popular development environments, with plug-ins available for *JBuilder*, *NetBeans*, and *Emacs*. Refer to the AspectJ site for information on where to obtain these and other plug-ins.

## The AspectJ Compiler

AspectJ supports compile-time weaving, with version 1.1.2 offering limited support for load-time weaving.

The AspectJ compiler builds on the capabilities of Eclipse's Java compiler, thereby firmly tying the language to the open source community and cutting its initial ties with `javac`. The Eclipse compiler is highly sophisticated and offers capabilities such as incremental compilation. By using the Eclipse compiler as its base, AspectJ leverages these capabilities for its own builds. Classes produced by the AspectJ compiler run on any Java-compatible platform.

## AspectJ Example

To understand how some of the fundamental concepts of AOP are applied, let's look at an example built using AspectJ. The example covers the main concepts of AOP and introduces the new language constructs AspectJ adds to the Java language to support AOP.

The code for the example adds aspects to an imaginary stock-control system. Stock items are contained within a central warehouse, and the stock-control system is responsible for managing all stock going into the warehouse. A single class encapsulates warehouse functionality. Listing 11–1 shows the implementation of the Warehouse class.

### Listing 11–1   The Warehouse Class

```
package stock;

import java.util.ArrayList;

/**
 * Warehouse class for storing stock items.
 */
public class Warehouse {

  private ArrayList stockItems;

  public Warehouse() {
    stockItems = new ArrayList();
  }
```

```
/**
 * Add a new stock item
 */
public void add(String stockItem) {
  stockItems.add(stockItem);
}

/**
 * Return the number of items in stock
 */
public int itemsInStock() {
  return stockItems.size();
}
}
```

The warehouse is nothing more than a wrapper around an `ArrayList`. However, the intention of the code is to demonstrate the concepts of AOP, not to build a fully featured stock-control system.

Our rudimentary stock-control system adds a number of stock items to the warehouse. Listing 11–2 shows the code for the stock-control example.

## Listing 11–2   The Main StockControl Class

```
package stock;

/**
 * Adds stock items to the warehouse
 */
public class StockControl {

  public void processStockItems() {

    //  Create the warehouse
    //
    Warehouse warehouse = new Warehouse();

    // Add some stock
    //
    warehouse.add("Washing Machine");
    warehouse.add("Microwave Oven");
    warehouse.add("Television");
  }

  public static void main(String[] args) {
    StockControl stockCtrl = new StockControl();
    stockCtrl.processStockItems();
  }
}
```

The example application is very simple, but it is easy to imagine a production version on a much grander scale. The concept of encapsulating the warehouse functionality into a component accessed via a common interface from all parts of the system is a design in keeping with object-oriented architecture.

To illustrate how AOP weaves in functionality, we introduce an auditing (or logging) concern into the system. The following use case defines the new auditing requirements:

1. All stock items must have an audit-log entry before going into the warehouse.
2. After adding a stock item to the warehouse, the number of items in the warehouse must be written to the audit log.

To incorporate the new requirements into the system using AOP, the first task is to specify the join points in the program where the auditing concern crosscuts the main concern. Achieving this task requires the declaration of a *pointcut designator*.

A pointcut designator is a special AOP language construct that specifies join point collections and precisely defines where a crosscutting concern intersects the main concern. AspectJ supports the declaration of pointcuts at a number of different locations in a program's execution:

- Method and constructor call
- Method and constructor reception
- Method and constructor execution
- Field access
- Exception handler execution
- Class and object initialization

Complying with the auditing requirements requires the declaration of a pointcut occurring at the point of the call to the add() method on the Warehouse class. We need to weave in the auditing advice ahead of the add() method's invocation and upon returning from the call.

Listing 11–3 shows the code for the aspect that specifies the pointcut declaration and the advice for weaving into the system.

## Listing 11–3    Auditing Aspect AuditingAspect.java

```
package stock;

import org.aspectj.lang.reflect.SourceLocation;

/**
 * Aspect to add auditing to the stock control system.
 */
public aspect AuditingAspect {

  // Pointcut declaration
  //
```

```
pointcut auditStockItem() : call(* Warehouse.add(..));

// Advice to execute before call
//
before() : auditStockItem() {
  System.out.println("<--Audit log entry start-->");

  // Log the name of the calling class
  //
  SourceLocation sl = thisJoinPoint.getSourceLocation();
  Class myClass = (Class)sl.getWithinType();
  System.out.println("\tCaller: " + myClass.toString());

  // Log the stock item description
  //
  Object[] args = thisJoinPoint.getArgs();
  for(int i=0; i < args.length; ++i) {
    System.out.println("\tAdding item: " + args[i]);
  }
}

// Advice to execute after call
//
after() : auditStockItem() {
  Warehouse warehouse;
  warehouse = (Warehouse)thisJoinPoint.getTarget();
  System.out.println("\tItems in stock: " +
                     warehouse.itemsInStock());
  System.out.println("<--Audit log entry end-->");
}
}
```

Examining the code in Listing 11–3 reveals a number of syntactic differences from standard Java, with the AOP keywords shown in bold text. The AspectJ keyword `aspect` specifies that we are defining an aspect and not a Java class. AspectJ uses aspects as a unit of modularization for crosscutting concerns. Aspects are similar to classes in that they have a type and can extend classes and other aspects. The main difference between the two constructs is that aspects cannot be instantiated with the new operator. They are also not directly interchangeable with classes.

The keyword `pointcut` declares the pointcut designator for the auditing advice and assigns the pointcut the name of `auditStockItem()`. Here is the full declaration of the pointcut:

```
pointcut auditStockItem() : call(* Warehouse.add(..));
```

The syntax following the pointcut name is of greatest interest because this captures the join points for the auditing concern. It is defined as `call(* Warehouse.add(..)`, where `call` specifies the join point as the point at which the method is invoked. The remainder of the pointcut designator specifies the method signature for matching the join point at runtime. From the example, a match will be found for all `add()` methods on instances of the `Warehouse` class, regardless of access, return type, or arguments. AspectJ provides a rich syntax for defining join points, enabling the definition of sophisticated matches that go well beyond the simple example shown.

Having identified the join points in the program, the next step is to provide the auditing advice AspectJ will weave into the main concern. AspectJ has three options for associating advice with a join point: `before()`, `after()`, or `around()` the join point.

Our auditing advice has to both precede and follow the call to the `Warehouse` instance. The AspectJ syntax of `before()` and `after()` details precisely where the advice is to be injected once the join point is reached. This syntax gives the following method signatures for the auditing advice:

```
before() : auditStockItem() {
  ...

after() : auditStockItem() {
  ...
```

Examining the code for the before and after advice highlights the use of the `thisJoinPoint` object, which provides a context for the join point and makes information relating to the join point available to the advice. The example uses this information to log the name of the calling class and the arguments to the `Warehouse.add()` method, and to invoke the `itemsInStock()` method on the `Warehouse` instance.

The code for the example was compiled and run on the Eclipse platform using the Eclipse AJDT plug-in. The use of an aspect-aware development environment offers significant benefits over a plain code editor and build script. In addition to syntax coloring of keywords and content-assist on AspectJ types, aspect-aware environments, such as AJDT for Eclipse, provide a visual cue to where join points occur within the application. This is an invaluable aid for determining the impact of a pointcut declaration upon the code of the core concerns.

Figure 11–1 depicts this feature of the AJDT, which shows the code from the example open as a project on the Eclipse platform.

The upper right pane shows the code for the `StockControl` class open in an aspect-aware editor. Marks on the left border of the editor denote where the join points of the `Auditing-Aspect` aspect crosscut the `StockControl` concerns. The content of the outline view, seen in the lower left pane, displays a hierarchical view of the location of the aspect's injected advice. The lower right pane contains the console view, which shows the results of executing the program.

The example contains only a single class and aspect. However, in a larger system with thousands of files, the pointcut declaration is just as easily applied across all classes within the system. This ability to inject functionality directly into a large system and with a high degree of precision makes AOP an ideal candidate for a rapid development language. Moreover, the dynamic nature of the language makes it an ideal prototyping tool because new behavior is easily added or removed as system functionality is explored.

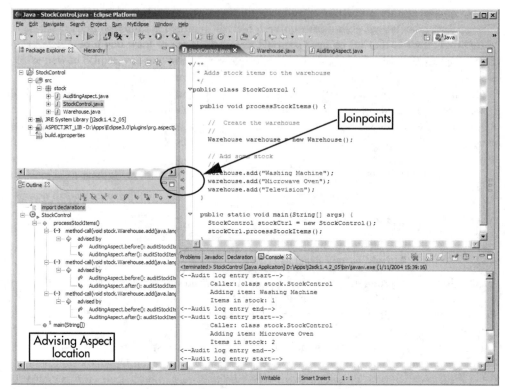

**Figure 11-1**    The Eclipse platform with an AspectJ project open.

tip

> AOP is potentially well suited to the development of evolutionary prototypes. Omitting concerns such as security, auditing, logging, and persistence, enables a prototype to be rapidly constructed using a conventional OOP approach. Once the prototype is accepted, aspects weave in these concerns to transform the prototype into a production-standard application.

AspectJ was the first release of an AOP language and still stands out as the most comprehensive AOP implementation available, offering unrivaled tool support in the form of the AJDT for Eclipse. Since its emergence from the research labs of Xerox PARC, a host of alternative AOP implementations has joined AspectJ. These newcomers to the AOP paradigm take a different approach to AspectJ. Instead of a new language, they provide a framework for defining aspects. The next section discusses this approach.

# Language Versus Framework

The designers of AspectJ elected to enhance the Java language to support AOP. Over the years, the AspectJ variant of Java has matured into a stable and complete AOP platform, with the AJDT offering excellent tool support.

However, changing the core Java language has met with a degree of criticism from some quarters. Some of the issues include the following:

- Learning Java becomes more difficult because the additional keywords mean developers new to Java must embrace the concepts and semantics of both the OOP and AOP paradigms.
- Compilation of Java and AOP hybrid languages requires the adoption of a new compiler.
- Moving to an AOP language is an issue when looking to employ AOP on an existing project, since migration of the complete code base to the new language is required.

Recent AOP implementations take the approach of defining aspects externally to the Java application using a framework in order to circumvent these issues. Frameworks enable the superimposing of AOP concepts onto existing Java applications without the need to move the entire application to a new AOP compiler. These frameworks typically use XML configuration files or J2SE 5.0-style metadata annotations to specify pointcuts and advice within the main application, ensuring AOP-specific keywords are isolated from the application. Advice is defined as standard Java classes, referenced by the framework's configuration.

A main advantage of these frameworks is that they bring AOP to vanilla Java, thereby easing the task of adopting AOP techniques within existing systems.

## AOP Framework Implementations

The number of open source AOP frameworks available is growing steadily as AOP continues to gain interest among the Java community. Table 11–1 lists a selection of the AOP frameworks available as open source.

To contrast AspectJ against a framework AOP implementation, we look at the approach to defining aspects taken by AspectWerkz.

**Table 11-1**    AOP Frameworks

| Name | Description | Reference |
|---|---|---|
| AspectWerkz | A popular, easy-to-learn AOP framework for Java. Features include both bytecode and load-time weaving. | http://aspectwerkz.codehaus.org |
| JBoss AOP | The JBoss AOP framework forms part of the JBoss application server and offers load-time and runtime aspect weaving. The framework is available standalone. | http://www.jboss.org/products/aop |
| Nanning | Nanning Aspects is a simple and scalable AOP framework for Java. | http://nanning.codehaus.org |
| CAESAR | Offers new AOP language that is compatible with Java. The CAESAR language compiles to standard Java bytecode. | http://caesarj.org/ |
| JAC | Java Aspect Components (JAC) is an open source project targeting the use of AOP for developing an aspect-oriented middleware layer. | http://jac.objectweb.org/ |
| Spring | Spring is an extensive Java-based framework in its own right based on the popular inversion of control (IOC) pattern. Spring also offers an AOP framework or is configurable to work with external AOP implementations. | http://www.springframework.org |

# Introducing AspectWerkz

*AspectWerkz* is a dynamic AOP implementation for Java, jointly developed by Jonas Bonér and Alexandre Vasseur. The framework is open source and available for download from the Codehaus site at http://aspectwerkz.codehaus.org. Check the site for full details of the license.

The AspectWerkz framework is not as comprehensive as AspectJ, but has a reputation as a workable and easy to learn AOP implementation. Unlike AspectJ, AspectWerkz does not extend the Java language to support aspects but instead defines aspects using either an XML definition file or J2SE 5.0-style metadata annotations. These methods for defining aspects avoid the need for an AOP-aware Java compiler.

note

> Before the release of J2SE 5.0, AOP frameworks like AspectWerkz used XDoclet-style metatags embedded within Javadoc comment blocks. With metatags now supported by J2SE 5.0 as annotations, the AspectWerkz team has stated it intends to update the AOP framework to use the new syntax for defining metadata in Java code.

> *Chapter 6 provides an overview of metadata annotations.*

To compare how the approach of the AspectWerkz framework to AOP differs from that of AspectJ, consider the code snippet in Listing 11–4, which depicts a plain Java implementation of the `AuditingAspect` from the AspectJ example.

## Listing 11–4    AspectWerkz AuditingAspect Class

```
package stock;

import org.codehaus.aspectwerkz.joinpoint.JoinPoint;

public class AuditingAspect {

  public void beforeAddStockItem(JoinPoint joinPoint) {
    .
    .
    .
  }

  public void afterAddStockItem(JoinPoint joinPoint) {
    .
    .
    .
  }
}
```

The code snippet in Listing 11–4 is devoid of any AOP language constructs, although there are a few hints such as the `JoinPoint` class. We look first at how an external XML definition file transforms the class into a full-fledged aspect.

# XML Aspect Definition

One of the first approaches of many of the AOP frameworks was to declare pointcut designators and the location of advice methods using XML definition files. Listing 11–5 shows a sample of an AspectWerkz definition file that turns the plain AuditingAspect Java class into an aspect.

## Listing 11–5    XML Definition File aop.xml

```xml
<aspectwerkz>
  <system id="stockcontrol">
    <package name="stock">

      <!-- Define the class implementing the aspect -->
      <aspect class="stock.AuditingAspect"
              deployment-model="perInstance">

        <!-- Named pointcut -->
        <pointcut name="auditStockItem"
                  expression="call(* Warehouse.add(..))"/>

        <!-- Bind aspect before method to pointcut -->
        <advice name="beforeAddStockItem"
                type="before"
                bind-to="auditStockItem"/>

        <!-- Bind aspect after method to pointcut -->
        <advice name="afterAddStockItem"
                type="after"
                bind-to="auditStockItem"/>
      </aspect>
    </package>
  </system>
</aspectwerkz>
```

Comparing the aspect definition in the XML file against the example from AspectJ reveals many similarities. Most notable is the syntax for the pointcut declaration. For example, here is the declaration for the pointcut in AspectJ:

```
pointcut auditStockItem() : call(* Warehouse.add(..));
```

Compare this to the corresponding declaration in the AspectWerkz configuration:

```xml
<pointcut name="auditStockItem"
          expression="call(* Warehouse.add(..))"/>
```

Supporters of AspectJ emphasize that these definition files present a similar learning curve to the new language constructs of AspectJ. This is a valid argument, but the strength of AspectWerkz lies in its ability to bring AOP to an existing system without requiring a move to an AOP compiler.

## Aspects as Metadata Annotations

Later versions of AspectWerkz offer an alternative mechanism for specifying aspects using metadata annotations. This method moves AspectWerkz closer to the AspectJ model by embedding AOP constructs as annotations within the language. The advantage of embedded annotations over an external XML file is that all code related to the aspect resides within a single file.

Listing 11–6 shows the `AuditingAspect` class but this time adorned with AspectWerkz annotations.

### Listing 11–6    AuditingAspect Class with Metatags

```
package stock;

import org.codehaus.aspectwerkz.joinpoint.JoinPoint;

/**
 * @Aspect perInstance
 */
public class AuditingAspect {

  /**
   * @Before call(* Warehouse.add(..))
   */
  public void beforeAddStockItem(JoinPoint joinPoint) {

    .
    .
    .

  }

  /**
   * @After call(* Warehouse.add(..))
   */
  public void afterAddStockItem(JoinPoint joinPoint) {

    .
    .
    .

  }
}
```

This new version of the `AuditingAspect` now bears a strong resemblance to the AspectJ version.

Here is the declaration of the *before* advice from the AspectJ example:

```
before() : auditStockItem() {...}
```

AspectWerkz produces a similar construct using metatags. The metadata also identifies the join points for the advice.

```
/**
 * @Before call(* Warehouse.add(..))
 */
public void beforeAddStockItem(JoinPoint joinPoint) {...}
```

Metadata annotations replace the previous XML definition file, although a smaller file is still required to alert the AspectWerkz framework to the presence of aspects within the application.

Precompilation of AOP metadata information into the application makes it available at runtime for the AspectWerkz weaver. However, moving to J2SE 5.0 removes the need for the precompilation step.

### tip

> The introduction of metadata annotations with J2SE 5.0 offers other interesting advantages to AOP frameworks. In addition to supporting the annotation model used by AspectWerkz, annotations make excellent join point candidates because they are unambiguous. For example, the declaration `call(@annotation * *(..))` offers the AOP developer more options when determining the location of join points within the application.

## AspectWerkz Weaving Options

The framework supports several weaving schemes, including bytecode and load-time weaving. AspectWerkz refers to these weaving schemas in terms of an operating mode: *offline* and *online* modes.

Offline mode is compile-time weaving and is a two-step process in AspectWerkz. The first step is the standard compilation of all source code with `javac`. The final step is the weaving process. Here, the AspectWerkz framework weaves the class files of the main application with the advice from the pertinent aspects. The result is a set of woven classes that run under any JVM, 1.3 or higher.

The online mode is more interesting, offering dynamic load-time weaving. In this mode, AspectWerkz hooks itself directly into the class-loading mechanism of the JVM. From this unique vantage point, AspectWerkz monitors class-loading activity and intercepts classes as they are loaded, weaving in advice at the bytecode level on the fly.

## Aspect-Oriented Middleware

AOP frameworks like AspectWerkz are gaining recognition for the advantages they bring to the development of enterprise software. The binding of application servers with AOP frameworks has given rise to a new term, *aspect-oriented middleware*.

The J2EE platform already takes care of many major system-level crosscutting concerns for the developer, providing services for handling threading, security, persistence, transactions, and component-location transparency. Despite this long list of services, the J2EE platform employs a static model for the management of crosscutting concerns. In comparison to AOP-based frameworks, the J2EE model is rigid and inflexible, with new concerns requiring ad hoc solutions. Aspects promise a fluid and dynamic model for development, and experts in the field believe aspects will revolutionize application server design and the way we develop enterprise software.

Major J2EE server vendors are investing in AOP technology in order to take advantage of the new dimension aspects bring to the middle tier. IBM sponsors AspectJ, and formal support for AspectJ in WebSphere and WebSphere Application Developer (WSAD) is expected in the near future. Meanwhile, BEA has hired the creators of AspectWerkz to add dynamic AOP capabilities to its JRockit JVM. JBoss is currently forging ahead and have come up with its own AOP framework, JBoss AOP, which is an integral part of its application server.

Aspect-oriented middleware is at the (cross) cutting edge and may in the future represent a fundamental change in the way we develop enterprise software.

# Adopting Aspects

Anyone involved in the development of business-critical systems is aware of the importance of a conservative approach when adopting new technology. Production systems must be robust, and a good architect takes all necessary steps to ensure the stability and reliability of any software that underpins an organization's core business processes.

Although AOP has been undergoing research for over 10 years, the paradigm has yet to establish itself within the software engineering community to the same degree as OOP. Indeed, some members of the IT community claim that we have yet to establish a complete set of best practices for developing with OOP. Undoubtedly, many mistakes are likely with AOP as people attempt to realize the full potential of the paradigm. This was certainly the case with OOP.

Given the constraint that the ongoing stability of a production-level system is sacrosanct, this section offers some advice for safely introducing AOP to either a new development project or as part of an established system.

## Development Aspects

One approach to adopting AOP is to constrain the use of the technology solely to the development process by targeting development aspects. Development aspects are those aspects primarily of interest only to the development team. They offer an excellent opportunity to deploy AOP in the relative safety of the development environment without impacting production software.

Examples of development aspects include the following:

### Tracing.

Adding trace statements to the code to follow the flow of a specific section of the application is an effective debugging method and supplements the use of a debugging tool.

### Profiling.

AOP enables the instrumentation of the application with code to gather performance data from the executing program. Profiling techniques identify bottlenecks within the application that prevent the system from achieving its performance objectives.

### Testing.

In addition to injecting advice for profiling applications, AOP can add advice as part of a white-box testing approach. Advice in this context reveals the internal state of the class under test.

Development aspects serve only as an aid in the development process and do not target production-level systems. The dynamic nature of the AOP paradigm makes it very easy to remove development aspects from a system prior to its release into a production or preproduction environment.

> *The different types of system environments are described in Chapter 15.*

Removing aspects from a system using AspectJ is simply a case of omitting aspects from the build process. For AOP frameworks that rely on load-time weaving, the production system has the AOP framework disabled.

tip

> Placing aspects under their own source directory or within their own package structure makes it easy to create build scripts that omit aspects from production builds.

Using AOP for only development aspects therefore offers a low-risk, incremental approach to introducing AOP to a project. The next step is to use AOP to implement production aspects of the system.

## Production Aspects

Unlike development aspects, production aspects form an integral part of the system delivered into production and actively contribute to the behavior of the system.

Taking AOP to this level carries a higher level of risk, but they are manageable by taking sensible steps in the introduction of AOP. These same steps apply when looking to introduce any new technology into a production environment.

A few common issues raised against the use of AOP in a production environment include the following:

* System performance degradation due to runtime weaving
* Emergent system behavior resulting from inaccurate pointcut declarations

A comprehensive testing process should address both of these issues, which is a standard approach when releasing any system into a production environment. You should also make the declaration of pointcut designators more accurate by enforcing rigorous coding standards.

Here are some ideas to consider if you are looking to deploy an AOP-based system into production:

* Experiment with development aspects.
* Define coding standards for working with aspects.
* Ensure all staff are knowledgeable in the use of AOP techniques.
* Build prototypes to validate the selected AOP framework from both a functional and performance perspective.
* Thoroughly test the system and the configuration of the AOP framework before deploying into production.

By following a methodical and incremental approach to the adoption of AOP, you should be able to successfully make AOP-based applications a part of your enterprise environment.

## AOP and Other Paradigms

AOP is not limited to just the OOP paradigm but is equally applicable to other programming types. Research is underway to investigate the suitability of AOP with procedural and rule-based languages. One area of interest is in the twinning of AOP and Model-Driven Architecture (MDA).

*MDA is covered in Chapter 8.*

AOP is complementary to working with the MDA paradigm, and the combination of the two technologies may point to an exciting direction for the future of application development. Code resulting from an MDA process is particularly well suited for defining pointcuts, due to the ability of MDA tools to generate standard method signatures and adhere to coding standards. An MDA-generated application therefore forms an ideal candidate for evolving into a final system by weaving in advice.

Taking this scenario further, the MDA tool could generate an application built purely from system-level concerns. Business concerns would be implemented as aspects that could then be woven into the framework created by the MDA tool. Theoretically, this approach would result in a completely platform-neutral application, as the only handwritten code would be the business logic in the aspects.

Switching platforms—for example, moving to the new EJB 3.0 model—would simply involve plugging in a new MDA cartridge and redefining some of the pointcuts for the final weave. Indeed, the MDA cartridge could potentially generate the new pointcut declarations, leaving the developer with even less work to do.

The benefits of MDA with AOP are still just idle speculation, and more research is required to ascertain if the approach is workable. However, potentially the two paradigms have the ability to work well together, meaning the future of developing business software could lie in the skills of modeling and weaving.

# Summary

AOP is an emerging programming paradigm that augments the benefits of existing paradigms by providing language constructs that support the modularization of crosscutting concerns.

Interest in AOP is growing steadily within the developer community, and AOP is starting to penetrate the mainstream with major application server vendors moving to integrate the technology within their products.

Following are some of the main reasons to consider adopting AOP:

* Improved designs and more easily maintainable applications due to the modularization of crosscutting concerns
* Systems offering greater flexibility in the face of changing requirements
* The ability to effect widespread change to an application's code base rapidly and dynamically
* Complementary to the development of solutions for the J2EE platform

Despite the benefits, AOP has yet to be universally accepted by the Java community, with some high-profile software engineers urging a cautious approach to what still is an emerging technology. However, moving to AOP does not require an *all-or-nothing* approach, and a low-risk incremental adoption of the paradigm is possible.

Perhaps the core strength of AOP lies in the new dimension it brings to existing programming paradigms. We briefly discussed the possibilities surrounding the twining of AOP with MDA.

Another interesting combination would be AOP with rule-based languages. This scenario sees business analysts using business-domain languages to describe business processes, while software engineers weave in aspects to turn business descriptions into software solutions. With this future vision of software development, business analysts become the hunchbacks, while the software engineers are the dragons. Personally, I'd rather be a dragon than a hunchback.

## Additional Information

AOP is an extensive subject, and it has been necessary to be very selective in order to cover the topic within the confines of a single chapter. Further information on AOP is available from the aspect-oriented software development Web site at `http://aosd.net`.

Ramnivas Laddad's "*I Want My AOP Series*," a three-part article on AOP based on AspectJ, can be found on the JavaWorld site. See `http://www.javaworld.com/javaworld/jw-01-2002/jw-0118-aspect.html`.

# Part IV: Dynamic Environments

Part IV covers a select range of practices and tools for building and testing enterprise software. We look at ways to design an efficient build process that provides the entire project team with a productive working environment. In addition, the benefits of integrated development tools for helping improve productivity are examined, with examples using the popular open source development platform Eclipse.

Part IV also addresses the issues surrounding software quality and rapid development, and describes how a test-driven approach can produce high-quality systems and facilitate rapid application development.

We conclude with a look at the formal testing process and evaluate open source tools that reduce testing times without compromising the accuracy or rigor of the testing process.

# 12

# Optimal Builds

O ne of the first tasks you'll undertake during the construction phase of a project is the design of the development environment. A well-designed environment is paramount to ensuring the entire project team can work productively and effectively.

In this chapter, we focus specifically on one aspect of the development environment that is critical to a successful rapid application development project, the build process. We cover in detail the importance of a fast, accurate, and maintainable build process, and examine the use of the Apache Ant build utility for producing optimal build environments for J2EE applications.

This chapter covers several areas regarding the build process:

- The importance of an efficient build process for rapid development
- The advantages of Ant as a build tool
- How to manage build dependencies in order to reduce build times
- The use of the open source tool *Antgraph* for graphically viewing dependencies in Ant files
- Guidelines for organizing the code artifacts of J2EE projects
- Suggested best practices for working with Ant

We conclude by revisiting the Jython scripting language and demonstrating how Jython scripts can readily extend the features of Ant.

## Time and Motion

Anyone who has worked on a manufacturing production line is familiar with the concept of *time and motion*. A time-and-motion study involves the analysis of the operations needed to manufacture an item in a factory, with the intention of reducing the manufacturing time per item and thereby increasing the rate of output. The study calls for every step of the manufacturing process to be scrutinized in order to identify any inefficiency in the production method.

A production line has to be the epitome of efficiency, and production engineers use time-and-motion studies as a technique for streamlining the manufacturing process. Consider a car manufacturing plant, with vehicles rolling off lines in huge numbers. If one step of the process is suboptimal, the result could be a substantial increase in the cost of production as well as fewer cars being available for market.

Manufacturing time is not the only concern of the production engineer. Another factor is quality, as the process must ensure an acceptable and consistent level of build quality for every item rolling off the line.

Although a time-and-motion study is a technique used by the manufacturing industry, the efficiency-focused mindset of the production engineer is relevant to the task of designing a build process for software.

## The Software Production Line

Few people would perceive the software development process as being similar to a production line. Developing software is a creative task and is different for each system. Nevertheless, the many and varied activities that make up a software development project are common to all projects and are frequently repeated by each member of the team on an almost daily basis.

A software engineer's tasks include such common activities as pulling down the latest version of the application from source control; building, deploying, and testing new application functionality; and checking the defects log for errors raised against previous releases. These tasks and many more make up a typical developer's day.

Similar recurring tasks exist for other project roles. The quality assurance team has a process for installing the latest releases from the development team and preparing a suitable environment for testing. The team may perform this task manually or rely upon a script for creating a clean environment for each test cycle.

For rapid development to take place, all of these activities must run smoothly and efficiently.

## Time and Motion for Software Development

The software development environment and the processes and procedures that drive it must ensure all team members can work expediently and accurately. To achieve this optimal state for the project, teams should look to the practices of production engineers and perform their own time-and-motion studies on those everyday activities that are performed so frequently.

This shouldn't be a matter of hiring production engineers with stopwatches to come in and time people as they work. Instead, efficiency is the responsibility of all team members, and everyone should seek ways to improve the process.

Feeding this information back into a company's development practices is critical to maintaining a companywide adaptive foundation for rapid development, as passing these process improvements from project to project helps establish productive environments for future applications.

With the importance of time and motion in mind, let's consider the intricacies of the build process.

# The Build Process

A good build process is more than just a script for compiling software. Instead, a build process performs and automates many of the common activities on a project. Examples of common activities include the following:

- Retrieving code from source control
- Installing the correct versions of libraries and software
- Compiling application libraries and components
- Running automated test suites
- Generating Javadocs
- Packaging components and libraries
- Setting up development and test environments, including updating database schemas and creating test data
- Deploying applications into a development environment
- Creating versioned releases of software components
- Deploying releases into a test environment

Having a ready-made build process in place before a project commences is a major time-saver. Build processes are sophisticated pieces of software that require careful design, construction, and testing. Consequently, investment in the development of build processes that are reusable between projects is a key factor in the makeup of a company's adaptive foundation for rapid development.

The next sections offer some guidelines for creating a build process that is conducive to the practice of rapid development.

## Designing a Build Process

Like software systems, build systems require careful design. Regardless of the type of software under development, the requirements for a build system tend to be common between projects. Here is a summary of some of the main requirements:

**Accurate.**

The build process must be consistent between builds, producing the same result from a given set of source files for all developers on the team.

### Rapid.

With builds running frequently, the process must be streamlined to ensure undue time is not lost waiting for the process to complete.

### Automated.

All steps of the build process must be under the control of a suitable build tool that ensures the entire build can be automated. If developers are required to undertake manual steps, such as copying files or building individual modules, then the possibility of introducing build errors into the process is increased. Furthermore, manual scripts cannot be set up to run as scheduled tasks that can operate overnight.

### Standardized.

How the build process is used should be consistent across projects and within teams.

### Parameterized.

A build for a developer is likely to be subtly different than a build destined for a formal test environment. These differences could be compiler options or the omission of build steps. The build process must be able to generate a consistent release for each type of environment.

### Maintainable.

Build environments have a tendency to increase in size and sophistication to the point that maintenance becomes a major headache, not to mention a black hole for lost time. The build system must be simple enough to be easily maintained yet capable of handling complex build tasks. Unfortunately, these two requirements are not complementary.

These requirements are common to most software projects. The development of enterprise-level software introduces a further set of requirements peculiar to the J2EE platform.

## J2EE Build Requirements

The build process for a conventional Java-based application often builds only a single target, thereby making for a simple build environment. Unfortunately, a J2EE application is not so straightforward; it involves numerous intricate steps to generate multiple targets.

Unlike its J2SE counterpart, a J2EE application comprises a set of components, which collectively make up the whole application. Each component can have vastly different build requirements. EJB components require specialized compilation tasks for the generation of stub and skeleton implementations. Code generation tools such as XDoclet are becoming increasingly popular for the effort they save, but add additional steps and complexity to the build process.

> *XDoclet is covered in Chapter 6.*

In addition to these specialized tasks, J2EE components require *packaging*. EJB components are wrapped in JAR files, and Web applications are packed in a Web archive (WAR) file. Finally, all components can be bundled in an enterprise resource file (EAR), the format recommended for J2EE deployments by application servers.

To summarize, a J2EE build typically includes the following tasks, which are additional to traditional Java builds:

- Execution of code generators
- Component-specific compilation, such as for Enterprise JavaBeans
- Packaging, for example, in JAR, WAR, and EAR files
- Deployment

All of these tasks devour time. Packaging, which requires moving files around the file system into a structure where they can be bundled into a format ready for deployment, is a particularly time-consuming process. Likewise, the process of deploying components to the server and placing them in an executable state is also potentially time consuming.

Shortening the length of time spent building and deploying is a case of reducing the amount of work the build system has to undertake. This gives rise to the concept of a build system capable of performing *minimal builds* and *minimal deployments*. We consider each concept in turn.

## Minimal Builds

Generating source, compiling code, and packaging binaries into JAR files are all resource-intensive tasks. If the number of times these tasks have to be performed as part of the build can be reduced, savings in build times result.

Achieving these savings involves ensuring the build system can undertake *incremental* tasks, building only those components impacted by a particular code change. Therefore, if a source file is changed, the build system should not have to regenerate the full system. Instead, it should be able to determine from dependency information those components affected by the change, and accordingly build, package, and deploy only those modules that are affected.

## Minimal Deployments

Minimal builds are only part of the story. It is also necessary to consider how a built application transitions into a state in which it can be run and tested. For J2EE solutions, this involves deploying components to the application server.

A minimal deployment approach looks to reduce the total number of steps that must be taken by the software engineer in order to deploy a change to the server. A typical worst case is that the server must be stopped, the entire application redeployed, and then the server restarted. This type of delay is unacceptable. Thankfully, most J2EE application server vendors acknowledge the importance of being able to turn around change quickly and efficiently, so they offer support for the *hot deployment* of applications. The practice of hot deployment requires further explanation given its importance to the build process.

## What Is Hot Deployment?

Hot deployment is a concept embraced by most application server vendors and refers to the ability of the server to deploy an updated J2EE application into a live environment without having to shut down either the server or the running application.

For a production system, hot deployment has obvious benefits for system availability. For development teams, however, we require a slightly different form of hot deployment that is perhaps better called *automatic deployment*.

This concept has the application server continually polling for new files. On detecting a new file, the application server immediately loads the change and integrates it into the current application.

warning

> Automatic deployment is unsuitable for a production environment because the need for the server to poll its deployment directories continually is an unacceptable performance overhead.

In a fast-paced development environment, this functionality is a major timesaver for the software engineer, as no manual steps are needed for the application server to apply the software changes other than deploying the changes to the server.

Automatic deployment is a proprietary feature and is not covered by the J2EE specification, which only stipulates the deployment of EAR, WAR, JAR, and RAR files. Application servers, such as WebLogic from BEA, have gone beyond the J2EE specification and provide support for the deployment of applications in an expanded, or exploded, format rather than an archive file. This approach, which BEA recommends for deployment to its server, provides support for the minimal deployment approach.

WebLogic server supports automatic deployment if the server is running in development mode. This is achieved by setting the system property `-Dweblogic.ProductionModeEnabled` to false.

You must check the details of your particular application server to determine what it provides in terms of minimal and hot deployment capabilities.

Having covered some of the main requirements for a build system, we can now look at producing the build process itself. For this, we need to adopt a suitable build tool.

# Introducing Ant

Ant is an extensible build utility from Apache Software Foundation that uses an XML-based syntax for creating build scripts. The build utility is open source and is available for download from the Apache Website at `http://ant.apache.org`.

Ant almost needs no introduction, as it has become the de facto standard for Java builds. As discussed in earlier chapters, *XDoclet*, *Middlegen*, and *AndroMDA* all rely on Ant for execution.

> *Chapter 7 discusses Middlegen and*
> *Chapter 8 introduces AndroMDA.*

Ant's success is due to a number of features that see the build tool ideally suited to Java development. Ant's use of XML documents for defining build files offers a clean and readily understandable syntax, making it possible for developers to get quickly up to speed with the tool. This was a significant problem with earlier Make tools whose declarative semantics were often difficult to grasp.

Furthermore, Ant is implemented in Java and runs under any compliant JVM. This makes Ant a crossplatform build utility, an important factor when working with the J2SE platform. This is also a big advantage over previous Make tools, which rely on platform-specific shell commands for performing build operations.

Due to its huge uptake, Ant has grown into a mature build tool that offers an extensive range of features for performing just about every conceivable build task. Under Ant, build files invoke build operations by calling *Ant tasks*.

Ant provides a set of core inbuilt tasks that perform many of the common build operations, including:

* Compiling Java source
* Defining build classpaths
* Generating Javadocs
* Copying and deleting files
* Changing file permissions
* Creating JAR files
* Executing external applications
* Invoking build steps in other Ant build files
* Working with archive formats, such as ZIP and TAR
* Sending mail
* Accessing source control repositories

Where Ant does not support a specific build operation, developers can implement their own custom Ant tasks, which are then accessible from within the build file.

Most major Java software vendors supply Ant tasks for controlling the build process when using their software. The code generators of XDoclet, Middlegen, and AndroMDA all supply Ant tasks specifically for this purpose.

With Ant's ubiquity in the Java world, you will likely use Ant for controlling all of your builds. Consequently, the next sections focus on the use of Ant for designing and implementing optimal build solutions.

## Key Features of Ant

Here are some of the reasons Ant has proven so popular:

- *Ease-of-use* through a simple XML-based scripting language
- *Crossplatform support*—Ant executes under any compliant JVM
- *Extensive functionality* through a wide range of built-in tasks
- *Extensible model* through the definition of custom Ant tasks in Java
- *A de facto standard*—software vendors supply Ant tasks by default
- *A large user base*, meaning most software engineers have experience with Ant build files

# Minimal Builds with Ant

For a build tool to support the concept of minimal, or incremental, builds, it must be able to identify the dependency relationships that exist between the various project artifacts that make up the application.

Prior to Ant, most Java developers used Make tools for creating build files. Make tools employ declarative programming language semantics for defining dependency rules between build artifacts. With this approach, the Make tool infers the build tasks to perform following a change to a particular source file or component.

> *Declarative programming is described in Chapter 10.*

The inference capabilities of the Make tool support a minimal build approach but at the expense of build-file complexity. Ant uses a simpler syntax for its build files than Make, but does not intrinsically support a declarative approach to the build process.

# The Importance of Build Dependencies

To appreciate the impact of build dependencies, let's consider the example build.xml in Listing 12–1. In this example, the build file instructs Ant as to the build order of each of the targets.

## Listing 12–1    Ant Example build.xml

```
<project name="ant-build" default="compile">

  <target name="compile"
          description="Compile all Java source">
    <javac srcDir="."/>
  </target>

  <target name="clean"
          description="Removes all class files">
    <delete>
      <fileset dir="." includes="*.class"/>
    </delete>
  </target>

  <target name="build"
          depends="clean, compile"
          description="Rebuilds all source"/>

</project>
```

The example build file in Listing 12–1 contains three build targets: compile, clean, and build. The compile target is set as the default for the project and is run whenever Ant is executed unless an alternative target, such as ant build, is explicitly specified.

Running the build file for the first time with the default compile target results in the compilation of all Java source in the base directory. For this example, assume we have a single HelloWorld.java file.

Running the build file a second time is distinctly quicker, as Ant determines all class files are up-to-date and no compilation is necessary. How is this possible given the build file provided no dependency information between HelloWorld.java and HelloWorld.class?

The secret lies in the <javac> task, used to compile the Java source. This task has built-in dependency rules and knows to associate *.java and *.class files. Therefore, for Java compilations, Ant supports the minimal build approach we require for fast builds. Unfortunately, Ant is not as knowledgeable about other file types. This is a problem, especially for J2EE builds that rely on many custom build steps.

Listing 12–2 revises the previous example to illustrate the problem.

## Listing 12–2    Build File with Dependent Target

```
<project name="ant-build" default="compile">

  <target name="generate"
          description="Long running build task">
    <ejbdoclet>
      .
      .
      .
    </ejbdoclet>
  </target>

  <target name="compile"
          depends="generate"
          description="Compile all Java source">
    <javac srcDir="."/>
  </target>

  <target name="clean"
          description="Removes all class files">
    <delete>
      <fileset dir="." includes="*.class"/>
    </delete>
  </target>

  <target name="build"
          depends="clean, compile"
          description="Rebuilds all source"/>

</project>
```

A new target, <generate>, has been added to the build. This target invokes a code generator, for example, XDoclet, which processes those files containing annotations.

Before the <compile> target can begin, the <generate> target must have completed. This dependency between the two targets is expressed using the special Ant attribute depends. With this dependency defined, Ant always runs the <generate> target ahead of <compile>.

The relationship specified between the two targets is procedural: Ant does not check file timestamps to determine if the <generate> target must be run.

Assume our example project comprised 10,000 source files, with 5,000 of them marked up with XDoclet-style annotations or attributes. Modifying an annotated file requires running XDoclet to pick up the change. However, if a file without annotations is changed, then we can safely skip the <generate> task and run only <compile>. Because the <compile> target uses the <javac> task, only the affected source file is compiled.

tip

Virus checkers slow down builds. Turning your virus checker off noticeably speeds up the build process. Unfortunately, the threat to unprotected machines from malicious viruses means companies tend to insist all machines run virus protection software at all times.

If you can't turn off your virus checker, another option is to change the setting of the virus software so it ignores all files written to build directories. Most virus checkers are configurable to enable the exclusion of certain files and directories from the scanning process. Refer to the manual of your particular virus-protection software for more information.

Ideally, we want our code generator, be it XDoclet or some other tool, to have the same functionality as the <javac> task. If only one of our 5,000 annotated files is modified, then the code generator should process only a single file.

With this approach, the steps of the build process are as follows:

1. Developer modifies a single annotate file.
2. XDoclet generates new program source from only the file that has changed.
3. <javac> task compiles only the files generated by XDoclet.

As it stands now, the <generate> target will pick up all 5,000 files, thereby resulting in the need for <javac> to undertake a significant recompilation effort.

This is a problem. Our build process does not support the concept of minimal builds, and our time-and-motion expert is far from pleased.

Using a Make tool, we could have defined build rules to instruct Make to run the code generator against modified files only. Unfortunately, Ant does not support this form of deterministic build process directly. More importantly, neither does the XDoclet Ant task.

Nevertheless, the authors of Ant recognized the importance of build dependencies and added support for this feature as a set of core tasks. We still have work to do if we are to make use of this functionality, as it is not default behavior. To understand how build dependencies can be enforced, let's leave XDoclet and consider another example.

## Defining Build Dependencies in Ant

The build.xml file shown in Listing 12–3 demonstrates the use of the <uptodate> task to define a conditional build dependency between two targets. In this example, the dependency defines the need to package Java binaries into a single JAR file.

## Listing 12–3   Ant Build File with Conditional Build

```
<project name="depend-example" default="make">

<!-- Build file with dependency defined between
     package and compile targets -->

<property name="src.dir"  location="src"/>
<property name="bin.dir"  location="bin"/>
<property name="dist.dir" location="dist"/>

<target name="compile"
        description="Compiles all Java source">
  <javac srcdir="${src.dir}"
         destdir="${bin.dir}"/>

  <!-- Check if files have been updated -->
  <uptodate property="package.notRequired"
            targetfile="${dist.dir}/app.jar">
    <srcfiles dir="${bin.dir}" includes="**/*.class"/>
  </uptodate>
</target>

<target name="package"
        depends="compile"
        unless="package.notRequired"
        description="Produces JAR file">

  <jar destfile="${dist.dir}/app.jar"
       basedir="${bin.dir}"/>
</target>

<target name="clean"
        description="Removes all class files">
  <delete>
    <fileset dir="${bin.dir}"/>
    <fileset dir="${dist.dir}"/>
  </delete>
</target>

<target name="make"
        depends="package"
        description="Incremental build"/>

<target name="build"
        depends="clean, make"
        description="Rebuilds all source"/>

</project>
```

The build process shown in Listing 12–3 involves two steps. First, the compile target compiles all code in the src directory with <javac>, directing all output to the bin directory. Second, the package target collects the contents of the bin directory into a single JAR file, placing the archive in the dist directory ready for deployment.

Two top-level build targets are responsible for performing these steps:

* The build target deletes all built files and compiles and packages the application from scratch.

* The make target performs an incremental build and creates a distribution only if any source has been updated.

Packaging large numbers of files into JAR files is a time-consuming process, so it is of benefit to perform this task only when needed. We make the running of the package target conditional with the use of the unless attribute.

The unless attribute instructs Ant to skip the execution of the target if the associated property has been set to any value. Conversely, the if attribute of <target> instructs Ant to run the target if the property is set.

With properties and the if and unless attributes of the <target> task, we can control at build time which targets are run. From the example in Listing 12–3, the package target references the package.notRequired property to determine if it should generate a JAR file. This property is set as the final act of the compile target upon which the package target is dependent.

The task <uptodate> is used to set the package.notRequired property in the example. This conditional task sets the property identified with the property attribute if the target file is more up-to-date than the source. In this case, the <uptodate> task checks to see if any class files have been generated since the JAR file was last produced. If any class files prove to be more recent than the JAR file, then the package.notRequired property is left unset and the package target is allowed to execute.

The conditional support provided by Ant makes it is possible to create sophisticated build scripts that support incremental builds. However, adding conditional behavior to the build process can significantly increase its complexity. The example in Listing 12–3 covers a very basic case. A typical J2EE build involves many more targets, and adding dependency information therefore adds significant complexity to the build process.

To prevent additional build logic making build files unduly complex, good design dictates the build process be broken down into discrete blocks, or modules. With this approach, modules of the system can be built in isolation, and dependencies can be more easily defined between build targets.

# Working with Subprojects

Good software design sees a large application broken down into smaller modules that exhibit the characteristics of loose coupling and high internal cohesion. A build script is itself a software artifact, so the same rules apply when designing a build process, and we should look to break large builds down into smaller, self-contained units known as subprojects.

Ant provides a number of options for breaking down large build files into smaller, more manageable modules. One approach is to have a central, controlling build file responsible for delegating build tasks to each of the subprojects. Ant allows targets to be invoked between build files using the <ant> task.

The following extract depicts the use of the <ant> task to kick off a target in a separate build.xml file.

```
<ant antfile="build.xml"
     dir="${subproject.dir}"
     target="package"
     inheritAll="no">
  <property name="package.dir"
            value="${wls.url}"/>
</ant>
```

Attributes of the <ant> task specify the name of the build file, its location, the name of the target to be invoked, and whether the subproject is to have access to all the properties of the caller. The default for this final attribute is to have the called build file take on all the properties of the caller. In the example shown, this behavior is disabled, and instead, specific properties are passed in using the nested <property> element.

Breaking up build files in this manner is not to everyone's liking. Some people prefer keeping all the build processing in one location. Ant can support this preference by allowing build files to pull in other build files rather than delegate out to them.

Ant can achieve the include-type functionality of Make in one of two ways. Ant files are first and foremost XML documents, so we can leverage the power of XML to pull in build snippets. Listing 12–4 demonstrates this approach.

## Listing 12–4   Including Build File Snippets

```
<?xml version="1.0" encoding="UTF-8"?>

<!DOCTYPE project [
  <!ENTITY properties SYSTEM "file:./config/properties.xml">
  <!ENTITY libraries SYSTEM "file:./config/libraries.xml">
]>

<project name="include-example" default="make" basedir=".">

  &properties;
  &libraries;

  .
  .
  .

</project>
```

From the example shown in Listing 12–4, the contents of the two files properties.xml and libraries.xml are inserted directly in the build.xml file at the location marked with &properties and &libraries respectively.

Ant 1.6 provides a second method for pulling in external build files. The `<import>` task, which pulls in an entire build file, has the advantage over the previous example in that it enables build files to inherit from other build files. Thus, we can use this behavior to override targets in imported build files if required.

# Viewing Build Dependencies

Dependencies within build files can become very complex and involved. Thankfully, Eric Burke has come up with *Antgraph*, a very convenient open source utility for graphically viewing Ant build files. Antgraph is available from Eric's Web site at `http://www.ericburke.com/downloads/antgraph/`. The software is very easy to install and run, and is available for several platforms.

Figure 12–1 shows an example of the output from Antgraph.

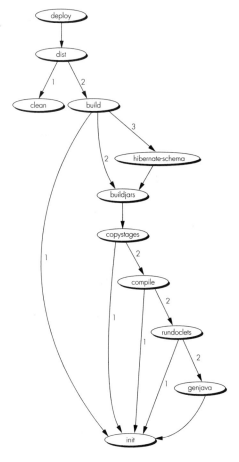

**Figure 12–1**    Ant build file dependency information produced by Antgraph.

The example in Figure 12–1 is a graphical representation of the Ant build file supplied by AndroMDA for producing a Hibernate-based AndroMDA project. The graph depicts each target within the build file, with the arrows showing the calling hierarchy between the targets. The numbers on the arrows are a count of the dependencies for each target. For example, build is dependent on three targets: init, buildjars, and hibernate-schema.

Antgraph relies upon *Graphviz*, a freely available graphics engine, for rendering the graph. Graphviz supports a number of different graph types, so you can experiment with the different options. The graph shown uses the standard *dot* layout engine, but other options include the *neato* and *twopi* layout engines. You might want to experiment to find your favorite.

# Standard Build Targets

It's a good idea to try to standardize on the targets across build files. Adopting a target-naming convention ensures all build files between projects are consistent and more easily understood and maintained by members of the project team. Table 12–1 offers some naming suggestions for the common Ant build targets.

**Table 12–1**   Naming Suggestions for Ant Build Targets

| Name | Reference |
| --- | --- |
| init | General utility target for performing any setup tasks, for example, creating directories, copying files, or performing dependency checks. This target is seldom invoked directly from the command prompt but is instead called by other Ant targets. |
| clean | The clean target removes all generated build artifacts, thereby ensuring any subsequent builds regenerate all targets. |
| compile | This target compiles all source files. It may also be dependent on a generate target, which invokes any code generators that are part of the build process. |
| package | The package target takes the output from the compile phase and packages up all files ready for deployment. This target is sometimes named dist. |
| make | Use the make target for initiating incremental builds. This target requires conditional dependencies to be correctly set up between the different build targets. |
| build | Performs a clean followed by a make, thereby ensuring the entire application is built from scratch. |
| deploy | Deploys the built application to the designated application server. An undeploy task is also useful for removing the application from the server. |
| test | Use this target for running all unit tests. The test target should be run regularly and preferably included as part of an overnight build process. |
| docs | Generates all the Javadoc documentation for the project. |
| fetch | Retrieves the latest version of the project from source control. You might want to consider defining an overarching target that fetches the latest code, performs a complete build, and then runs all unit tests. |

These suggestions are for a minimal set of build targets; your project will probably have many more. For example, you could add a run target to launch any client applications as well as start and stop targets for controlling the application server.

Applying a consistent naming convention becomes more important with Ant 1.6, as the use of <import> makes it possible to override the targets of other build files within an inheriting Ant build file.

tip

> Ensure you provide a good level of help for all targets within the build file. Use the description attribute of the target element for this purpose. You can then launch Ant with the -projecthelp option to see a list of all targets, complete with descriptions, that are supported by the build file.

You must specify dependencies between each target. Figure 12–2 shows the output from Antgraph based on the targets defined in Table 12–1.

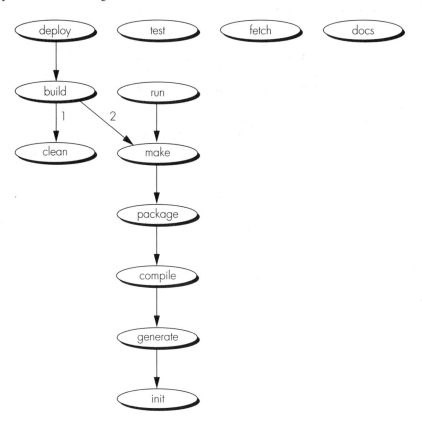

**Figure 12–2**    Target hierarchy as generated by Antgraph.

For larger projects comprising multiple modules, we need to consider how the overall project is organized. The next section provides guidelines for addressing this issue.

# Project Organization

A well-organized project directory structure makes both the code and the build process easier to manage. A number of factors, including the requirements of the target application server and the needs of the development tools used by the project team, drive the exact structure of your particular build process. However, the concepts presented here provide an outline that you can tailor for your specific project environment.

note

> The project structure becomes more elaborate as the application grows in size. By keeping things simple from the start, you can help avoid undue complexity as the system evolves.

For J2EE development, the project structure falls logically into the four separate areas: source, build, external libraries, and distribution. Each area is normally contained within its own directory on the file system, with each directory sitting directly beneath a top-level project directory in the hierarchy.

Figure 12–3 depicts the top-level project structure.

We start by examining the structure of the source directory.

**Figure 12–3**   Top-level directory structure.

## Source Directory

The source directory contains all program artifacts involved in the construction of the application. This is not limited to Java source but encompasses such artifacts as build scripts, property files, deployment descriptors, database scripts, and XML schemas. Figure 12–4 shows the organization of the source directory.

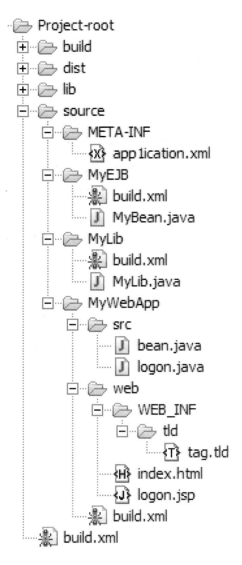

**Figure 12–4**    Source directory structure.

The project is structured around the creation of a single EAR file, with each module of the distribution being maintained as a subproject.

note

> All source code should reside under its package directory structure. You should also consider adding a parallel source directory for each component to maintain the code for unit tests.

From the directory structure shown in Figure 12–4, we have several modules:

- The META-INF directory holds all the files necessary to make up a deployable EAR file.
- EJB modules are placed in their own directory. An EAR file can be comprised of several modules. The example shown in Figure 12–4 contains a single EJB module, MyEJB.
- Common libraries built as part of the project should reside within the directory structure, as is shown with the library MyLib.
- Web applications have the most complex structure because they are made up of several file types. The Web application MyWebApp shows a possible layout for the organization of the different file types.

Each module that makes up the J2EE distribution possesses its own build.xml file. These are self-contained build files, capable of building each module in isolation. The build files are also aware of dependencies that may exist between the different modules. A Web application will likely call into a business layer and so may have a dependency on the EJB module. This should all be managed by each build file.

All build files should be consistent between modules, with each build file exposing the same set of targets. A single controlling build file resides at the top of the project directory structure. This is a *delegating* Ant build file, again exposing the same targets as the build files of each subproject.

Calls to targets in the project build file are cascaded down to the equivalent targets in each of the subprojects. Although each build file has the same set of targets, the work they perform is in context with the type of module they are responsible for building. On a Web module, the target package produces a WAR file, while on the top-level project build file, the package target generates an EAR file.

The build order of the subprojects is important and should commence with the low-level modules and work upwards. Building from bottom-to-top and ensuring hierarchical dependencies are in place provides a build system that is easy to maintain and consequently produces consistent results.

# Lib Directory

This directory holds all external libraries. The build scripts reference this directory structure during compilation. When assembling a distribution, libraries required at runtime are copied from this directory as needed.

# Build Directory

All output from the source directory is directed to the build directory. Keeping source files separate from built files is important for good housekeeping. A clean separation of the two directories means the build directory is disposable and can simply be deleted at any time. This makes the writing of the clean target a trivial task.

The structure of the build directory should mimic that of the source for consistent navigation of all built files. It is considered good practice to direct all output from the build process to the build directory, including output from code generators such as deployment descriptors and remote interfaces. The simple rule to follow is to place all output that will be created each time a full build is run under the build directory, regardless of whether the output is source or binary.

Figure 12–5 illustrates the structure of the build directory based on the project structure defined for the source in Figure 12–4.

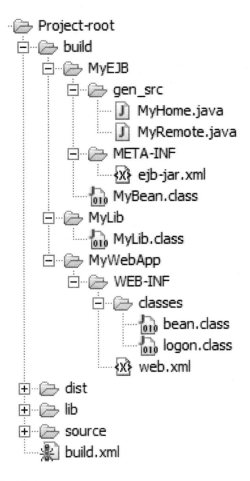

**Figure 12–5**   The build directory structure.

Having built all the necessary parts of the project, the next step is to package all components ready for deployment to the application server. For this task, we make use of the distribution directory.

## Distribution Directory

The distribution directory is convenient for packaging and deployment purposes. It is possible to undertake all of this work within the build directory, but having a separate directory for all packaged files simplifies the process of generating formal releases or passing new versions of the system onto a formal test environment.

Figure 12–6 depicts an example of a distribution directory. Again this directory structure adopts the module structure seen in both the source and build directories.

Having the distribution directory fall under the main project directory is optional. For development purposes, you may wish to generate the packaged files directly into the directory structure of the application server to take advantage of its hot deployment capabilities. In some cases, the application server may call for all modules to be deployed in an uncompressed format, bypassing the need for extensive packaging.

The project structure outlined is a guideline only. The requirements of your project dictate the workings of your build process, and you should design a project structure according to your specific needs.

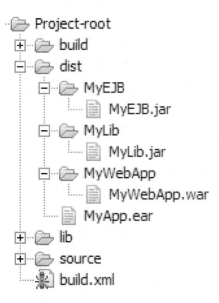

**Figure 12–6**   The distribution directory.

# Integration with IDEs

Although it is important to be able to build the entire application from the command line, the use of a build script should not preclude the use of the productivity features of your favorite integrated development environment (IDE). While is important that an IDE is able to interoperate with a build script, it is equally important that a build script can utilize the features of the IDE.

> *Chapter 13 covers the advantages of working with an IDE.*

Unfortunately, IDEs do not make good build tools. They tend to do only a very small subset of the build tasks required on most projects. They can perform such tasks as compilation and packaging, but fall short of supporting all the build tasks necessary for the development of enterprise software. In contrast, a good build script performs tasks such as stamping JAR files with version numbers, packaging applications ready for deployment, distributing applications into test environments, running unit tests, and so on.

Although IDEs do not perform all the essential build tasks required for a project, they do perform certain build tasks extremely well. Compilation of all source files is one example. A highly useful feature of an IDE is to have it continually compile and syntax-check code as you type. This feature traps syntax errors early on and is very productive.

To support this feature, the IDE must be configured with all the necessary information to compile the application. If the build script is also to perform the compile task, a duplication of effort exists between the IDE and build script. Such a duplication, as well as being an overhead to maintain, is a possible source of build inconsistencies, since different application characteristics may emerge from the different build approaches.

One way to circumvent this problem is to have Ant use the IDE to perform the build. With this method, builds initiated from the IDE are identical to those invoked from the build script.

In order for this approach to work, the IDE must be able to run a build from a shell command, preferably without launching the entire graphical development environment.

Here's how the Ant <exec> task can build the project using Borland's JBuilder.

```
<exec dir="."
      executable="${jbuilder_home.dir}/jbuilder.exe"
      failonerror="true">
  <arg line="-build myproject.jpx make"/>
</exec>
```

This approach relies on using the machinery of the JBuilder IDE, complete with the JBuilder project's classpath settings, to perform the build. This removes the need to duplicate build information between the project file of the IDE and the Ant build file. Check the manual of your favorite IDE to establish how to initiate the build process from the command line.

# Extending Ant with Jython

Though Ant comes complete with an extensive range of built-in tasks suitable for most build-related operations, you will likely encounter situations in the design of your environment that are not accommodated by the existing Ant tasks. In this scenario, we can use Ant's extensibility to define our own tasks.

Ant tasks are traditionally implemented in Java. However, as build tasks are usually the domain of scripting languages, another option is to use Jython. The advantage of this approach is that we get the rapid development benefits of the Jython scripting languages as well as access to Jython's extensive library of functions.

> Chapter 9 covers the basics of the
> Jython language.

## Creating a New Ant Task

Implementing a basic Ant task involves the following steps:

1. Define a Java class that extends `org.apache.tools.ant.Task`.
2. Provide public setter methods for all task attributes.
3. Implement a public `execute()` method.

Listing 12–5 shows an implementation of an Ant task in Jython. The task has a single attribute called `message`. Invoking the task from an Ant build file prints out the message held in the attribute and then prints further information on the owning target's dependency information.

You can use this example as a template for creating your own Jython Ant tasks.

## Listing 12–5   Jython Ant Task RapidTask.py

```
from org.apache.tools.ant import Task
from org.apache.tools.ant import Target

class RapidTask(Task):

  # Overrides the Task.execute() method
  #
  def execute(self):
    "@sig public void execute()"

    # Print out properties of task
    #
```

```
    self.log('Task Name: ' + self.taskName)
    self.log('Description: ' + self.description)

    # Print out the message property
    #
    self.log('Message: ' + self.message)

    # Get the owning target and list dependencies
    #
    target = self.owningTarget

    self.log('Target name: ' + target.name)

    for dependency in target.dependencies:
        self.log('\tDepends: ' + dependency)

# Ant attribute setter method
#
def setMessage(self, message):
    "@sig public void setMessage(java.lang.String str)"
    self.message = message
```

## Compiling Jython Classes

The Jython class shown in Listing 12–5 has a few differences from a normal Jython class, as it must be complied if Ant is to use it. Compiling Jython to standard Java bytecode involves moving from the type-less world of Jython to the strongly typed world of Java. This presents a few problems when defining methods on Java classes as Jython methods have no signature.

To get around this problem, it is necessary to embed a string in the __doc__ namespace of each method that defines the Jython method's Java signature. Here are the embedded method signatures for both the setMessage() and execute() methods on the RapidTask class:

```
@sig public void setMessage(java.lang.String str)
@sig public void execute()
```

The @sig preamble at the start of the string tells the jythonc compiler the Java method signature to generate. This is all jythonc needs to compile the class to bytecode.

The Jython class is compiled from the command line:

```
jythonc -a -c -d -j rapidTask.jar RapidTask.py
```

The parameters -a, -c, and, -d instruct jythonc to include the entire core Jython libraries in the build. The -j rapidTask.jar specifies to place the compiled classes into the named JAR file.

With the new task successfully compiled, it is ready for use from within a build file.

## Testing the New Task

The new task is included in the build script using the <taskdef>, which defines the name of the new task and the class to load. Listing 12–6 shows an example of an extract from a small test build file for the new Ant task.

### Listing 12–6   Test Build File for the Jython Ant Task

```
<target name="test"
     depends="clean, package"
     description="Access the Jython Ant task">

  <!-- Declare the new Jython task -->
  <taskdef name="Rapid"
           classname="RapidTask">
    <classpath>
      <pathelement location="${task.jar}"/>
    </classpath>
  </taskdef>

  <!-- Set a property on the task -->
  <Rapid description="Example task"
        message="My Jython Task" />

</target>
```

Invoking the <test> target generates the following output from the Jython Ant task.

```
test:
    [Rapid] Task Name: Rapid
    [Rapid] Description: Example task
    [Rapid] Message: My Jython Task
    [Rapid] Target name: test
    [Rapid]     Depends: clean
    [Rapid]     Depends: package

BUILD SUCCESSFUL
```

The Jython task uses methods on the Task class to obtain information about its environment, such as the name of the task, the name of the owning target, and a list of all dependencies. It also prints out the message attribute we added as part of the task.

That's all there is to building an Ant task with Jython. Mixing Ant and Jython gives us the structure and control of Ant coupled with the rapid scripting capabilities of Jython—the perfect combination for constructing build processes.

# Summary

The build process forms only part of the overall software development process. Nevertheless, the frequency with which the process is invoked is such that small inefficiencies result in substantial time penalties.

Designing a generic build process that is usable by all project teams is an important building block in the creation of an adaptive foundation for rapid development. Having an optimal and accurate build process in place at the start of the project provides a significant time saving.

The effort spent on defining a common build process is a good investment for the long-term success of all projects, so don't skip this vital development task. Remember to treat the build process as a time-and-motion study and remove any unnecessary steps.

With the build process covered, the next chapter looks at the development tools that should be a part of any software engineer's toolbox.

## Additional Information

Ant is a tool for building software. The folks at Apache chose Ant as the basis for *Maven*, a tool for performing project management, build, and deployment tasks. Maven provides a formal framework for developing software artifacts and strictly enforces dependencies between build targets.

For more information on Maven, and to download the latest version of the software, see `http://maven.apache.org`.

An important part of the software development environment not covered in this chapter is the mechanism for the integration of software produced by team members. Bringing together newly developed pieces of functionality can often result in a broken build process, a major source of wasted time on any project.

A solution to the software integration problem is to adopt a policy of continuous integration. This idea involves integrating software changes frequently, possibly several times a day, and is the brainchild of Martin Fowler and Matthew Foemmel. The pair wrote their ideas up in a paper that can be viewed at `http://www.martinfowler.com/articles/continuousIntegration.html`.

The concept of continuous integration is backed by the open source product *CruiseControl*, a framework that integrates with your build system to perform regular builds and reports on build status. The CruiseControl software is obtainable from `http://cruisecontrol.sourceforge.net`.

Finally, for anyone who wishes to experiment with *make files*, a copy of GNU Make is available from `http://www.gnu.org/software/make`.

# 13

# The Integrated Development Environment

The best craftsmen insist on the best tools. Craftsmen know producing quality work requires having the right tools and the expertise to use them effectively.

The software engineer has the same needs as the craftsman, and the right tools, coupled with the knowledge and skill necessary to use them, are essential ingredients for the rapid development of quality software. This chapter focuses on the importance of integrated development tools and covers the features a tool should offer to assist the software engineer in the task of developing J2EE solutions. It introduces the Eclipse platform as an example of an integrated development environment (IDE) and discusses the features a tool should provide to assist in the development of enterprise-level software for the J2EE platform.

Eclipse is covered because it fits the criteria of being open source. There are many other effective development tools available, such as JBuilder, IntelliJ IDEA, and NetBeans. Each offers a range of powerful features for software development. The concepts described using Eclipse are representative of the functionality you should look for in similar tools.

In addition to examining the benefits of IDEs for rapid development, we discuss how an IDE makes it possible to debug J2EE applications with the Java Platform Debugging Architecture (JPDA) and how this architecture supports the use of advanced techniques such as *remote debugging* and *hot swapping*.

## Why Use an IDE?

A fully integrated development environment is the ultimate toolbox for the software engineer. It combines all the tools necessary for producing software applications into a single, self-contained environment.

Having all tools under one roof provides a workbench for development; integration between tools such as the editor, compiler, and debugger enable code to be quickly assembled, syntax-checked, and debugged. This close integration of toolsets makes for a rapid development environment and avoids the need to work with different and disjointed development tools.

Despite the advantages of toolset integration, an IDE is not mandatory for software development. You can produce applications with a good code editor like *emacs* from GNU and an Ant build file. In the past, a valid alternative to the services of an IDE was to take a best-of-breed approach to development tool selection and create your own toolbox of top-of-the-line development tools.

The best-of-breed approach has merit, but as IDEs have matured, the tools provided in an IDE now match many of the features of these standalone tools. Moreover, the synergy afforded by having the tools integrated makes them far more effective than when used in isolation.

In the upcoming sections, we examine what features we should expect our chosen IDE to provide for effective J2EE development.

## IDE Core Features

A good IDE should provide all the tools and features necessary for developing, debugging, and testing an application. J2EE projects call for an enhanced feature set from the IDE beyond that of conventional J2SE applications. The IDE must contend with multiple file types, additional build steps, deployment concerns, and interaction with J2EE servers. Some products also support the design phase and provide additional modeling features.

Whatever IDE you select, one of the most important selection criteria is whether the product can support the way you work. We have covered software engineering practices that can greatly assist in the rapid development of J2EE solutions. Here is a summary of some of the techniques covered:

* Use of multiparadigm development languages such as Jess, Jython, and AspectJ
* The importance of frameworks
* Modeling techniques with UML diagrams
* Active and passive code generation with tools such as Velocity, XDoclet, and Middlegen
* Transparent data access with O/R mapping products
* Model-Driven Architecture using AndroMDA
* Incremental build processes with Apache Ant

The ideal IDE should support us in applying these techniques and working with the products and frameworks listed. In addition, the IDE must also be J2EE-specific and have built-in support for all the J2EE artifacts we are likely to work with.

So, what can we reasonably expect an IDE to provide beyond a standard code editor? The following lists some of the core features an IDE should offer for J2EE development.

### Language-aware editors.

Support for syntax coloring for different languages in code editors was seen as a major step forward in editor functionality when it first appeared. Now syntax coloring is an expected feature. A good editor should intrinsically understand the language it supports, offering such features as code assistance, instant error detection, source formatting, and essential refactoring capabilities.

### Code wizards.

Passive code generators can remove much of the drudgery from development tasks. The IDE should provide wizards and code templates for standard tasks such as creating Java classes and Enterprise JavaBeans. Code wizards that allow code for common design patterns to be laid down are a powerful feature in any IDE. In addition, an IDE should support customized wizards implemented by the development team.

### Debuggers.

The ability to inspect code in a running state is an effective means of investigating defects and understanding the behavior of the executing code. For a J2EE project, debugging support is also required for languages other than Java, with JSP being toward the top of the list. Support for debugging—and remote debugging particularly for J2EE servers—is an important feature of an IDE supporting a J2EE development.

### Deployment.

To test and debug a J2EE application, it must be packaged and deployed to a J2EE server. The IDE should support this package-and-deploy phase and allow the execution of the target server to be controlled from within the IDE. Control of the server involves not just startup and shutdown, but also having the server executing in a state whereby the deployed application can be tested and debugged.

### Integrated help.

Quick access to the help on any of the various APIs that make up the J2SE and J2EE specifications removes the need to go hunting through the documentation for the semantics of a particular API call. This feature is an immense time saver and assists the software engineer in selecting the most appropriate features from the API for the current task.

### Refactoring support.

Refactoring code has become a watchword for agile development. Refactoring patterns must be applied consistently across the entire code base. An IDE should support a number of refactoring options, allowing the sweeping changes refactoring calls for to be applied consistently and accurately.

### Source control integration.

The use of a source control system, such as CVS, is fundamental to any software development project. An IDE must be able to work seamlessly with your choice of source control repository.

**Testing.**

A fully integrated development environment should support the unit testing of components. The ability of an IDE to autogenerate unit tests, run test suites, and report on the success of test runs has gained significant attention since the rise of the XP-style *test-driven* approach to development.

> **The use of an IDE for unit testing is covered in Chapter 14.**

**Reliability and accuracy.**

Finally, no matter how long the feature list of an IDE, it must provide a robust platform for development. Few things are more frustrating than losing work due to an unreliable editor.

These features are in no way a comprehensive list, and we should expect to see most IDE vendors providing development productivity features that add additional functionality to the workbench. Such additional functionality might include metrics-gathering, code quality analysis, and profiling support.

To showcase the features we would expect to find in an IDE targeting J2EE projects, the remainder of this chapter concentrates on the Eclipse IDE.

## Key Features of an IDE

- Language-aware editors offering syntax coloring and code completion facilities
- Code wizards for generating program artifacts
- Application debugging support
- Facilities for deploying J2EE applications
- Online help for the J2SE and J2EE APIs
- Refactoring tools
- Integration with source control systems
- Ability to generate and run unit test suites
- High reliability and accuracy

# Introducing Eclipse

The argument as to which is the best IDE for Java development can reach religious fervor, and most software engineers have their own particular favorite. This chapter features Eclipse because it meets the criteria of being open source and offers most of the features necessary for a productive development platform.

It is also very popular with the Java development community and one of the slickest-looking Java development tools around—a factor which, in combination with its free status, may account for its huge popularity.

## What Is Eclipse?

Eclipse is not strictly an IDE but is instead a generic Java-based platform for hosting development tools. The Eclipse Platform uses pluggable tools to build IDEs for supporting the development of a range of applications using a diverse set of technologies. The base Eclipse platform provides the functionality to detect, load, and integrate different development tools known as plug-ins into an Eclipse workbench. Collectively, these plug-ins form an IDE for a specific development technology, for example, Java, Smalltalk, or C++.

Eclipse's pedigree can be traced back to IBM. In producing tools for the IBM range of development products, the project teams at IBM found themselves continually producing IDEs from scratch for each new product. Recognizing this approach as wasteful in both time and effort, IBM focused its attention on developing a generic IDE platform that could be tailored for each new product. The Eclipse Platform was the result of this effort. IBM then contributed the source for the platform to the open source community and established and funded the Eclipse Foundation to encourage the development of the platform.

In its basic state, Eclipse is too generic for developing applications. To make Eclipse usable, the download comes complete with Java Development Tooling (JDT), a collection of tools targeted at the development of Java applications. The JDT provides the Eclipse Platform with all the features necessary for developing, running, testing, and debugging Java applications. In this chapter, we look at additional plug-in tools for supporting the development of J2EE solutions.

## Installing and Running Eclipse

The Eclipse Web site is located at `http://www.eclipse.org`. This site provides the news on the Eclipse platform, articles, documentation, and the latest versions of Eclipse ready for download. The full Eclipse download comes complete with the JDT, so Eclipse is all ready to go for Java development.

note

Because Eclipse is a Java application, you must have a suitable JVM installed. Eclipse works with multiple versions, but check the site for details.

For the installation, you may either pick up the designated formal release or take a build from the current development stream. Certain development builds are periodically flagged as being stable, so if you want to see all the latest features, then go for one of these. However, if you're new to Eclipse, you may wish to download a reliable formal release.

Eclipse is downloaded as an archive and extracted into an appropriate local directory. On a Microsoft Windows platform, launch Eclipse using the `eclipse.exe` executable.

Although Eclipse runs directly from this file, it is advisable to set a few configuration parameters before starting the IDE. Specifically, you can tell Eclipse the JVM to use with the `-vm` flag. Explicitly stating the JVM is useful for machines with multiple JVM versions installed and avoids problems when upgrading to new versions of the J2SE platform.

Here is an example of the command line for running Eclipse with this option set:

```
eclipse.exe -vm c:\jre\bin\javaw.exe
```

You can set the option on the Windows platform by creating a desktop shortcut and providing the additional command-line arguments.

## tip

> You can specify several parameters on the command line for optimizing the JVM to squeeze out extra performance from Eclipse. You may find the following settings result in Eclipse starting up considerably quicker on your system: -vmargs -Xverify:none -XX:+UseParallelGC -XX:PermSize=20M -XX:MaxNew-Size=32M -XX:NewSize=32M -Xmx256m -Xms256m.

Note that the setting of all these parameters is optional and serves purely to enable the customization of the Eclipse platform for your specific environment. Eclipse runs perfectly well straight out of the box.

## The Eclipse Workspace

Eclipse adopts the concept of a user's *workspace* for managing applications under development. A workspace comprises a series of *projects*, and each project maps directly to a directory on the file system. Under a project directory resides all the source files for building a specific application or component.

Within a workspace, dependencies can be expressed between projects that govern build order. This makes workspaces an effective mechanism for organizing applications and allows large systems to be broken down into smaller subprojects.

warning

> The build constraints imposed by an IDE may prevent the implementation of your desired project structure. It is necessary to ascertain how an IDE organizes its directory structure and determine if the structure will scale to enable large project teams to work effectively.

From version 3.0, Eclipse supports the use of multiple workspaces and allows you to create a new workspace or select an existing one at startup. Alternatively, the location of the workspace can be passed to Eclipse on the command line with the –data argument. For example, eclipse –data c:\myproject\workspace.

## The Eclipse Workbench Paradigm

Developers interact with Eclipse using the *workbench* paradigm, which is based on the concept of *editors*, *views*, and *perspectives*:

- Editors allow the opening, modifying, and saving of files.
- Views present additional information on the object being worked on within the workbench.
- Perspectives are an arrangement of editors and views.

An example of an editor and a view is the Java source editor and the accompanying outline view. Here the outline view displays the structure of the Java class open in the editor.

Perspectives are a common source of confusion when learning the intricacies of Eclipse, since they are a concept not normally found in IDEs. Essentially, perspectives are a convenience for organizing editors and views according to a logical grouping, such as Java development or debugging.

Figure 13–1 shows the Eclipse workbench with a Java file open for editing. In addition to the editor, three views are visible in the perspective: the package explorer, which shows the Java project's package structure; the outline view, which provides an at-a-glance overview of the methods and attributes of the class being edited; and the console, responsible for displaying all output.

Perspectives can take a little time to become familiar with, but after some experimentation, you'll find them a useful way of organizing the workbench.

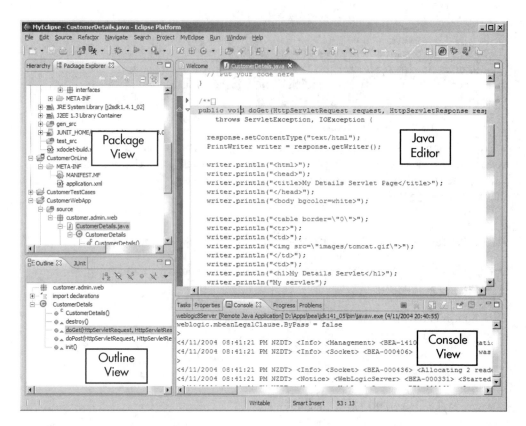

**Figure 13–1**    The Eclipse workbench.

# Extending the Workbench with Plug-in Tools

The ability to tailor an IDE for a particular environment with custom plug-in tools is an important feature. The Eclipse Platform takes the use of plug-ins to the extreme and relies on plug-ins to provide the workbench with the development features required for a particular language or technology.

Plug-in tools are both the Eclipse Platform's main strength and its Achilles' heel. Heavy reliance on modular development tools makes the platform infinitely extendable and customizable. On the downside, the use of multiple tools can lead to integration problems, with badly behaving plug-ins causing instability within the workbench. Such instability, if it occurs, is extremely frustrating, especially as reliability must rank as one of the top requirements for an IDE.

When selecting a plug-in, you should determine the version of Eclipse the new tool supports. Tool versions that target a formal Eclipse release are likely to be more stable than those targeting a milestone, and hence a beta, version of Eclipse—user beware!

Numerous plug-in tools are available for the Eclipse Platform, with a highly active Eclipse community engaged in the development of both open source and commercial tools. The teams involved in tool development are required to "commune" away from the main Eclipse site. Sadly, this can make tracking down appropriate plug-ins difficult.

Two sites that carry an extensive list of tools are `http://www.eclipse-plugins.info` and `http://www.eclipseplugincentral.com`. Each of these resources provides searching facilities and sorts plug-in tools by category. The sites also rank each tool according to activity and download rate, making it easy to see which tools developers are actively using.

This chapter introduces a number of tools for enhancing Eclipse for performing J2EE development tasks. Table 13–1 gives a selection of popular open source and commercial tools available for the workbench.

**Table 13–1**    Eclipse Plug-in Tools

| Name | Description | Reference |
|---|---|---|
| MyEclipse | MyEclipse is a collection of tools for J2EE development that transforms the Eclipse platform into a full J2EE workbench. | http://www.myeclipse.com |
| Lomboz | Lomboz is a comprehensive suite of tools for J2EE development, including EJB wizards and a JSP editor. | http://www.objectlearn.com/products/lomboz.jsp |
| Exadel Struts and JSF studio | The Exadel tools support the development of Web applications using either the Struts or Java Server Faces MVC frameworks. The tools offer an excellent graphical representation of page flows. This considerably simplifies page navigation configuration. | http://www.exadel.com |
| Quantum DB | A lightweight but effective database access tool for querying databases and executing SQL statements. Supports syntax highlighting of SQL scripts. | http://quantum.sourceforge.net |
| Sysdeo | Popular plug-in for controlling the Tomcat servlet engine. | http://www.sysdeo.com/eclipse/tomcatPlugin.html |
| Veloedit | Velocity template editor with syntax highlighting and code assist. | http://veloedit.sourceforge.net |
| Hibernate Synchronizer | This plug-in supports the Hibernate O/R mapping tool, and automatically generates Java source when the Hibernate mapping files are changed. | http://www.binamics.com/hibernatesynch |

**Table 13–1**    Eclipse Plug-in Tools (continued)

| Name | Description | Reference |
|---|---|---|
| JadClipse | Brings JAD support to the workbench, allowing Java classes to be decompiled from bytecode and viewed as source. | http://sourceforge.net/ projects/jadclipse |
| XMen | XML editor. | http://sourceforge.net/ projects/xmen |

The next section looks at the features of an IDE necessary for supporting J2EE projects.

# IDE Features for Enterprise Development

The tools of the JDT provide a comprehensive range of features for supporting the development of Java applications. In a nutshell, the JDT supports the following:

* Organization of Java projects, with each project containing standard Java build artifacts

* Browsing of Java projects and Java package hierarchies

* Code wizards and templates for creating Java artifacts such as classes and interfaces

* A Java-aware editor

* Refactoring of Java source and packages

* Full text-based searching capabilities

* Incremental Java compilation

* Automated unit testing

* Integration with Ant files

* Debugging of Java applications

These features for supporting the construction of Java applications are only a subset of those required for effectively developing J2EE systems. The tools of the Eclipse JDT do not accommodate J2EE components. For this task, the Eclipse workbench requires the installation of plug-in tools that supplement the Java development capabilities of the JDT. Fortunately, a range of Eclipse tools is available for this very purpose.

Two J2EE toolsets that consistently rank toward the top of the active plug-ins lists on various Eclipse Web sites are *Lomboz* from Object Learn, and *MyEclipse* from Genuitec. Each product transforms the Eclipse workbench into a J2EE development platform, adding all the wizards, editors, and views necessary for producing J2EE applications.

Lomboz is available as open source. Full details of this tool, including documentation and installation instructions, can be found at http://www.objectlearn.com/products/lomboz.jsp.

MyEclipse is a commercial product, with licenses available on a yearly subscription basis. Surprisingly, for a product aimed at enterprise-level development, MyEclipse does not carry an enterprise-sized price, being relatively low-cost per developer seat. A fully featured version of the software is available for download on a 30-day trial from the MyEclipse Web site. See `http://www.myeclipse.com` for download details and licensing information.

For our discussion on IDE enterprise development features, the functionality shown uses Eclipse 3.0 with the MyEclipse 3.7 tools installed. The discussion covers the following:

- Code wizards for generating J2EE program artifacts
- Working with multiple file types
- Integration with the build process
- Using code generators as part of the IDE
- Integration with the J2EE server
- Including modeling tool support
- Accessing the database

Collectively, these features provide a highly productive J2EE development environment.

## Code Wizards

Code wizards rely on passive code generation to generate much of the boilerplate code associated with the task of programming. They offer a significant saving in terms of time and effort.

To take advantage of the productivity gains passive code generation affords, it is worthwhile selecting an IDE that provides code wizards for some of the more common J2EE operations.

> *Passive code generation is described in Chapter 6.*

The base JDT provides wizards for generating common Java artifacts such as classes and interfaces. Installing MyEclipse enhances the Eclipse workbench with an additional set of wizards that target J2EE components.

The wizards available include *project-level* wizards for generating Web applications (WAR), EJB components (JAR), and enterprise application (EAR) deployments. MyEclipse also adds wizards for generating *code-level* artifacts, including support for generating the following:

- Session, entity, and message-driven beans using XDoclet
- Hibernate mapping files
- Web components for the Apache Struts framework

* Standard Web components such as JSP files, HTML pages, and servlets
* XML documents and schemas

> *Chapter 6 covers XDoclet, and Chapter 7 introduces Hibernate.*

Figure 13–2 shows the MyEclipse EJB Wizard, used for generating XDoclet based EJB components.

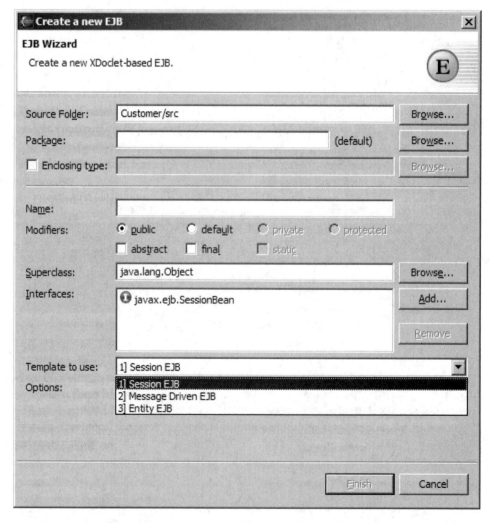

**Figure 13–2**   MyEclipse EJB Wizard.

The EJB wizard provided by MyEclipse is template based. From the templates available, enterprise bean types of session, entity, and message-driven beans can be autogenerated. Note that the code generated is XDoclet based, and the code wizard generates a single bean implementation adorned with XDoclet annotations.

> *Design options for working with EJB technology are discussed in Chapter 4.*

## Editor Support for Multiple File Types

The editor is the tool around which the workbench revolves. A powerful code editor contributes immensely to developer productivity. In this regard, the Eclipse Java editor is very advanced and offers a number of time saving features. As an example, here are some of the features from the Eclipse editor's *source* menu that you may find particularly useful.

### Organize imports.

This operation neatly orders all import statements and removes all redundant import declarations.

### Add import.

Automatically creates an import declaration for the referenced type.

### Format.

Arranges, or beautifies, the code based on a specified layout configuration. Using a common source formatter is a way to ensure compliance with company coding standards.

### Override/implement methods.

Code wizard for selecting the methods of a superclass or interface to override or implement. This feature both saves time and increases accuracy by removing the opportunity for inadvertently creating a new method in a deriving class with a typing error.

### Generate getters and setters.

This operation removes the tedium of implementing getters and setters for class attributes.

### Surround with try/catch block.

Wraps a code selection with a try/catch block and explicitly catches all exceptions types. It also adds import declarations for the necessary exception types.

You should expect most Java development tools to offer similar time saving features.

tip

> Learning the keyboard mappings for invoking these features without having to resort to pointing and clicking with the mouse makes coding a faster process.

J2EE applications require editor support for file types other than Java source. A typical J2EE project could comprise the following:

- JSPs, HTML pages, and style sheets
- SQL scripts
- Deployment descriptors
- Property files
- Velocity templates
- Ant build files
- XML documents and schemas

The editor should help us to quickly and accurately write files of all these types and should afford features such as context-sensitive help, syntax highlighting, and code assist (sometimes called code completion).

> *The Apache Velocity template engine is covered in Chapter 6.*

note

> *Code assist*, or *code completion*, is the ability of the editor to display context-sensitive information relating to a particular element in the editor. For example, in the Java editor, a code assist feature would prompt the developer with a list of the available methods for an instance variable of a given type. This functionality is given various names by various IDE vendors. This chapter uses the Eclipse term *code assist*.

The plug-in model of the Eclipse platform makes it ideally suited for dealing with the various file types of J2EE projects. One primary file type not directly supported by Eclipse is JSP. Here, the MyEclipse plug-in adds JSP editor support, providing code assist and syntax highlighting features, and allows the JSP to be syntax-checked and previewed prior to deployment.

## Ant Integration

A prerequisite for any IDE is its ability to integrate with Apache Ant for performing build tasks. An IDE is an unsuitable tool for constructing a reliable and repeatable build process because most development platforms lack the functionality to cover all of the eventualities required of a build system. For the majority of projects, the Apache Ant build utility is used for this purpose. In order for an IDE to integrate with the build process, it must be able to invoke Ant build file targets directly.

> *The Apache Ant build utility is described*
> *in Chapter 12.*

The ability to integrate an Ant build file into the IDE is especially significant if code generation tools such as AndroMDA and XDoclet form an integral part of the build process, as these tools require Ant for invocation.

> *The MDA tool AndroMDA is covered in*
> *Chapter 8.*

The Eclipse developers recognize the importance of Ant's role in Java software engineering and ensure that Ant is well supported by the Eclipse workbench. No additional plug-in is required to support Ant integration.

Figure 13–3 illustrates the Ant view, which forms an integral part of the Eclipse workbench.

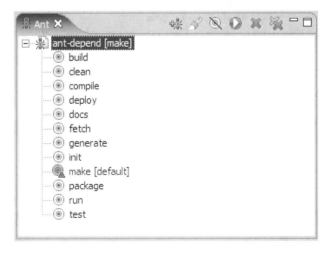

**Figure 13–3**    Eclipse Ant build file view.

The Ant view lists all targets in a build file. Build targets can be invoked directly from the workbench using the Ant view. All output generated by Ant is written to the Eclipse workbench's console.

For writing build files, the Eclipse workbench comes with an Ant file-aware editor, which can be associated with all XML file types and provides syntax coloring and code assist for Ant tasks.

This level of integration with Ant makes it possible to write and run build files within the confines of the Eclipse workbench, thereby providing a single environment for project development work.

# Working with Code Generators

If a project is using a code generator, then the chosen IDE should both integrate with the code generator and work with the generated code.

A major criterion for integrating the IDE with a code generator is the ability of the IDE to invoke the generator by executing targets in an Ant build file. As we learned in the previous section, Eclipse is very accomplished in this area. Furthermore, the IDE should be able to contend with multiple source paths, because it is good practice to output generated source to a different directory than that of handwritten code. This is possible with Eclipse because Java projects may define multiple source paths.

## Velocity Templates

For working with template-driven code generators, it is desirable for the IDE to provide support for editing the template files. An open source editor for Velocity templates is available for Eclipse. The plug-in *Veloedit* can be downloaded from `http://veloedit.sourceforge.net`.

Figure 13–4 shows Veloedit editing an AndroMDA cartridge template. The editor supports both syntax highlighting and code assist for Velocity files.

Velocity is becoming widely used for code generation, so the Veloedit plug-in enjoys a high number of downloads—currently, about a thousand downloads a month, which is a significant amount.

**Figure 13–4**    Editing a Velocity template with Veloedit.

## XDoclet

The MyEclipse plug-in makes extensive use of XDoclet for generating J2EE components. As we have seen, the EJB wizard generates a bean class annotated with XDoclet attributes.

MyEclipse extends the workbench to ensure XDoclet is well supported and adds code-assist support to the editor for the embedded XDoclet tags. Execution of the XDoclet engine for a MyEclipse project is controlled by a project Ant build file named xdoclet-build.xml. The contents of this build file should not be edited directly. Instead, MyEclipse associates the XDoclet settings with the properties of the EJB project. These properties can be accessed by right-clicking on the project and selecting the *Properties* menu item. Figure 13–5 displays the various XDoclet properties dialog used for controlling code generation in the project.

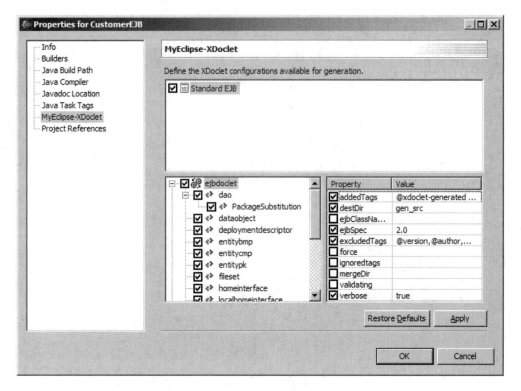

**Figure 13–5**    Setting XDoclet properties with MyEclipse.

warning

The setting for the destDir attribute that specifies the location of generated source defaults to the same location as the Java source directory.

Accepting this configuration would see generated source mixed up with hand-written code. In line with code generation best practice, you should consider changing this setting to a directory dedicated to holding the generated source. Add this new directory as a source path to your Eclipse project.

Having established a suitable configuration, the XDoclet build script is run via a MyEclipse menu item, available by right-clicking on the project in the package explorer view.

## Server Control and Application Deployment

To operate as a fully integrated environment, the IDE must have the capability to deploy J2EE applications. It should also offer the functionality to control the target J2EE server, allowing the developer to start and stop the server without the need to leave the IDE.

note

> These integration features require the IDE to keep pace with new versions of the different application servers. You must also check that your chosen IDE or Eclipse plug-in supports your particular application server.

Eclipse relies on plug-in tools for incorporating this functionality into the workbench. For deployment, MyEclipse adds a deployment wizard to the workbench that enables J2EE modules to be deployed to a number of J2EE server types. Figure 13–6 shows the MyEclipse deployment dialog with a J2EE EAR project selected. The packaged application targets instances of the JBoss and WebLogic servers. For each server selected, you may specifying the deployment type. From the example deployment setup in Figure 13–6, an exploded deployment is specified for WLS, while for JBoss the application is deployed as an EAR file. The type of deployment selected depends on what the application server supports.

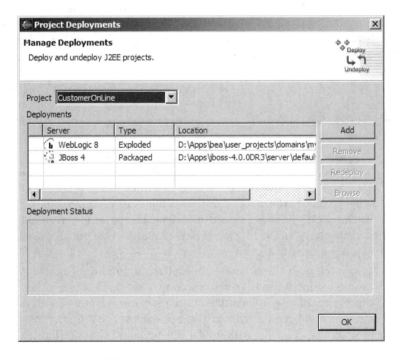

**Figure 13–6**    MyEclipse J2EE project deployment dialog.

MyEclipse allows J2EE servers to be configured within the IDE and adds toolbar items to enable each configured server to be started or stopped from within the Eclipse workbench. This level of integration between application server and IDE provides for the rapid transition of newly written code into a running state, where it can be tested and debugged.

## Modeling Support

Eclipse's use of plug-in tools enables the integration of UML modeling tools into the workbench. A number of modeling tools are available as Eclipse plug-ins. Omondo offers Eclipse-UML, available from `http://www.omondo.com`. In addition, Borland produces an Eclipse modeling tool as part of its Together family of products; see `http://www.borland.com`.

> *Chapter 5 provides an overview of the main UML diagrams and discusses modeling tools.*

Modeling tools generally add their own perspective to the Eclipse workbench. Switching between the modeling and Java perspectives offers a convenient means of moving from model to code, and vice versa. This approach ensures the model is closely associated with the code, thereby helping to prevent the model from being neglected as development progresses.

## Database Access

Few J2EE solutions are constructed without an underlying data repository; most enterprise systems use a relational database.

One area where many IDEs are still trailing the best-of-breed tools is in database support. Few. if any, IDEs offer the same level of functionality as specialized database tools such as *DBArtisan*, *ERwin*, or *TOAD*. These tools support such features as writing stored procedures and database triggers, generating database performance statistics, and in some cases modeling entity relationships for schema designs. Some IDE products offer limited support in this area. For example, Together ControlCenter can generate ER diagrams reverse-engineered from the database and can generate DDL scripts from an ER diagram.

Although they do not offer the same level of sophistication as the best-of-breed database tools, most IDEs offer some form of database access. A few open source database tools are available for Eclipse. One offering is Quantum DB, a useful query editor that allows the execution of SQL statements and the contents of database tables to be interrogated via a JDBC driver. MyEclipse also includes a tool with similar functionality. Although limited, this simple functionality comes in very useful and can be a great time saver when it comes to checking the results of test runs or preparing test data on the database.

Over time, mainstream database-management products may migrate to the Eclipse platform, making a fully integrated development environment possible.

# Debugging J2EE Applications with Eclipse

A debugger is one of the most powerful tools available to the developer and can assist immensely for both tracking down defects and helping to understand an application's core behavior. Despite the benefits debugging tools offer, my experience is that few developers take advantage of these tools and so miss out on one of the biggest productivity gains an IDE can offer. In many cases, the common debugging practice is to adorn the application with strategically placed log messages and examine the output at the console as the application executes.

This method of fault-finding and discovery is workable but is a slow and ponderous means of analyzing code. With a suitable debugging tool, you can set breakpoints within the application and then step through the code from that point on, line by line. With the debugger invoked, a wealth of information is available, the state of threads can be viewed, the contents of variables observed, and the call stack of the application monitored. The ability to replicate this level of information through log messages at the console is highly unlikely. Armed with a full array of information, it is possible to get to the root of a problem quickly and easily.

To understand the full benefits a debugger can offer, this section walks through how this useful tool can be put to best effect on a J2EE solution. First, let's look at the technology in the JVM that makes debugging tools possible.

## Java Platform Debugger Architecture

The Java Platform Debugger Architecture (JPDA) was introduced as of JDK 1.3, enabling a debugging tool to attach to a JPDA-compliant JVM. The JPDA has the debugging tool execute in a separate JVM from that of the application being debugged. This architecture has significant advantages over running a debugging tool in the same JVM as that of the application being debugged. For optimal debugging, it is often necessary to suspend the JVM of the debugged application, a process that is not possible if both debugger and debuggee are collocated in the same JVM.

The JPDA defines two interfaces and a protocol:

### Java Debugging Interface (JDI).

This interface is used by the debugging tool to make requests and receive notification events from the application being debugged in the target JVM.

### Java Virtual Machine Debug Interface (JVMDI).

The JVMDI interface is implemented by a JVM in order to allow the debugging of an application under its control.

### Java Debug Wire Protocol (JDWP).

The JDWP ties the two debugging interfaces of JDI and JVMDI together and allows the two interfaces to communicate over a given transport mechanism.

Implementations of the JDI and JVMDI interfaces interoperate via two software components, which are imaginatively called the *front end* and *back end* in the JPDA documentation. Figure 13–7 illustrates the JPDA debugging model.

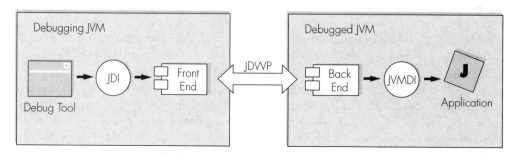

**Figure 13–7**　The Java platform debugger architecture.

A debugging tool submits requests to an attached JVM through the JDI. The front-end component forwards all JDI requests over the communications channel in accordance with the JDWP. The receiving end of the communications channel is the back-end component, which translates JDWP packets and submits them to the JVMDI of the JVM. The entire process is bidirectional because the JVM being debugged must be able to report events back to the debug tool, for example, when a breakpoint is triggered.

The function of the back-end and front-end components is similar to the approach used for marshaling RMI calls and so should be familiar.

> ### RMI is discussed in Chapter 4.

## Local and Remote Debugging

JDWP is independent of the underlying transport mechanism used to move requests between both ends of the conversation. This independence allows a JVM to be debugged on a machine separate from the JVM running the debugger. This process is known as *remote debugging* and is achieved by specifying a suitable transport mechanism, known as a *transport* in JPDA terminology, for carrying traffic between the two machines.

Sun Microsystems' reference implementation for JDPA provides two transport types: a socket transport and a shared memory transport. The socket transport uses TCP/IP for supporting remote debugging between machines. The shared memory transport supports inter-process communication between JVMs running on the same box.

## JVM Debug Configuration

The details of configuring a JPDA-compliant JVM are mostly taken care of for us by Eclipse. However, to take advantage of remote debugging, you must understand how a JVM is configured to support debug tools attaching remotely to the JVM.

JVM configuration is proprietary to the target VM, and you should refer to the documentation for your specific implementation. The following instructions refer to the Sun Java HotSpot VM 1.4.2.

Debug support is enabled in the JVM by providing the arguments -Xdebug and -Xrunjdwp. The -Xdebug argument instructs the JVM to listen for debugging connections. The -Xrunjdwp argument is a little more complicated and is used to configure the transport for incoming debug connections. To start the JVM so that it can accept remote connections, this argument is set as follows:

```
-Xrunjdwp:server=y,transport=dt_socket,address=8000,suspend=n
```

The suboptions require some explanation:

* server—if set to y instructs the JVM to wait for connections rather than search for them.
* transport—specifies the transport mechanism.

Options are dt_socket for TCP/IP or st_shmem for shared memory.

* address—port address for the connection.
* suspend—if set to n, the JVM starts in a running state; otherwise, the JVM remains suspended, waiting for a connection.

These settings also need to be provided to the debugger so it can attach to the target VM. Under Eclipse, a remote debugging configuration is created for this purpose. Figure 13–8 shows the Eclipse dialog for configuring remote debugging for an application.

The Eclipse dialog makes it easy to configure remote debugging once the target VM is set up correctly. The dialog shown offers a single connection type of socket for the transport. The connection properties specify the host machine name, and the port the target VM listens for incoming connections.

Now that we've covered the basics of the JPDA, let's look at the features Eclipse, with some help from MyEclipse, provides for debugging J2EE solutions.

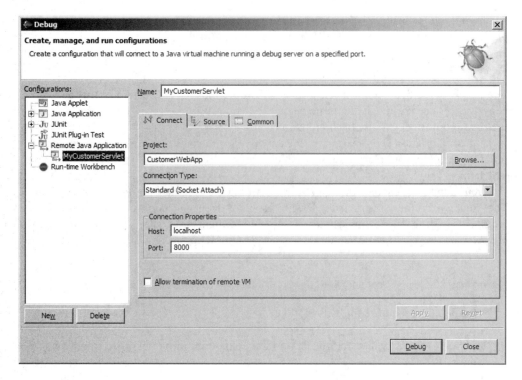

**Figure 13-8**    Eclipse configuration dialog for remote debugging.

## Debugging a J2EE Application

With JPDA support, Eclipse lets us set breakpoints in J2EE components that are under the control of the J2EE server. Thus, we can break in on the execution of components such as servlets and EJBs to observe their behavior in an executing state. Moreover, if the source is available, we can debug the implementation of the J2EE server itself.

JPDA-compliant debugging tools remove the need to scatter log messages, shotgun style, throughout the code, and provide a superior level of diagnostic reporting than is possible with the use of logging and console messages.

note

> Logging messages still have their uses, as it is highly unlikely you'll get the opportunity to use a debugger for tracing faults in a production environment.

To debug a servlet under Eclipse involves setting a breakpoint in the editor, then starting the servlet engine and deploying the application. Deployment of the application and the startup of the server can all be performed from within the IDE using the services MyEclipse provides.

With the application deployed and the target server running, accessing the page associated with the servlet from a browser causes the breakpoint to be hit. This triggers Eclipse to switch to the debug perspective, displaying the debugger's editor and views. Figure 13–9 shows the Eclipse debug perspective with an active breakpoint for a servlet running under Tomcat 5.0.

The different views provided in the debug perspective allow the state of variables to be inspected and the current instruction pointer in the code to be advanced line by line. Figure 13–9 shows the debug, variables, code, and outline views. The debug view displays the processes, threads, and stack frames. The variables view allows the state of all object instances to be inspected. The source being debugged is displayed in the editor, while the outline view shows the code structure. Each represents the state of the code as at the current line of execution.

The inclusion of the Java code editor in the debug perspective allows us to take advantage of another JPDA feature—hot swapping.

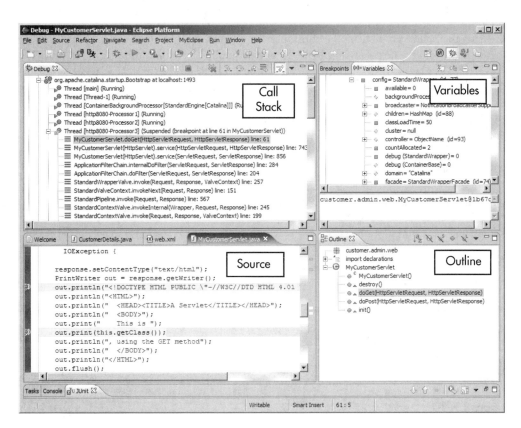

**Figure 13–9**    The Eclipse debug perspective.

## Hot Swapping

The hot swapping feature was introduced with the release of JDK 1.4 and enables code to be modified from within a debugger while executing under a JVM.

Hot swapping technology makes it possible to apply changes quickly, bypassing the normal build-and-deployment cycle, and thereby allowing for a swift resolution to defects within the code.

There are limits, however, to the extent to which changes can be made. The main rule is that the structure of the method cannot be changed, so the method signature, including the return type, is immutable if hot swapping is to work. This type of functionality is also called *fix-and-continue* debugging.

Hot swapping is implicitly supported by Eclipse and can be used to fix-and-continue code running under a J2EE server that is executing under a JPDA-complaint JVM with dynamic class-loading support. Hot swapping is a feature of the JVM, not the J2EE server.

Following from the example shown in Figure 13–9, where a servlet running under Tomcat is being debugged, changes can be made to the servlet using the open code editor in the debug perspective.

Using the MyEclipse plug-in, the Tomcat server is launched as a remote Java application, and the debugger is attached. Having deployed a Web application containing a simple servlet, a breakpoint can be set in the Java editor. Note the breakpoint does not need to be set in the debug perspective. It can be set in any perspective with the source open in the Java editor. Eclipse automatically switches to the debug perspective when the breakpoint is triggered.

Figure 13–10 shows the presence of the breakpoint annotation in the code editor. The breakpoint can be set by double-clicking on the left edge of the editor, on the line where execution is to be interrupted. Note a mouse-over tool tip is visible in the screenshot to denote the location of the breakpoint.

**Figure 13–10**　Servlet code with breakpoint set.

With the Tomcat server started from the Eclipse workbench, the Web application deployed, and the breakpoint set, the page associated with the servlet can be accessed from a Web browser.

Loading the page in the browser triggers the breakpoint, and the Eclipse debugger is activated. Within the body of the method, any line of code under or ahead of the breakpoint can be changed. Once a modification has been made, the action of saving the file has Eclipse load the changed class into the target VM. Resuming the execution of the application from the debugger executes the changed code and the changes are immediately visible in the browser.

note

> Hot swapping should not be confused with hot deployment. Hot deployment refers to the ability of a J2EE server to reload updated parts of an application dynamically, without the need to shutdown or interrupt the running application. Hot swapping is a feature of a JPDA-compliant JVM, not the J2EE server.

# JSP Debugging

Earlier, we discussed the need for an IDE to support various file types in order to be suitable for J2EE development. The ability to work with a variety of file types applies equally to the debugger as to the code editors.

Under JDK 1.4, JPDA has been extended to support the debugging of languages other than Java. This ability is addressed by JSR-045, *Debugging Support for Other Languages*.

JSPs benefit greatly from this advancement, making it possible to set breakpoints and inspect the running state of a JSP as if it were Java code.

A plug-in such as MyEclipse is required to support this functionality on the Eclipse workbench. However, the process of running a JSP under the debugger is identical to that of debugging Java components such as servlets and Enterprise JavaBeans.

# Debugging Guidelines

This section offers some suggestions to help you get the most out of the debugger. The techniques described all rely on standard JPDA features found in most debugging tools.

## Check All New Code with the Debugger

A debugger isn't just a diagnostic tool for locating defects; it can also help improve the quality of your software. In his book *Code Complete* [McConnell, 2004], Steve McConnell recommends the approach of debugging all new code before it is placed under source control.

This practice allows the developer to confirm the code is operating as designed, rather than passing tests on pure luck. For example, a common code error is to have a loop statement either perform an extra iteration or skip a final iteration. You can verify the correct termination of the loop by using the debugger to step through the loop construct while monitoring the state of the count variable.

## Set Conditional Breakpoints

A conditional breakpoint is triggered when an expression associated with the breakpoint evaluates to true. This is a common feature of most debuggers and is especially useful when tracking down problems that do not occur on the first run through of the code.

In the example of an error you suspect is occurring on exiting a loop, rather than stepping through every iteration of the loop, have the breakpoint triggered by providing an expression for the breakpoint that sees the debugger interrupt execution when the loop's exit condition is reached.

Conditional breakpoints are set in Eclipse by right-clicking on the breakpoint and selecting its properties from the context menu. You can set a condition for the breakpoint in the resulting properties window.

## Use the Watch Functionality to Monitor Specific Variables

The debugger can display so much information about the state of the executing program, it becomes difficult to monitor those variables that are of interest. In this situation, using the *watch* functionality enables the placing of specific variables in a separate view where they are easily observed.

To do this in Eclipse, with execution of the program suspended in the debugger, highlight the variable and right-click to bring up its context menu. Selecting *Watch* from the menu adds the variable to the Expressions View.

## Modify the State of Variables for Testing Purposes

With execution of the program suspended at a breakpoint, you can use the debugger to change the value of a variable. You can use this feature to turn the debugger into a testing tool by setting a breakpoint on entry into a method and then populating the method's parameters with test data.

Modifying the program's internal state at runtime is useful for test scenarios for which test data is not readily available.

To modify a variable in the Eclipse debugger, double-click on the variable in the Variables View. This displays a dialog box from which you can enter a new value.

## Explore the Code by Stepping Into and Out of Methods

In addition to stepping through code line by line, you can step into a method. This approach allows you to burrow down into the depths of the application to determine its inner workings. The approach is particularly useful when exploring other people's code, as would be the case on an XP project where code ownership is discouraged.

When you have gone deep enough into the code base, to step back out, use the *Step Return* debug menu command. This returns you to the calling method and places you at the line of code immediately following the call into which you initially stepped. This is a handy feature when you don't want to step through to the end of a method before returning.

## Debugging Tips

- Check all new code with the debugger.
- Set conditional breakpoints.
- Use the watch feature to monitor specific variables.
- Modify the state of variables for testing purposes.
- Explore the code by stepping into methods.

# Summary

An IDE provides an integrated suite of tools for improving team productivity and software quality. It can also help simplify the task of developing systems for the J2EE platform with code wizards and online help for API reference material. You will likely use an IDE more than any other tool, so selecting an IDE that meets all your development needs is a critical decision.

When making that decision, ensure the tool supports the full development lifecycle of a J2EE application. The IDE should provide code wizards for generating J2EE program artifacts and powerful editors for all the main Java and J2EE file types, and it should integrate seamlessly with your choice of application server.

Regardless of the cost of the tool, an IDE represents a substantial investment in terms of time and effort. You must determine how the IDE can complement your development practices and what impact it will have on existing build processes.

To get maximum benefit from the tool, set time aside for training. Like any craftsman, you need to be skilled in the use of a tool to get the most from it. Gaining the expertise and knowledge to use a tool effectively is an important part of establishing a firm foundation for conducting rapid development.

The next chapter covers the benefits of test-driven development for RAD and explains how this approach promotes both agility and accuracy in the software development process. We also return to Eclipse to examine the important role the IDE plays in supporting a test-centric approach.

## Additional Information

The MyEclipse plug-in was featured in this chapter. However, for anyone interested in open source alternatives, a tutorial on the use of the Lomboz equivalent is available from `http://www.tusc.com.au/tutorial/html`.

For information on IDEs other than Eclipse, see `http://www.jetbrains.com` for details on IntelliJ IDEA and `http://www.borland.com` for Borland's JBuilder and Together range of products.

These are both commercial products. For an open source product, visit the Web site for the NetBeans IDE at `http://www.netbeans.org`.

# 14

# Test-Driven Development

The best candidates for rapid development are systems for which requirements remain constant throughout the lifetime of the project. Sadly, such projects are a rarity, possibly to the extent that like such mythical beasts as the Yeti and the Loch Ness monster, their existence is questionable at best, and most likely fictitious.

Software projects have proven themselves prone to change at even the latest stage of the development process. A change can strike a project from a variety of directions: requirements are subject to change when use cases are enhanced, removed, or added; the system design may also change, either to reflect an update to the requirements or because of an initial discrepancy or shortcoming. Furthermore, an application's code base is constantly in a state of flux, as mistakes are made and rectified, and enhancements and optimizations are applied.

We've already covered techniques that seek to both assess the impact of change and mitigate its disruptive effects. Models offer a low-cost option for measuring the consequences a change will have on the ability of the design to execute the system, while code generation helps build an adaptive foundation for the project in order that changes can be absorbed without unduly stretching out the project schedule. We've seen that a layered design is also important, as it confines the potential ripple effects of a change to a single part of the architecture.

Another software engineering method can be added to this arsenal of techniques to further strengthen the base of our adaptive foundation: *test-driven development*.

Test-driven development is an approach in which the project is protected from change by a shield of unit tests. In this chapter, we examine the benefits of test-driven practices for rapid development and identify how testing techniques contribute to productivity and agility.

The testing activity is critical to the successful delivery of a software system, and we discuss over the next two chapters the various aspects of the testing process and the role it plays in rapid development.

The focus of this chapter is on the advantages and application of test-driven development, and we introduce the unit-testing framework *JUnit*. Methods for the autogeneration and running of unit tests are covered, as are the role of *mock objects* in the testing process.

# Testing as a Development Paradigm

Software engineers generally regard testing as a necessary evil. While all developers acknowledge the important role of testing in producing quality software, few admit to relishing the task of testing their own code, or anybody else's for that matter.

XP has turned this perception of the testing process around, breathing new life into the art of software testing. XP has achieved this turnaround by making the writing and running of tests central to the development effort.

> *The practices of XP covered in Chapter 3.*

For many developers, testing prior to the practices of XP was a laborious process. A test case had to be written, test data prepared, and expected results documented before any test could be executed. To make the testing process more palatable, XP seized upon the notion of using automated scripts for all developer-related testing. With XP, developers write code to test code, and writing code is something every engineer enjoys.

The XP approach to testing differs from traditional processes in that the test is written before any implementation code is produced. With the test in place, the next task is to write the minimal amount of code to pass the test—no more, no less. Writing the code to pass a test has the test driving the development process, hence the term test-driven development, or test-first development, as it is also known.

This test-driven approach moves the testing process to the forefront of the engineer's attention. The result of this emphasis on testing is tests that prove the implementation meets the requirements and code built to pass these tests.

Test-driven development existed before XP. However, XP has popularized the practice and helped gain widespread acceptance of the merits of test-centric development.

Adopting test-driven development does not require you to embrace the XP process. XP embodies a range of interlocking practices, of which test-driven development is only one. Instead, a test-first approach to development is a valuable addition to any methodology, and its use is actively encouraged as part of the IBM Rational Unified Process (RUP).

> *Chapter 3 covers the IBM Rational Unified Process.*

## The Benefits of Test-Driven Development

Following a test-driven approach to development enables the production of a comprehensive suite of automated tests over the course of the project that can be run quickly and easily. By including the testing in the build process, the impact of an application change on the code base can immediately be gauged. The cost of identifying implementation errors at the construction stage is far less than discovering them during a formal testing process by a separate quality assurance team.

Here is a summary of the benefits a test-driven approach can provide:

- Testing requirements are considered early.
- Tests are not omitted, since they are written first.
- The act of writing testing serves to clarify requirements.
- Writing testable code tends to produce better organized software.
- The usability of interfaces is improved because developers are required to work with the interface under test.
- Code changes can be validated immediately as part of the build process.
- The practice of refactoring is supported.
- A higher quality deliverable is provided to the quality assurance team, since unit tests catch defects earlier in the process

A test-driven approach therefore provides a project with the agility it needs to incorporate change into its structure. Changes can be made quickly, accurately, and with impunity on behalf of the software engineer.

Having a comprehensive test suite in place allows invasive techniques such as refactoring to be followed safely. Thus, engineers can undertake sweeping changes to the code base, safe in the knowledge that any errors introduced by such a process will be detected immediately.

## The Cost of Test-Driven Development

A test-driven approach to development can significantly improve the quality of software delivered into formal testing. However, while the theory behind test-driven development is attractive, the practice is not without its pitfalls. The writing of code, whether it is for adding functionality or writing tests, still consumes valuable project resources, namely a developer's time. The implementation of an effective automated test suite is not a trivial task. Some of the factors to consider are these:

### Complexity.

Each test that forms part of a greater test suite must operate in isolation. It must not exhibit side effects that have an impact on the behavior of other tests within the suite. Achieving this level of isolation between tests is a technical challenge, since the use of common resources, specifically the database, increases coupling between tests.

### Test coverage.

A strategy should exist to define the scope and distribution of all tests. A project with a poorly structured test strategy is liable to *unit test bloat*, whereby developers generate an excessive volume of unit tests with overlapping test coverage. To avoid test duplication, ensure you define your testing strategy early in the project and communicate it to all members of the team.

### Maintenance.

As the code base of the application grows, so does the number of automated unit tests. Requirement and design changes are likely to result in the need to update numerous test cases. Although the benefits of the automated test may justify the maintenance overhead of tests, this additional time and cost must be factored into the project schedule.

### The build process.

To be truly effective, a regularly scheduled build process should execute all unit tests as part of the build. The process needs to be able to run all unit tests and report test failures accordingly. The effort required to establish and maintain unit tests as part of the build process must be factored into the project's timeline.

Test-driven development can be undertaken effectively with the application of a sound test strategy and the use of a suitable testing framework. In the next sections, we look at the use of the open source testing framework JUnit for building test suites.

# Introducing JUnit

For writing unit tests for Java, we have to look no further than JUnit, an open source testing framework initially developed by Kent Beck and Erich Gamma. JUnit has become the de facto standard for Java unit testing. It is well supported by most development tools, and a wealth of reference material, tutorials, and other literature is available on its use.

The JUnit framework provides a ready-made test harness for executing unit tests as well as an API for reporting the success or failure status of a test. The JUnit framework is available for download from http://www.junit.org.

The success of JUnit is due in part to its simple design, as JUnit is both easy to learn and work with. Listing 14–1 shows the basic structure of a JUnit test case.

### Listing 14–1    JUnit Test Case

```
package customer.admin.ejb;

import junit.framework.TestCase;

public class CustomerAdminBeanTest extends TestCase {

  protected void setUp() throws Exception {
    super.setUp();
  }
```

```
protected void tearDown() throws Exception {
  super.tearDown();
}

public CustomerAdminBeanTest(String arg0) {
  super(arg0);
}

public final void testValidateAccount() {
  //TODO Implement validateAccount().
}

}
```

The example unit test shown in Listing 14–1 was automatically generated using Eclipse for a session bean with a single business method, validateAccount(). In its current state, the code shown isn't going to be performing much of a test, as we still have to add the testing functionality to the class. Nevertheless, the code does illustrate the structure of a JUnit test case.

To create a test that can be executed by the JUnit framework, you must write a test class responsible for conducting the individual test. This is achieved by defining a subclass of TestCase.

For each method on the class under test, a test method is required in the testing class. The method name should be prefixed with test. Methods must also be public, have no parameters, and return void. Adhering to these rules means the JUnit framework can use Java *reflection* to identify the test methods on the class dynamically. Without this approach, it would be necessary for all test methods to be registered with JUnit for execution. Reflection therefore simplifies the process of setting up a test case.

The basic test shown in Listing 14–1 contains only a single test method, testValidateAccount(). All the preparation work for the test can be done inside of this method—for example, instantiating objects required for the test or creating database connections. All of this test preparation, however, clutters the test code—something we must avoid, since a test should be easily readable.

For this reason, TestCase has two protected methods that can be overridden to provide setup and housekeeping tasks. The setUp() method is run before each test, while tearDown() is run once the test has completed.

tip

> The setUp() and tearDown() methods are run before every test method in the TestCase. If you have a setup-type operation that needs to be performed just once for all tests within the TestCase, then you must do this in the constructor. However, be wary of all code that is placed within the constructor, as JUnit simply reports that the test case could not be instantiated if an error occurs. A more detailed stack trace can be obtained from JUnit if setUp() is used.

You can confirm expected results at each step of the test's execution with the JUnit API. JUnit provides a number of assert methods for this purpose, where a failed assertion causes JUnit to report that the test has failed. Table 14–1 lists the different assertion types provided by JUnit for determining the status of an executing test.

**Table 14–1**  JUnit Assertion Types

| Assert Type | Description |
| --- | --- |
| assertEquals | Asserts that two items are equal. |
| assertFalse | Asserts that a condition is false. |
| assertNotNull | Asserts that an object isn't null. |
| assertNotSame | Asserts that two objects do not reference the same object. |
| assertNull | Asserts that an object is null. |
| assertSame | Asserts that two objects refer to the same object. |
| assertTrue | Asserts that a condition is true. |
| fail | Fails a test unconditionally. |

Listing 14–2 shows a complete test. In the example, the CustomerAdminBean session bean is tested from outside of the container using the remote interface of the enterprise bean.

**Listing 14–2  CustomerAdminBeanTest.java with Complete Test**

```
package customer.admin.interfaces;

import java.util.Hashtable;
import javax.naming.InitialContext;
import junit.framework.TestCase;
import customer.domain.Customer;
import customer.factory.CustomerFactory;

public class CustomerAdminBeanTest extends TestCase {

  private CustomerAdminBean customerAdminBean = null;

  /**
   * Obtain a remote interface to the Customer EJB.
   */
  protected void setUp() throws Exception {
    super.setUp();

    Hashtable props = new Hashtable();

    props.put(InitialContext.INITIAL_CONTEXT_FACTORY,
        "weblogic.jndi.WLInitialContextFactory");
```

```
    props
        .put(InitialContext.PROVIDER_URL, "t3://localhost:7001");

    customerAdminBean = CustomerAdminBeanUtil.getHome(props)
        .create();
}

/**
 * Expects the class under test to declare the Customer does not have a valid
 * account, i.e. method should return false
 *
 * @throws Exception
 */
public final void testValidateAccount() throws Exception {

    Customer customer = CustomerFactory.getCustomer(1);

    assertFalse(customerAdminBean.validateAccount(customer));
}

} // CustomerAdminBeanTest
```

The setUp() method obtains the remote interface for the session. The tearDown() method has been removed, as we won't be performing any housekeeping in this example. The actual test is provided in the testValidateAccount() method. The expected result from the test is that the validateAccount() method on the session bean will correctly determine the Customer has an invalid account and will return a value of false. To verify this condition, the call to the session bean is wrapped in an assertFalse() statement.

With the test created, the next step is to execute the test and examine the results. Running unit tests should be as quick and painless as possible. The next section discusses some of the options for invoking test cases.

## Running JUnit Tests with Eclipse

For executing test cases, JUnit uses a TestRunner. Three versions of TestRunner are available, depending on how you wish to execute the tests:

- junit.textui.TestRunner directs all test output to stdout.
- junit.awt.ui.TestRunner provides a graphical AWT-based user interface for running tests.
- junit.swingui.TestRunner provides a Swing-based graphical user interface for executing tests.

Although the JUnit framework provides the necessary tools for executing tests, it is preferable if the testing process integrates into your chosen development workbench.

Having an IDE that can run unit tests leads toward the goal of a single workbench as a one-stop shop for J2EE development. Rather than jumping out of the IDE in order to execute test cases, it is far more productive to have the IDE perform this operation.

The Eclipse workbench, like most IDEs, has excellent support for JUnit and comes with all of the necessary JUnit libraries as part of the install. Using an IDE like Eclipse, it is a trivial matter to execute all test cases and receive immediate feedback of the results of a test run.

> An overview of the Eclipse workbench is
> provided in Chapter 13.

Figure 14–1 shows the Eclipse JUnit Fast View. This view is displayed after telling Eclipse the `TestCase` instance is to be run as a JUnit test. This action is invoked from the Eclipse *run* menu.

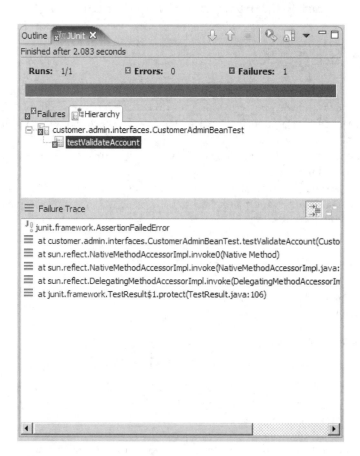

**Figure 14–1**    Eclipse JUnit Fast View.

The results of the `CustomerAdminBeanTest` test case are displayed in Figure 14–1, and in this instance, it is a failed test. The results of the test run are represented by a colored bar at the top of the view. Green is a pass and red is a fail. Figure 14–1 shows a red bar indicating failure. The reasons for the failure are given in the lower pane. In the example, we have an assertion failure: the `validateAccount()` code failed to correctly recognize an invalid customer account.

Having Eclipse make the running of tests so convenient allows for a rapid development cycle. The developer can update code and launch the test for immediate feedback on the success of the change.

Being able to run tests quickly is one factor in building a rapid development environment. Another is the time taken to write the test case. If we are going to embrace a test-first approach as part of a development methodology, then we need to consider how to reduce the time taken to write the tests.

Now that you have an appreciation of what is involved in writing a JUnit test, let's look at some of the options for expediting the development of a test suite.

# Generating Unit Tests

To have a comprehensive regression-testing suite in place requires writing a lot of test cases. Full-bore test-driven development requires a unit test for every class. Taken to these levels, an approach is required to prevent the creation of test cases from becoming a chore for the developer. Given the boilerplate nature of unit tests, they are ideal candidates for code generation techniques.

## Generating Unit Tests with Eclipse

In addition to running unit tests, Eclipse makes it easy to generate a unit test for any given class. A wizard is used to lay down the code, and it inspects the methods on the class under test to determine which test methods are to be included in the test case.

The Eclipse JUnit test wizard is shown in Figure 14–2.

The wizard offers several options for configuring the JUnit test generated. It is possible to specify which methods from `TestCase` should be overridden, define the class under test, and nominate the package for the test. When defining the package, it is considered best practice to use the same package as the class under test. With this approach, the relationship between test and implementation is unambiguous.

Note the warning from Eclipse at the top of the wizard dialog about generating a test case for an interface. Ideally, we want a test case for each class. An interface can be implemented by any number of classes. Nevertheless, this approach does make sense if we are testing a session bean via its remote interface from outside of the EJB container. Methods of the bean itself, such as `setSessionContext()`, cannot be called by the test case, only by the container. It is therefore nonsensical to generate a test case based on the class, because we cannot test these container-only methods.

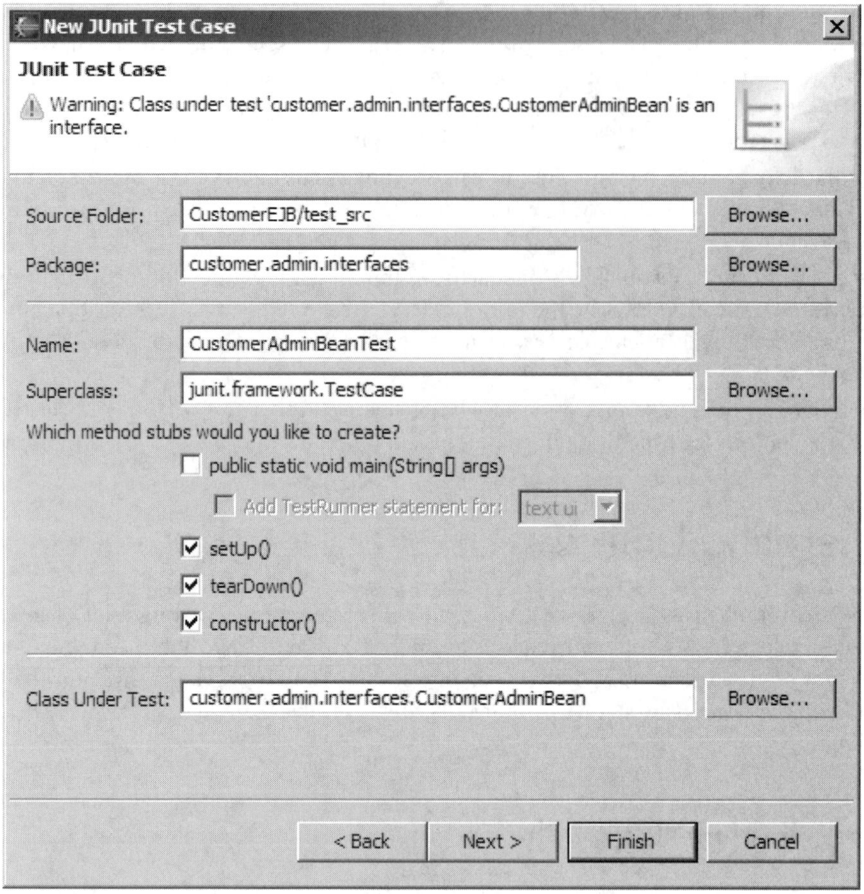

**Figure 14–2**    Eclipse JUnit test case wizard.

tip

> It is a good idea to place all test cases in the same package as the class under test but in their own source directory. This makes packaging easier and avoids inadvertently deploying test cases in J2EE modules.
>
> This tactic also provides the testing class with access to the package-level members of the class under test.

The final dialog for the wizard is shown in Figure 14–3. This screen allows the exposed methods on the class or interface to be selected for inclusion in the test case. Based on the methods selected, Eclipse creates the method stubs for writing the test, leaving the job of providing the test detail to the developer.

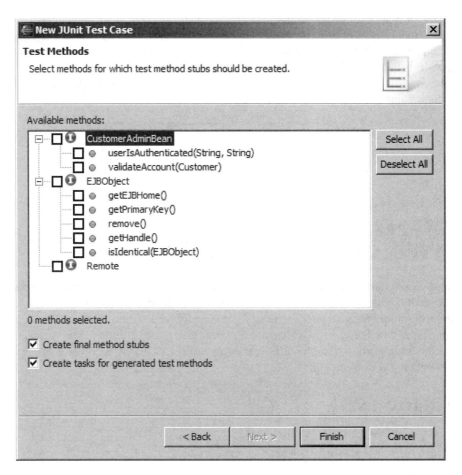

**Figure 14–3**  Eclipse test method selection dialog.

Generating tests in this manner may seem contrary to the principles of test-driven development. Previously, it was explained that a true test-driven approach to development involves writing the test case ahead of the class under test. How, then, can the Eclipse code generator be used for laying down the test case based on the class under test, when according to the principles of test-driven development, no actual class should exist?

There are perhaps two factors surrounding the rationale for including test code generators in IDEs. First, test case generators like the one offered by Eclipse are an indication that while developers are using JUnit for writing tests, in many cases engineers are falling back on the traditional approach of writing the test case after the class under test has been written. This *test-second* approach has value, but it does not emphasize the importance of the test case, and inadequate test cases may be the result.

The second factor is a question of whether we should be using test-driven development to drive the design or drive the implementation effort. There are many differing opinions on this topic.

My thoughts are that the best designs are produced by modeling, not by coding, particularly when extremely large systems are involved. Combining a model-based approach with a test-driven approach would see a minimal set of architecturally significant interfaces and classes, along with their responsibilities, defined before the main coding effort commences. With this approach, test-driven development is used to both ratify the interfaces being promoted and guide the writing of the code that sits behind each interface.

> *Chapter 5 covers the benefits of UML models in software design.*

note

A model-based approach to design does not preclude the use of code-level refactoring to further advance and refine the design.

Using a combination of modeling and testing techniques to drive the development means all architecturally significant interfaces can be legitimately defined ahead of the test cases. Ideally, our modeling tool will have generated the structure of the application for us. This raises the question as to whether the modeling tool can also generate the test cases in tandem. This approach has implications if a Model-Driven Architecture (MDA) paradigm is adopted, a subject we cover in the next section.

## Unit Tests and MDA

An MDA approach enables a large percentage of the code needed for an application to be generated from a high-level platform-independent model.

> *Model-Driven Architecture is covered in Chapter 8.*

It is possible to leverage the power of MDA tools in order to support test-driven development during the construction, or implementation, phase of a project. This can be achieved by having the MDA tool generate all necessary test cases on our behalf.

This approach has significant advantages that go beyond the time-savings made by having the test cases autogenerated in an IDE. Many software projects fail to build up a comprehensive test suite for the application. Often, the result of unit test development efforts are a patchwork of tests spread unevenly across the application. Consequently, some areas of the system are overtested,[1] while other areas are completely overlooked.

---

1. Some people would argue that you can never have enough testing.

This problem arises because the responsibility of producing unit tests traditionally is placed on the developer. Each developer is likely to take a different view of the value of unit tests. Some developers might diligently generate tests for all their work, while others may be far less rigorous in their approach to testing.

Standards that stress the importance of testing and provide guidelines to the necessary test coverage expected can help. Nevertheless, it still falls to the individual to follow the standards and work within the guidelines.

With MDA, it is possible to make the development of a consistent test suite much less of a hit-or-miss affair. The architect should be thinking strategically as to where test coverage is required for the design. Based on these decisions, an MDA transformation mapping can be used to generate test cases for the appropriate elements within the model.

Using the MDA tool in this manner ensures a consistent approach to test coverage is taken. Developers simply need to fill in the implementation detail for each generated test case.

## Generating Test Cases with AndroMDA

The cartridge system of AndroMDA makes it easy to add the capability to the tool to generate test cases. Two options are available: either develop a new test cartridge or extend one of the existing cartridges by adding a new Velocity template.

> *Velocity templates and the Velocity template language are described in Chapter 6.*

Updating one of the existing cartridges is perhaps the easiest method for getting something in place quickly, while building a new cartridge from scratch allows tests to be built for any project type by adding the test cartridge to the AndroMDA classpath. Note, however, that the latter option is a far more challenging and time-consuming, undertaking.

Regardless of which approach is taken, a Velocity template lies at the heart of the solution. To get you started, Listing 14–3 provides an example `UnitTest.vsl` template.

### Listing 14–3   UnitTest.vsl AndroMDA Cartridge Velocity Template

```
#set($packagename=$transform.findPackageName($class.package))
#set($remoteInterface=$str.lowerCaseFirstLetter(${class.name}))
package $packagename;

import java.util.Hashtable;
import javax.naming.InitialContext;
import junit.framework.TestCase;
```

```
public class ${class.name}Test extends TestCase {

  private ${class.name} $remoteInterface = null;

  /*
   * Perform all set up work here
   *
   */
  protected void setUp() throws Exception {
    super.setUp();

    Hashtable props = new Hashtable();

    props.put(InitialContext.INITIAL_CONTEXT_FACTORY,
        "weblogic.jndi.WLInitialContextFactory");
    props
        .put(InitialContext.PROVIDER_URL, "URL_AS_PROPERTY");

    // Obtain remote interface to the session bean under test
    //
    $remoteInterface = ${class.name}Util.getHome(props).create();
  }

  protected void tearDown() throws Exception {
  }

#foreach ($op in $class.operations)
  #set($testMethod = $op.getName())

  public final void test$testMethod() throws Exception {

    // TODO Add your test here

  }
#end

}
```

In the configuration of the MDA cartridge, associate the template with all model elements with a stereotype of Service. The template applies to any cartridge that generates EJB components for all classes stereotyped as a Service.

> *Refer to Chapter 8 for information on the specifics of configuring AndroMDA cartridges.*

The template generates a test case for each service element from the model. Tests take on the name of the service with `Test` appended to the name.

Walking through the example template, the `setUp()` method follows from the previous example and obtains the remote interface to the session bean generated by AndroMDA for the service. The remote interface is intended for use in each of the test methods.

A Velocity Template Language (VTL) `#foreach` statement is used to iterate through each operation on the model element. The name of the operation is obtained by interrogating the model. From the list of operations, the test methods for each business method on the service can be built up.

You can use the example shown in Listing 14–3 as a basis for further experimentation. AndroMDA makes all model metadata accessible from within the template, allowing the generation of sophisticated test cases. The trick is to avoid getting carried away and making the generated tests overly complicated. You'll find a little goes a long way.

tip

> Be devious and add a `fail("Test not implemented")` in every test method. This ensures tests fail unless the developer corrects the problem by supplying a valid test.

# Testing from the Inside Out

The concept of a test-driven approach to development is extremely attractive if the full benefits of the paradigm can be realized. An exhaustive set of automated tests provides the safety net necessary for rapidly accommodating change on the project. In addition, it raises software quality, which in turn reduces the number of defects detected in formal systems testing. All of these benefits combine to facilitate a rapid development process.

While the concept of test-driven development is sound, the practicalities of implementing a suite of automated unit tests at the level required represents a sizeable technical challenge for the project team.

Writing valid unit tests is not a trivial task. In some cases, writing the test can prove a greater technical challenge than writing the class under test.

One of the greatest difficulties lies in isolating the class under test. Within the boundaries of a system, an object collaborates with other objects in order to execute specific functionality. For example, an object may require a number of domain objects returned from the persistence layer. The state of these domain objects determines the behavior of the class under test.

Designing a test that provides a class with all the information it needs to perform a specific operation can be an involved process, as dependencies between components make the testing of objects in isolation problematic. Good design practice that sees component coupling carried out through strongly typed interfaces can help ease the burden of writing unit tests. However, pulling an object out from a nest of collaborating instances is far from a trivial exercise in even the most well-designed system. Moreover, complete test coverage requires that a number of different scenarios be run. This involves setting the state of collaborating objects for each test scenario.

Object isolation is not the only issue with a test-driven approach. If we stick rigidly to the rule that each class is fully tested before proceeding to the next class to be developed, we are forced to adopt a bottom-up approach, whereby all foundation classes must be implemented ahead of any classes relying on those foundation services.

A bottom-up approach is not always the most practical approach. Project scheduling may dictate that classes in upper layers of the architecture must be implemented in parallel with classes from the lower layers. This raises the question of how to test an object when the classes upon which it is dependent have yet to be written, a problem inherent to even traditional development approaches.

One solution to the problem of how to test objects in isolation and undertake a top-down approach is to use *mock objects*, familiarly known as *mocks*.

## What Is a Mock?

A mock object is best described as a dummy, or stub, implementation of an actual class. Mocks take the place of the real objects a class under test relies upon. Thus, if the class under test requires a domain object in a particular state for a specific test scenario, then you can substitute the domain object with a mock. Likewise, if the domain object has yet to be implemented, a mock can take its place.

The term mock was first coined in a notable paper by Tim Mackinnon, Steve Freeman, and Philip Craig, *Endo-Testing: Unit Testing with Mock Objects*, [Mackinnon, 2000]. The authors invented the term *endo-testing* as a play on endoscopic surgery, a process that enables the surgeon to work on the patient without having to make a large incision to allow access.

Mocks may sound very similar to test stubs in that they *stub out* the real code. Like test stubs, a mock can be configured to return a specific result in order to conduct a test scenario. This approach makes it easier to simulate events that are difficult to produce in a real environment, for example, a database connection being unavailable or an exception being thrown from a method call.

The comparison with test stubs is valid, but mocks go beyond what is offered by the typical test stub. Units test operate on the public- and package-level members of a class. Although they should exercise all execution paths within the code and test all boundary conditions, they do not interact directly with the internals of the class. However, using mocks, the internals of a class can be inspected as part of the test; hence the reference to endoscopic surgery—mocks enable testing from the inside.

For the class under test, we can predict what calls we expect to be made on a mock object for a given test scenario. The mock object can record these calls. If an expected call fails to be made or the calls are made in the wrong order, then the mock can elect to fail the test. Thus, mocks allow a form of *white-box* testing to be undertaken as part of the unit testing process.

White-box testing is testing inside the methods of a class. Unlike black-box testing, which tests what a class does, white-box testing focuses on how a class performs its tasks. It is usually an invasive process and requires the class to be implemented in such as way that the internals can be examined while executing. Mocks offer a mechanism to inspect the internals of the class without having to structure the code in a manner that directly supports white-box testing.

## Working with Mocks

Mocks require that we follow good design practices and architect our system around the use of interfaces. Divorcing an object's implementation from its interface is sound software engineering. It also facilitates the use of mock objects because the approach enables mocks to be easily substituted in place of the real object.

When it comes to writing mocks for a unit test, you can write the mock from scratch, implementing all the methods on the interface as needed for the test. This approach is labor-intensive and means the amount of code dedicated to testing the system is prone to bloating in size. Thankfully, a number of frameworks are available that can help reduce the effort involved in producing mocks. We consider these next.

## Mock Flavors

Mocks take on the interface they are mocking. With an interface defining the shape of the mock, the mock object is another ideal candidate for code generation.

Although numerous options exist for generating mock objects, there are essentially two distinct approaches: *static* mocks and *dynamic* mocks.

Static mocks can be either handwritten or the output of a mock object code generator. Several code generators for mock objects are available; *MockCreator* and *MockMaker* are two notable examples. Each of these generators creates a mock object for a given interface. Optional Eclipse plug-ins are available for each generator.

For more information on MockCreator, see `http://mockcreator.sourceforge.net`. To obtain MockMaker, visit the site at `http://www.mockmaker.org`. Both code generators are freely available. In addition, XDoclet provides a mock generator, `<mockdoclet>`, which generates mock objects from the `@mock.generate` tag.

---

*Chapter 6 covers the use of XDoclet.*

---

By now, you should be well versed in the use of code generators and how XDoclet attributes can drive code generation. We now look at dynamic mock objects, which typically rely on Java reflection to work their magic.

## Dyna-Mocks to the Rescue

As with static mock generators, a number of freely available dynamic mock implementations exist. Again, we have two notable examples: *jMock* and *EasyMock*. Both enjoy a level of popularity among developers. and each provides a reasonable level of documentation. In selecting between the two, your best option is to perform your own bake-off and determine which best suits the needs of your particular project.

JMock is maintained under the Codehaus project. so see `http://jmock.codehaus.org`. For EasyMock, pay a visit to `http://www.easymock.org`.

To show how mocks can assist in the process of unit testing and to demonstrate how dynamic mocks work, we go through an example unit test that uses a dynamic mock as the collaborating object for the class under test. The example uses EasyMock for defining the mock object.

The objective of the example test is to validate that the class under test calls the correct methods on the collaborating object. The example is based on two classes: the class under test, `Invoice`, and the collaborating object, which is an implementation of the interface `ICustomer`. Listing 14–4 shows the `ICustomer` interface.

## Listing 14–4   The ICustomer Interface

```java
public interface ICustomer {

    /**
     * Customer's discount entitlement
     */
    public abstract double discountRate();

    /**
     * Customer's interest on credit sales
     */
    public abstract double creditRate();

} // ICustomer
```

Listing 14–5 has the implementation of the `Invoice` class.

## Listing 14–5   The Invoice Class under Test

```java
public class Invoice {

  private double    invoiceAmount;

  private ICustomer customer;

  /**
   * Associate the invoice with a customer
   *
   */
  public Invoice(ICustomer customer) {
    this.customer = customer;
  }
```

```
/**
 * Set the invoice amount
 */
public void setInvoiceAmount(double invoiceAmount) {
  this.invoiceAmount = invoiceAmount;
}

/**
 * Calculate the customer's discount for the invoice amount
 */
public double discount() {

  return invoiceAmount * (customer.creditRate() / 100);
}

} // Invoice
```

The `Invoice` class doesn't do much, but a mistake has still been made. The `discount()` method returns the value of the discount the customer receives off the total invoice amount. The calculation is based on the customer's special discount rate. In this system, loyal customers get a better discount. A customer's discount percentage is returned from the method `discountRate()` by the object implementing the `ICustomer` interface. Unfortunately, in this case, the `discount()` method on the `Invoice` class has been incorrectly implemented by using the customer's credit rate in place of the discount rate.

It's a silly error, but problems of this type can easily arise if care isn't taken when using code-editor productivity features like *code assist* or *code completion*. Here the developer has inadvertently selected the wrong method from the list. Code assist is an invaluable editor feature, but you have to be careful not to get too lazy.

To detect this type of error, a test is required that confirms the correct methods are being called on the collaborating objects, in this case `ICustomer`. This is easily done with mocks.

Listing 14–6 gives the test case for the test, using a dynamic mock object in place of the implementation for the `ICustomer` interface.

## Listing 14–6    The InvoiceTest Unit Test Case

```
import junit.framework.TestCase;
import org.easymock.MockControl;

public class InvoiceTest extends TestCase {

  protected void setUp() throws Exception {
    super.setUp();

    // Create mock based on interface
    //
    control = MockControl.createControl(ICustomer.class);
    customerMock = (ICustomer) control.getMock();
```

```
    // Prepare the class under test
    //
    invoice = new Invoice(customerMock);
    invoice.setInvoiceAmount(200.0);
}

public final void testDiscount() {

    // Configure the mock ready for the test
    //
    customerMock.discountRate();
    control.setReturnValue(10.0);

    // Place mock in the active state
    //
    control.replay();

    // Run the test
    //
    assertEquals(20.0, invoice.discount(), 0.0);

    // Ensure test class calls discountRate() method
    //
    control.verify();
}

private MockControl control;
private ICustomer   customerMock;
private Invoice     invoice;

} // InvoiceTest
```

The setUp() method of the test case is where the dynamic mock is created. Using Easy-Mock, two classes are created: an instance of MockControl, which takes the type of interface to be mocked as a parameter and is used for controlling the mock object, and the mock object itself, which is returned from the MockControl instance with a call to the factory method get-Control().

The mock returned from the MockControl exposes the ICustomer interface, so we can substitute the mock for the real object. MockControl achieves this feat of impersonation by using java.lang.reflect.Proxy under the covers.

The final act of the setUp() method is to create an instance of Invoice for using in the test. The mock is passed to the Invoice object via its constructor. The Invoice instance is then seeded with an invoice amount for the test. This value is used for checking against our expected results.

The final steps for setting up the test are completed within the testDiscount() method on the TestCase. At this stage, the newly created mock is in *record* mode. In this state, the methods that must be invoked on the mock when the test is run can be specified. EasyMock enables this information to be specified in detail. You can specify the order of calls, the number of times each call should be made, and the expected parameters. Refer to the EasyMock documentation for a full list of its capabilities.

The test in the example isn't overly complex. Next, we ensure that the correct method is invoked on the collaborating object and that the class under test returns the expected result.

For defining the expected method invocation, the required method is called on the mock object with the mock in the record state. In this case, the method is `discountRate()`.

The next step is to set the result returned by the mock when the class under test invokes the method. This is achieved by calling `setReturnValue()` on the `MockControl` instance.

Now that the mock is configured, it is placed in the active state with a call to `replay()` on the `MockControl`.

A call to `discount()` on the `Invoice` object initiates the test. The called method is wrapped in a JUnit `assertEquals` so the expected results can be confirmed. The final call to `verify()` on the `MockControl` instructs the mock controller to assert if the methods specified when the mock was in the record state are not invoked. All that remains to do is run the test.

Here is the error reported when the test case is run.

```
junit.framework.AssertionFailedError:
  Unexpected method call creditRate():
    creditRate(): expected: 0, actual: 1
```

The mock asserts during the execution of the test that an unexpected method, `creditRate()`, has been called. We've found our bug. The troublesome code can be corrected and the test rerun to achieve the green bar indicating a successful test.

Based on the example, you can see that mocks add another dimension to the type of unit testing you can perform. Not only can the mock stand in for the real collaborating object, as is possible with a traditional test stub, it can also validate the class under test from the inside. This all leads to a rigorous testing process and hence higher quality code.

## Choosing Between Static and Dynamic Mocks

Dynamic mocks are attractive—they offer the ability to create powerful test stubs at runtime. All the code relating to a test can be maintained within the test case itself, avoiding the need to support further test code for the implementation of the mock.

Despite these benefits, mocks are not suited to all test scenarios. The example shown cannot be used to test an EJB component through its remote interface, as the dynamic proxy cannot be marshaled as part of the call. Moreover, as has already been stated, testing is not a trivial undertaking, and it is likely a combination of static and dynamic mocks will make up the overall test suite.

A general heuristic to follow when working with mocks is to use dynamic mocks where possible for their convenience and setup speed. Dynamic mocks help keep the size of the code base down and can be localized to a single test. For situations in which this cannot be achieved, look to generate the mock, and if all else fails, simply write your own implementation. Static mocks can be used to test Enterprise JavaBeans, and the strong typing of a static interface can be an advantage because it enables the compiler to detect errors in the test suite.

# Summary

After reading this chapter, you should have an appreciation of the important role testing has to play throughout the software development lifecycle. The testing activity is more than a backstop at the end of the project for catching defects. It is critical to rapid application development, which can be greatly facilitated by putting in place an automated unit test suite for the project. The presence of this test suite and the adoption of a test-driven approach to development offers two major benefits:

**Agility.**

The project team can respond quickly and accurately to any changes, whether in the form of updated end-user requirements or design modifications. All changes can be immediately validated with the unit test suite, thereby providing a safety net for potentially sweeping changes to the design and code base.

The ability to absorb changes without adversely impacting the project's timeframe and compromising quality is an essential ingredient for successful rapid application development.

**Accuracy.**

The cost of resolving defects in a system increases as the application progresses through the stages of the software development lifecycle. Defects detected during a formal system test by a dedicated quality-assurance team incur a far higher penalty than those detected early in the process during implementation. By having the development team adopt a rigorous, upfront approach to testing, the quality of releases into the formal test environment is improved, thereby reducing the number of defects detected at the later stages of the project.

Unit tests also reduce the time it takes to resolve a defect, since unit tests make it easily reproducible. Furthermore, adopting a test-driven approach helps instill the importance of testing for producing quality software within the project team.

In the next chapter, we keep the focus on the testing effort but broaden the scope to include tools and techniques for automating the process of conducting functional and load-based testing.

# Additional Information

The process of writing unit tests has gathered a critical mass of knowledge thanks to the large take up of JUnit, and a set of best practices has emerged from the wider developer community for writing effective units tests. To find out more about the intricacies of automated unit testing, the JUnit site found at `http://www.junit.org` is an excellent starting point and provides an extensive set of links to literature on the subject.

Kent Beck has published a book, *Test Driven Development by Example* [Beck, 2002], on test-driven development that illustrates the entire process with a complete example.

For more details on mocks, the uncontested home of mock objects on the Web is `http://www.mockobjects.com`. The site provides an extensive amount of information on anything and everything relating to mock objects.

# 15

# Efficient Quality Assurance

Properly testing a system requires a sizeable effort, with typically a quarter of the project schedule being set aside for the testing process [Brooks, 1995]. Consequently, any method that facilitates the various testing activities directly impacts the project timeframe, helping to speed up the delivery of the software. If you can reduce the time to undertake all aspects of the testing process, you'll achieve the RAD objective of delivering the application to the customer in a shorter timeframe.

Despite the advantages test-driven development provides, it is not a replacement for a rigorous quality assurance (QA) process. This still has to be undertaken, as a test strategy based purely on unit testing falls well short of the goal of delivering a comprehensively tested solution.

The primary focus of this chapter is on functional and system-load testing. Predominantly, we examine how test automation tools can assist in reducing testing times and improving test accuracy. Two open source tools are introduced: *HttpUnit* for creating test scripts for the functional testing of a Web application, and *JMeter* for conducting load and stress testing.

## Quality Assurance

Quality assurance involves the auditing, monitoring, and management of all aspects of software quality throughout the entire project lifecycle. A rigorous QA process demands a range of testing types to ensure an acceptable level of quality for the system delivered to the customer.

Here are the different types of test an enterprise system commonly undergoes before being released into a production environment.

### Unit tests.

The objective of unit testing is to validate a component's conformance to the design. These tests form the backbone of a test-driven approach and are the responsibility of the developer. They are fine-grained tests and typically exercise the functionality of a single class or component via its public and package-level methods and data.

Unit tests can be a combination of *black-box* and *white-box* testing methods. Under a black-box test, the unit test confirms the class under test meets its specified requirements. A white-box test looks at the internals of the class to verify how the requirements are met.

> *Unit testing is covered in Chapter 14.*

### Integration tests.

Unlike unit tests, which focus on a single class or component, integration testing takes a wider view, operating at a higher level. They confirm components are able to collaborate in order to deliver the required functionality.

### Functional tests.

Functional tests verify the system's conformance to the end-user requirements. They usually align with individual use cases, which themselves provide a starting point for a test case. Larger projects tend to charge a dedicated QA team with the responsibility of producing and executing all functional tests.

### Load tests.

Load, or performance, tests target the nonfunctional requirements and confirm the ability of the system to meet the specified performance criteria under a given load.

### Stress tests.

Stress testing places the system under a load that exceeds its designed operational capacity. The purpose of the stress test is to observe the system's failsafe behavior under excessive load.

### System tests.

A system test is carried out on a completely integrated system and looks to prove that the system meets all requirements, both functional, as defined in the use cases, and nonfunctional, such as meeting specific performance criteria.

### Regression tests.

This is a combination of the different testing types that together measure the impact of a modification upon a system. Full regression testing can be a lengthy process, involving the rerunning of all unit, integration, functional, and system tests. Depending on the nature and extent of the change, a partial regression test may be preferable.

### Acceptance tests.

An acceptance test confirms the system meets the acceptance criteria agreed with the stakeholders. It is common for the customers of a system to undertake this type of testing with their own QA team, as acceptance testing is closely linked to the terms of the contract under which the system was developed.

The focus of this discussion is on functional, load, and stress testing. Performing these tests correctly requires the establishment of a suitable QA environment. The next section examines the different environments necessary for developing and testing enterprise software.

## The Project Environment

Enterprise projects commonly require three distinct working environments: development, testing, and production.

Figure 15–1 illustrates the three environments.

In the *development* environment, software engineers write, unit-test, and integrate all source code for the system. This environment is likely to comprise developer workstations with additional machines for performing integration builds and housing source-control repositories.

The *testing* environment is where all formal testing takes place against regular, versioned releases of the system from the development environment. For tests to be meaningful, the test environment must closely resemble the production environment.

### note

The testing environment is sometimes called the *staging area* or *preproduction* environment.

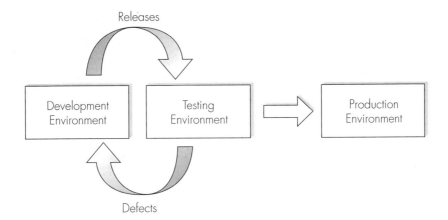

**Figure 15–1**   Environment setup.

*Production* is the target environment for the system, and the testing effort must validate the system is capable of meeting all functional and nonfunctional requirements when operating in this final environment. Testing is unlikely to be possible in production because live systems are involved, hence the need for the testing environment to closely mirror that of production.

## The Testing Process

Testing as part of an iterative development methodology such as Extreme Programming (XP) or the IBM Rational Unified Process (RUP) is an ongoing process conducted throughout the entire software development lifecycle.

> *Chapter 3 covers iterative development processes, including XP and the RUP.*

An iterative development process has a running version of the system available from the early stages of the project. This allows the project team to continually submit the system to a barrage of functional and nonfunctional tests. This constant and ongoing testing effort is a key strategy in reducing risk by confirming the system under development is able to meet customer requirements and design goals.

Formal testing should commence toward the end of each iteration. The process starts by delivering a versioned release into the test environment

note

> It is important the testing environment is reproducible between tests so the environment's hardware, configuration, and test data remains constant for each test cycle. This is essential for meaningful comparisons of test results between releases.

Each release is subjected to a full range of functional and nonfunctional tests, and any arising defects and issues are logged for the attention of the development team. The release and testing process continues until the system is of an acceptable standard. The final iterations of a project focus intensely on the testing effort and look to deliver the finished system into production.

It is common for systems with a high defect rate to spend a substantial amount of time bouncing between the developments and testing environments. A long and involved testing process causes lengthy delays in getting the application into production.

## Testing for RAD Projects

Supporting rapid application development requires meeting two objectives:

- Improving the quality of software releases in order to reduce the number of testing cycles
- Reducing the time taken to complete the testing process

A test-driven approach to development results in higher quality software with fewer defects. This point has critical implications for rapid development, as the number of defects found during testing directly relates to the project's duration. Put bluntly, the more defects discovered, the longer the system takes to deliver to the customer. Moreover, a problem detected during the formal testing process is more expensive to rectify than if discovered during development. Rigorous testing during development pays dividends by enabling the detection and correction of defects close to their point of origin.

Reducing the time taken to execute all of a system's functional and nonfunctional test cases is achievable with test automation. This approach speeds up the testing process without comprising the quality of the test performed. The benefits of automated testing for rapid development make this the main topic for this chapter.

# Automated Testing

According to Robert Binder, author of the definitive testing guide *Testing Object-Oriented Systems*, for tests to be effective and repeatable, they must be automated [Binder, 1999]. This is an added bonus: by adopting test automation techniques, you not only help to reduce the project timeframe but also apply best-practice testing methods.

The arguments for writing automated tests have close parallels with the arguments used to justify the creation of code generators during development:

> *Code generators are introduced in Chapter 6.*

### Accuracy and repeatability.

Test scripts are usually executed more than once during the course of a project. Even the most careful developers fail to prevent every defect from finding a way into the system. Although a single test cycle must be the goal, several test cycles are often required.

Accurate system testing relies on tests being repeatable between cycles. Repeatability is easier to achieve with test automation. By comparison, manual testing is labor-intensive and subject to both human error and oversight. A test strategy based completely on manual testing procedures carries the risk that errors introduced between testing cycles will escape detection. An automated test that is 100 percent repeatable avoids this danger.

### Reduced timeframes.

The time available to fully test a complex enterprise system, with numerous interoperating subsystems and countless points of integration between collaborating components, may be such that test automation is the only plausible option for realizing an effective test strategy in a timeframe that is acceptable to the customer.

### Improved test effectiveness.

Certain types of testing are difficult to achieve without the use of automated tools. Load and stress testing fall firmly within this category. Here, sophisticated tools are required that reproduce the same level of throughput upon a system as a large number of users all accessing the system concurrently. Unless the project's budget runs to hiring potentially thousands of testers, then the use of these tools is a necessity.

### Removal of mundane tasks.

Testers, like developers, get bored if they are required to perform the same type of tests repeatedly. As with the use of code generators, automated test scripts remove the drudgery from the testing effort, leaving the QA specialist free to focus on other aspects of the system.

note

> The adoption of test automation does not completely remove the need for manual testing processes. Expert testers can, and should, continue to perform invasive manual tests in an effort to break the system. An effective test strategy is a combination of automated and manual tests that together comprehensively test a system prior to its delivery to the customer.

A question that often arises in relation to test automation is whether the time taken to write the automated test script is justifiable in terms of the effort saved in running an automated test. Despite the benefits, test automation does consume effort and hence incurs a cost to the project. Nevertheless, these costs are usually recoverable within two or three test cycles, especially when including the added benefits of improved test accuracy and consequent increase in software quality. Furthermore, the same test scripts are reusable in the long term, as the system enters a maintenance phase.

tip

> The creation of test scripts can start in the early stages of a project iteration by using a prototype as a starting point for the creation of automated test scripts.

# The J2EE Testing Challenge

An enterprise-level distributed J2EE application presents some very unique challenges to the tester, and regardless of whether manual or automated tests are used, the testing of a distributed application is an involved and complex process.

First, an application built on the J2EE platform employs a variety of Java-based technologies for the development of system components, which are distributed over remotely distinct tiers. Thus, the tester immediately has a multimachine environment to contend with, plus the headaches a network brings in the form of firewalls and corporate security policies.

> *Chapter 4 examines some possible software architectures for creating J2EE applications that do not depend upon the remote method invocation services of Enterprise JavaBeans.*

In addition to the distributed environment, by leveraging the full capabilities of the J2EE platform, the architecture of a J2EE enterprise application could potentially involve the use of asynchronous messaging between systems, long-running business transactions being fired between heterogeneous systems, and critical business functionality being exposed to other systems as part of a wider service-oriented architecture.

Besides the sophisticated architectures made possible by the J2EE platform, enterprise systems present their own special challenges to the tester, with system operational attributes such as security, performance, scalability, and robustness requiring intensive test coverage. The sensitivities revolving around security alone often demand the skills of specialized QA experts.

Collectively, these points make the task of testing an enterprise system as complex for the tester as the task of development is for the software engineer.

# Test Automation Tools

Fortunately, test automation tools are available to help address the challenges presented in thoroughly testing J2EE solutions. These tools aim to both simplify the testing process and improve the quality of the tests conducted.

Tools that support the testing process fall into the following general categories:

### Test coverage.

These tools analyze the entire code base and report on the depth and breadth of existing test cases.

## Quality measurement.

Measurement tools operate either statically, analyzing such artifacts as the design model and the source code, or dynamically by inspecting the runtime state of the system under test. The output from these types of products enables metrics to be compiled on the application in terms of complexity, maintainability, performance, and memory usage. This information can then be used to drive the production of a suitable test strategy.

## Test data generators.

One of the harder aspects of testing is the generation of suitable test data. This is especially the case where a new system is under development and no existing legacy data is available. Test data generators will produce test data from such artifacts as the design model, database schema, XML schemas, and the source code.

## Test automation tools.

This general-purpose category covers the tools that execute prepared automated test scripts. Products are available that support the automation of the full range of testing types, including unit, integration, functional, load, and stress tests. Methods employed by these tools include record and playback of events for GUI testing and programmatic testing for specific GUI types.

Various testing tools are available as open source, although few offer the same level of functionality as the high-end commercial products. Table 15–1 lists some of the open source testing tools available to the Java enterprise tester for undertaking test automation.

**Table 15–1**   Open Source Java Testing Tools

| Name | Description | Type | Reference |
|---|---|---|---|
| Cactus | Cactus is a unit/integration test framework from the Apache Software Foundation. It is used for the testing of server-side Java code and offers a means of undertaking in-container testing on J2EE components. | Unit/Integration | http://jakarta.apache.org/cactus/ |
| Grinder | The Grinder orchestrates the activities of a test script in many processes and across many machines, using a graphical console application. Test scripts use client code embodied in Java plug-ins. The Grinder comes with a plug-in for testing HTTP services, as well as a tool that allows HTTP scripts to be automatically recorded. | Load/stress | http://grinder.sourceforge.net/ |

**Table 15–1**    Open Source Java Testing Tools (continued)

| Name | Description | Type | Reference |
|------|-------------|------|-----------|
| HttpUnit | HttpUnit offers a Java API for developing a suite of functional tests for Web applications. | Unit/Functional | http://source-forge.net/projects/httpunit/ |
| Jameleon | Jameleon is an acceptance-level automated testing tool. Jameleon claims to separate applications into features, which are then tied together as test cases. | Functional | http://jameleon.source-forge.net/ |
| JFCUnit | An extension to the JUnit framework that enables you to execute unit tests against code that presents a Swing GUI–based interface. JFCUnit offers a record and playback facility to enable novice GUI developers to generate and execute tests. | Unit/Functional | http://source-forge.net/projects/jfcunit/ |
| JMeter | Apache JMeter is a 100 percent pure Java desktop application designed to load-test functional behavior. | Load/stress | http://jakarta.apache.org/jmeter/ |
| Solex | Solex is an Eclipse plug-in for testing Web applications. It provides functions to record client sessions, adjust parameters as required, and then replay later as part of a regression suite. | Functional | http://solex.source-forge.net/ |

The next sections cover the use and application of two of these tools: HttpUnit and JMeter. We first look at HttpUnit, an API that provides support for functional testing.

# Functional Testing

Functional tests focus on proving the system exhibits the behavior requested by the customer. A system's functional behavior can be detailed in a series of use cases, as is the practice with a use-case-driven process like the RUP, or as a set of user stories when following an agile method such as XP.

The ability of the system to meet the customer's business requirements is obviously a key concern. The owners of the system use functional tests to assess the application's conformance to their requirements as part of their *acceptance tests*.

Under XP, the customer works with the development team to generate an automated suite of acceptance tests. Larger projects following the RUP are likely to use a QA team to build test scripts from the system's use cases.

Functional testing is a black-box technique, and for business systems relies on test cases that exercise system functionality via the user interface, although testing of batch functionality is also a concern.

Tools offer several approaches for automating the functional testing of systems via the user interface. One approach uses event capture and replay to rerun recorded keystroke sequences against the GUI. However, this approach is fragile and susceptible to even very small changes in the system's user interface.

Another approach is to take control of the user interface programmatically using a script. This approach is the subject of the next section, which introduces the functional testing tool *HttpUnit*.

# Introducing HttpUnit

HttpUnit is an open source testing tool for undertaking the functional testing of Web applications. Unlike its namesake JUnit, HttpUnit is not a testing framework but a Java API. The HttpUnit API provides a means of programmatically interacting with a Web application and enables the automation of sophisticated test scenarios.

> *The JUnit framework is covered in*
> *Chapter 14.*

The HttpUnit API centers around four core classes, described in Table 15–2.

**Table 15–2**   Main HttpUnit Classes

| Class | Description |
|---|---|
| WebConversation | Acts as the Web browser during the test and maintains all conversation state associated with the running test case and the Web application under test. |
| WebResponse | Represents the HTTP response received from the Web application and provides methods for conveniently inspecting the contents of the response. |
| WebForm | Used to represent an HTML form and enables a request to the server to be built up by specifying values to be submitted for the form. |
| WebRequest | Represents an HTTP request submitted to the Web application. |

Using this API, all facets of an interaction with a Web application are controllable. The API provides an elegant mechanism for constructing and submitting Web requests and analyzing the response. This functionality alone makes it a useful utility for Web application development, not just for testing purposes.

Although HttpUnit is suitable for building unit tests, its ability to engage in a dialog with a Web application places it in the category of a functional testing tool. HttpUnit test cases are written from the perspective of the end user, and key business scenarios can be orchestrated and tested, making the tool ideally suited for constructing acceptance tests.

As a testing tool, HttpUnit is very simple. Its main strength is a clean and easily understandable API. Unlike many of the commercial Web functional testing tools, the feature set of HttpUnit is distinctly limited in comparison. HttpUnit offers no reporting capabilities or graphical analysis features for deciphering the results of test runs. However, all of these bells and whistles carry a price tag. Consequently, the open source nature of the HttpUnit distribution, combined with its effectiveness as a functional testing tool, has made it a highly popular choice for testing Web applications.

The latest version of HttpUnit can be downloaded from `http://sourceforge.net/projects/httpunit/`.

## HttpUnit and JUnit

As HttpUnit is not a framework but an API, a method is required for running the tests. Although HttpUnit is independent of the JUnit framework, it is perfectly acceptable to use HttpUnit in conjunction with JUnit. With this approach, a standard JUnit `TestCase` is produced, and HttpUnit calls are used within the test to submit requests and evaluate responses to and from the Web application. Based on the responses received, JUnit assertions confirm whether the interaction with the Web application is behaving in accordance with its requirements.

The advantage of piggybacking HttpUnit tests on the back of the JUnit framework means JUnit now serves as a common mechanism for running both unit and functional tests on the project. This allows all functional tests to be run against a system before its release into a formal testing environment. Ideally, the functional test suite should run as part of a continuous integration build process.

## Writing a Test with HttpUnit

To illustrate the use of the HttpUnit API for constructing functional tests, you must have a Web application ready for testing. Rather than select a public Web site, the example operates against the Avitek Medical Records (MedRec) example that comes with the BEA WebLogic Server installation.

The MedRec application allows physicians, patients, and administrators to log in to the system and perform activities according to their role. Physicians, for example, can log in and perform a search for patients, and then view a patient's details.

As every interaction with the application involves submitting a username and password via a login page for authentication, we build a test around this functionality. Specifically, we test the physician login process with the following scenario:

1.  Access the physician application via the login page.
2.  Confirm reaching the correct login page.
3.  Obtain the physician login form.
4.  Submit the login form with a valid username and password.
5.  Confirm reaching the physician search page.

To write a test for this scenario using HttpUnit, it is not necessary to have access to the code for the MedRec application. Instead, the test case is constructed by examining the source for each page through the *view source* option available from the browser. Tests confirm the presence of expected elements for each page.

Listing 15–1 illustrates a test case for the physician login scenario.

## Listing 15–1   Physician Login Test Case

```java
import junit.framework.TestCase;

import com.meterware.httpunit.WebConversation;
import com.meterware.httpunit.WebForm;
import com.meterware.httpunit.WebRequest;
import com.meterware.httpunit.WebResponse;

/**
 * Login test for Physician MedRec application
 */
public class PhysicianLoginTest extends TestCase {

  private WebConversation conversation;

  /**
   * Establish an instance of WebConversation for
   * running the test
   */
  protected void setUp() throws Exception {
    super.setUp();

    conversation = new WebConversation();
  }

  /**
   * Ensure search page is reached on valid physician login
   */
  public void testPhysicianLogin() throws Exception {
```

```
// Establish connection with Web page
//
WebResponse response = conversation
    .getResponse("http://localhost:7001/physician/login.do");

// Check we have the right application
//
assertEquals("Avitek Medical Records", response.getTitle());

// Get the form for the login
//
WebForm form = response.getFormWithName("userBean");

// Build up a request from the form
// Ensure we specify the action button for the submit
//
WebRequest loginRequest = form.getRequest("action");

// Submit a valid username and password
//
loginRequest.setParameter("username", "mary@md.com");
loginRequest.setParameter("password", "weblogic");

WebResponse loginResponse = conversation
    .getResponse(loginRequest);

// Check we are successfully through to the search page
//
String destinationPath = loginResponse.getURL().getPath();
assertTrue(destinationPath.endsWith("search.do"));
    }

} // PhysicianLoginTest
```

The MedRec application launches from the WebLogic Quick Start menu, which conveniently starts the WebLogic server and deploys the MedRec application. With the system up and running, initiate the test case as for a standard JUnit test from either Eclipse or using one of the JUnit test runner applications.

> *Chapter 14 provides information on*
> *how to run a JUnit test.*

The test starts by establishing a conversation with the physician application. Normally, we do this from a Web browser, but as this is an automated test, the equivalent of an automated browser is required. The WebConversation class serves this purpose and acts as the browser component in all communications with the application. The login page is accessed via a single call to `getResponse()` on the instance of `WebConversation`, passing in the URL. A `WebResponse` object is the result of a successful call. Methods on the `WebResponse` class enable the inspection of the response from the physician application in order to confirm we have received the expected response.

From the example, we can see how a JUnit assertion verifies the page's title to confirm we have accessed the MedRec application.

```
assertEquals("Avitek Medical Records", response.getTitle());
```

It is one thing to validate a response from a Web application, but a proper test requires submitting requests. For the test in the example, we must supply both the username and password for the physician.

Using the `getFormWithName()` method on the `WebResponse` object, we can produce an instance of `WebForm` that enables us to build up a request to the server. The login page has only a single form, but the test requests the form explicitly by name.

```
WebForm form = response.getFormWithName("userBean");
```

From the `WebForm` object, a `WebResponse` is constructed. Note that we must specify the name of the submit button used for the form, because the form contains two buttons: a *submit* and a *cancel*. The call to `getRequest("action")` on the `WebForm` instance provides a readymade `WebRequest`.

```
WebRequest loginRequest = form.getRequest("action");
```

Using the `WebRequest` object, you can specify the username and password, and submit the request to the MedRec physician application. The `setParameter()` method on the `WebRequest` object allows the contents of the form to be built up. Submit the request by invoking the `getResponse()` method on the `WebConversation` instance and passing the request in as a parameter.

```
loginRequest.setParameter("username", "mary@md.com");
loginRequest.setParameter("password", "weblogic");
WebResponse loginResponse = conversation
        .getResponse(loginRequest);
```

A valid username and password should take us to the search screen. The final act of the test is to confirm the page we have sent to by interrogating the path of the URL associated with the latest response from the application.

```
assertTrue(destinationPath.endsWith("search.do"));
```

The example should serve as a useful template for building more complex test scenarios. HttpUnit is an effective tool for creating exhaustive, automated functional tests for Web applications. HttpUnit is not suitable for testing Swing- and AWT-based fat clients. In this situation, consider using *JFCUnit*, which is designed for this very purpose.

The next section moves on to testing nonfunctional requirements and examines methods for conducting load and stress tests.

# Load and Stress Testing

Load and stress tests are part of the process of validating that a system meets its nonfunctional requirements, which typically define such operational attributes for the system as performance, reliability, scalability, and robustness.

Load testing validates the system's *performance* in terms of handling a specified number of users while maintaining a defined transaction rate. Stress testing assesses a system's reliability and robustness when its design load is exceeded. Although the system may decline some requests when overloaded, it should still have the resilience to keep functioning without suffering a potentially embarrassing outage.

Load tests also test for system scalability. This testing takes the form of proving that through an increase in processing power, whether by adding processors or additional machines to the production environment, the system can scale to keep pace with the anticipated increase in load.

The expected system performance criteria can be detailed precisely in a number of ways but are typically stated as a required transaction rate with the system under a stated load. For example, the requirements could state that a request must be handled within two seconds when 10,000 users are accessing the system. For contractual reasons, the specification of load criteria must be highly detailed, taking into account such operational elements as environment, database size, network speed, and hardware configuration, to name but a few.

## warning

Be wary of vague performance criteria, such as *"Requests must be handled in a timely manner."* Such statements are impossible to quantify and hence impossible to accurately test. Remove any ambiguity and make sure you have hard figures for defining the performance measures your system must meet.

## Performance Concerns

A key failing on many projects is that performance testing is not carried out until near the end of the project. If performance problems are not detected until later iterations in the project, drastic changes to the system's underlying architecture may be necessary. Last minute efforts to correct performance-related problems put the quality and stability of the finished application at great risk. Moreover, such late changes could result in unacceptable delays in the delivery of the system.

A good test strategy combined with a software architecture that considers performance upfront in the development process guards against this danger.

You should use early project iterations for building exploratory prototypes that seek to validate the ability of the software architecture to meet all nonfunctional requirements. Tests constructed against such prototypes validate the architecture. Furthermore, these same tests remain available throughout the development of the system to ensure compliance with performance objectives as the application evolves.

Testing of this nature requires a suitable test automation tool. You can develop your own load-testing tool by building a framework to execute your automated functional tests multiple times from independently executing threads. Fortunately, the Apache Software Foundation has already developed such a tool in the form of *JMeter*.

# Introducing JMeter

Like some of the best software tools, JMeter was built out of necessity. Stefano Mazzocchi originally created the application for testing the performance of Apache JServ, the forerunner to Tomcat.

JMeter is a Java application for load testing functional behavior. Initially, JMeter only supported the testing of Web applications. However, since its inception, the product has evolved to support the load testing of different parts of the system architecture, including database servers, FTP servers, LDAP servers, and Web Services. JMeter is extensible, so can you can easily add to this list.

JMeter is available from the Apache Software Foundation under the Apache Software License and can be downloaded from `http://jakarta.apache.org/jmeter`. Our example uses version 2.0.1.

Unlike HttpUnit, which is purely an API, JMeter is a complete framework and offers a Swing-based user interface for defining and executing load and stress tests. It also provides graphical reports for analyzing test results.

Load testing with JMeter involves using the JMeter user interface to define a number of functional test cases. JMeter uses these test cases to simulate multiple-users accessing the system by running each functional test repeatedly from a number of concurrent threads.

The test cases, the number of threads, and the number of times each test case is executed are all configurable elements of a JMeter *test plan*. JMeter takes responsibility for executing a test plan against the system under test, spinning up threads as needed in order to generate the required load.

We examine the elements of a test plan and the fundamental concepts behind JMeter by building up a simple example. Continuing from the previous discussion of HttpUnit, we stay with the MedRec system but this time put the application through its paces from a performance perspective.

## Testing MedRec with JMeter

The functional tests created in the HttpUnit example verified the behavior of the application for a physician entering a username and password at the login page and navigating to the patient search page. To test the system under load, we use a functional test scenario that goes one step further and initiates a patient search after passing the login page. The objective of the test is to evaluate the patient search under load.

The steps for the performance test scenario are as follows:

* Access the physician application via the login page.

* Submit the login form with a valid username and password.

* From the search page, initiate 100 patient searches.

Like JUnit, JMeter supports the use of assertions in the creation of its functional test cases. These assertions verify the results returned by the system under test. We do not use assertions in the example, but it is good practice to confirm functional behavior in tandem with performance. A well-performing system that has incorrect functionality isn't much use to anyone. Furthermore, unexpected behavior may occur with the system under load.

Figure 15–2 shows the JMeter GUI with a test plan open for executing our load test. Over the next sections, we examine how this test plan is built up and the purpose of each of the plan's elements.

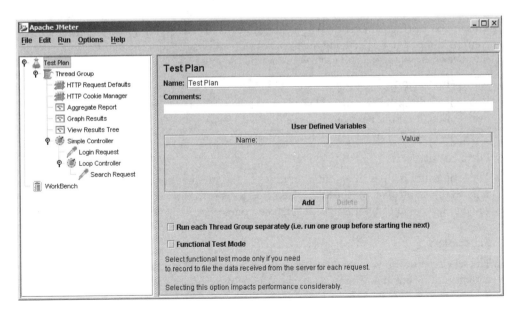

**Figure 15–2**    JMeter with the MedRec test plan open.

The test plan is comprised of test elements that control the execution of the load test. Elements are added to the test plan as nodes to the tree in the left pane of the JMeter GUI.

The tree structure enables the hierarchical organization of plan elements. Here is a description of the main element types we use in the MedRec test plan:

- A *thread group* is the starting point for the test plan and controls the number threads for executing the functional test cases.
- A *sampler* sends requests, such as HTTP requests, to the server.
- A *logical controller* allows you to instruct JMeter when to issue server requests.
- A *configuration element* can add to or modify server requests.
- A *listener* provides a view of the data JMeter gathers from a running test plan.

You add new elements to the plan by right-clicking a node in the tree and selecting the *Add* menu item from the element's context menu. The action presents a menu of all child elements available for selection. We begin by adding a thread group to the top-level test plan node.

## Creating a Thread Group

A thread group represents a *virtual user*, or tester, and defines a set of functional test cases the JMeter virtual user executes as part of the test plan. The JMeter GUI displays configuration options for the thread group element in the right pane.

There are several options of interest for a thread group:

### Number of threads.

This option instructs JMeter as to how many threads to allocate for the thread group for running the load test. Specifying the number of threads is the equivalent of defining the number of simultaneous end users who run the test cases.

### Ramp-up period.

Specifying a ramp-up period has JMeter create the threads in the thread group gradually over a given duration. For example, you may wish to have 10 threads spinning up over 180 seconds. This option is useful for monitoring performance as the load increases.

### Loop count.

The loop count defines the number of times to execute the thread group's test cases. The default is to run continuously. When creating a test plan, it's a good idea to set this value to just a single iteration, as this makes troubleshooting considerably easier.

### Scheduler.

The scheduler option is a checkbox. In the checked state, additional fields appear in the configuration pane that allow setting of the test's start and end time.

The example contains only a single thread group, but the test plan node supports the addition of many thread groups, each with its own configuration and test cases.

For the example, the number of threads is set at 100 with a ramp-up period of one second. The thread group is set to run continuously.

A JMeter test plan can have many thread groups, each running a different functional test scenario. As the example is concerned with a only single test scenario, our plan contains just the one thread group element.

# The Configuration Elements

Configuration elements modify requests sent to the server. They work closely with the *sampler* elements, which are responsible for sending requests. The MedRec test plan uses two types of this element: an *HTTP request defaults* and a *cookie manager*. We add both of these elements to the plan as immediate children of the thread group node.

## The HTTP Request Defaults

Like the HttpUnit example, testing a Web application requires submitting HTTP and HTTPS requests to the Web server. The requests sent to place the Web application under load will likely share a common set of configuration options.

JMeter provides the HTTP request defaults element as a convenience for storing these common options. Here are some of the main settings you may wish to set for each request:

**Protocol.**

This option specifies the protocol for sending each request, either HTTP or HTTPS.

**Server name or IP.**

Use this field to set the domain name, or IP address, of the server running the system under test.

**Path.**

The path option sets the Universal Resource Identifier (URI) for the page. You can also set default parameters for sending with the request, but it is likely these will be set for each individual request.

**Port number.**

Set this option if your Web server is listening on a port other than port 80 (which is the default).

The example sets the Server Name or IP to the machine hosting the MedRec application and the Port Number to 7001. All other options remain unset.

## Creating a Cookie Manager

The *HTTP cookie manager* does exactly as its name implies: it manages all cookies sent to the thread group from the Web application. Failing to add a cookie manager to the thread group is the equivalent of disabling cookies within the browser.

For the purposes of the example, the cookie manager element uses the default settings.

## Logic Controllers

Logic controllers let you determine when JMeter issues requests. They direct the execution order of test plan elements, and so orchestrate the flow of control for a test.

JMeter provides a range of different logic controllers. Table 15–3 lists those that are available.

**Table 15–3**　Logic Controllers

| Controller | Description |
| --- | --- |
| ForEach | Iterates through all child elements and supplies a new value on each iteration. |
| If | Makes the execution of child elements conditional. |
| Interleave | Executes an alternate child sampler element on each loop of the Controller's branch. |
| Loop | Iterates over each child element a given number of times. |
| Module | Offers a mechanism for including test plan fragments into the current plan from different locations. |
| Once Only | Runs elements of the Controller only once per test. |
| Random | Randomizes the execution order of subcontrollers. |
| Recording | Placeholder for indicating where the *HTTP proxy server* element should record all data. |
| Simple | Placeholder for organizing elements. |
| Throughput | Used for throttling the requests sent by its child elements. |
| Transaction | Times the length of time taken for all child elements to run, then logs the timing information. |

For the example, the flow of control sees the test case log in to the application and perform 100 patient searches. To achieve this, we use two types of controller: a *simple controller* and a *loop controller*.

## The Simple Controller

Adding a simple controller provides a placeholder for organizing the sampler elements of the plan. The element type has no configuration options other than a name.

The simple controller in the example has two child elements: an HTTP request sampler for the login page and a loop controller. When JMeter executes the test plan, the login request under the simple controller executes first, followed by the elements of the loop controller.

## Adding a Loop Controller

Unlike the simple controller, the loop controller is more than a placeholder. The loop controller states the number of times to iterate through each of the controller's child elements.

For the example, the loop controller's Loop Count property is set to 100. Thus, we have the login request being sent once, followed by 100 search requests. Of course, we still have to add a suitable HTTP request sampler element for the search request to the loop controller, as well as a sampler for the login request as a child of the simple controller. We look at the configuration of these sampler elements next.

# Samplers

Up until now, the test plan doesn't do much. To put the MedRec application under some strain, we need to start sending some actual requests. For this, we need a *sampler* element.

A sampler submits requests to the target server. JMeter supplies several types of sampler elements, making it possible to test systems other than Web applications. Table 15–4 describes each sampler provided as part of the JMeter installation.

**Table 15–4**    JMeter Samplers

| Sampler | Description |
| --- | --- |
| FTP Request | Sends an FTP get request to the server to retrieve a file. |
| HTTP Request | Submits an HTTP or HTTPS request to a Web server. |
| Java Request | Allows you to control any Java class that implements the JavaSamplerClient interface. |
| JDBC Request | Enables the execution of SQL statements against a database. |
| LDAP Request | Issues an LDAP request to a server. |
| SOAP/XML-RPC Request | Supports sending a SOAP request to a Web Service or allows an XML-RPC request to be sent over HTTP. |

Because MedRec is a Web application, we must generate HTTP requests, and JMeter provides the *HTTP request sampler* for this purpose.

Our test scenario calls for two HTTP request sampler elements, one for making the login request and another for initiating the patient search.

## Making a Login Request

The first page accessed as part of the test is the physician login. Navigating past this page requires submitting a login request to establish our security credentials for the session. This process involves issuing the appropriate parameters as part of the request: a username and password.

The login process was covered in the HttpUnit example for the login page using an instance of WebForm in Listing 15–1. JMeter works very differently from HttpUnit, but rather than cover the login page twice, let's leave the discussion on how to submit request parameters with JMeter until we reach the search page.

For now, Figure 15–3 shows the configuration of the sampler for the login page.

Notice that some of the options for the request are blank. These include the Server Name or IP, Port Number, and the Protocol. You can ignore these options because the HTTP request sampler inherits these settings from the HTTP request defaults element created earlier and added to the top-level of the thread group.

Add the sampler for the login requests as a child of the simple controller. To complete the test case, we need a final sampler for the search request.

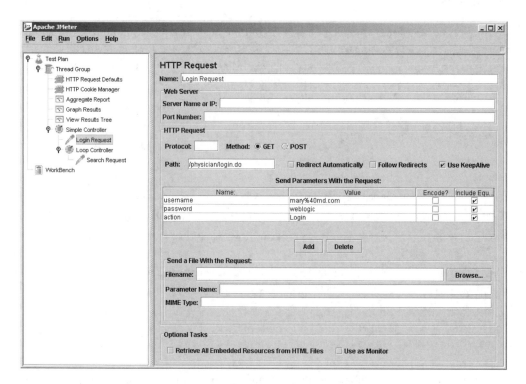

**Figure 15–3**    HTTP login request settings.

## Submitting a Search Request

The patient search requires an HTTP request element as a child of the loop controller. This element sends the parameters for the patient search. The search page uses an HTML form element for sending search requests, so the sampler needs to mimic the action of the form.

Here is an edited extract of the HTML source for the patient search page showing the form:

```
<form name="searchBean"
     method="POST"
     action="/physician/searchresults.do">
  <input type="text" name="lastName" value="">
  <input type="text" name="ssn" value="">
  <input type="submit" name="action" value="Search">
</form>
```

The searchBean form takes either the patient's name or social security number. Our test case uses the name for searching. Figure 15–4 shows the configuration of the HTTP request element for the form.

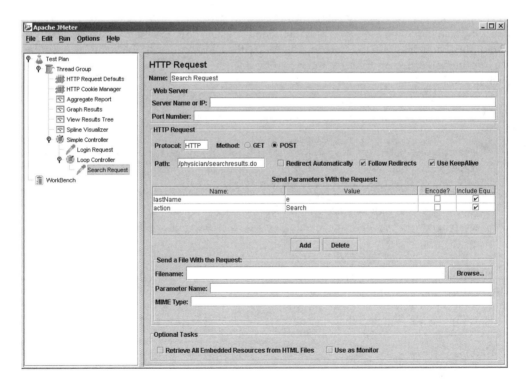

**Figure 15–4**    HTTP search request settings.

The HTTP request sampler in Figure 15–4 simulates the sending of the searchBean form as if submitted from a browser. To match the form, you first need to switch the method from a GET, which is the default, to a POST. The HTTP request sampler provides a handy set of radio buttons for making this change.

Next, the path setting for the request must correspond to the value of the action attribute from the form. Set this to /physician/searchresults.do.

For the final task, add the form's parameters to the HTTP request. We are searching on the patient's last name, so you can ignore the social security number.

Two parameters are required to initiate a search. The first is the lastName parameter and specifies a string for matching against patient surnames. The second parameter is the value associated with the submit button, in this case the action parameter, which is assigned a value of Search. Don't forget to add this value, or the MedRec application will not know how to handle the request correctly.

The search request completes the setup of the test plan for running the test. However, the test plan is still not complete: we need to tell JMeter how we wish to view the data gathered from running the test. This is accomplished using a *listener* element.

## Listeners

JMeter uses listener elements for analyzing data gathered from the test. A selection of listeners is available, each providing a different presentation format for the data gathered during the execution of the test. In addition to rendering the data gathered by JMeter, each listener type can log the information collected to file for interrogation after the test plan has completed using other analysis tools.

tip

> JMeter stores test results as either an XML document or a comma-separated value (CSV) file. XML is the default, but the CSV format is very useful for importing the data into spreadsheets like Microsoft Excel.
>
> To change the format, locate the jmeter.save.saveservice.output_format entry in the jmeter.properties file and set its value to csv.

The listeners elements interpret data for their parent thread group. Add a listener to the thread group node by right-clicking on the node and selecting *Add*, then *Listener*, and then choosing from the listener elements available.

The example test plan uses these listeners:

### View results tree.

This listener presents a text-based hierarchical view of the requests and responses sent and received during the test.

**Aggregate report.**

The aggregate report is a text-based listener that displays summary information for each separately named request used in the test.

**Graph results.**

This listener provides a simple graphical view of the test results, including the average response time and throughput rate.

Refer to the JMeter documentation for a full list of listeners.

tip

> The view results tree listener is especially useful when initially building the test plan for determining if the plan is executing as expected. It is of less value when intensive testing is underway due to the volume of data presented.

With the listeners in place, the test plan is complete and ready to run.

## Executing the Test Plan

Before running a test, it is highly advisable to save the test plan first. The JMeter engine can potentially spin up a large number of threads, and things can go wrong. Always save the plan before starting the test just in case.

Set the thread group so it loops forever, and start the test from the *Run* menu with the *Start* item. You can stop the test with the *Stop* item from the same menu. By clicking on the different listener elements, you can observe the status of the test while it is in progress.

## Analyzing the Results

The listeners display the data gathered for the test. These next sections examine the information presented in the aggregate report listener and the graph result listener. Although JMeter provides a number of other inbuilt listeners, these two are indicative of the type of information JMeter generates for a load test.

### Aggregate Report Listener

The aggregate report displays the following summary information for the login and search requests.

* Number of requests
* Average response time

- Minimum response time
- Maximum response time
- Error percentage
- Throughput rate in terms of requests per second

Figure 15–5 shows the results from the aggregate report listener for the example test plan.

The report provides a concise and easy-to-read representation of the data in table format. In this case, the MedRec application has maintained a high throughput for the given load.

Because the aggregate report listener displays summary information, it is not possible to see how the Web application behaved during the running of the test. Viewing this information requires a graphical listener.

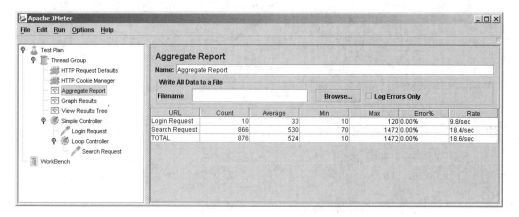

**Figure 15–5** Aggregate Report Listener.

## Graph Result Listener

For a graphical display of the test results, the graph result listener plots several types of performance information, including data samples, the average and median sample times, standard deviation, and throughput.

Showing all of this information in black and white is hard to read, so the graph result listener shown in Figure 15–6 plots only the data samples and the average response times during the test.

The graph has the duration of the test on the X-axis and the server response times for HTTP requests on the Y-axis. The black dots are the individual timings for each request. Ideally, the time taken for the application to handle a request should be uniform. A reasonably tight grouping of the dots represents a consistent response time for each request. The load on the server was quite light, and MedRec coped with the load—illustrated by the X-axis topping out at only 552ms.

The line through the dots is the average. Again, this should be fairly even. Apart from the step curve at the start where the test was ramping up, this is certainly the case.

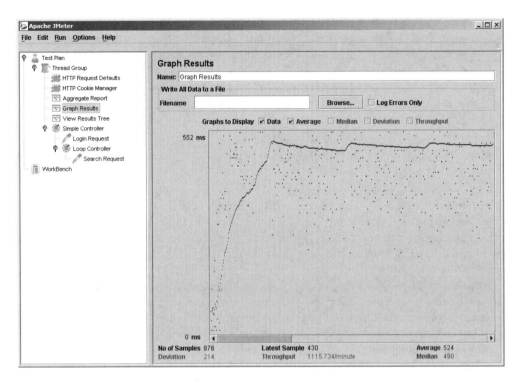

**Figure 15–6**    Graph Result Listener.

# JMeter Guidelines

Here are some guidelines you should find helpful when load testing a system with JMeter:

- Use meaningful test scenarios, and construct test plans with test cases that represent real-world situations. Use cases provide an ideal nucleus around which to build your load tests.

- Ensure you run JMeter on a separate machine from the system under test. This prevents JMeter from affecting the results of the test.

- Testing is a scientific process, so conduct all tests under carefully controlled conditions. If you are working with a shared server, check first before starting a test that no one else on the team is also running a JMeter test plan against the same Web application.

- Ensure you have adequate network bandwidth for the workstation running JMeter. You are testing the performance of the application and server, not your network connection.

- Use several instances of JMeter running on different machines to add additional load on a server. This setup might be necessary for stress testing. JMeter can control instances of JMeter on other machines for this purpose. Refer to the JMeter documentation on *distributed testing* for more information.

- Leave a JMeter test plan running for long periods, possibly several days or longer. This tests system availability and highlights any degradation in server performance over time due to poor resource management.

- Don't run JMeter test plans against external servers for which you are not responsible. The owners may consider this a denial of service attack.

HttpUnit can also assist in the process of load testing. Although JMeter and HttpUnit are different types of testing tools, the two can complement one another to assess the performance of a Web application under load.

Using this combined approach, a JMeter test plan places the Web application under load while running the HttpUnit functional test suite. Assertions raised from the functional tests are an indication of load-sensitive defects.

When designing and executing load tests, remember every system has its limits. By running JMeter on enough machines, it is possible to exceed those limits. This is a valid test in itself, as the system should exhibit failsafe behavior for this scenario. However, the objective of load testing is to prove the ability of the application to meet the performance criteria stipulated in the nonfunctional requirements.

Design tests to prove a system's compliance with the customer's performance specifications. Simply deluging the system with requests will not confirm this, so make your testing scientific. Set yourself a target, and carefully design a test plan that will either prove or disprove whether the system meets the stipulated criteria.

## Summary

Formal testing of an enterprise-level system is often a time-consuming process. Using an automated approach improves the effectiveness of the testing process, resulting in shorter development timeframes and greater test accuracy.

Getting the most from test automation requires the definition of a carefully planned test strategy. Following are some important points to consider when formulating a suitable strategy.

- Don't leave testing to the end of the project. Early testing prevents nasty surprises that are expensive and time consuming to correct in the final iterations of a project. Test early and test often.

- Design the system to be tested, and devise the test strategy in tandem with the software architecture.

- Use an array of testing types. No single type of testing will adequately validate an enterprise-level system. Apply a barrage of different testing schemes, including unit, integration, functional, load, and stress testing.

- Automate the testing process. The time taken to build automated test scripts will more than pay off in terms of testing accuracy and test speed.

Thoroughly testing a J2EE application is as hard a process as the development itself: do not underestimate the task. Give quality assurance the attention and respect it deserves.

## Additional Information

The testing of object-oriented systems is a huge topic and appropriately, Robert Binder has written a huge book on the subject. For an in-depth discussion on all matters relating to the testing process, *Testing Object-Oriented Systems: Models, Patterns, and Tools* [Binder, 2000] is an extremely inclusive read and has the honor of being the thickest publication on my bookshelf.

To find out about other open source testing tools, visit `http://www.opensourcetesting.org`.

# A

# Acronyms

This appendix lists all the acronyms used in the book.

| Acronym | Meaning |
|---------|---------|
| API | Application Programming Interface |
| AOP | Aspect-Oriented Programming |
| AWT | Abstract Windowing Kit |
| BMP | Bean-Managed Persistence |
| CGI | Common Gateway Interface |
| CLIPS | C Language Integrated Production System |
| CMP | Container-Managed Persistence |
| CMR | Container-Managed Relationships |
| DBA | Database Administrator |
| DBMS | Database Management System |
| DDL | Data Definition Language |
| DOM | Document Object Model |
| DTD | Document Type Definition |

| Acronym | Meaning |
| --- | --- |
| EAI | Enterprise Application Integration |
| EAR | Enterprise Archive |
| EIS | Enterprise Information System |
| EJB | Enterprise JavaBean |
| EJB-QL | EJB Query Language |
| ER | Entity Relationship |
| ERD | Entity Relationship Diagram |
| ESS | Expert System Shell |
| GUI | Graphical User Interface |
| HTML | Hypertext Markup Language |
| IDE | Integrated Development Environment |
| IIOP | Internet Inter-ORB Protocol |
| JAD | Joint Application Development |
| JAD | Java Decompiler |
| JCA | J2EE Connector Architecture |
| J2EE | Java 2 Enterprise Edition |
| J2SE | Java 2 Standard Edition |
| JAR | Java Archive |
| JCP | Java Community Process |
| JDBC | Java Database Connectivity |
| JDK | Java Development Kit |
| JDO | Java Data Objects |
| JFC | Java Foundation Classes |
| JMS | Java Messaging Service |

| Acronym | Meaning |
|---------|---------|
| JNDI | Java Naming and Directory Service |
| JPDA | Java Platform Debugger Architecture |
| JRE | Java Runtime Environment |
| JSP | JavaServer Pages |
| JSR | Java Specification Review |
| JSTL | JSP Standard Tag Library |
| JVM | Java Virtual Machine |
| MDA | Model-Driven Architecture |
| MDD | Model-Driven Development |
| MOF | Meta-Object Facility |
| MOM | Message-Oriented Middleware |
| MVC | Model View Controller |
| ODMS | Object Database Management System |
| OMG | Object Management Group |
| ORB | Object Request Broker |
| POJO | Plain Old Java Object |
| RAD | Rapid Application Development |
| RAR | Resource Archive |
| RDBMS | Relational Database Management System |
| RMI | Remote Method Invocation |
| RMI/IIOP | Remote Method Invocation over Internet Inter-ORB Protocol |
| RUP | IBM Rational Unified Process |
| SAX | Simple API for XML Processing |
| SDK | Software Development Kit |

| Acronym | Meaning |
|---------|---------|
| SQL | Structured Query Language |
| SSL | Secure Sockets Layer |
| SOAP | Simple Object Access Protocol |
| SWAT | Skilled With Advanced Tools |
| TDD | Test-Driven Development |
| TLD | Tag Library Descriptor |
| UML | Unified Modeling Language |
| URI | Uniform Resource Identifier |
| URL | Uniform Resource Locator |
| VTL | Velocity Template Language |
| WAR | Web Archive |
| WLS | WebLogic Server |
| WSAD | WebSphere Application Developer |
| XML | eXtensible Markup Language |
| XP | eXtreme Programming |
| XPath | XML Path Language |
| XSL | eXtensible Stylesheet Language |
| XSLT | XSL Transformations |

# B

# Bibliography

Alur, Deepak, Dan Malks, & John Crupi. *Core J2EE Patterns, 2nd ed.* Prentice Hall PTR, 2003.

Ambler, Scott. *Agile Database Techniques.* John Wiley & Sons, 2003.

Beck, Kent. *Extreme Programming Explained.* Addison-Wesley, 1999.

Beck, Kent. *Test Driven Development.* Addison-Wesley, 2002.

Bill, Robert. *Jython for Java Programmers.* Pearson Education, 2001.

Binder, Robert V. *Testing Object-Oriented Systems: Models Patterns and Tools.* Addison Wesley, 1999.

Boehm, Barry. *"Making RAD Work for Your Project".* Computer, 32(3): 113–114, 117, March 1999.

Boehm, Barry. "A Spiral Model of Software Development and Enhancement." *Computer,* 21(5): 61–72, May 1988.

Boehm, Barry, & Richard Turner. "Using Risk to Balance Agile and Plan Driven Methods." *Computer,* 36(6): 57–66, June 2003.

Booch, Grady, James Rumbaugh, & Ivar Jacobson. *The Unified Modeling Language User Guide.* Addison-Wesley, 1998.

Brooks, Frederick P., Jr. *The Mythical-Man Month, Anniversary Ed.* Addison-Wesley, 1995.

Brooks, Frederick P., Jr. "No Silver Bullet: Essence and Accidents of Software Engineering." *Computer,* 20(4): 10–19, April 1987.

Forgy, Charles L. "Rete: A Fast Algorithm for the Many Pattern/Many Object Pattern Match Problem." *Artificial Intelligence,* 19: 17–37, 1982.

Fowler, Martin. "The New Methodology." Online: http://www.martinfowler.com/articles/new-Methodology.htm, July 2000.

Fowler, Martin. *Patterns of Enterprise Application Architecture.* Addison-Wesley, 2002.

Fowler, Martin. *UML Distilled, 3rd ed.* Addison-Wesley, 2003.

Gamma, Eric, Richard Helm, Ralph Johnson, & John Vlissides. *Design Patterns.* Addison-Wesley, 1995.

Glass, Robert L. *Facts and Fallacies of Software Engineering.* Addison-Wesley, 2002.

Gottesdiener, Ellen. "Business Rules Show Power and Promise." *Application Programming Trends.* 4(3), Online: http://www.adtmag.com/article.asp?id=4566, March 1997.

Gradecki, Joseph D., & Nicholas Lesiecki. *Mastering AspectJ: Aspect-Oriented Programming in Java.* Wiley, 2003.

Highley, Timothy, Michael Lack, & Perry Myers. "Aspect Oriented Programming: A Critical Analysis of a New Programming Paradigm." Online: http://citeseer.ist.psu.edu/highley99aspect.html, 1999.

Hunt, Andrew, & David Thomas. *The Pragmatic Programmer.* Addison-Wesley, 1999.

Hutchings, Edward (editor), Ralph Leighton, & Richard Phillips Feynman. *Surely You're Joking, Mr. Feynman!* W.W. Norton & Company, 1997.

Johnson, Rod. *Expert One-on-One J2EE Design and Development.* Wrox, 2002.

Kiczales, G., J. Lamping, A. Mendhekar, et al. "Aspect-Oriented Programming". In ECOOP'97---Object-Oriented Programming, 11th European Conference, LNCS 1241: 220–242, 1997

Kiczales, Gregor, Erik Hilsdale, Jim Hugunin, Mik Kersten, Jeffrey Palm, & William G. Griswold. *An Overview of AspectJ.* In Proc. of ECOOP '01, LNCS 2072, pp. 327–353, Springer, 2001.

Kruchten, Philippe. "Planning an Iterative Project." Online: http://www-106.ibm.com/developerworks/rational/library/2831.html, 2002.

Kruchten, Philippe. *The Rational Unified Process: An Introduction, 3rd ed.* Addison-Wesley, 2003.

Kruchten, Philippe. "The 4 + 1 View Model of Architecture." *IEEE Software*, 12(6): 42–50, November 1995.

Larman, Craig, Philippe Kruchten, & Kurt Bittner. "How to Fail with the Rational Unified Process: Seven Steps to pain and Suffering." Online: http://www.agilealliance.org/articles/articles/How_to_Fail_with_the_RUP_-_Kruchten_and_Larman.pdf, 2002.

Mackinnon, Tim, Steve Freeman, & Philip Craig. "Endo-Testing: Unit Testing with Mock Objects." Online: http://www.connextra.com/aboutUs/mockobjects.pdf, 2000.

Martin, James. *Rapid Application Development.* Macmillan, 1991.

McConnell, Steve. *Rapid Development.* Microsoft Press, 1996.

Steve McConnell. "Cargo Cult Software Engineering." *IEEE Software*, 17(2): 11–13, March/April 2000.

McConnell, Steve. *Code Complete, 2nd ed.* Microsoft Press, 2004.

Pedroni, Samuele, & Noel Rappin. *Jython Essentials.* O'Reilly, 2002.

Reilly, John P. "Does RAD Live Up to the Hype?" *IEEE Software*, 12(5): 24–26 September, 1995.

Roman, Ed. *Mastering Enterprise JavaBeans*. John Wiley & Sons, 1999.

Singh, Inderjeet, Beth Stearns, Mark Johnson, & Enterprise Team. *Designing Enterprise Applications with the J2EE Platform*. Addison-Wesley, 2002.

Snyder, Carolyn. *Paper Prototyping: The Fast and Easy Way to Design and Refine User Interfaces*. Morgan Kaufmann, 2003.

# Index

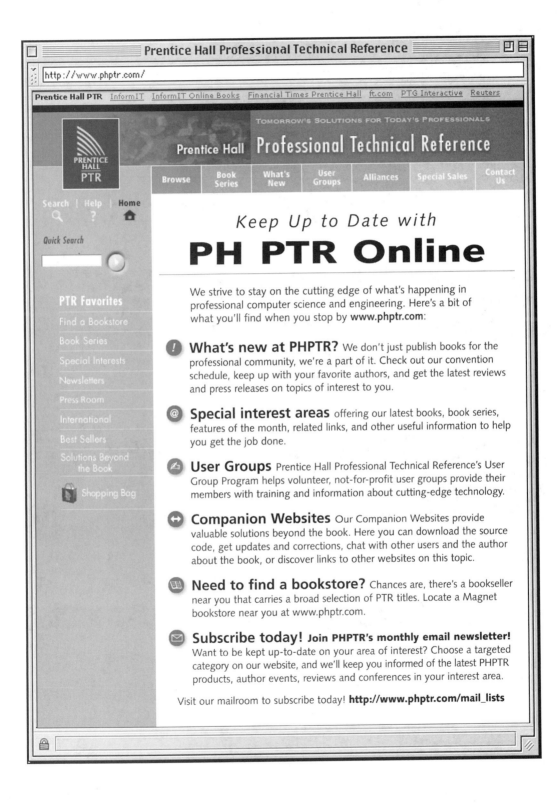

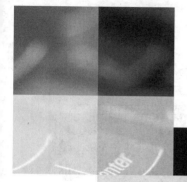